THE JEWISH NOVEL IN
THE ANCIENT WORLD

A volume in the series

MYTH AND POETICS

edited by GREGORY NAGY

A complete list of titles appears at the end of the book.

THE JEWISH
NOVEL IN THE
ANCIENT WORLD

Lawrence M. Wills

CORNELL UNIVERSITY PRESS

ITHACA AND LONDON

First published 1995 by Cornell University Press.

Printed in the United States of America

⊗ The paper in this book meets the minimum requirements
of the American National Standard for Information Sciences—
Permanence of Paper for Printed Library Materials, ANSI Z39.48-1984.

Library of Congress Cataloging-in-Publication Data

Wills, Lawrence M. (Lawrence Mitchell), 1954–
    The Jewish novel in the ancient world / Lawrence M. Wills.
        p.   cm. — (Myth and poetics)
    Includes bibliographical references and index.
    ISBN 0-8014-3075-5
    1. Bible. O.T.—Criticism, interpretation, etc.   2. Bible as literature.   3. Narration in the Bible.   4. Bible. O.T. Apocrypha—Criticism, interpretation, etc.   5. Jewish fiction—History and criticism.   6. Literature, Ancient—History and criticism.   I. Title. II. Series.
    BS1171.2.W58   1995
    809'.935224—dc20   94-40788

The novel is the most hazardous genre because the novel—unlike other genres—has a caricatural twin almost indistinguishable from itself: the entertainment novel. . . . Superficial likeness can almost lead to the caricature being mistaken for the real thing. But a closer look will always reveal the caricature for what it is.

—Georg Lukács, *The Theory of the Novel*

Contents

Foreword

GREGORY NAGY

The ancient Jewish novel, as described by Lawrence M. Wills, is a bridge between the Hebrew Bible and the genre known to Classicists as the Greek novel. As familiar parts of Jewish sacred scripture, books like *Daniel* or *Esther* may elude levels of analysis which apply to such overtly secular productions as *Daphnis and Chloe,* in vogue among the reading public of the late Hellenic world. Conversely, the study of the Greek novel in its historical context is impoverished by the neglect of comparable media in neighboring cultures. Such a medium is the Jewish novel, as Wills reconstructs it in its own historical context. His reconstruction gives rise to a rigorous comparison between the Greek and the Jewish forms of the novel, which yields important new insights into the mythology and poetics of this evolving genre.

Preface

When I began this enterprise, the Jewish novels as a category were unknown to laypeople and barely known to scholars in the various fields concerned with this period. As the Greek novels experience something of a renaissance among scholars, I hope that the Jewish novels, along with all the other indigenous novelistic literature of the ancient world, will be permitted to join them.

This work has taken me through several academic fields that usually remain segregated: Jewish and early Christian studies, classics, history, folklore, gender studies, literary theory. The breadth of this study would not have been possible had it not been for a number of very patient people who have helped me enter into a comparative enterprise. I especially thank Gregory Nagy, editor of Myth and Poetics. Few authors are fortunate enough to have such a generous, critical, and engaged series editor.

Richard Pervo's study of the ancient novel and the Acts of the Apostles, *Profit with Delight,* was also very influential. Many of my theoretical considerations are attempts to articulate in some detail what he suggested in a few lines. He perceived, in fact, the need for a fuller study of the Jewish novels, and I hope my own book begins to fill that need. I have also learned much from the responses of other scholars, especially Bernadette Brooten, Ross Kraemer, Jon Levenson, Margaret Miles, Theodore Hiebert, Christine Thomas, David Biale, and the members of the Cross-Cultural Poetics and Rhetoric Seminar of the Harvard Center for Literary and Cultural Studies. The editors and staff of Cornell University Press have been very conscientious and helpful. And last, my wife and family, as ever, deserve special thanks for taking such an interest in my work; I dedicate this book to Shelley, Jessica, and Daniel.

L. M. W.

THE JEWISH NOVEL IN
THE ANCIENT WORLD

Introduction

In 1967 the professor of Jewish studies Elias Bickerman published a highly entertaining yet scholarly work titled *Four Strange Books of the Bible,* on *Daniel, Esther, Koheleth* (or *Ecclesiastes*), and *Jonah.* These books are strange, he seemed to suggest, because they do not fit comfortably in the biblical categories of history, prophecy, wisdom, and so on, and they assault our preconceptions of what biblical books should say. We experience a genre problem when reading these books, and we do not know quite what to make of them. Although Bickerman went a long way toward explaining them and elucidating some of their salient literary characteristics, the strangeness of two of them, *Esther* and *Daniel,* is somewhat alleviated if we compare them, not with other biblical books, but with similar works of the same time period—in which they are perhaps less alien—and analyze them in terms of their literary genre, the Jewish novel.

Between about 200 B.C.E. and 100 C.E., Jewish authors wrote many entertaining narratives marked by fanciful and idealized settings, adventurous tone, happy endings, and important women characters. They were probably considered "fictitious," not in the sense of bad or credulous history that misrepresents the past but in the sense of prose writings that involve a new sort of reading experience, the creation of invented worlds that are nevertheless like our own. As David Konstan notes, whereas history has a referent in a real or presumed event of the past (no matter how inexactly that referent may be described), fiction has no referent.[1] In the mind of the author and the audience, a fictitious account

---

[1] David Konstan, "The Invention of Fiction," address at the annual convention of the Society of Biblical Literature, November 20, 1993. See also Ducrot and Todorov, *Encyclopedic*

is not about any situation that really existed or any event that really occurred (even if the characters represent real historical personages). Greek *Esther,* Greek *Daniel, Judith,* and *Tobit,* all in the Old Testament Apocrypha, and *Joseph and Aseneth* constitute the genre of Jewish novels and, before being canonized, were likely perceived by their audiences as fictions. Closely related to these, though not likely considered fictitious according to the definition just applied, are several "historical novels" from the same period: the *Tobiad Romance* and the *Royal Family of Adiabene* from Josephus's *Antiquities; Third Maccabees;* and fragments of others. Despite the similarities, the novels *as a group* have almost completely evaded serious scholarly scrutiny. What little work has been done on them has focused primarily on the individual writings and rarely on two or more in comparison. By failing to recognize the genre, many critics have held the writings at arm's length, separated them from their rightful function, and denied them their one overriding characteristic: their popularity.[2] The authors of these works, indulging in many of the

---

Dictionary of the Sciences of Language, 259–60. Differing definitions of fiction utilized by scholars sometimes complicate the comparison of texts. Alter suggests that the Hebrew Bible should be analyzed as "fiction" because it achieves a high level of narrative art, and the poetics that was developed to study narrative fiction is the most appropriate methodological tool to use in analyzing it (*The Art of Biblical Narrative,* 23–46). Here he is opposing the historicizing tendencies of biblical scholars who would dispense with any aesthetic criteria in addressing ancient Hebrew literature. Veyne also blurs the distinction between the credulousness of historians and intentional fiction to underscore the relativism of historical objectivity (*Did the Greeks Believe in Their Myths?,* esp. 21–22, 103–4). In both cases, the usual sense of fiction as a special, "marked" mode of discourse with its own particular reading experience is lost; I much prefer Konstan's definition.

[2] Some have recognized the similarities among this group of writings. Hengel, in a groundbreaking study that emphasized the interrelatedness of Judaism and Hellenism after Alexander the Great, acknowledged the influences of Greco-Roman genres on Jewish literature (*Judaism and Hellenism,* 110–12). Furthermore, Smith, who emphasized the parallels between Jewish and Greek literature for the period before Alexander the Great, also touched on popular literary genres that encompassed many of the novels studied here (*Palestinian Parties and Politics That Shaped the Old Testament,* 158–62). The most important step, however, in the development of the study of Jewish novels was Pervo's 1979 Harvard dissertation on the comparison of Acts of the Apostles with the Greek novels. Published as *Profit with Delight: The Literary Genre of the Acts of the Apostles,* it provides an excellent treatment of the ancient novel genre as a whole, including Jewish and other indigenous novels. Bickerman was also far ahead of most scholars in detecting in these writings the genres of popular literature. In addition to his *Four Strange Books of the Bible,* see *The Jews in the Greek Age,* 51–65, on the Aramaic narrative tradition in Judaism, and also Altheim and Stiehl, *Die aramäische Sprache unter den Achaimeniden,* 1:183–213.

The targums to *Esther* will not be included in this study, as they are very likely much later and fall outside of the genre delineated here. Likewise, rabbinic midrashic traditions were collected and edited much later and, more important, do not come down to us as separate, extended narratives. On these see most recently Kugel, *In Potiphar's House;* Stern, *Parables in Midrash;* and Stern and Mirsky, *Rabbinic Fantasies.*

devices of literary manipulation current in ancient narrative literature, created works that were transmitted widely, altered, and expanded, ultimately to constitute an entire tradition of popular Jewish literature. It is quite possible, even likely, that Jewish novels were read by more Jews than was any other type of literature, except perhaps the biblical scrolls themselves. This bears repeating: It is possible that Jewish novels were read by more Jews than any other type of literature. Although we shall never have firm data on readership, the number of different novels preserved and the wide variety of known textual versions (there being rarely any institutional imperative for them to be copied by professional scribes) indicate that a broad popular market existed for these writings.

To generate interest, many entertaining techniques and motifs are utilized in these works. The sweep of history and the importance of place are often evoked. Nineveh, Babylon, the Persian court, and great military campaigns are described with relish and excitement, much as they are in the popular novels of other cultures of the period. The historical interest is, at the same time, playfully undermined by a cavalier approach to dates and personages: Esther becomes a Jewish queen for King Xerxes, Daniel serves under the nonexistent "Darius the Mede" (Darius was Persian), Judith opposes "Nebuchadnezzar, king of the Assyrians" (Nebuchadnezzar was Babylonian)—a set of narrative "facts" that would have been instantly recognized by the audience as historical impossibilities. These discrepancies from the received tradition are so great and so obvious that they evidently reflect a new sort of reading experience in which the purportedly historical text is understood by the audience as fanciful, that is, fiction. Grave dangers are also encountered in these works, dangers that often threaten Jews as a group: Esther steps in to oppose an empirewide threat to her people, Daniel remains stalwart while facing possible martyrdom, Judith stops the advance of Holofernes, Tobit's son Tobias must overcome the evil demon Asmodaeus, and Aseneth, after her internal struggles, thwarts the plot of Joseph's brothers to kill him. The interior life of characters is also explored, sometimes through narrative devices, such as the exchange of messages between Esther and Mordecai, but more often through prayers and hymns, whether short, as in Susanna's sigh at her moment of decision, or long, as in the Greek additions found at crucial points in *Daniel* or *Esther*. The depiction of emotion, a common element in Greek and Roman art and literature of this period, appears in the novels as well. The narrative innovation that is the most striking above all, however, is the sudden predominance of women characters, who become the focus of the emotional issues of the drama.[3] A vulnerable woman, placed in jeopardy, experiences fully the threats that rise up against her and her people.

The increase in literacy in the Hellenistic age is a crucial component of the social context for novelistic literature of all kinds. In both Greek and Jewish society there existed a rich literary tradition, but until the second century B.C.E., reading and writing had never really transformed culture. Throughout most of its history, human culture has been principally an oral culture, even if a learned class of scribes also conducted official business in the written medium. Walter J. Ong describes the significant changes that are effected in thinking and social patterns when a society moves from relying principally on oral transmission to relying on written,[4] and it is precisely at just such a period of great transformation that we find the birth of Jewish novels and their adaptation to an increasingly literate society. Although Ong and others sometimes refer to the transformation of culture from oral to written as a long, slow growth that only culminates in the modern world,[5] there

---

[3] These tendencies in the art and literature of the Hellenistic period are described by many authors. In addition to the standard treatments of Hellenistic art, such as J. J. Pollitt, *Art in the Hellenistic Age* (Cambridge: Cambridge University Press, 1986), see Michael Grant, *From Alexander to Cleopatra* (New York: Scribner's, 1982), 149–213, and John Winkler, "The Novel," in Michael Grant and Rachel Kitzinger, *Civilization of the Ancient Mediterranean,* 3 vols. (New York: Scribner's, 1988), 3:1563–72. An interesting catalog of the artistic motifs that proliferate during the Hellenistic period can be found in Fowler, *The Hellenistic Aesthetic,* and for a fascinating glimpse into the projection of femininity in Hellenistic art see Jaimee P. Uhlenbrock, *The Coroplast's Art: Greek Terracottas of the Hellenistic World* (New Rochelle, N.Y.: A. D. Caratzas, 1990). To be sure, R. R. R. Smith cautions us that the *development* of style in Hellenistic sculpture is not uniform but progresses quite differently at different social levels and with different subjects (*Hellenistic Sculpture* [London: Thames and Hudson, 1991], 269–73). Here he puts his finger on an issue of the various levels of popular and aristocratic or state art that should be kept in mind throughout this study.

[4] Ong, *Orality and Literacy.*

[5] Ibid., 144. Compare also Alfred North Whitehead: "Writing was an invention which took about two thousand years to make its effect felt" (in Graham, *Beyond the Written Word,* 19). See also Graham's treatment of the issue in general (pp. 9–44). Ong also notes (p. 24) that a literate-culture perspective is already initiated with Plato (the latter's protests to the contrary notwithstanding), and Graham emphasizes the importance of Aristotle in defining literate methods (pp. 34–35). To be sure, for a literate revolution to have taken place it is not necessary to posit *general* literacy, only a literate class within society. A high literacy rate is not necessarily correlated closely to the production of novelistic literature. The existence of novelistic writings in ancient Israel or Egypt can be attributed to the literary production of a scribal subculture. Furthermore, the cultures that have produced the *longest* novels are nineteenth century Russia and medieval China and Japan, all of which had low literacy rates. In general on the issue of ancient and comparative literacy, see Havelock, *Origins of Western Literacy;* Terence A. Boring, *Literacy in Ancient Sparta* (Leiden: Brill, 1979); and Goody and Watt, "Consequences of

is also a huge spike in the graph of world literacy, beginning in Athens in the fifth century B.C.E., continuing throughout the Hellenistic world from about the second century B.C.E., and lasting until the fall of the Roman Empire. This major achievement in the spread of writing has to be taken into consideration for a study of ancient novelistic literature. The literacy that was thus one of the hallmarks of the late Hellenistic period was available to Jews as much as to anyone (whether in Greek, Aramaic, or Hebrew) and perhaps more so. Furthermore, the rise of a larger class of entrepreneurs, merchants, and state bureaucrats—that is, a bourgeoisie—created an audience for a new art form: novelistic popular literature. The term *novelistic* as used here, however, is intentionally broad, covering written prose narratives of different regions and ethnic groups, whether short or long, simple or highly developed. Where it derives its specificity is in the focus on the new (novel) application of older narrative forms to a *written* medium for a *popular* audience. The Jewish novels arose from story-telling traditions that were mainly oral, influenced by Persian traditions, and also from the interpretation of biblical precedents, but we are here following the evolution of these narratives into an era of a new written literature. The new genre that is created out of old ones is the novel, and although it is difficult to describe, we may begin with a tentative definition of the novel as a work of prose narrative fiction, composed (or reedited) and transmitted in the written medium and read primarily as entertainment. Its attainment of some extension in length allows for the development of plot and subplot and the fuller exploration of the interior life of the characters, that is, their psychological and moral dimension and their motivation.

Central to the rise of the popular novel is what I term the novelistic impulse: the tendency under certain social conditions for authors to transfer oral stories over to a written medium, to embellish them and create others, using description, interior psychological exploration, dialogue, and other narrative devices that can be easily manipulated in written prose but are not as often utilized in oral. Popular written prose narrative, where it occurs, arises as a result of the novelistic impulse, but its creatures are quite varied. Under some conditions, longer works can

Literacy." Harris gives a low estimate for the number of people in the ancient West who were literate (*Ancient Literacy*), but see also James G. Keenan's review, "Ancient Literacy," *Ancient History Bulletin* 5 (1991): 101–7. Some scholars who are skeptical about the high rate of literacy in classical Athens nevertheless grant that literacy was much higher in the Roman period; see Thomas, *Literacy and Orality in Ancient Greece*, 158–70, and James L. Franklin, Jr., "Literacy and the Parietal Inscriptions of Pompeii," in Beard et al., eds., *Literacy in the Roman World*, 77–98.

arise, as in the case of the novels of ancient Greece and Rome, medieval China and Japan, or modern Europe. In other cases, this level of investment by author and reader is not reached or maintained; nevertheless, a similar novelistic impulse is discernible.

The structural variety of novels is great, and formal conventions are few. It is in the very nature of prose narrative, in fact, to resist a *formal* definition. In the rise of both scholarly and entertaining prose writing there is generally the same attempt at verisimilitude, that is, the plastic exploration and extending of the medium of writing to conform to the many shapes and textures of reality. It is what Ian Watt refers to as "the correspondence between the literary work and the reality which it imitates" or what Elizabeth Deeds Ermarth terms the "rationalization of consciousness."[6] Watt emphasizes the comprehensiveness of the novel in presuming to describe "all" of reality, whereas Ermarth, like many other recent literary critics, focuses on the unity and rationalization of vision attained by the deliberate sequencing of events and the ordering of reality. This logical and temporal progression of events that is associated with the novel is precisely what Ong points to as the major difference between literate-culture thought and that of oral culture.[7] Although this distinction can be overly schematized and some scholars romanticize the literate-culture development as the culmination of an evolution of reason, it can still be stated descriptively that the novel is the inevitable art form of literate culture. Behind written prose narrative, as opposed to poetry, there is the presumed need—and the operative pretense—to "mirror" reality and to describe it as it is. One need not protest that reality could never be described accurately, much less fully, or that the most objectifying prose is still full of ideological prejudices and distortions; in prose writing there is generally the pretense that reality is being described fully and accurately.

Like the novel of any place or period, the Jewish novel had a tendency to blend on all sides with other sorts of writings. It can be seen variously as a commentary on scripture or a vulgarization of history writing (as biblical scholars have consciously or subconsciously treated it), a continuation of the oral folktale into the written medium, or an

---

6 Watt, *The Rise of the Novel*, 11; and Elizabeth Deeds Ermarth, *Realism and Consensus in the English Novel* (Princeton: Princeton University Press, 1983), 5. Regarding the issue of the ordering of events in narrative, see Rimmon-Kenan, *Narrative Fiction*, 43–58.

7 Ong, *Orality and Literacy*, esp. 78–116. Recent discussions of the problems of overvaluing the "literate revolution" (with bibliography) can be found in Nagy, "Homeric Questions," 32, and "Mythological Exemplum in Homer," 318–19.

early version of the larger Greek novel. The exact contours and formal characteristics of the novel thus remain ambiguous. The lack of a term in the ancient world for the Jewish novel—or for the Greek and Roman novel—forces us to utilize, in place of any known ancient genre category, a hermeneutical model of our own naming that can explain the data before us. To be sure, *novel* as a genre title could be criticized as conveying more to the modern reader than is actually intended here. The Jewish novels, for example, are shorter than modern novels or even Greek and Roman novels. Yet other terms do not seem quite appropriate. The term *novella,* for instance, in the modern idiom generally refers to carefully crafted literary works that are too short to be novels and too long to be short stories and that are often seen as derived forms of the more rambling novel. Indeed, some of the greatest novelists of the nineteenth and twentieth centuries, such as Henry James, D. H. Lawrence, Herman Melville, Leo Tolstoy, and James Joyce, also turned their attentions to the creation of finely sculpted novellas. This is a recent development, however; the word goes back many centuries in Italy, where it was used to describe tales such as those found in Boccaccio's *Decameron.* The origins of novelistic literature in Europe from traditional stories might offer more parallels to the ancient Jewish novels than would carefully constructed modern novellas. In the study of ancient literature and culture, *novella* is often used for oral narratives that are short and entertaining, set in the real world instead of the make-believe world of the fairy tale, and focused on a single unexpected turn of events. In either case, then, this term may bring with it many different associations from other fields.[8] Likewise, *short story* should properly be restricted to the modern experiment in narrative fiction that investigates in a few pages a carefully circumscribed dramatic universe and that cannot contain the broad gestures and pretensions of a worldwide perspective that the Jewish novels often present. Despite the fact that Jewish novels lie between the short story and modern novella in size, they actually have a social and literary function that is closer to that of the novel, whether ancient or modern, as this study will try to show.

To be located in the context of literary history, the Jewish novels

---

[8] The study on the Joseph story as novella by Humphreys ("Novella") relies quite heavily on modern "high literary" novellas for its definition of terms and thus has difficulty placing the Joseph narrative in an ancient literary tradition. On the use of novella for traditional narratives, see, for example, Weimar, "Formen frühjudisher Literatur"; Trenkner, *The Greek Novella in the Classical Period;* Benno von Wiese, *Novelle,* 6th ed. (Stuttgart: Metzlersche Verlagsbuchhandlung, 1975); and the references to Jason in the notes that follow.

should first be compared to the earlier biblical literature. The rich tapestry of the literature of the Hebrew Bible is derived from many genres, woven, more than likely, over a full millennium. The best literature of the Bible, however, at least as far as prose narrative is concerned, is usually dated from the period of the reign of Solomon in the tenth century B.C.E. down to the destruction of Judah by the Babylonians in the sixth and consists of the Pentateuch (five books of Moses) and the earlier historical works (Former Prophets: *Joshua, Judges, First* and *Second Samuel*, and *First* and *Second Kings*). The style of the Jewish novels, whether of those within the Jewish canon (*Esther* and *Daniel*) or those without (*Tobit, Judith, Joseph and Aseneth*), is easily contrasted to the "classical" biblical prose. The latter, to be sure, is hardly homogeneous in style. The Pentateuchal narratives are episodic, whereas some parts of the historical books, such as the Succession Narrative of *Second Samuel* 9 to *First Kings* 2, are more continuous; God is present and active as a character in the former but often hidden in the background in the latter; and the sense of awe and lack of distance between the realms of the natural and the supernatural is strong in the Pentateuch, whereas the Succession Narrative is more realistic and "typical" of human experience.[9] For our purposes, however, they still share one important trait: the artistry of expression is achieved through the most judicious restraint. There is little detail or description, little direct reporting of interior emotional states.[10] When emotions are displayed as a result of some great loss, such as the death of Sarah (*Genesis* 23), they are communicated by the external actions of the characters at appropriate dramatic moments, in a "classical" separation of levels. The whole artifice is carried forward by plot[11] and also by characterization but rarely through the twin techniques

---

[9] Folklorists have tried to account for the different ways in which the otherworldly is present in various kinds of narratives. See Jason, "Aspects of the Fabulous in Oral Literature."

[10] Auerbach, *Mimesis;* Alter, *Art of Biblical Narrative,* 12, 17; Chase, *Life and Literature in the Old Testament,* 95–118. Note also, however, the important caution of Scholes and Kellogg (*The Nature of Narrative,* 167) that it is incorrect to romanticize the value of "restraint" in archaic narrative: "There is no restraint involved in not doing something which it does not occur to one to do." Even if the restraint is not a conscious choice, it nevertheless resonates with modern readers as a positive aesthetic achievement. Put another way, the present study is concerned precisely with this process of learning the *lack* of restraint.

[11] Sternberg has shown (in *The Poetics of Biblical Narrative*) that plot is more subtle and complicated than previously recognized. Sternberg, it should be noted, insists (232, 268) that Auerbach overemphasizes the economy of biblical prose, but as a *general* statement I believe that Auerbach's is quite accurate.

that are the stock-in-trade of novelists: internalizing psychology[12] and discursive description.

A "golden age" that would produce such classical restraint, however, could not last; the fall of Israel, first to Assyria in 721 B.C.E. and then to the Neo-Babylonian Empire in 587 B.C.E., brought about the end of this age of achievement. The prose narrative that derives from the Babylonian Exile and after is very important historically but in general lacks the ambition to describe reality at a high artistic level through the medium of prose.[13] In terms of continuous prose narrative, the productions of the postexilic period—at least the ones we are aware of—come to a curious halt at about 400 B.C.E., after the composition of *Ezra* and *Nehemiah*. From this point down to about 200 B.C.E. is a period scholars have considered a "dark age." There is not one Jewish prose work that can be dated with confidence to this period, and few can even be considered. We possess fairly full historical information about the major empires of the period and fascinating information about Jews from archaeological finds, but the lacuna in Jewish literary history is more than two centuries long.[14] The end of this "dark age" is the date at which we

---

[12] Lukács (*The Theory of the Novel*, 66, 88, 118–19) laid great store by the exploration of the interior life of the protagonist as a defining characteristic of the novel. This issue will be taken up again in Chapter 6.

[13] The historical divisions adopted here represent the common consensus of the field, but note that John Van Seters (*In Search of History* [New Haven: Yale University Press, 1983], 209–362) would assign the entire production of biblical literary prose to a much later date. Other revisions of the dating of the pentateuchal sagas, especially in regard to the Joseph narrative of *Genesis* 37–50, will be considered in Chapter 6. Tamara Cohn Eskanazi (*In an Age of Prose: A Literary Approach to Ezra-Nehemiah* [Atlanta: Scholars, 1988]) also proposes to find literary and aesthetic qualities in *Ezra-Nehemiah*, but surely nothing that could compare with the earlier literature.

[14] On the scarcity of Jewish narrative and historical writings in this period, see Smith, *Palestinian Parties*, 148–92, and Michael Stone, *Scriptures, Sects, and Visions*, 23–35. Some prose works are practically undatable, such as *Jonah, Ruth*, or the prose frame of *Job*, and for this and other reasons (their brevity, for example), they are omitted from my analysis; how they relate to the novels must be addressed elsewhere. *Esther* or its sources may have been written in the "dark age," as well as the sources of *Daniel* 1–6, *Tobit, Judith*, or *First Enoch*, but no complete document can be stated with assurance to have been written between the fifth and second centuries B.C.E.

Ironically, this "dark age" was evidently a period of peace and prosperity for Jews, who lived comfortably under the shadow of the Persian and Hellenistic kingdoms; pottery finds from this period in Palestine indicate a lively mix of Greek, Egyptian, and Asiatic styles (M. Rostovtzeff, *Social and Economic History of the Hellenistic World*, 3 vols. [Oxford: Oxford University Press, 1941], 3:1325), and David Biale, *Power and Powerlessness in Jewish History* [New York: Schocken, 1986], 18). Important glimpses into Jewish social and economic life of this period have also been afforded from three major textual discoveries: the papyri from the Jewish mili-

take up the study of the Jewish novels, for they were all likely written or edited after the Maccabean Revolt in 167–164 B.C.E. Novelistic experiments may have occurred in Judaism before 200, but they are difficult to trace, and the high period of the novels begins some time after that.

The differences in style between the novels and the preexilic masterpieces of Hebrew literature might at first sight be attributed to an internal degeneration of the Jewish creative spirit, but the explanation is more to be found in the common aesthetic of the Hellenistic Age. Where the classical Hebrew literature lacks description, the Jewish novels paint with a broad brush; where the classical literature lacks discursive treatment of theme, the novels are certain to impress the reader with a pious or deeply felt message; where the classical literature reveals characters' emotions externally and with a classical hierarchy of scale, the novels open up the characters' souls to allow a complete examination of the *Sturm und Drang* of their inner lives. These tendencies are also found in Hellenistic literature even before the novel, as well as in visual art, and should not surprise us here. A full appreciation of the Jewish novels requires us not simply to compare these writings with other biblical narratives but to see them for what they are: popular writings of the late Hellenistic and Roman periods, written for entertainment and enjoyed and transmitted widely.

The Depiction of Women in the Jewish Novels

The difference between preexilic Hebrew narrative and the Jewish novels is nowhere more clearly in evidence than in the depiction of women. The number of important women characters in both bodies of literature is truly striking, but the *ways* in which women are depicted are very different and reflect quite different sets of social circumstances.

---

tary colony at Elephantine, Egypt; the business letters of Jewish entrepreneurs among the Zenon papyri from Egypt; and the banking records of Jews found among the Murashu tablets in Persia. See on Elephantine, Bezalel Porten, *Archives from Egypt* (Berkeley and Los Angeles: University of California Press, 1968), and A. E. Cowley, *Aramaic Papyri from the Fifth Century* B.C. (Osnabrück: Zeller, 1967); on the Zenon papyri, Tcherikover, *Hellenistic Civilization and the Jews,* 60–72; on the Murashu tablets, Michael David Coogan, "Life in the Diaspora: Jews at Nippur in the Fifth Century B.C.," *Biblical Archaeologist* 37 (1974): 6–12. On the historical reconstruction of this period in general, see John H. Hayes and J. Maxwell Miller, *Israelite and Judaean History* (London: SCM, 1977); W. D. Davies and Louis Finkelstein, eds., *Cambridge History of Judaism,* 2 vols. (Cambridge: Cambridge University, 1984–89); and Trebilco, *Jewish Communities in Asia Minor.*

In the preexilic biblical narratives, women often appear in the most forceful and dramatic roles. The account of the victory of the Hebrew prophetess Deborah over Sisera, in both its prosaic and poetic versions (*Judges* 4, 5), places first Deborah and then Jael resolutely in control of their destinies in a time of crisis. Other women emerge as fully formed dramatic characters of import, such as Sarah (*Genesis* 18–21) and Tamar (*Genesis* 38), or who wield political power within the royal court, such as Bathsheba (*First Kings* 1). Their sex, or the limitation of their gender, though often clearly discernible, is rarely discussed as an issue. Reading these narratives, one would assume that in both the Pentateuch and the preexilic history books women walk about over the same stage with men, act and speak their lines as forcibly, and are as much involved as men—if not more so!—with the shaping of their own destiny. In reality, women probably did not enjoy such freedom of speech and significant, public action, but in the narrative world they do; this contrast has prompted some feminist scholars to try to explain the intriguing roles of these women characters. Tikva Frymer-Kensky suggests that in this narrative world, which is unreal and only partially drawn, the actual social relations of men and women are not described.[15] Women are allowed to play out their parts as dramatic characters in the public realm, while men are often surprisingly active in the private. Preexilic

[15] Frymer-Kensky, *In the Wake of Goddesses,* 118–43, esp. 120–21. My remarks here are necessarily quite general. Feminist analysis of the individual passages often searches out nuances with very intriguing results. Regarding Deborah and Jael, for example, Hackett has suggested that such strong women leaders as these may arise during periods of instability, decentralized power relations, and "social dysfunction" and that the entire distinction of public and private spheres may be inappropriate in more primitive economic and political formations ("In the Days of Jael," 22–26). Phyllis Bird would also point out ("The Place of Women in the Israelite Cultus," in *Ancient Israelite Religion,* ed. Patrick D. Miller, Jr., Paul D. Hanson, and S. Dean McBride [Philadelphia: Fortress, 1987], 401–9) that the role of *prophet,* which Deborah has assumed, was not a hereditary office limited to men but a charismatic role that could on occasion be carried out by exceptional women. On the role of women in general, see also Niditch, "Portrayals of Women in the Hebrew Bible"; Trible, *Texts of Terror;* and J. Cheryl Exum, "Mother in Israel: A Familiar Figure Reconsidered," in *Feminist Interpretations of the Bible,* ed. Letty M. Russell (Philadelphia: Fortress, 1985), 73–85.

The theoretical issues raised by the discrepancy between the depiction of women in art and the actual social relations of women and men are illuminated also by studies of other eras. See Roberta L. Krueger, "Double Jeopardy: The Appropriation of Women in Four Old French Romances of the 'Cycle de la Gageure,'" in *Seeking the Woman in Late Medieval and Renaissance Writings,* ed. Sheila Fisher and Janet E. Halley (Knoxville: University of Tennessee Press, 1989), 21–50; Penny Shine Gold, *The Lady and the Virgin: Image, Attitude, and Experience in Twelfth-Century France* (Chicago: University of Chicago Press, 1985), xv–xxi; and Alice Jardine, *Gynesis: Configurations of Woman and Modernity* (Ithaca, N.Y.: Cornell University Press, 1985).

biblical narrative, says Frymer-Kensky, is not so much gender-neutral as it is gender-blind.[16]

In classical Greek drama as well, women characters rise to great prominence in the artistic world of the stage, even though their actual social role was quite limited. Greek women, unlike Roman women several centuries later, had almost no social function in the public world of the city. Much the same situation may obtain in classical Greek literature as in classical Hebrew. In the abstracted image of the dramatic world, women characters emerge from the inner chambers of the home to challenge the male hegemony in the government of the city. Nicole Loraux points out, however, that in this liminal state in which women emerge from obscurity to take dramatic action, they usually come to a violent end: they commit suicide if they are married, or they are sacrificed if they are virgins. When the liminal state is traversed, there is a resolution of the dramatic tension by an expiatory sacrifice, reaffirming the typical, mundane social relations.[17] The strong presence of women characters in classical Hebrew and Greek literature, therefore, should not be taken as a direct reflection of their actual social roles; in fact, it is quite possible that strong roles for women derive from male projections of an archetypal dramatic world in which women, like goddesses, have power and substance.

The new developments in the Hellenistic period, however, present a different situation altogether. In Greece and in Rome and among Jews as well, women really did begin to interact with men on a social and business level, if somewhat less on a political level. The increased presence of women in everything from philosophical schools to business dealings to public works can be documented, both in the society at large and among Jews.[18] The open city of the Hellenistic world was open to a limited degree to women also. One might expect, then, that the lit-

[16] Fuchs ("Who is Hiding the Truth?") also cautions us to mark clearly the conditions under which the women characters in the Hebrew Bible gain entry into men's power relations. If a woman really does have more control over her destiny than a man, it is because in the narrative world a woman often rises through deceit to the effective action usually denied her.

[17] Nicole Loraux, *Tragic Ways of Killing a Woman* (Cambridge: Harvard University, 1987), 4. Compare also Frye, *The Secular Scripture,* 70–71; Lefkowitz, "Influential Women"; and Helene P. Foley, "The Concept of Women in Athenian Drama," in Foley, ed., *Reflections of Women in Antiquity* (New York: Gordon and Breach, 1981), 127–68.

[18] On the partial openness to participation by women, see Grant, *From Alexander to Cleopatra,* 149–213. Concerning Jewish women, see Kraemer, "Jewish Women in the Diaspora World of Late Antiquity"; Levine, ed., *"Women Like This";* and Bernadette Brooten, *Women Leaders in the Ancient Synagogue* (Chico, Calif.: Scholars, 1982).

erature of the period would fully embrace this social fact and depict women as they were. A new social realism, however, transparent to the actual roles of women, was not to occur in this literature. The women depicted in Jewish novels do not so much move onto the stage of the human drama as take total possession of it. Even where there are other male characters, the dramatic tension is focused on the heroine, and the evolution of the novels moves consistently in this direction. The last novel, *Joseph and Aseneth,* is devoted almost entirely to the heroine's emotional turmoil.

We shall find, in addition, that the heroine is much more than a new stock figure in the repertoire of characters; she is the medium through which certain obsessions of the author and audience are expressed. At a crucial moment in the narrative, near the middle but before the decisive action of the climax, the female protagonist enters into a process of cleansing and self-abasement. She must debase the sexually attractive parts of her body, as if to expiate the sin that pertains to her gender. In Greek *Esther,* for example, when Haman's decree against the Jews becomes known, Esther's reaction is developed beyond that found in the version of Esther in the Hebrew Bible: "Esther the queen, gripped by the fear of impending death, turned to the Lord for refuge; she took off her rich garments and robed herself in clothes of mourning and tribulation, covering her head with ashes and dung in place of her expensive perfumes. She utterly humbled her body, and every part that she had earlier adorned with such delight she now covered with her fallen tresses." (14:1–2) This motif is often greatly expanded in the Jewish novels, as in the case of *Joseph and Aseneth,* where Aseneth wallows in ashes and her tears for hours, repenting of her idolatry. These scenes are depictions of ritualized grief, based on the ritualized gestures of mourning: rending one's clothes or wearing sackcloth, and befouling one's head with ashes. In some cases, as in Greek *Esther* and *Joseph and Aseneth,* there is a past sin that could be seen as giving rise to this need for purgation, but in the case of *Judith* there is none. Men are also depicted enacting the symbols of mourning as a protestation of their grief (for instance, Mordecai in *Esth* 4:1), but the action takes on a deeper psychological meaning in regard to the female protagonist's private scene of prayer and penitence; her sexual attractiveness becomes a central issue, as do her change of identity and even her death and rebirth. Death and rebirth are not really new elements imported into the symbol system of the mourning process; it had long been felt in Israel that the mourner also dies symbolically and is reborn when he or she is reintegrated into society.[19] What appears to be new, however, is the combination of the death and rebirth of the mourning event with a change of identity.

In addition, the female protagonist of the novel, like the heroine of a Gothic novel, is at the same time often placed in jeopardy. This surprising comparison invites a closer look, for the Gothic novels of the late eighteenth and early nineteenth centuries share a curious feature with the Jewish novels: they portray a similar debasing of the heroine's body. Compare with the quotation above this account of the Gothic heroine Agnes, condemned to a dungeon with her child, from Matthew Lewis's *The Monk.* "Sometimes I felt the bloated toad, hideous and pampered with the poisonous vapours of the dungeon, dragging his loathsome length along my bosom. Sometimes the quick cold lizard roused me, leaving his slimy track upon my face, and entangling itself in the tresses of my wild and matted hair. Often have I at waking found my fingers ringed with the long worms which bred in the corrupted flesh of my infant." [20] The debasing of her sexually attractive parts, her bosom and hair, is similar to what is found in the Jewish novels. In the Gothic novel, the refinement associated with women is stripped away in horror. Novalis, influenced by the same ethos as that of the marquis de Sade, could aver, "It is strange that the association of desire, religion and cruelty should not have immediately attracted men's attention to the intimate relationship which exists between them." [21] The eroticism of the Jewish novels and the heroine's purging of her sinful desires lead one to suspect that the association of desire, religion, and cruelty is present here as well.[22]

Though such passages clearly suggest a male projection of the erotic

[19] Gary A. Anderson, *A Time to Mourn, a Time to Dance: The Expression of Grief and Joy in Israelite Religion* (University Park: Pennsylvania State University Press, 1991), 87–91.

[20] Quoted by Mario Praz, *The Romantic Agony* (London: Oxford, 1951), 111.

[21] From Novalis's *Psychological Fragments,* quoted by Praz, "Introductory Essay," in *Three Gothic Novels* (Harmondsworth: Penguin, 1968), 11.

[22] Though the Gothic heroines are apparently not being purged of their sexuality or the taint of sin, they are not the agents of their own debasement, as is the case in the Jewish novellas. See Raymond W. Mise, *The Gothic Heroine and the Nature of the Gothic Novel* (New York: Arno, 1980), 245–51. The perception of the woman's role as a "subversive" stance vis-à-vis normal gender relations is a common temptation—see, for example, Lacocque, *The Feminine Unconventional,* and Chapter 5, on *Judith*—but the danger inherent in this is noted by Krueger, "Double Jeopardy," 44: "But what is significant about . . . the modern theorists' inscription of 'woman' is that they deploy her to explore a crisis in male culture. Precisely because historical woman is marginal to the structures of masculine power, the figure of 'woman' comes to represent opposition and subversion. . . . Male critics and clerics embody their highest poetic aims in the metaphor of woman."

and of the sin perceived to be inherent in women's attractiveness, on another level the scenes may *function* similarly for male and female readers. The new Jewish piety of the age, intensely personal and often internalizing, gave rise to a new penitential literature.[23] Added to *Daniel* in the Greek versions, for example, is the *Prayer of Azariah*. Along with his two companions, Azariah was thrown into Nebuchadnezzar's furnace. Although he and his friends have been models of piety in the narrative, he prays to God begging forgiveness, saying that their own punishment and the destruction of Jerusalem were deserved. The intense penitential piety, associated in the novels with the debasement of the woman's physical body, constitutes the beginnings of a new turn in Jewish religious psychology that is likely related to Jewish and Christian asceticism.[24] The novels present a "narrative asceticism" (though in the beginning probably lacking a corollary in actual practice) focusing on the woman but equally exemplary for both men and women. We shall return to this question in the concluding chapter.

The sensibility of the Gothic heroine placed in jeopardy bears more than a passing resemblance to the heroines of the Jewish novel. Among the elements added in Greek *Esther* vis-à-vis Hebrew *Esther* are her swooning and fainting at the rise of King Ahasuerous:

> Thus clothed in splendor, she called upon the all-seeing God and savior and chose two of her maids to accompany her. On one she leaned gracefully for support, while the other trailed behind her carrying her train. She was blushing and in the full bloom of her beauty, her face bright and cheerful, as though she were basking in her love's delight; within, however, her heart was frozen with fear. Making her way through each of the doors, she came before the presence of the king, as he sat upon his royal throne, dressed in the awesome radiance of his majesty and covered with gold and precious jewels—a formidable sight! He lifted his face, flushed with the power of his bearing, and glared at her in anger. The queen suddenly swooned, turning pale and faint, and collapsed upon the maid at her side. (15:2–7)

---

[23] Shaye J. D. Cohen, *From the Maccabees to the Mishnah* (Philadelphia: Westminster, 1987), 115–16, and Nickelsburg, *Jewish Literature Between the Bible and the Mishnah*, 28–30, 109–14. David Biale charts some of the shifts in sexual ethics among Jews in the period in question (*Eros and the Jews*, esp. 34–42). Although he gives relatively little attention to the Jewish novels, his conclusions are very suggestive for the present study.

[24] Asceticism was practiced by the Therapeutae, a Jewish communal sect that Philo describes in *On the Contemplative Life*, and evidently by the Essenes as well.

Esther's characterization here has attributes that come very close to those that one critic assigns to the Gothic heroine: youth, beauty, sensibility, innocence, propriety, delicacy, and filial obedience.[25] One important difference emerges, however, if we observe this last virtue closely. In the Gothic novel, filial obedience becomes a problematic virtue for the heroine, supplanted in the course of the novel by conjugal devotion. The breakdown of traditional extended-family relationships and the rise of an urban, bourgeois nuclear family appear to be reflected in the Gothic novel, as in the early modern novel generally.[26] In this respect, then, the Jewish novels stand significantly apart. Filial obedience and the extended family remain paramount, much more important as a virtue in the Jewish novels than is generally recognized.

Jewish Novels and the Greek Novel

The novels that we are studying are not derived forms of the Greek novel but a series of manifestations of popular art, some predating the Greek novel, that reflect the play of the novelistic impulse. These Jewish writings must bear some distant family relation to the Greek novels, and I will try to specify what that relation might be. They arise at about the same time, under similar conditions, in parts of the world that are ruled by the same successors of Alexander the Great. Greek novels are larger, written in a florid, self-consciously "literary" style, perhaps appealing to the literary pretentions of their audience. The five fully extant Greek novels, Chariton's *Chaereas and Callirhoe,* Xenophon's *An Ephesian Tale,* Achilles Tatius's *Leucippe and Clitophon,* Longus's *Daphnis and Chloe,* and Heliodorus's *An Ethiopian Story,* tell the story of the overpowering love of two surpassingly beautiful young people who are separated and overtaken by any number of threats and torments, dragged all around the Mediterranean, and finally reunited to find perfect marital bliss.[27]

---

[25] Mise, *Gothic Heroine,* 246–51.

[26] Ibid., 5–6, 144–45, 154.

[27] To be sure, the "typical" plot elements mentioned here are not found in each novel, a point that is often mentioned as a problem in defining the genre. However, MacQueen (*Myth, Rhetoric, and Fiction*) argues convincingly that each of the novels presumes a stable "model" of the genre and in some cases intentionally alters it.

The five complete novels or romances—the terms are used interchangably by most scholars studying the ancient period—and many fragments are now available in Reardon, ed., *Collected Ancient Greek Novels.* All translations of the Greek novels in the present study are from Reardon's collection. The best introductions to the recent study of the Greek novel

The quality of these novels varies, but some are exciting enough, with a compelling enough love story, to have secured considerable popularity down to the present day.

The popularity of the novels in the ancient period is usually attributed to the breakdown of the old city and clan structures, which defined each person in terms of strong local ties and allegiances. The independent *polis,* or city-state, of the classical period, the basic unit of Greek cultural and political life, had given way to a new conception of the city. The free citizens of the classical city had felt themselves bound by ties of intense loyalty to extended family and clan as well as to the city structure itself, but the strains on this aristocratic system of loyalties were already being felt when Alexander the Great, in a few eventful years, extended his father's control of Greece to include the entire domain of the Persian Empire as well, that is, all the lands from the eastern Mediterranean to India. This huge expanse came to be known as the *oikoumene,* the "entire civilized world." The Hellenistic cities that were created or reconstituted throughout the East were not independent but interdependent, tied together in a single sweeping economic system that stretched from Europe into Asia. The residents of these new cities came to view themselves no longer as *politai,* citizens of one city, but *kosmopolitai,* citizens of the world. As the world horizon grew larger and the importance of local ties diminished, there arose a new emphasis on individualism, even the interior life of the individual. As B. E. Perry describes this development:

> In the vastly expanded world of Hellenistic and Roman times, the individual lost nearly all his quondam importance and representative significance, having become too tiny to be tragic, or heroic, or poetic, or symbolical of anything more than himself or a particular segment of contemporary society. . . . The bigger the world the smaller the man. Faced with the immensity of things and his own helplessness before them, the spirit of Hellenistic man became passive in a way that it had never been before, and he regarded himself instinctively as the plaything of Fortune. All this is conspicuous from first to last in the Greek romance.[28]

include Reardon's *Form of the Greek Romance,* Hägg's *Novel in Antiquity,* and Morgan and Stoneman, eds., *Greek Fiction.* Still indispensable are Rohde, *Der griechische Roman und seine Vorläufer;* Merkelbach, *Roman und Mysterium in der Antike;* and Perry, *The Ancient Romances.* Of great interest for the scholar of comparative literature is Tatum and Vernazza, eds., *The Ancient Novel.*

[28] Perry, *Ancient Romances,* 47–48, quoted in Reardon, *Form of the Greek Romance,* 172. See also Pervo, *Profit with Delight,* 111–13. Many years ago, Bruno Lavagnini ("Le origini del ro-

As we shall see, there is some reason to question whether the "Hellenistic man" in every class or ethnic group reacted in precisely this way, and others have also asked whether the "Hellenistic man" in the audience of the novels was not more likely a woman.[29] For now, however, we note with approval Perry's attention to the social conditions that gave rise to the novel, and we also note, incidentally, that the same social conditions are often adduced to account for the rise of the *modern* novel as well.[30]

Although it is a commonplace to say, with Perry, that the social conditions of the late Hellenistic period gave rise to a focus on the isolated individual, reflected in the rootless protagonists of the novel, it is also true that there is a focus on the conjugal couple. One naturally gives rise to the other. The new "home" for the rootless individual is in the arms of the lover, where, at the beginning of the novel, erotic love is perfect and where, at the end, the beginnings of nuclear family life are established. Changes in Roman society in regard to such things as the sanctity of marriage and the strictures of chastity before marriage

---

manzo greco," in his *Studi sul romanzo greco* [Messina: G. D'Anna, 1950], 98–104) had drawn attention to the importance of the shift from the city-identity to a new identity that was at the same time universalized and individualized. It can also be expressed in terms of the breakdown of the strict public/private distinction of the older *polis*. The private world, especially that of women, became the center of the novel's interest just as it had in New Comedy (Williamson, "The Greek Romance," esp. 33–34; Hägg, *Novel in Antiquity*, 81–108).

[29] Pervo, *Profit with Delight*, 83–84, and Hägg, *Novel in Antiquity*, 94–95 (with reservations). The centrality of the female protagonist, as well as the female readership of modern romances, has suggested to many that women were well represented in the audience. Not all of the Greek novels need have the same audience, however. One can much more easily imagine the eroticism of *Daphnis and Chloe* appealing to women than, say, the discussion of sexual partners in *Leucippe and Clitophon* 2.37. See Winkler, *The Constraints of Desire*, 101–26, and for a cautious assessment of the function of the female character, see Williamson, "Greek Romance," 36–37. For various perspectives on the readers of Greek novels, see Brigitte Egger, "Looking at Chariton's Callirhoe," in Morgan and Stoneman, eds., *Greek Fiction*, 31–48; H. Elsom, "Callirhoe: Displaying the Phallic Woman," in Richlin, ed., *Pornography and Representation in Greece and Rome*, 212–30; Susan A. Stephens, "Who Read Ancient Novels?" in Tatum, ed., *The Search for the Ancient Novel*, 405–18; and Ewen Bowie, "The Readership of Greek Novels in the Ancient World," ibid., 435–59. The modern novel is often associated with female sensibilities and with a female audience, on which see Watt, *Rise of the Novel*, esp. 43–47, 151–4; Terry Eagleton, *The Rape of Clarissa: Writing, Sexuality, and Class Struggle in Samuel Richardson* (Minneapolis: University of Minnesota Press, 1982,) passim, but esp. 14–15 and 95–100; and Danahy, "Le Roman est-il chose femelle?"

[30] Watt, *Rise of the Novel*, passim, and George Steiner, *Language and Silence* (New York: Atheneum, 1967), 387–89. Lukács (*Theory of the Novel*, 80) emphasizes especially the focus on the individual at the center of the modern novel: "The inner form of the novel has been understood as the process of the problematic individual's journeying towards himself, . . . towards clear self-recognition." The more precise sociological reformulation of Watt's thesis by McKeon (*The Origins of the English Novel, 1600–1740*) seems plausible to me, but the data from the ancient world will probably not allow a precise comparison.

have been well documented. Thus, a marriage institution was created that was at the same time a very public affair and one that isolated the partners in a very private relationship: "It appears that marriage became more general as a practice, more public as an institution, more private as a mode of existence—a stronger force for binding conjugal partners and hence a more effective one for isolating the couple in a field of other social relations."[31] The pattern appears to be in general the same in the major eastern cities of the Greco-Roman world as in Rome itself, and the preoccupations of such a pattern can readily be seen in the Greek novel.

The question of the origins of the Greek novels has been illuminated by finds of early papyrus fragments of these novels and others, such as the story of *Ninus and Semiramis*. The explanation of the rise of the novel, however, and of its relation to previously existing genres has been much controverted. Similarities can be found between novels and many of the other genres that existed in antiquity. New Comedy, lyric and epic poetry, historiography, and biography all betray signs of transformations in the Hellenistic period that parallel the themes and structures of romance, such as emotional intensity and introspection, alienation or separation from old civic structures, individualism, domestic setting, love, and, most of all, the gaudy triumph of happiness over suffering. Most scholars who treat ancient Greek novels nevertheless feel confident that the special "attitude" of romance differentiates the five extant novels from other literature, and a definition of romance can be agreed upon. Bryan Reardon's, for example, is the following: "Extensive narrative fiction in prose, destined for reading and not for public performance, describing the vicissitudes and psychological torments of private individuals, culminating in their ultimate felicity, and achieving through the presentation of their fears and aspirations the satisfaction of similar emotions in the reader."[32] The definition of novel that I offered above is not very different, but one wonders whether the ethos of the romantic novel (and therefore most of the ancient novels) is captured more economically by Jean Radford when she calls it a "non-mimetic (that is, non-realistic) prose narrative focusing on emotion."[33] Indeed, the element of emotion as a constitutive element of the novel has been proposed before, by Elizabeth Hazelton Haight. She distin-

---

[31] Michel Foucault, *The History of Sexuality*, 3:77. See also Veyne, "La famille et l'amour sous le haut-empire romain."

[32] Reardon, *Form of the Greek Romance*, 100.

[33] Radford, "Introduction," in Radford, ed., *Progress of Romance*, 8.

guishes two kinds of short narratives that were current in Greece and the East and that may have influenced the development of the novel: cynical and realistic rogues' tales or erotic adventures on the one hand, which had "interest of episode, plot or behavior" but were "uncolored by emotion," and romantic, usually tragic love stories on the other, which were "fundamentally colored by emotion." In her view, there was an evolution and merging of these two types toward a realistic novel with scenes "surcharged with emotion."[34] This surfeit of emotion comes close to the essence of the Greek novel and will be a key parallel between the Greek novels and their relatives, the Jewish novels.

Despite the modern scholar's relatively clear sense of the parameters of the Greek novels, it is still surprising that there are almost no references to these works in antiquity, either individually or as a genre. The Greek novel was not recognized among ancient intellectuals as a fit subject for literary analysis.[35] Genre, then, in regard to the Greek novel or to the Jewish, is not a category that arises from ancient canons; the novel is a modern hermeneutical construct that allows us to group and describe certain ancient writings according to their similarities. Genres "operate" within society even when they are not named, giving coherence to a certain contract between author and reader, to some extent conditioning both of them to the sort of experience that is to be expected. Genres are perhaps most "alive" and effective when they are subconscious and are often only named after they are dead.[36]

Furthermore, some writings in the ancient world, though not considered novels, nevertheless stretch their own genre boundaries and share some important characteristics with novels. The *Cyropaedia,* of Xenophon of Athens, for example, is a "biographical novel" of Cyrus's life, the *Alexander Romance* is a "historical novel," Philostratus's *Apol-*

---

[34] Haight, *Essays on Ancient Fiction,* 16–43. An example of the former type would be the Treasury of Rhampsinitus in Herodotus 2.121, and of the latter, the collection of stories in Parthenius's *Love Stories.* Once again, the parallel with the division of modern novels into the "serious" and the "picaresque," a division both Watt and McKeon exploit, is fascinating. MacQueen (*Myth, Rhetoric, and Fiction,* 117–37) would prefer to distinguish the body of serious Greek novels from the cynical *Leucippe and Clitophon* by Achilles Tatius, and from the more gentle but equally arch and subversive *Daphnis and Chloe.*

[35] Reardon, *Form of the Greek Romance,* 46–53.

[36] Ducrot and Todorov, *Encyclopedic Dictionary,* 149. This is also what Nagy has in mind when he says that "the very concept of *genre* becomes necessary only when the *occasion* for a given speech-act . . . is lost"—that is, the original performance situation of genres is often lost by the time the genres are given a name, canonized, *and imitated.* (*Pindar's Homer* 362–63 n. 127; see also p. 9; and Nagy, "Homeric Questions.")

lonius of Tyana is an "aretalogical novel" (or an account of a person's extraordinary qualities), and so on. These two points should serve as a cautionary restraint on those who would presume that a totally clear picture has emerged. Yet the poetics of the Jewish novels, that is, the set of rules by which they achieve their communicative ends, is inextricably tied up with the question of defining the parameters and significance of the genre, and the present work will consist of an attempt to group and describe a single genre, the Jewish novel.

The theoretical, even metaphysical, controversies over the difficulty of defining genres cannot be treated here in detail, even though they are inevitably just beneath the surface of any such endeavor. A basic distinction in the *kinds* of genre definition that are possible must be stated at the outset, however, and will be quite useful for our purposes. Frederic Jameson has noted, for example, that most genre classifications are based on an accounting either of the *semantic* elements present in the members of a genre or of the *syntactic* relationships among the elements.[37] Semantic elements are the separable motifs, themes, or techniques that tend to characterize a writing and indicate the *mode* of the work of art, its overriding and unmistakable ethos. To Jameson, Northrop Frye is the quintessential theorist of mode, specifically in regard to his study of romance. Syntactic relationships, by contrast, become the focus for many contemporary theorists, who look instead at the *model* of the interrelationships among the semantic elements. The relationships among the semantic elements in this approach become more important than the elements themselves. Vladimir Propp represents the classic expression of this approach to genre. Although the syntactic approach has held sway in recent scholarship, I shall argue in the following chapters that the semantic elements are equally valuable in discerning the nature and meaning of the genre at hand. I shall also suggest, in agreement with

[37] Jameson, "Magical Narratives," esp. 136–50. Similar distinctions have often been made in recent decades, using various terms for the two approaches, such as "etic" and "emic" (based on the analogy of "phonetic" and "phonemic") and "metaphoric" and "metonymic." On the latter, see Jakobson, "The Metaphoric and Metonymic Poles." Cawelti utilizes the same distinction between formula as motif and formula as plot structure in *Adventure, Mystery, and Romance*, 5–6. His terminology, however, does not have quite as wide an application as does Jameson's, nor does he intend it to. See also Radford, "Introduction," in Radford, ed., *Progress of Romance*, 8–12.

For a historical survey of the question of genre through 1972, see Paul Hernadi, *Beyond Genre: New Directions in Literary Classification* (Ithaca, N.Y.: Cornell University Press, 1972), and, more recently, Adena Rosemarin, *The Power of Genre* (Minneapolis: University of Minnesota Press, 1985).

the work of Rick Altman, a film historian whose work on genre has influenced discussions of literary genres,[38] that the two approaches can be reconciled and that this is the most adequate means of describing the poetics of this or any genre. Indeed, the definition of genre utilized here will be a body of works that reflect similarities on both the semantic and syntactic levels and that create a similar contract between the author and audience concerning the expected reading experience.

No less important than defining the nature of a particular genre is an account of its rise and development. The standard surveys of the early history of the Greek novel, to which the Jewish novel is related, place the origins in the first century B.C.E., the date of a fragment of *Ninus and Semiramis*.[39] It would be natural to conclude that the Greek novels evolved by their own internal logic from the small pieces of narrative tradition that existed in the second and first centuries B.C.E. The shifting demographics and the growth of a literate middle class provided an audience that was increasingly eager to have the pleasure of reading about the erotic attachments and narrow escapes of a beautiful young couple. The similar themes and interests of Hellenistic art and New Comedy could be adduced as additional evidence that an evolutionary trajectory for the novel was inevitable. The evolutionary model, however, has often been rejected as an inappropriate influence of the biological sciences on a question of the history of art. Major genres, according to Perry, do not "evolve" by increments out of the bits and pieces of a thousand different novelistic experiments. They are created in one burst of inspired innovation, and a new model of artistic expression is born.[40] In the case of the Greek novel, it was likely one anonymous author who independently created a long, episodic novel of love and adventure, utilizing, to be sure, many of the same motifs and techniques of the popular storytellers. And Perry has one very strong piece of evidence in support of his theory: the modern domestic novel arose along precisely these lines. Samuel Richardson, a businessman who composed guidebooks on proper letter writing, came upon the notion of creating an epistolary novel narrating a domestic drama, and the first true modern novel, *Pamela,* was thus composed in 1740. It could be countered that some of the groundwork of the novel had been laid by Cervantes, Boc-

[38] Altman, *The American Film Musical,* 90–128. Altman is in turn indebted to Jameson, "Magical Narratives." See also Ralph Cohen, "Genre Theory, Literary History, and Historical Change."

[39] Reardon, ed., *Collected Ancient Greek Novels,* 1–15, and *Form of the Greek Romance,* 3–14.

[40] Perry, *Ancient Romances,* 3–43, 149–80.

caccio, Swift, and Defoe, or that some evolution had already occurred in Richardson's own creative processes that led to the creation of the novel. His guidebook on letter writing, in fact, already contained more model letters to and from women and covered more personal, domestic matters than did other such guides, and these were precisely the interests we find in his novel.[41] It was nevertheless the one bold step of his epistolary novel, not his guidebook, that launched a totally new literary vehicle destined to establish the realistic novel as the modern literary form par excellence. The ancient Greek novel, according to Perry, likely originated in a similar way.

This view requires closer scrutiny, however. An evolutionary approach does not necessarily entail a biological model of accidental mutation and a consistent process of adaptation. An evolutionary model can account for changes in great leaps, not just in incremental steps, and without denying the importance of individual achievements. In terms of the one burst of inspired innovation, it is not simply a question of how the author may have found his or her voice; one can always posit a rare creative genius. The more pressing question is, Where did the audience come from? It is the relationship between a changing audience and the changing, experimental means of representing reality that presses art forward. To return to the example of Richardson, it is interesting that just as the first English domestic novel came on the heels of the author's guide to writing letters, so also Madame de La Fayette, the creator of the first French novel *The Princesse de Clèves,* was likely influenced by her association with the great epistolographer Madame de Sévigné. The relationship between the collection of domestic letters and the domestic novel is analogous in the two cases. Furthermore, the unique place that Richardson's *Pamela* holds as the herald of the new form is partly achieved by excluding all comers, from Defoe and Fielding to Madame de La Fayette.[42] Both Perry and Watt, in roughly contemporary books but looking at vastly different epochs, eliminate what they view as minor competitors to champion the lone creator of the novel genre. In the present study, the hermeneutical value of a diachronic model is seen as more justifiable, especially as the database of novels and novel-

---

[41] William M. Sale, Jr., "Introduction," in Samuel Richardson, *Pamela* (New York: Norton, 1958), vi.

[42] McKeon, *Origins of the English Novel.* The relationship of letter writing and the origins of fiction in the ancient world has also been explored by Patricia A. Rosenmeyer, "The Epistolary Novel," in Morgan and Stoneman, eds., *Greek Fiction,* 146–65, especially 147: "Epistolary technique always problematizes the boundary between reality and fiction."

istic fragments is broadened. *Diachronic* does not, however, simply refer here to an account of a succession of texts or historical events; it refers to a model whose structure can be accounted for in evolutionary terms: an evolutionary model versus a static model.[43] Perry, by contrast, proposes a historical succession of static models.

Perry's antievolutionary view is still echoed in many treatments of the Greek novel, although the search for literary antecedents and genealogies continues. Most scholars, as Bruce D. MacQueen has noted,[44] agree with Perry that literary forms do not evolve by an internal logic; such a view is perhaps the idealist-romantic affirmation of an earlier generation of literary historians, against which Perry was reacting. Many critics, with Perry, do, however, emphasize the social dimension of literary forms, and since society does change, the new demands for literary forms can be seen as evolutionary, exerting a constant forward pull on a succession of new authors. Perry, more than most, was able to give a compelling account of the social world of the novel and the reasons why new social forms would welcome it. His concern was to avoid a specious explanation of the rise of the novel by recourse to previous forms. A new form was created for a new age, but in his mind it really was *new;* its distinctiveness was to be emphasized. Only an oversimplification, however, can reduce all literary innovations to the "one bold step" of literary history. This would not do justice to the thousands of smaller shifts and innovations, which, in response to changing social conditions, exhibit a directional progression that can only be called "evolutionary," even if they are not in and of themselves the kind of daring new composition that would constitute the larger Greek novel. The sum total of these minor innovations stands as evidence of a novelistic impulse: the coordinated desire of an author and audience from a middle-class, literate social stratum to engage the new art form of prose narrative fiction.

Parallels, then, with the Greek novel on the one hand or the Gothic novel on the other compel us to consider the novelistic impulse transhistorically and cross-culturally, as many scholars have indeed treated it. The modern novel, according to Lennard Davis, originated in an ambivalent relationship with the recently invented means of printing and dispensing journalistic information, a discourse between "novels" and "news." Prose narrative *nonfiction* was being used to describe actual

---

[43] See Nagy, *Pindar's Homer,* 21 n. 18; Ducrot and Todorov, *Encyclopedic Dictionary,* 144–45.

[44] MacQueen, *Myth, Rhetoric, and Fiction,* 204–24; see also 144–45 for a questioning of Perry's denial of a connection between historiography and the novel.

events, and prose *fiction* arose as a reflective art form for a new class that read about these events: "The novel is about reality and at the same time is not about reality. . . . It is a report on the world and an invention that parodies that report."[45] Davis's theory is suggestive for the rise of prose fiction in the ancient world. Given the definition of fiction as literature that provides a reading experience based on the enjoyment of imagined worlds or a narrative without a referent in past events, one wonders if ancient novels had a similar dialectical relationship with literature that conveyed truth claims. Neither the ancient Greek novel nor the Jewish novel had such a relationship with journalism per se, but they may have with history writing. For our purposes, history writing may be defined as an account of past events, presumed by the author and audience to have actually occurred, in which the author engages in a critical reflection on the reliability of conflicting sources. The rise of history writing in Greece corresponds to a new and precise delineation of the contrast between truth and opinion or hearsay. This observation has been developed along separate lines by three different scholars but with remarkably corroborative results. Gregory Nagy finds in Herodotus's distinction between truth and legend (*aletheia* and *mythos*) a concern for ferreting out historical traditions that are truly panhellenic and therefore "universal" or canonical, not mere local legend. B. P. Reardon emphasizes the importance of Thucydides' stated goal to write only what is "fact," and Northrop Frye attributes to Plato the fundamental Western metaphysical axiom that true statements are ones that correspond to the world.[46] Herodotus, Thucydides, Plato—all writing at about the same time (fifth to fourth century B.C.E.), using different language to articulate a new precision about historical and philosophical investigation, all giving the necessary underpinnings for history writing. And where there is a concern for precision about *fact,* communicated in prose, an art form written in prose is likely to arise which is playful about fact—that is, fiction. Reardon suggests that this reaction begins almost immediately in Greece, with the experiments in prose fiction found in Xenophon's *Cyropaedia.*[47] It is interesting, however, that many of the histories from

---

[45] Lennard J. Davis, *Factual Fictions: The Origins of the English Novel* (New York: Columbia University, 1983), 212.

[46] Nagy, *Pindar's Homer,* 52–67; Reardon, *Form of the Greek Romance,* 59–69; and Frye, *Secular Scripture,* 17–20. J. R. Morgan argues ("*Daphnis and Chloe:* Love's Own Sweet Story," in *Greek Fiction,* ed. Morgan and Stoneman, 73–74) that the prologue of *Daphnis and Chloe,* by intentionally subverting the stated principles of Thucydides' prologue, blurs the boundary between truth and fiction and thus makes a programmatic statement about fiction.

[47] Stewart Flory (*The Archaic Smile of Herodotus* [Detroit: Wayne State University, 1987], 49–79) finds a possible origin of this spirit even earlier, in Herodotus's *Histories,* where the

the two centuries after Herodotus, Thucydides, and Xenophon have not been preserved. There is a sort of "dark age" here as well, contemporary with that in Israel mentioned above, created by the canonizing of intellectual history writing.[48] MacQueen's argument that the Greek novel arose against the background of history writing[49] receives some corroboration, then, in Davis's theory concerning the modern novel.

Among Jews the period of the novels may mark a similar reaction to the canonizing of some of their own classical prose as sacred history. Ezra evidently promulgated the five books of Moses as a holy book near the end of the fifth century B.C.E. (Nehemiah 8), and the main historical books had been edited somewhat earlier. A new compilation of historical works arose, consisting of First and Second Chronicles, Ezra, and Nehemiah, that reflects a new mindset, celebrating both the creation of a "book" and a "people of the book." It is unclear whether this canonization to some extent creates the "dark age" of prose production that follows, but, at any rate, when the dark age comes to an end, novelistic works are among those that begin to appear. The novels that we are analyzing are not merely a degenerate stage of biblical literature, nor, despite all of their biblical allusions, are they "midrashic" compositions at the particular stage we are studying.[50] They are to biblical literature what fiction is to history, that is, they lack a referent in the presumed events of the past. They were probably perceived by their audiences as new fictional undertakings that evoked a romanticized era, imbued with pressing issues of contemporary Jewish identity.

Although there are many advantages to be gained by comparing the Greek and Jewish novels, important differences remain between them. The Jewish novels are entertaining fictions that, like Greek novels, play upon the alternation of a descent into the threat of chaos and an ascent

---

"Father of Lies" often moves playfully over several "false" traditions of an event, only to settle dutifully and humorlessly on the one supposedly true account.

[48] Smith, *Palestinian Parties*, 149. As Smith points out (271 n. 95), the rationalizing and harmonizing of dates and the "fixing" of historical data by the inclusion of genealogies occurs among intellectuals both great and small in Greece and in Israel. Such minor Jewish historians as Demetrius the Chronographer (ca. 210 C.E.) must have sent readers scurrying in search of new potentialities for prose.

[49] MacQueen, *Myth, Rhetoric, and Fiction*, 144–45.

[50] This statement requires careful qualification. It has been argued that certain parts of *Esther, Daniel,* or *Joseph and Aseneth* are midrashic compositions, that is, texts that are based on and inspired by some passage in scripture. Whereas this may very well be true for certain *stages* of their development, it is not characteristic of the freer, novelistic stages. On the process of midrashic composition in the Joseph tradition (including *Joseph and Aseneth*), see Kugel, *In Potiphar's House*, 11–155, and Chapter 6.

to deliverance and create a surfeit of emotions in the reader's response. There is, however, no element of travel in the Jewish novel as there is in most of the Greek novels, and the beautiful young couple who are the protagonists of the Greek novel are generally replaced by a beautiful young Jewish woman and her extended family members: Esther is swayed by her cousin Mordecai; Susanna, it is emphasized in the story, is shamed before her whole family and servants; Sarah and Tobias unite two families in Tobit; Judith is the pride of her dead husband's family; and Aseneth must be reconciled to Josephs family. Still, the same gaudy triumph of happiness over suffering that was noted above for the Greek novels applies here as well. The differences must nevertheless be outlined as carefully as the similarities.

The most obvious difference is that the Jewish novels are shorter. Greek Esther contains about 5,500 words, Tobit 6,500, and Judith 9,000, compared to about 15,000 words for Xenophon's *Ephesian Tale,* the shortest of the Greek novels (although even this may be an epitome of a longer novel), 35,000 words for Chariton's *Chaereas and Callirhoe,* the second shortest, and a hefty 80,000 words for Heliodorus's *Ethiopian Story,* the longest. Aside from their interesting similarity in length, the Jewish novels clearly have a literary function at a somewhat different level of society.[51] Despite classicists' neglect of the Greek novels as popular and sometimes base literature, these works are still relatively higher in the social, educational, and economic scale than most of the novelistic literature we shall be examining. In terms of social level, the Jewish novels look up at the Greek novels from below.

The second most important difference is language. Whereas the five fully preserved Greek novels are written in a somewhat elevated, florid Greek style, the Jewish novels were composed either in a Semitic language (Hebrew or Aramaic) or, for the last of the series, *Joseph and Aseneth,* in less educated Greek. This points up one of the most fascinating problems of our study: How did novelistic techniques shift along with the change from Semitic and Persian story structures to Greek? We are

[51] Regarding the size of the Jewish novels, it is interesting to include here the report of Milik that the fragments of some of the novelistic works from Qumran (otherwise unknown to us) are printed on scrolls in a small-page format, a format not used for other genres ("Ils meritent bien l'appelation d' 'éditions de poche' de l'antiquité" ["Les modèles araméens du livre d'Esther dans la grotte 4 de Qumrân," 363–65]). Milik misleadingly refers to the fragments as "proto-Esther," suggesting that they reflect some prior stage in the development of the Esther tradition; rather, they are *parallels* to Esther, of the sort Bickerman would call "harem-intrigues" (see Chapter 4). Milik had also earlier reported three fragments of a parallel to Susanna ("Daniel et Susanne à Qumrân?").

fortunate to possess in the Jewish novels the evidence of a large number of steps from ancient Near Eastern narrative traditions to novels with a self-consciously Hellenistic form. At the end of the process, we find in the additions to *Esther* two extremely pretentious and rhetorical Greek passages: the king's letter to annihilate the Jews and his second edict rescinding the first. At this stage in the composition of the Esther narrative, a "showpiece" was needed that would go further than the other additions in creating a version of *Esther* worthy of the level of style of Greek novelistic literature.

Novels and Historical Novels

It is not the thesis of this book that the Jewish novels are themselves the direct forerunners of the Greek novel, though S. West goes almost this far in regard to *Joseph and Aseneth*.[52] Jewish novels are perhaps more similar to the many other indigenous novelistic writings that have often been touted as true forerunners of the Greek novel. This body of adventurous narratives, attested from the first centuries B.C.E. in different geographical areas and among different ethnic groups, represents the broad stream of popular literature out of which both the Jewish novel and the Greek novel arose. The many experiments in the application of prose narrative that are attested internationally indicate the breadth of a late Hellenistic novelistic impulse that reshaped older stories and created new ones. *Ninus and Semiramis* was popular among native Syrians and descendants of the Babylonians, *Sesonchosis* and *Petubastis* among Egyptians, *Alexander Romance* most likely among Hellenized Egyptians, Artapanus's *Moses Romance* among Jews, and *Life of Aesop* among alienated Greeks. Martin Braun has grouped all of these (except *Aesop*) together as "national hero romances," popular romances that champion the early heroes of a people.[53] Love, as a motive force of the narrative,

---

[52] West, "Joseph and Asenath," 81. Compare the even more audacious claim of John Wintour Baldwin Barns, to the effect that all of the elements of Greek romance are already present in ancient Egyptian literature ("Egypt and the Greek Romance," *Mitteilungen aus der Papyrussammlung der Österreichischen Nationalbibliothek*, n.s., 5 [1956]: 29–36).

[53] Braun, *History and Romance in Graeco-Oriental Literature*, see also Hadas, *Hellenistic Culture*, 90, and Stoneman, *The Greek Alexander Romance*, 23: "The *Alexander Romance* is Cecil B. DeMille's Gospel of Alexander." Stoneman also notes (p. 19) the ethnic propaganda value of Jewish novels. Bickerman, however, believes that *Ninus*, like the *Story of Ahikar*, is essentially international in appeal and lacks the national propagandistic slant of these other works (*Jews in the Greek Age*, 51–52). English translations of the *Alexander Romance* and the fragments of *Ninus*

is sometimes absent in these writings and has a "transgeneric" history of its own, found in such places as New Comedy, lyric poetry, and Parthenius's *Love Stories*. The love theme and the novel form, then, are not coterminous. The Jewish novels may directly or indirectly reflect— or perhaps even subvert—an erotic interest, but they are actually more like these contemporary indigenous novels, which still derive some narrative energy from ethnic or antiaristocratic propaganda. By contrast, the somewhat later Greek novels espouse a "universal" value, romantic love, and are emphatically pro-"Hellenic" and anti-"barbarian." Just as Herodotus sought a panhellenic and therefore (to his mind) universal perspective, the Greek novels espouse a universal Hellenic motif, love, and look down on barbarians.[54] The following analysis of what is "novelistic" in the Jewish novels, however, will still rely heavily on

---

and Semiramis and *Sesonchosis* can be found in Reardon, ed., *Collected Ancient Greek Novels* (see also Stoneman for the first mentioned), whereas the *Petubastis* fragments (under the name of Pedikhons; cf. also the *Setne Khamwas* cycle, 3:125–51) are collected in Miriam Lichtheim, ed., *Ancient Egyptian Literature*, 3 vols. (Berkeley: University of California, 1973–80), 3:151–56, and the works by Artapanus in James H. Charlesworth, *Old Testament Pseudepigrapha*, 2 vols. (Garden City: Doubleday, 1985), 2:889–904. Pervo, *Profit with Delight*, is very responsible toward the many fragmentary novels from antiquity; see passim and esp. his table on p. 114. Although one recent study of the *Gospel of Mark* (Tolbert, *Sowing the Gospel*, 48–79) makes significant advances by comparing it to the Greek and Roman novel, the conclusions could have been stated even more strongly if the author had compared Mark with the more similar novelistic works that exist at a lower social class level, such as *Life of Aesop, Alexander Romance,* or the Jewish novels. In conversation she has suggested that her research is also moving in this direction and that further comparisons could be made between Mark and the indigenous novels.

Life of Aesop has been unjustly ignored in the discussion of ancient novelistic literature, but see Nagy, *The Best of the Achaeans*, 280–91; Nagy, *Pindar's Homer*, 322–25; and Winkler, *Auctor & Actor*, 286–91. An English translation can be found in Lloyd W. Daly, *Aesop without Morals* (New York: T. Yoseloff, 1961). The *Dream of Nectanebos* has also been considered a novelistic experiment, but Ludwig Koenen, "The Dream of Nectanebos," *Bulletin of the American Society of Papyrologists* 22 (1985): 171–94, argues against this idea. Philo of Byblos's Phoenician history is also in some respects novelistic (on which see R. A. Oden, Jr., "Philo of Byblos and Hellenistic Historiography," *Palestine Exploration Quarterly* 110 [1978]: 115–26), and another indigenous narrative fragment may be reflected in an Aramaic text in Demotic script (Richard C. Steiner and Charles F. Nims, "Ashurbanipal and Shamash-shum-ukin: A Tale of Two Brothers from the Aramaic Text in Demotic Script," *Revue Biblique* 92 [1985]: 60–81). Iambulus's *Empire of the Sun* (summarized in Diodorus Siculus 2.55–60) is very interesting for purposes of comparison, but the nature of this work is unclear in the fragment we possess, since it is broadly summarized. It appears to fall into the category of *Reisefabulistik*, or an account of travel wonders, much like Antonius Diogenes' *The Wonders Beyond Thule;* so Hägg, *Novel in Antiquity*, 117–18, and Stoneman, *Greek Alexander Romance*, 18. As an early fragment, it is nevertheless intriguing for what it suggests about the popular appeal of utopian travel narratives. On the Jewish counterparts to some of these writings, see especially Chapter 7 below.

[54] See Reardon's introduction to Chariton in his *Collected Ancient Greek Novels*, 18–19, and cf. Chariton 2.6: "You are a Greek, you live in a humane community, you are a civilized man—please don't be like the tomb robbers."

comparisons with the Greek novels, since in them we see most clearly the techniques and themes that could be realized in this new genre.

Alongside the Jewish novels and these national hero romances, we may also introduce other Jewish writings of the Greco-Roman period that share some characteristics with these popular works but that should nevertheless be placed in a slightly separate orbit: the "historical novels," such as *Third Maccabees, Second Maccabees* 3–4, and the *Tobiad Romance* and *Royal Family of Adiabene* from Josephus's *Antiquities*. The Jewish novels proper discussed above are set in a much earlier historical period relative to the author's own day and generally portray only characters from *outside* the canon of historical figures (often women placed in stress and jeopardy): Esther and Mordecai, Judith, Tobit and Sarah, Daniel and Susanna. Joseph, in the last of the novels, is a historical, "canonical" figure from the ancient past, but the interest of the story has shifted to a relative unknown, Aseneth. The novels were probably read by the audience as fictions and share other features that will be adumbrated in the course of this study. Historical novels cover the recent, as opposed to the ancient, past and were evidently presumed to be truthful and factual or at least to have a historical referent (to use Konstan's phrase). Women characters are rarer here, though not unknown. The category of historical novels also seems to go beyond the Jewish sphere, since the Christian *Acts of the Apostles* and apocryphal acts can be included, as can the early stages of the *Alexander Romance*.[55] The category of popular novelistic literature in the Hellenistic period, then, consists of several separate subgenres, among them novels, historical novels, and national hero romances. Despite all their variations, they occupy a similar social level and function.

The Poetics of the Popular Jewish Novel

Poetics is the analysis of the techniques of composition of a work of literature that define it as art, as opposed to a functional writing such as a list, court summons, or treaty. Any aspect of a literary work that

---

[55] Hägg ("The Beginnings of the Historical Novel") uses the term *historical novel* quite narrowly to mean a novel that takes a historical event or personage as part of its dramatic structure; he bases the definition largely on the modern historical novel and would include only Chariton and *Metiochus and Parthenope*. A more useful category—at the very least, a larger category—would be those works that deal with history in a novelistic way. Note, however, that in this usage a novel is fiction, whereas a historical novel is nonfiction.

pertains to its artifice, its imaginative composition, can be considered an appropriate part of the subject matter of poetics.[56] Poetics can also be expanded beyond an analysis of the text to a consideration of the role of the reader in interpreting the text, but in this book I set aside this level of analysis. Rather, I focus here on the text and not the reader, attempting to address what appear to be the most pressing questions of the character of popular indigenous novels in the ancient world. This approach often entails moving beyond some of the typical concerns of poetics as an analysis of isolated texts (or of "text" in the abstract) and reintroducing issues of literary history. The preoccupation of much of recent poetics with narrative grammar or a universal language of narrative inevitably leads to a different emphasis from that found in studies that look for genera among the wealth of narratives and their relation to social formations.[57] It could be argued that the latter entails a separate field of inquiry—literary history, as opposed to poetics— but the special methods and techniques that constitute the "novelistic" are the subject matter of both fields. With the novel—a gross, lumbering, seemingly formless type of literature—the larger tendencies and devices characteristic of its "envelope" are a crucial if sometimes unconscious part of the novelist's technique. This forces us to examine not just the "micropoetics" of the narrative grammar—valuable as that undoubtedly is—but the "macropoetics" as well. Here I intentionally broaden the scope of recent studies of biblical poetics and look at the correlation between narrative poetics and social function. My approach is diachronic in addition to synchronic, cross-cultural and comparative rather than culture-specific.[58]

---

[56] Rimmon-Kenan, *Narrative Fiction*, 2; Ducrot and Todorov, *Encyclopedic Dictionary*, 78–80.

[57] Compare, for example, the approach of Brichto, *Toward a Grammar of Biblical Poetics*, 3–5, 19–27. To a certain extent, the present study does utilize humanistic and sociological methods, which hold up as an attainable goal the contextualizing of the literary productions in their milieux. It is also influenced, however, by the results of more recent criticism to emphasize cross-cultural comparisons, to look for relationships within the text, and to distrust specious historical connections. Literary criticism at the edge of the twenty-first century has become increasingly eclectic, or it has simply recognized the value of eclecticism. Cf. here David Perkins, ed., *Theoretical Issues in Literary History* (Cambridge: Harvard University Press, 1991), and especially Ducrot and Todorov, *Encyclopedic Dictionary*, 144–45: Literary history is concerned with "literary discourse, not [individual] *works;* thus literary history is defined as part of poetics." The main epochs of twentieth-century literary criticism are characterized quite nicely, albeit briefly, by Cornel West, "On Georg Lukács," in *Keeping Faith* (New York: Routledge, 1993), 143–64.

[58] Many of these interests were characteristic of earlier literary theorists, such as Mikhail Bakhtin. See especially his *The Dialogic Imagination;* Bakhtin and P. N. Medvedev, *The Formal Method in Literary Scholarship: A Critical Introduction to Sociological Poetics* (Baltimore: Johns Hop-

Most important, however, is my insistence that the appropriate poetics to investigate this genre is to be derived from *popular* literature. Recent investigation of poetics has concerned itself largely, though not exclusively, with the great classics of modern European and American literature—Flaubert, Proust, Dostoevsky, Joyce, and Faulkner[59]— and has treated issues appropriate to those works, such as the order and manner of narration of events, "gaps" in narrative information, ambiguity of the narrator's voice and persona, and so on. These questions are certainly valid for the study of popular literature, but many of the acute and subtle, not to mention "modern," literary techniques of a Joyce or a Proust are not likely to emerge as significant artistic expressions in popular novels. To be sure, the distinction imposed here between popular and high literature may appear more subjective than objective, but it is important to emphasize throughout the present discussion that these categories are not based on aesthetic distinctions as much as on the social tendencies of two different modes of discourse. Most popular art inhabits a different world from that of high art—a world of mass production; repeatable, formulaic plots and characters; and market-driven concerns for immediacy of impact. To the extent that ancient novels participate in this popularity (and I argue here that they do), the poetics that are employed to describe them must address the ethos and compositional grammar of *that* body of literature. The poetics of popular literature must ultimately be sought through analysis of popular works, whether ancient or modern, and not through the analysis of high literary works alone.

Certain characteristics of popular literature can be mentioned at the outset to guide our study. Susan Niditch has addressed the pervasive influence of traditional narrative patterns in the written texts of the Bible and in doing so has produced some of the best recent work on this topic, but she does not analyze the popular transmission of written texts.[60]

---

kins University Press, 1978); and the brief introduction to Bakhtin's work by Todorov, *Mikhail Bakhtin,* esp. 80–85.

[59] Important exceptions to this nineteenth- and twentieth-century focus among literary critics include Bakhtin, who treats the ancient novel; Sternberg, *Poetics of Biblical Narrative;* Alter, *Art of Biblical Narrative;* and Bal, *Narratology.*

[60] Note, however, Niditch's remarks in *Underdogs and Tricksters,* xi–22, esp. 16, and "Legends of Wise Heroes and Heroines," 450–51. Other valuable recent studies of folklore analysis of biblical texts include Niditch, ed., *Text and Tradition;* Milne, *Vladimir Propp and the Study of Structure in Hebrew Biblical Narrative;* Kirkpatrick, *Old Testament and Folklore Study;* and Ronald S. Hendel, *The Epic of the Patriarch: The Jacob Cycle and the Narrative Traditions of Canaan and Israel* (Decatur, Ga.: Scholars, 1987). Christine Thomas is completing a doctoral dissertation at Har-

In terms of the distinction between oral and written culture, popular written narrative poses a special problem for scholars. On the one hand, a "literate" culture or subculture is presumed, even if the number of people in the society who can read and write is still a minority, and many of the techniques utilized in popular written literature are also found in "high literature." Extended use of dialogue, interwoven plots, explicit statements of a character's motivation, and interiorizing psychology are more commonly encountered in written than in oral narrative.[61] On the other hand, other aspects of popular narrative reflect similarities to the oral folklife of a culture and can be analyzed in those terms. Lack of a fixed text, anonymous authorship, conventional and repeatable plot motifs, one-dimensional moral characterizations (often balanced good against evil), and the easy appropriation of oral folk themes all bespeak a closeness with folk narrative.

Folklorists have begun to turn their attention to the level of cultural transmission that lies on the cusp of the oral level and the high literary level, and it has also been investigated by sociologists and scholars of literature under the category of "popular culture." John G. Cawelti has analyzed the modern formula story in several genres, focusing on the repeatability of the plot structures and their function in escape and relaxation.[62] He defends the standardization of genre in the formula story, noting among other things that it allows a prolific production by art-

---

vard University on the apocryphal *Acts of Peter* as a popular novel, and I have learned much from conversations with her on the nature of popular texts. It was she who pointed out to me the correlation between anonymity and the lack of a fixed text in Greek and Christian novelistic literature. These two properties, anonymity and the lack of a fixed text, raise issues of the "authority" of a popular textual tradition that I will address in this study.

[61] Axel Olrik, "Epic Laws of Folk Narrative," in *The Study of Folklore*, ed. Alan Dundes (Englewood Cliffs, N.J.: Prentice-Hall, 1965), 129–41, indicates some of the tendencies of oral narrative and, by contrast, written narrative. See also Ong, *Orality and Literacy*, and on explicit motivation, Propp, *The Morphology of the Folktale*, 75–76. Whereas Olrik misleadingly calls general tendencies of oral narrative "laws," Propp is much more nuanced: "Motivations often add to a tale a completely distinctive, vivid coloring, but nevertheless motivations belong to the most unstable elements of the tale. . . . Motivations formulated in words are alien to the tale on the whole."

[62] Cawelti, *Adventure, Mystery, and Romance;* see also Ducrot and Todorov, *Encyclopedic Dictionary*, 151: "The good detective story . . . does not attempt to be original (if it did, it would no longer deserve the name), but attempts, on the contrary, to apply the formula well." (For a critique of the view that formula works are not "original," see below, this chapter.) On modern romances in particular, see Tania Modleski, *Loving with a Vengeance: Mass-Produced Fantasies for Women* (New York: Methuen, 1984); Radway, *Reading the Romance;* and Radford, ed., *Progress of Romance.* On some of the difficulties of the division between oral and written in Greek literature, see Nagy, *Pindar's Homer*, 57–60, 80–84, 215–20.

ists in the field—Georges Simenon, for example, managed to write a vast number of best-selling detective novels—and also that escape and relaxation depend on a predictable genre and reading experience. Popular, formulaic literature provides a form of escape by transporting the reader from the uncertainties of the present world to an idealized world. Cawelti contrasts this with high art, which forces the reader to confront the troubling questions of existence and to return to the present world with no illusions.[63] Once escapist literature leaves the atmosphere of our real world, it does not look back again to comment or endow us with a greater degree of awareness of the tragic dimension of life. If it did, it would not be escapist, and we would find no relief in it.[64]

Heda Jason, a folklorist, also gives some attention to this *tertium quid* between oral narrative and high written literature. High literature and popular literature are similar in addressing a private reader, unlike oral narrative, which exists only in individual performances.[65] High literature also possesses a fixed text, whereas oral prose narrative is different with each performance and is not confined to a fixed text. Popular written prose narrative, Jason points out, is only semistable; various renditions of a written narrative can be created, and there is no sense of a single text.[66] This is certainly the case with the Jewish novels, most of which are attested in very different text recensions. Oral prose narrative, though not confined by a canon of a fixed text, is, however, confined by a canon of fixed rules of composition and performance

[63] Cawelti, *Adventure, Mystery, and Romance,* 18–19.

[64] This same distinction readily applies in ancient Jewish literature, although we would also have to distinguish high art (our example would perhaps be the *Book of Job*), the goal of which is to explore ambivalences about the world as we experience it, from apocalypticism, which harbors no ambivalences: the world is thoroughly corrupt and will be deservedly swept away by God. In this respect popular art is the opposite of apocalypticism; it springs from an ever-hopeful attitude about the possibilities for this world.

[65] Jason, *Ethnopoetry,* 5–7; see also her "Genre in Folk Literature" and "Aspects of the Fabulous in Oral Literature" and Jason and Kempinski, "How Old Are Folktales?"

[66] The equation of written with fixed text and oral with unfixed is thus a questionable rule. Nagy describes the process of the stabilization and crystallization of oral epic in ancient Greece (*Pindar's Homer,* 53, 55; also "Homeric Questions"). In addition, it is not clear whether we must introduce the "performance" criterion into written popular prose as well, especially in regard to *Esther,* which most likely developed as a narrative for the Purim celebration. Cf. also Derek Pearsall on medieval popular literature: "Each act of copying was to a large extent an act of recomposition, and not an episode in a process of decomposition from an ideal form" ("Texts, Textual Criticism, and Fifteenth-Century Manuscript Production," in *Fifteenth-Century Studies,* ed. Robert F. Yeager [Hamden, Conn.: Archon, 1984], 126–27).

Note also that Jason uses the term *novella* as it is used generally by folklorists and classicists, that is, as an *oral* story that focuses on human characters and powers in a real-world setting (*Ethnopoetry,* 27–29, 147, 197).

appropriate to its "setting-in-life." Although the distinctions between oral and written narrative are sometimes drawn in an overly schematic way, the tendencies of the two modes of discourse can be described fairly clearly. Oral narrative is traditional, with a repeated repertoire of plots, characters, and themes. The high literary narrative is theoretically unlimited and characteristically strives for novelty, both in form and content. The claim to uniqueness may of course be pure pretense in many cases, but our concern is with the ethos of the art form, not its achievements.[67] Concerning novelty in the novel, Hans-Robert Jauss goes so far as to suggest that the distance between an audience's expectations of a literary work—determined by the genre—and the demand the author introduces by challenging those expectations is a measure of the work's artistic merit.[68] As a criterion of aesthetics, this may seem to romanticize the social role of the modern artist as prophet, but as a sociological observation on the distinction between high and popular art, it is very helpful and should be compared with Cawelti's observations above. Corresponding to this are other aims of high art: for instance, to attain "classic" or universalizable status, to be understood across the centuries or by people of different cultures. Whether the art is universalizable or not is generally a matter of indifference to the popular artist. If the "classic" is a work of art that rises above the horizon of the period of its creation to become universalizable, popular art remains embedded in its social origins. A "classic" work may of course begin as popular, but the moment it rises above the immediate interests of popular entertainment, it ceases to be "popular" by definition and takes on a different social function. It may transcend the time and place of composition to the extent that it continues to entertain, but it will place a different challenge before the audience a century or millennium later from that which it presented at the first performance.[69] The

---

[67] See Harold Bloom, *The Anxiety of Influence* (New York: Oxford University, 1973), and Martin, *Recent Theories of Narrative*, 83–85. Martin intriguingly associates the "unique" pretension of high modern novels with the assumption that the conclusion of the work occurs as the result of a logical necessity, as if to suggest that it could not have ended any other way.

[68] Hans-Robert Jauss, "Literary History as a Challenge to Literary Theory," *New Literary History* 2 (1970): 15.

[69] See also Frank Kermode, *The Classic: Literary Images of Permanence and Change* (New York: Viking, 1975). There also exist, on the far end of the spectrum from "the classic," entertaining works that are so embedded in their context of origin that they cease to entertain in a new context and can barely be comprehended. Robert Darnton argues in *The Great Cat Massacre and Other Episodes in French Cultural History* (New York: Vintage, 1984) that such examples reveal the peculiarities of different times and places: "To get the joke in the case of something as unfunny as a ritual slaughter of cats is a first step toward 'getting' the culture" (p. 262).

work, however, that does not "rise" to classic status but is composed from the beginning as high art is governed by an unstated principle that the plot is unique and the characters real and unrepeatable; there could not, for example, be a cycle of stories about Madame Bovary. As Jason says bluntly, "The individual poet (of high literature) is an innovator, the folk poet a conformist. The individual poet may cross genre boundaries, . . . the traditional folk poet cannot change nor innovate."[70] Her dichotomies, intentionally schematized, could be contradicted by numerous counterexamples; in addition, taken out of context they appear to ignore the possibilities of creativity and change within folk genres. They do, however, point up some general differences in the poetics of oral and written narrative.

But where do popular written narratives fall in this division? They, like oral narratives, are likely to be guided by traditional plots and themes, and, as I will show, although the Jewish novels change and move toward new characters, roles, and plots, the movement does not evidently result from a conscious desire for uniqueness. With possible exceptions, the Jewish novels appear to be composed and recomposed, without the canon of a fixed text but with the canon of a traditional set of plots and characters. The study of ancient novels thus places the scholar in a difficult position between the analysis of oral and written tradition, oral and literary culture. We are addressing neither oral culture nor written culture but "popular literary culture." This problem is not restricted to ancient novels but is true of popular literature today, the part of the literary industry aimed at a large market. Comic books, science fiction novels, and drugstore romances occupy a similar position in modern society. A certain flexibility of approach is required, along

---

[70] Jason, *Ethnopoetry,* 13. Her comments, taken out of context, could be misinterpreted as being prejudicial to oral culture. She merely wishes to emphasize the limits imposed by tradition on the folk poet, who generally creates and innovates *within established forms.* Watt, who states dichotomies that are similar (*Rise of the Novel,* 13–19), has in general valued the literate revolution over oral culture. For a critique of older romanticizing views of folk tradition, see Hermann Bausinger, *Formen der "Volkspoesie,"* 2d ed. (Berlin: Erich Schmidt, 1980), 11–12, 41–55. Some folklorists challenge any overly schematized distinction of oral versus written, and it is certainly true that this simple dichotomy will have to give way to much more subtle models. See, e.g., Foley, *The Theory of Oral Composition* and *Oral Tradition in Literature.* In my present study, I am invoking a number of distinctions to illuminate a kind of written literature that is not easily placed in a dichotomy between oral and written.

Jason also points out (p. 7) a strong disagreement between her method and that of the French semioticians and Russian formalists, such as A. J. Greimas, *Semantique structurale* (Paris: Larousse, 1966), and Tzvetan Todorov, *Grammaire du Decameron* (The Hague: Mouton, 1969), who would assert that high literature is equally "formalistic," even reflecting the same formal patterns as the oral equivalents. This assertion, to Jason, is much too abstract and simplistic.

with an awareness of the "everydayness" and the repeatability of the popular novel. We must also condition ourselves not to despise popular literature, ancient or modern, for being what it is. It is a reflection of ourselves in an unguarded moment.

Several other common notions of oral versus written narrative must also be dispelled. The first is that oral narratives were never fixed or unchanging. Homeric oral epic, to be sure, was not fixed when it was first composed and performed; it was probably composed anew and performed differently at each recital. It probably became increasingly fixed during diffusion, however, attaining the status of a canonical text for a panhellenic culture in Athens during the sixth century B.C.E.[71] Conversely, written literature was often a mere record of oral truth, as when Herodotus recounts, in writing, how he discerns the difference between true oral accounts (*aletheia*) and mere local legend (*mythos*). Elsewhere, written narratives at the popular level are often extremely fluid or unfixed, as in the Greek *Life of Aesop* or *Alexander Romance,* which are attested in several different ancient versions (and these more than likely only a small sampling of the variety). The solemnity and permanence, even canonicity, that we attach to the written word is not generally recognized in popular literature.[72] This phenomenon is equally in evidence in the Jewish novels. The various ancient translations of *Esther,* for example, all represent different narrative traditions. We possess one Hebrew version, two different Greek versions, an Old Latin version (separate from the Vulgate), and two very different Aramaic translations. Something like this variety exists also for *Daniel, Tobit,* and *Joseph and Aseneth.*[73] Most popular written texts in the ancient world were

[71] See the discussion in Nagy, "Homeric Questions."

[72] This lack of fixity in popular literature is not limited to the ancient world but is found at times in the modern novel as well. Richardson, for example, put *Pamela* and *Clarissa* through several editions, making substantial changes. As Eagleton describes it (*Rape of Clarissa,* 20–21): "The whole of this dangerously labile writing is merely one enormous spare part, permanently capable of being recycled into something else." Furthermore, Richardson's novels are "great unwieldy containers crammed with spare parts and agreeable extras, for which the manufacturer (Richardson) never ceases to churn out new streamlined improvements." Not only does Richardson's literary activity reflect a lack of concern about the publication of a fixed text; it also shows the "baggage car" nature of the novelistic impulse, parallel to the "novel by agglutination" described for *Daniel* below. Richardson's text, however, has now *become* classic, just as *Daniel* has, and both are generally read in fixed versions.

[73] Earlier biblical literature likely remained unfixed as well until it was canonized. Thus, *First* and *Second Chronicles* utilize the books of *Samuel* and *Kings* to rewrite an account of Israel's history, and the texts of *Jeremiah* and *Proverbs* were very fluid until their canonization. Among Christians, the authors of *Matthew* and *Luke* were quite willing to use *Mark* as a source to create a gospel more to their liking. Nobody, it appears, was interested in fixing these texts until some time after their composition.

composed in a state of "free adaptation," their authors often guilty of what we would call plagiarism. Of all ancient literature, however, the Jewish novels provide perhaps our best laboratory for the study of the growth and change of unfixed, popular texts and for the interaction of oral sources and written narratives.

The Daniel tradition is an excellent case in point. The biblical book can be divided into six short episodes that relate the experiences of Daniel and his three companions in the court of the Babylonian and Persian kings, told in the third person (*Daniel* 1–6), and a series of apocalyptic visions, told in the first person (*Daniel* 7–12). The narratives of *Daniel* 1–6 are likely derived from oral legends of the pious heroes, legends that circulated independently in the fourth to third centuries B.C.E. in the eastern Diaspora. A scribal interest in court wisdom is also reflected, and it was perhaps Jewish scribes who gathered these subsequently expanded by the addition of other narratives, *Susanna* and *Bel and the Dragon*. The latter were likely oral, but *Susanna* may already represent a written novelistic addition; certainly, *Daniel* as a whole begins to look more like a novel. Peter Weimar argues that even when short oral narratives are grouped in a cycle, they still cannot become a novel. He is, however, too rigid on this point. *Daniel* is novelistic, especially in its Greek versions, in the sense that the originally oral legends have been processed through a new medium and are growing by written accretions into something that will serve, at one level of society, as pleasure reading.[74] A female character in distress has been added, and the psychological states of the main characters are explored both through the narrative and through the prayers and hymns added at various points in the text (see Chapter 3 below). At every level we see the easy passage of motifs and narratives from oral to written activity, and at the written stage the versions vary and the text is far from fixed. The Daniel tradition, as we shall see, constituted a major subcurrent in the flow of Jewish literature, taken up by a broad spectrum of parties and interests, coexisting in both oral and written media, undergoing constant changes. Before it became scripture, *Daniel* was popular culture.

To accomplish my ends, then, I treat the Jewish novels both individually, noting how they most likely came into existence, and in comparison, isolating the salient characteristics that describe their genre. I begin with *Daniel,* since it can be analyzed most easily into "building blocks" and contains the clearest datable references (that is, to the Maccabean

---

[74] Weimar, "Formen frühjudischer Literatur."

Revolt). Next I discuss *Tobit,* which may derive from one of the oldest core narratives and has the most affinity with recognized folktale traditions. *Esther* follows, which, like *Daniel,* is based on court narratives that have evolved into longer popular novels. *Judith* is taken up next; it provides a contrast to *Daniel* in the method of composition. There is no easily discernible source or narrative disjunction in *Judith,* but on the contrary, despite its two separate "acts," it is an intentionally integrated whole. The last of the novels is *Joseph and Aseneth,* which, along with the *Testament of Joseph* and other writings, reflects both an active Joseph narrative tradition in the genre of a national hero romance and a novelistic adaptation. I devote one chapter also to the writings related to the novels—the national hero romances (Artapanus on Moses and Joseph) and the historical novels (*The Tobiad Romance, The Royal Family of Adiabene, Third Maccabees,* and *Second Maccabees* 3–4). In the conclusion I bring together some of these threads of discussion, and aim also to substantiate the contention that, whereas the early versions of the novels all reflect quite different origins, the endpoints in the development of each reflect changes of a similar nature and share many important traits. In other words, the novelistic experiments appear to be moving toward a common goal, and what the genre becomes can best be seen by charting the separate developmental histories of the novels. Here we find that the novel comes into existence with a poetics all its own, related to other genres to be sure but reflecting an internal experimental trajectory, a Jewish novelistic impulse.

CHAPTER 2

The Daniel/Susanna Tradition:
From Legend to Novel

During the postexilic period there arose a vibrant tradition of narratives and visionary materials concerning the figure of Daniel. In addition to the *Book of Daniel* as it stands in the Masoretic Text (the basis of the Jewish and Protestant canons of the Bible), two other ancient versions are known in Greek translations, the Old Greek text and the text of Theodotion, the latter of which became standard in the Eastern Orthodox and Roman Catholic Bibles.[1] They differ from the Masoretic version by the inclusion of three additions, relegated to the Apocrypha in modern editions of the Bible: *The Prayer of Azariah and the Song of the Three Young Men, Susanna,* and *Bel and the Dragon*. In addition to these recensional differences between the most important ancient versions, there are also fragments of Daniel stories and visions found at Qumran. For our purposes, the significance of these varied writings in the name of Daniel is to show that a very active tradition of stories and visions about this figure existed and that the corpus of traditions was still known and considered of some significance at the end of the first century C.E. [2] The *Book of Daniel* in its various texts provides a marvelous

---

[1] The Old Greek text of *Daniel* is sometimes misleadingly called the Septuagint text, even though the Theodotionic recension supplanted it in the Septuagint, the common name for the Greek translation of the Bible.

[2] Josephus, writing at the end of the first century C.E., does not allude to the additions to the Greek Bible, but he does include some stories about Daniel that are not attested in the Hebrew Bible (*Antiquities* 10.11.6–7). On narratives and visions concerning Daniel that were found in fragmentary form at Qumran, see Milik, " 'Prière de Nabonide' et autres écrits d'un cycle de Daniel," and "Daniel et Susanne à Qumrân?"

opportunity to study the novelistic impulse at work, for here we have very clear evidence concerning the evolution of the work from individual narratives into a Jewish novel. Novelistic elements are added as the corpus expands, and we are granted many insights into the separate steps of this process.

The Masoretic version of *Daniel* consists, first, of six legends (*Daniel* 1–6) recounting Daniel's rise and ultimate success in the courts of the great ancient Near Eastern monarchs, told in the third person. These legends are followed by a series of apocalyptic visions (*Daniel* 7–12), described with first-person narration. The latter reflect the embattled situation of the Maccabean Revolt of 167–164 B.C.E., whereas the former do not make any clear reference to this watershed event. Not only are the narratives of chapters 1–6 apparently ignorant of the persecution of Antiochus IV Epiphanes (the ruling monarch at the time of the Maccabean Revolt); they are not even consistently negative toward the pagan kings, even Nebuchadnezzar. It seems clear, then, that the narratives were composed at a time prior to the Maccabean Revolt and are closely parallel with other court narratives of the Persian and Hellenistic periods, which were also composed far from the heat of persecution.

The legends of *Daniel* 1–6 and other court narratives have been divided by scholars into "contests" and "conflicts."[3] In the contest, the protagonist, a member of the court, rises to prominence before the king by solving some problem or interpreting some sign or dream that none of the other courtiers can interpret. The conflict, which also concerns a courtier, provides more tension and drama. The protagonist in this narrative also begins within the court but is persecuted or conspired against

---

[3] The terminology is derived from Humphreys, "A Life-Style for Diaspora," and is taken up especially by Collins, *The Apocalyptic Vision of the Book of Daniel*, 33–59; Collins, "The Court-Tales in Daniel and the Development of Apocalyptic"; and Wills, *The Jew in the Court of the Foreign King*; but nuanced and critiqued by Niditch and Doran, "The Success Story of the Wise Courtier."

The theme of persecution and vindication at court of course transcends cultural and historical boundaries. There is an entire tradition of the trials of Queen Constance, retold by Chaucer, as well as other cycles of stories, such as those concerning Genevieve of Brabant or the French "wager" romances. Margaret Schlauch (*Chaucer's Constance and Accused Queens* [New York: New York University Press, 1927]) distinguishes in these stories two types of the accused queen: one, associated with oral fairy tales, who is accused by a jealous mother-in-law and the other a courtly romance type who is accused of treason or infidelity by a jilted lover within the court; the former emphasizes the family intrigue typical of fairy tales, the latter the administrative figure of the opposing courtier, precisely the type we encounter in the ancient court conflicts. I wish to thank Nancy Jones of the Romance Languages department at Harvard University for pointing out to me these later European court parallels.

by the other courtiers, only to be finally vindicated before the king. Analyzing *Daniel* 1–6, therefore, in terms of contests and conflicts, we find that *Daniel* 1 can be considered a contest. It introduces Daniel and his three companions, who are Jews carried into the Exile, to the court of Nebuchadnezzar. Though they are provided rich food, they refuse it since it is not kosher, yet to everyone's surprise they remain fat and healthy and are found by the king to be the wisest of the youths who are trained for courtly service. This court contest is followed by another, *Daniel* 2, in which the king demands that his counselors must interpret his dream. He also insists, however, that the one who interprets it must first describe it to him. Daniel rises to the occasion, relates the dream in detail, and then interprets its meaning to the king. Despite the fact that it is bad news for Nebuchadnezzar—it foretells the fall of his dynasty— the chipper monarch showers Daniel with honors. *Daniel* 3 is a court conflict in which Daniel's three companions, Shedrach, Meshach, and Abednego, refuse to bow down to a golden image that Nebuchadnezzar has erected. They are accused by other courtiers and are thrown into a fiery furnace. They emerge unharmed, however, and the king acclaims their God and promotes them over the land. *Daniel* 4 and 5 are two contests; in the first, Daniel is able to interpret Nebuchadnezzar's dream, and in the second, Daniel interprets the words written on the palace wall by a ghostly hand. In *Daniel* 6 we have another conflict story, in which the tension is created by Daniel's refusal to pray to the new king, Darius the Mede (a wholly fictitious personage). Daniel is cast into the lions' den but is taken out unharmed and, now vindicated, is promoted while his accusers are eaten by the lions. These narratives, probably composed separately during the fourth to third centuries B.C.E. under Persian or Hellenistic rule, were likely combined with the apocalyptic visions of *Daniel* 7–12 during the Maccabean Revolt in 167–164 B.C.E. This text is the canonical text of the Jewish and Protestant Bibles.

Daniel was evidently a popular hero in postexilic Judaism but was depicted in two separate social roles. In the narratives, Daniel is a wise and righteous courtier, much like the heroes of other court narratives. In *Daniel* 7–12, however, he is an apocalyptic visionary whose insights are interpreted to a small group of sectarian pietists called *maskilim* (11:33, 35; 12:3, 10). Thus, the canonical *Book of Daniel* can be divided roughly in half, into two depictions of Daniel, the courtier and the visionary, which derive from different periods and social groups within Judaism. What holds the two disparate roles together and makes their combination possible in one book is Daniel's "mantic" or "prophetic wisdom."[4] Daniel the courtier-sage does not just dispense statesmanlike advice but has insight into God's revealed purposes and is called to a higher degree of witnessing to God's sovereignty. Thus, the dream Daniel interprets in *Daniel* 2 shows some similarities to the vision in *Daniel* 7. The emphasis on mantic wisdom is greater in *Daniel* 1–6 than in most court legends and, in fact, may have increased as the corpus took shape.[5] It is also the case that apocalyptic works often incorporate materials of other genres, including narrative frameworks.[6] What is unusual here is that the proportions are so evenly divided. This provides extra credence to the theory that *Daniel* 1–6 already existed as an independent corpus before the addition of chapters 7–12. For the study of the development of the narrative, therefore, the interesting question is, What was the Daniel collection of narratives like before the Maccabean Revolt, at which time the visions were added, and what happened to it afterward?

The Daniel tradition from before the Maccabean Revolt can be reconstructed with some degree of certainty from several clues in the texts of *Daniel* 1–6. It has been theorized, for example, that chapter 1 was composed as an introduction to the other legends. Daniel and his three companions, who figure separately in the legends of chapters 2–6, are here introduced together, and we are told how they came to be in Babylon. This chapter is also in Hebrew, whereas all of the other legends (and the vision in chapter 7) are in Aramaic. It further differs from the other narratives in reflecting more of a consciousness of the Exile and the separation from the Judaean motherland and in focusing on Jewish food laws, a more specific issue of Jewish ethnic identity, found also in later Jewish texts such as Greek *Esther*.[7] There is also evidence that some of the other narratives may have circulated first in smaller groups. The Old Greek and Theodotionic versions of *Daniel* are very similar except for chapters 4–6. The difference indicates that these three chap-

---

[4] Collins, "Court-Tales," 229–34; Hans-Peter Müller, "Magisch-mantische Weisheit und die Gestalt Daniels," *Ugarit-Forschungen* 1 (1969): 79–94, and "Mantische Weisheit und Apokayptik," *Vetus Testamentum Supplement* 22 (1972): 268–93. On the difficulty of the two languages in Daniel, Hebrew and Aramaic, which do not correspond precisely to the two halves, see the discussion in Collins, *Apocalyptic Vision,* 15–19.

[5] Wills, *Jew in the Court,* 75–152, esp. 144–48.

[6] John J. Collins, *Daniel, with an Introduction to Apocalyptic Literature* (Grand Rapids, Mich.: Eerdmans, 1984), 5.

[7] Jürgen Christian Lebram, *Das Buch Daniel* (Zürich: Theologischer, 1984), 22–23, 43, 48, 51–52; and Kratz, *Translatio imperii,* 148–50.

ters circulated in a separate corpus, either as an earlier collection that evolved by accretion into chapters 1–6 or as an apocopated selection of a larger corpus. The former suggestion is more likely; it is much easier to imagine the need to expand the corpus than the need to abbreviate it, and certain differences between the two recensions, especially the cross-references between chapters, can more easily be explained as the redactional changes that were introduced in the making of a larger literary corpus.[8] Either way, it is clear that more than one corpus was in existence. The most likely process of development for the Daniel narratives, therefore, is that a group of independent, oral legends of Daniel and his three friends were written down and grouped together into a series of expanding corpora, first as *Daniel* 4–6 and later as 1–6 (possibly with 2–6 as an intermediate stage). The various steps in this reconstruction do not necessarily depend on one another, however. The pieces of evidence for each step are quite different; the reconstruction does not collapse if a single step proves untenable. For our purposes, the most important consideration is that the narratives of chapters 1–6 were probably independently composed and circulated and edited together into one or more different corpora before the Maccabean Revolt.

The independent narratives are charming, even humorous stories, and one might ask why they are not considered little novels in themselves. Chapter 3, for example, the story of the three young men who refuse to bow to Nebuchadnezzar's image and are thrown into the fiery furnace, was probably intended as a humorous satire of the king.[9] The comic effect is achieved in several ways: by the repetition of the jawbreaker names Shedrach, Meshach, and Abednego (thirteen times with no variation!), by repetition of the pomp and ceremony surrounding the edict (3:2, 3, 5, 7, 15), and by the strutting and histrionics of the famous Nebuchadnezzar. This form of satire, however, is quite typical of oral tales. The individual narratives that make up *Daniel* 1–6 belong to the genre of court narratives that can be found circulating in the ancient Near East in the Persian period. But despite the wide occurrence of these narratives in Herodotus, the Hebrew Bible, and elsewhere, they were not adequate to the new needs experienced by the more literate

---

[8] With Haag, *Die Errettung Daniels aus der Löwengrube,* and contra James A. Montgomery, *The Book of Daniel* (New York: Scribner's, 1927), 37. See also Wills, *Jew in the Court,* 87–152, and Rainer Albertz, *Der Gott des Daniel.*

[9] A view put forward in slightly different forms by Good, "Apocalyptic as Comedy," and Hector Avalos, "Comic Elements in Daniel 1–6," unpublished seminar paper at Harvard University, fall 1986.

social classes in the late Hellenistic period. As delightful as these stories are, they are not, in themselves, "novelistic." They were, first of all, too short and were probably orally composed and transmitted. They also reflect a fundamentally different depiction of the protagonist from that found in the later novels. It is the nature of legends, that is, oral narratives that glorify the pious cultural hero of the past, to create a one-dimensional protagonist who rises resolutely above life's threats. The protagonist of legend is invulnerable and is not buffeted by events, unlike the protagonist of the novel. Such is the nature of Daniel in these narratives and, despite the humor in chapter 3, of his three companions as well.

Many scholars have studied the individual narratives as oral folktales, with intriguing results. That they are essentially independent narratives with few cross-references indicates that they were transmitted separately, and it is difficult to posit a function for the *separate* stories in the written medium. In varying degrees, they also correspond in form and content to oral narratives from other cultures. Earlier studies have focused on *Daniel* 3 as an oral legend and on *Daniel* 2, 4, and 5 as "success stories of the wise courtier."[10] Pamela J. Milne has analyzed *Daniel* 1–6 in detail, comparing them to the model of the "heroic fairy tale" which the folklorist Vladimir Propp isolated for Russian folktales, but the results she obtains are mainly negative: the pattern does not quite fit.[11] These works, however, have relied principally on folklore studies of *tales,* or fanciful narratives that do not have a definite historical or geographical setting; tales are set "once upon a time" in a "faraway kingdom." Much more similar to *Daniel* 1–6 are saints' legends from various cultures, such as the collected legends regarding Elijah and Elisha (*First Kings* 17–*Second Kings* 10), the early Christian Desert Fathers or medieval saints (from which we derive the word legend, from *legenda,* "things to be read"). The Daniel legends are not, however, "martyr accounts"; that categorization is a retrojection of a later genre back into the pre-Maccabean period.[12] The heroes in Daniel do not die, and the main point of the story is their miraculous rescue, not their suffering unto death. The study of *Daniel* 1–6 as *legends* has been more successful in terms of

---

[10] *Daniel* 3: Curt Kuhl, *Die Drei Männer im Feuer (Daniel, Kapitel 3 und seine Zusätze)* (Giessen: Töpelmann, 1930). *Daniel* 2, 4, and 5: Niditch and Doran, "Success Story."

[11] Milne, *Vladimir Propp.*

[12] Contra Aage Bentzen, *Introduction to the Old Testament,* 7th ed., 2 vols. (Copenhagen: Gad, 1967), 1:238, and "Daniel 6: Ein Versuch zur Vorgeschichte der Märtyrerlegends," in *Festschrift Alfred Bertholet,* ed. Walter Baumgartner et al. (Tübingen: Mohr [Paul Siebeck], 1950), 58–64.

identifying the themes and literary tone, though it is still inconclusive regarding structure.

Legends, to be sure, are quite different from the ancient Israelite sagas that are contained in the early biblical history. The latter constitute a highly developed art form that probably arose from oral epic traditions. They depict the history of Israel and the Hebrew people in terms of linear, progressive developments tied together by the family lineage of Abraham, Isaac, and Jacob and their descendants. Legends, by contrast, are generally self-contained and restricted in their historical sweep. They do not point beyond themselves to any larger historical developments, and the original legends in *Daniel* 1–6 are not exceptions. The protagonist of legend is normally a one-dimensional model of human ideals, with no imperfections and little fleshed-out character. He or she is essentially the conduit of God's miracle and little else. Curt Kuhl summed up the style of Daniel 1–6: "The presentation of the material shows little of the power of the old art of storytelling; the characters are shadowy and unreal; they do not impress us as human beings. But the narrator is not interested in so doing." [13] Daniel and his companions show little emotion, and there is no tension created concerning their perception of their situation. [14] It is evidently natural for legends to be collected into a repetitive cycle, as in the case of Elijah and Elisha or of Christian saints' legends. The result of placing these legends side by side, however, is the creation of the apparent absurdity of a king who is humbled to revere God and honor the heroic Jews at the end of one chapter, only to threaten them again in the next. Legends required credulousness on the hearers' or readers' part but little contextualizing. This is no continuous historical narrative in its original contours (the succession of kings is imposed during the later stages of the collection) but a collection of vignettes of triumph which do not offer many rewards to those who second-guess them. The only exception to this depiction of Daniel in the Masoretic version is in chapter 2,

[13] Curt Kuhl, *The Old Testament: Its Origins and Composition* (Richmond: John Knox Press, 1962), 274.

[14] Wills, *Jew in the Court*, 12–19; Müller, "Märchen, Legende und Enderwartung,": 339. Fewell's *Circle of Sovereignty*, despite many interesting observations, is flawed in part by trying to apply Sternberg's theory of the "gaps" in Pentateuchal literature to the narratives in Daniel; in the latter case the gaps are not nearly so suggestive as Fewell makes them out to be. The lack of detail in *Daniel* 1–6, rather than demanding some searching human response, merely ensures that the audience's mind will not wander while waiting for the miracle that is assuredly coming.

when Daniel, faced with the threat of the king's judgment, prays. This, however, is likely a later addition,[15] a presentiment of later insertions to follow in Greek *Daniel* (see below in this chapter), and a foreshadowing of parallel novelistic developments in Greek *Esther* and the novels in general.

Another surprising aspect of the six court legends in *Daniel* 1–6 has implications for the understanding of Daniel as history and novel: the failure to condemn Nebuchadnezzar. To be sure, the impression made on the modern reader is that Daniel 1–6 condemns Nebuchadnezzar outright, but this reading is influenced by other traditions about Nebuchadnezzar, such as the oracles against Baylon in *Isaiah* and *Jeremiah*. A close reading of the legends of *Daniel* 1–6 reveals that they do not reflect a consistently negative view of Nebuchadnezzar.[16] In *Daniel* 2, for example, the king is powerful and threatening, but he threatens Jewish and pagan courtiers equally. When Daniel succeeds in interpreting the king's dream, he is made minister over Babylon. In *Daniel* 3, Nebuchadnezzar tries to execute Daniel's three companions in the fiery furnace, but when they survive he praises God and sets them over the provinces. In *Daniel* 4, Nebuchadnezzar is overcome by hybris and vaunts himself before God, but after his seven-year punishment, he praises God and is restored to even greater glory than before. It is only in *Daniel* 5, with the appearance of Nebuchadnezzar's son and successor (actually vice-regent), Belshazzar, that we detect a more condemning tone. Belshazzar desecrates the Jerusalem temple vessels by using them in a toast to the gods of the palace. He is as a result cut down that night but not before rewarding Daniel and reappointing him as a high official. Thus, in *Daniel* 1–6 there is tension in serving the Babylonian kings, but it is not without its rewards for the loyal Jewish courtier protected by God against the vicissitudes of the monarch. This is, in fact, a theme of court narratives throughout the ancient world. The overall tone cannot be seen as negative.

To be sure, the oracle contained in *Daniel* 2 describes the demise of the present (Babylonian) kingdom, to be succeeded by the Medes, Persians, and Greeks. This oracle, however, is derived from a more condemning,

---

[15] L. F. Hartman and A. A. Di Lella, *The Book of Daniel* (Anchor Bible; Garden City, N.Y.: Doubleday, 1978), 139, 145; Lebram, *Buch Daniel*, 48.

[16] This surprising lack of condemnation is noted by Ginsberg, "The Composition of the Book of Daniel"; Bickerman, *Four Strange Books of the Bible*, 97; Collins, *Apocalyptic Vision*, 9–10, cf. 46–47; and Collins, "Daniel and His Social World."

eschatologically oriented source.[17] To our surprise, even though Daniel interprets the oracle to Nebuchadnezzar as predicting the fall of the Babylonian dynasty, the king is enthralled with Daniel's performance and reveres both him and his god. The *narrative* of *Daniel* 2, therefore, in contrast to the oracle contained within it, presents a more positive view of coexistence with the powers that be. *Daniel* 2 and the other narratives project exemplary action regarding rather everyday concerns: remaining kosher, praying, avoiding the temptation of foreign worship. The divinely mandated grand cycles of history, intimated to the pious in the form of the old oracle, are reduced in scale to cover the lives of a few individuals as exemplars of the observance of God's laws. Thus, although *Daniel* 1–6 is ordered on the dynastic succession of the oracle of *Daniel* 2, the oracle itself has become domesticated by the narrative and transformed into a mere opportunity for Daniel to dazzle us with his wisdom. Nebuchadnezzar can hardly be threatening—or even worthy of condemnation—in the comic triumph of these legends. The episodic nature of the legends contributes to this impression. No danger is so real that it is met just once, overcome, and relegated to the past; rather, Daniel has an opportunity to model his resolve again and again.

If the *Book of Daniel* allows for Nebuchadnezzar's repentance and a positive relationship with Daniel, rabbinic exegesis certainly corrects this lapse of historical vision. David Satran has shown in detail how the rabbis wrestled with this problem in *Daniel*.[18] His conclusions are, first, that the depiction of Nebuchadnezzar in *Daniel* 4 was consistently interpreted by the rabbis in light of the thoroughly negative view of *Isaiah* 14; second, that Nebuchadnezzar's repentance at the end of *Daniel* 4 was largely ignored; and third, that the rabbis thought that Daniel should be soundly condemned for taking such interest in this tyrant's welfare. It is only in Christian exegesis that a sympathetic view of Nebuchadnezzar as the repentant idolator emerges. Rabbinic literature brings moral criteria to bear in challenging the clear sense of the sacred text of *Daniel*.[19]

---

[17] Collins, *Apocalyptic Vision,* 34–46; Susan Niditch, *The Symbolic Vision in Biblical Tradition* (Chico, Calif.: Scholars, 1983), 185–89, and most recently, Kratz, *Translatio imperii,* 48–55.

[18] David Satran, "Early Jewish and Christian Interpretation of the Fourth Chapter of the Book of Daniel" (Ph.D. diss., Hebrew University, 1985).

[19] On the anthropocentric and ethical conception of history that underlies rabbinic literature, see P. Schäfer, "Zur Geschichtsauffassung des rabbinischen Judentums," *Journal for the Study of Judaism* 6 (1975): 167–88. The rabbis' historical consciousness sometimes appears confused, but they often tried to straighten out problems inherent in the biblical texts (cf., e.g., *bMegillah* 11b–12a). Their specific criticism of Daniel for remaining loyal to Nebuchadnezzar may be explained partly by the problems they were having with the Roman emperors.

From our vantage point, the coziness of Daniel with Nebuchadnezzar can be seen as part of the essentially comic worldview of the collection. There is a certain triumph over villainy in subordinating Nebuchadnezzar to Daniel, transforming the former into a comic foil, a *senex iratus* or "blustering old man" of comic tradition.[20]

The social world of these narratives can be hypothesized, but only if we paint with broad strokes. W. Lee Humphreys noted that Jewish court narratives in general present a "lifestyle for Diaspora," an affirmation of the possibility of peacefully coexisting with the pagan power structure while at the same time maintaining true Jewish piety and identity.[21] The court narratives probably reflect not a situation of governmental persecution but, rather, one of relative religious freedom, in which the tension derives from the social and economic competition with other ethnic groups. Especially in the court conflicts of *Daniel* 3 and 6, it is the other courtiers, not the king, who instigate the antagonism, even if the king is enlisted in their efforts. The Daniel stories do not necessarily presuppose an actual situation of violence and persecution between the various parties. The social reality that could give rise to such stories of conflict may simply be the day-to-day ethnic competition in the larger marketplace of the Hellenistic world, a situation reflected in the business records preserved in the Murashu tablets and Zenon papyri (see Chapter 1). The Daniel narratives depict a pious, brave, and resourceful Jewish hero who wins the position at the king's right hand by besting the courtiers of the rival ethnic group. Projected here are the wish fulfillments of a large cross-section of Diaspora Jews, in light of what they perceived as ethnic competition. John Collins suggests that the authors (if not the audience) were, "like Daniel, upper-class, well-educated Jews, who found careers in government service in the eastern Diaspora,"[22] but this description may be too specific. As noted in the introduction, the growth of a Jewish entrepreneurial class in the Diaspora gave rise to a possible audience for such stories, and we should not necessarily restrict the audience to the social milieu or class of the characters. Likewise, we should not overstate the moral statures of the authors and audience, as Collins does when he avers that the audience "maintained unwavering piety." The idealized protagonists and, pre-

---

Interestingly, Nebuchadnezzar's officer Nebuzaradan, who was responsible for actually taking Jerusalem, comes off positively in rabbinic exegesis and even becomes a proselyte (*bSanh* 96b).

[20] Avalos (n. 9 above) makes this connection.

[21] Humphreys, "A Life-Style for Diaspora."

[22] Collins, "Daniel and His Social World," 136–37.

sumably, the projected and idealized self-image of the authors and audience convey unwavering piety, but we cannot say whether the actual community would have been so steadfast. The narrative world reflects the values, not the accomplishments, of its author and audience.

The collection of these narratives into a corpus, whether of chapters 4–6 or 1–6, is an important step in the establishment of the novel. We are here witness to the desire to harness originally oral narrative to a written medium, accomplished at a popular level, much as Herodotus, at a more educated level, attempted to gather and interpret the largely oral narratives he encountered. The collected cycle has some analogues in biblical literature, specifically the collection of prophet legends concerning Elijah and Elisha, and it may be that this "new" genre owes something to the older collection of prophet legends. The identity of the kings in *Daniel* 1–6 is probably introduced into older Danielic legends that lacked them, in accordance with the cycle of kingdoms predicated in *Daniel* 2: Babylonian, Median, and Persian. Thus, there is an ordering of the Daniel cycle to create a new whole. The Elijah/Elisha legends in *First Kings* 17–*Second Kings* 10 likewise appear to be largely interchangeable, episodic accounts of the two prophets' miracles—and this is probably what they originally were. They are placed in a temporal order, however, more than anything else, by the kings of the northern kingdom against whom the prophets make their pronouncements. Thus, this cycle and *Daniel* both order the legends on the basis of a chronology of the royal "opponents."[23]

Other developments present in *Daniel* 1–6 foreshadow a new genre and indicate by what steps the novel would emerge. *Daniel* 1, for example, was likely composed especially to serve as the introduction of the collection, since it introduces Daniel and his three companions, gives both their Hebrew and Babylonian names, and explains how they came to be in Babylon in Nebuchadnezzar's court. Likewise, cross-references are evidently inserted into the older narratives of *Daniel* 1–6 to weave the pieces into a whole. At *Daniel* 5, for example, we are told by one of the

---

[23] The royal chronology is not the only ordering principle in either case, but it is the most obvious. Both the Elijah/Elisha cycle and *Daniel* 1–6 can appear to have interchangeable parts, like so many shirts on a clothes line, but important interchapter structural patterns can be detected. On *Daniel*, see Collins, *Daniel*, 28–32, and the literature cited there and Kratz, *Translatio imperii*, 84–99. On the literary editing of the Elijah/Elisha cycle, see Alexander Rofé, "The Classification of the Prophetical Stories," *Journal of Biblical Literature* 89 (1970): 427–40, and Burke O. Long, *1 Kings* (Grand Rapids, Mich.: Eerdmans, 1984), 175–77.

characters (the queen mother) all of the events that transpired in chapter 4.[24] *Daniel* 2 also incorporates a long "prayer-retreat" of Daniel and his companions—companions whose very presence in *Daniel* 2 probably represents a secondary cross-referencing with other chapters—and creates an internalizing moment that is paralleled by many other similar insertions in the Jewish novels analyzed below.

Most important for our discussion, however, are the historical difficulties that the text presents. In *Daniel* 5 and 6, we are told that the Babylonian kingdom fell to "Darius the Mede." Darius was a Persian ruler, a successor of Cyrus, and it was Cyrus who was finally responsible for the fall of Babylon, not Darius or a Mede. Commentaries on *Daniel* will, of course, try to account for this discrepancy from the known facts by suggesting the actual identity of the historical personage who is "intended" in Darius the Mede. H. H. Rowley's 1935 book *Darius the Mede* was a valiant, if unconvincing, attempt in this direction.[25] Others often note that a Median king is required by the succession of kingdoms propounded in *Daniel* 2, and Darius's name is supplied because he is strongly associated with the creation of satrapies or provinces, which figure prominently in *Daniel* 6. We are, however, still left with a historical absurdity hanging in the text. Specifically, the introduction of a plainly impossible king, Darius the Mede, may indicate that a conscious fiction is being presented to the audience,[26] we shall also see historically impossible royal figures in the other novels. My point is not that there is a discrepancy here from what we perceive to be the correct historical tradition; it is that there is almost assuredly a discrepancy from what literate Jews in the ancient world would have perceived as historical tradition. These are discrepancies involving what would have been the most important kings of history. Although each of these cases might be addressed separately—in fact, that is precisely how they have been addressed by scholars—it seems clear that the inclusion of historical blunders is related to the genre of novel. As we move through the novels, we shall see that a case develops to substantiate this hypothesis: the impossible royal personages are indicators of a fictional mode. The pious and edifying content of *Daniel* 1–6 does not contradict this obser-

---

[24] An account that has probably been expanded; see Wills, *Jew in the Court,* 125–26. Other interchapter references are discussed there as well, chapter 3 passim.

[25] H. H. Rowley, *Darius the Mede* (Cardiff: University of Wales, 1935).

[26] M. Delcor, *Le livre de Daniel* (Paris: Gabalda, 1971), 133; Norman Porteous, *Daniel,* 2d ed. (London: SCM, 1979), 83–84.

vation but gives a justification for the use of a seemingly "fraudulent" prose narrative.

This process in Daniel, however, which appears to have been so marvelously evolutionary, was abruptly rerouted by the advent of the Maccabean Revolt. The legends were attached to several apocalyptic visions, the literature of crisis of the day. No longer mere enjoyment, they portray the mantic abilities and divine favor of the man who is allowed to see God's will and to prophesy against the age. What had been humorous or celebratory is now divinely inspired opposition. And, thus, the *Book of Daniel* stands in the Jewish and Protestant canons. The diverting literature of this period, then, creates a fanciful atmosphere in which historical figures can be recast at will, Jews can become the most powerful officials in the land, and the tyrant Nebuchadnezzar is capable of repentance. *Daniel* 1–6 was an early example of the popular Jewish writings that exercised a different sort of appeal to Jewish consciousness than was the case before and that allowed for a bizarre appropriation of famous kings, who are effectively subordinated to Jewish characters and the execution of God's will.

The Growth of the *Daniel* Corpus After the Maccabean Revolt

Now we turn to what became of the *Daniel* corpus after the Masoretic Text version. Although other visionary texts have come to light among the Dead Sea Scrolls, they were never added to the *Daniel* corpus. Rather, the next stage in the development of the corpus, Greek *Daniel,* reflects another step in the direction of the novel, presumably in response to the new needs of a literate Jewish social class in the late Hellensitic era.[27] Added to *Daniel* 1–12 are the so-called additions to *Daniel:* the *Prayer of Azariah and the Song of the Three Young Men, Susanna,* and *Bel and the Dragon.* They have separate origins and developmental histories, but their inclusion in the text of *Daniel* clearly came after the Maccabean Revolt.

---

[27] In a recent literary-critical study, Marti J. Steussy remarks on the fact that the new Danielic narratives of *Susanna* and *Bel and the Dragon* were added to the corpus but new visions were not (*Gardens in Babylon: Narrative and Faith in the Greek Legends of Daniel* [Atlanta: Scholars, 1993], 181). Other Danielic visions were nevertheless still circulating elsewhere and indicate considerable interest in that side of the hero's persona. See Milik, " 'Prière de Nabonide' " and "Daniel et Susanne à Qumrân?"

The *Prayer of Azariah and the Song of the Three Young Men* is added to chapter 3 at the point in the narrative (3:23) where the three young men have been thrown into the fiery furnace by Nebuchadnezzar. The focus in the original, humorous tale of *Daniel* 3 was always on Nebuchadnezzar; his thoughts and feelings are described, including first his bluster and then, when he realizes that a miracle has taken place, his humbled demeanor. The three youths are mere ciphers in the Masoretic version, speaking only once. With the addition of the *Prayer* and the *Song*, however, the focus has now shifted to the heartfelt prayer of the protagonists and God's response to send an angel to their rescue. The *Prayer* is similar to such laments as *Psalms* 44, 74, 79, and 80, but it also introduces a new element of postexilic Jewish theology: a confession of sin as a means of reinstituting the covenant between Jews and God.[28] The interior experience of the Jews, therefore, is now plumbed, and their penance is recounted, even though they have, as far as we know, committed no sin. This guilt and confession is not only lacking in *Daniel* 1–6; it is totally out of character for the protagonist of legends in general, who is, in the narrative world of legend, without sin. The *Prayer* and *Song*, therefore, do not wholly reroute the legends, as the apocalyptic visions did, but push them along an evolutionary process, a process that manifests the novelistic impulse. An editor is once again placing oral materials into a written medium, but it is for a literary, even novelistic, end. The reader is introduced to the interior life of protagonists who are in a state of psychological jeopardy—a jeopardy not fully experienced in the older version of *Daniel* 3—in much the same way that the reader of Greek novels has access to the emotions of the protagonists through the inclusion of letters, prayers, and monologues.

Susanna

The other additions, *Susanna* and *Bel and the Dragon*, are not inserted into the narrative of *Daniel* but simply included as additional episodes. As noted above, two important Greek translations of *Daniel* existed,

---

[28] See Nickelsburg, *Jewish Literature Between the Bible and the Mishnah*, 28–30, and cf. *Nehemiah* 9:6–37, *Ezra* 9:6–15, and also the visions of Daniel, *Daniel* 9:4–19. It can also be compared to the *Prayer of Manasseh*, which is added to the text of *Second Chronicles* 33:11–19 in the Apocrypha. The novelistic interest in interior experience should not be sharply distinguished, therefore, from this same interest reflected in other genres or, for that matter, in other media such as visual art (see Chapter 1).

each of which contained the additions inserted at different points. In the Theodotionic text, *Susanna* is placed before *Daniel* 1, with *Bel and the Dragon* coming at the end (after the visions), whereas in the Old Greek and Old Latin versions, both are placed together at the end. It is not certain which order represents the original placement of the additions, but most scholars now favor Theodotion's arrangement as the original: *Susanna* placed at the beginning, introducing Daniel as a young lad, and *Bel and the Dragon* placed at the end.[29] They are in genre and length similar to the court narratives of *Daniel* 1–6, but they do more than simply expand the corpus further; each serves a special function in rounding out the biography of *Daniel*.

Susanna was most likely placed at the beginning of the group of narratives to depict the qualities of Daniel as a young man which would serve him in later life. The story begins, however, not with Daniel but with Susanna, a beautiful young Jewish woman who, through her marriage to a wealthy Jew, Joakim, is mistress of a large household where the leading Jewish citizens of Babylon gather. Susanna has the custom of walking in her garden each day at noon after the guests have departed, but on one occasion two wicked elders independently decide to return to the garden to get a better glimpse of her on her promenade. The two elders discover each other in the garden and confess their shared lust. Together they plot to force her to have sex with them. While she is bathing in the garden, they run to her and demand that she submit to their desires, threatening to accuse her of lying with a man if she refuses. Faced with the prospect of death if convicted of adultery, she decides nevertheless that she must remain loyal to God's law and refuse their demands. When brought the next day before the people, she is accused by the elders of having lain with a young man whom they had witnessed running away. The crowd is persuaded and condemns her to death. Susanna makes a fervent plea to God to protect her, and immediately God inspires the young Daniel to come to her aid. He insists that the two elders be cross-examined separately and asks them each under what tree they saw her with the young man. Daniel's cleverness is indicated by his use of puns during his cross-examination. To one, who asserts that he saw them under a clove tree, Daniel replies, "You have lied, and under a *clove* tree the angel of God will *cleave* you!"[30] To the

---

[29] Moore, *Daniel, Esther, and Jeremiah*, 90. See the recent discussion in Steussy, *Gardens in Babylon*, 163–65, where she is more cautious about assigning an original order.

[30] To retain a pun in English, the species here (and in the next line) is altered. The paraphrase here is based on that of Bruce M. Metzger in the *Oxford Annotated Apocrypha, Expanded*

other, who testifies that they were lying under a yew tree, he says, "You have also lied, and under a *yew* tree the angel of God will *hew* you in two!" The two are thus condemned by the discrepancies in their testimony and are sentenced to death according to Jewish law; Susanna is restored to her family, and Daniel is respected by all.

The story, which probably circulated independently, is well constructed, allowing about equal time for the plight of Susanna and the courtroom heroics of Daniel. The two halves can each be compared to common folklore motifs, the falsely accused chaste wife and the wise child who prevents an unjust action of his elders. In its present composition, however, the two motifs are wonderfully harmonized. The tension is skillfully built up and dramatically resolved as the puns in Daniel's pronouncement provide an effective punch line, at the same time that they reflect Daniel's authority to pass judgment based on his charisma. The overall structure of threat and vindication is very similar to the court conflicts of *Daniel* 3 and 6, *Esther,* and *Bel and the Dragon,* although in this case, the "court" is not the highest court in the land but the local, self-governing Jewish court. The ethnic competition of Jews and non-Jews is totally absent, but, more to the point, the setting has been democratized and brought closer to a normal setting in everyday life (even though it is still quite idealized).[31] This development is a crucial step in the creation of a novel.

A closer comparison of the Theodotionic and Old Greek versions reveals other fascinating transformations of the popular story. In the conclusion of the Theodotionic version, Susanna is restored to her husband and her parents, while Daniel is established as a man of highest regard in the community; these events set the stage for the narratives that follow in *Daniel.* The Old Greek version, however, has nothing of this. The conclusion of the latter is an encomium to the ability of young people and the importance of respecting their *haplotes,* sincerity

---

Edition (New York: Oxford University Press, 1965), ad loc. Although the use of a pun indicated to Julius Africanus (and many subsequent Christian exegetes) that *Susanna* must have been written in Greek, it is easily created in other languages, as Metzger's translation proves. See also Moore, *Daniel, Esther, and Jeremiah,* 81–84.

[31] Steussy argues (*Gardens in Babylon,* 146–55) that Susanna reflects larger tensions of Jews as resident aliens in Babylon. This is mainly to be found in the Hebrew Bible quotations and not in the narrative itself. Are the quotations secondary to the narrative, or is there, as Steussy suggests, an intentional shading of the larger intent by the use of everyday characters? "Precisely the folkloric ordinariness makes Susanna an effective framework for interpretation of the troubling statements in Jeremiah 29" (p. 154). Either way, the development of novelistic techniques can be noted.

or innocence, and raising them properly. True to the form of Jewish and Christian sermons of the period, the Old Greek version ends on a pious and uplifting note: "And there shall be in them a spirit of understanding and discernment forever and ever."[32] In this context, we also see that the contrast that is played upon in the story is not just that between innocence and evil but also that between young and old. It is very likely that the Old Greek version was originally not about Daniel at all but about an unnamed youth who becomes a model of the young. Daniel is not named in either version until verse 45, but in the Old Greek version his name is awkwardly inserted. He does not appear at all in the encomium to youth in the conclusion. It is for these and other reasons that most scholars take the Old Greek version to be closer to the original and that the Theodotionic version reflects a more thoroughgoing attempt to relate the story of Susanna to the rest of the *Daniel* corpus.[33] In addition to this obvious difference, other more subtle changes were introduced into the Theodotionic text. It plays up the erotic element in a manner typical of Greek novels.[34] The bath scene did not occur in the Old Greek, and the lively action of the running and shouting that occurs when the elders claim to have caught Susanna *in flagranti* is also lacking. Further, Marti J. Steussy has demonstrated that there is a stronger narratorial presence in the Theodotionic version, where we find more explicit characterization and use of indirect dialogue.[35]

In one particular, however, the Old Greek retains a more strongly erotic element: Susanna is actually stripped in her trial scene, whereas in Theodotion she is only unveiled (v. 32).[36] Richard I. Pervo suggests

---

[32] On the sermonic form of the Old Greek *Susanna,* see Lawrence M. Wills, "The Form of the Sermon in Hellenistic Judaism and Early Christianity," *Harvard Theological Review* 77 (1984): 277–99, esp. 294, and *Jew in the Court,* 76–79. Translations of the two versions can be found in R. H. Charles, ed., *Apocrypha and Pseudepigrapha of the Old Testament,* 2 vols. (Oxford: Clarendon, 1912), 1:647–51, and also in Steussy, *Gardens in Babylon,* 101–14. She notes (140–41, 171) the hortatory nature of the ending and considers it "sermon-like."

[33] Joachim Schüpphaus, "Das Verhältnis von LXX- und Theodotion-Text in den apokryphen Zusätzen zum Danielbuch," *Zeitschrift für die alttestamentliche Wissenschaft* 83 (1971): 49–72; Engel, *Die Susanna-Erzählung.*

[34] Pervo, *Profit with Delight,* 152 n. 105; Robert Dunn, "Discriminations in the Comic Spirit in the Story of Susanna," *Christianity and Literature* 31, no. 4 (1982): 19–31, and Steussy, *Gardens in Babylon,* 142.

[35] Steussy, *Gardens in Babylon,* 101–43, esp. 140 (but note also 174, where the limitations of the characterization in these writings are conceded).

[36] The Greek verb *apokaluptein,* "to uncover," which appears in both texts, could conceivably mean either, but the Theodotionic text restricts it by adding, "for she was veiled." In the Old Greek it more likely means to expose completely, especially in light of the parallel mentioned below.

that the Theodotionic text softens the indignity inflicted on Susanna in a way that would be in keeping with Greek novels: the heroine would never be allowed to be shamed by appearing nude in public; her chastity would be threatened but ultimately protected.[37] Her unintended exposure during her bath—before the elders *and* the reading audience— would not have brought ritual shame upon her. The stripping of an adulteress in the Old Greek, however, had a correlation not in narrative practice but in actual legal practice. The Mishnah, edited in about 200 C.E., contains a provision for stripping a convicted adulteress, based on *Numbers* 5:11–31, exposing the parts of the body in the order that they were exposed in the sexual act.[38] Ritual shame is evidently the motive behind this practice, since it is noted that a woman's servants would have already seen her nude and need not witness her being stripped, but one might speculate that the woman also becomes a sort of sexual scapegoat, a permissible object of male erotic attention who is then stoned by the community (according to the provisions of *Leviticus* 20:10), taking away, as it were, the sexual sins of desire of the community. The story of *Susanna,* in that case, would be a narrated expression of this same psychological need to play out sexual tensions and desires in a permissible fashion. The author makes use of a common technique in psychologically oriented narrative. The two elders act upon their forbidden desires (male desires that are extrapolated as normative and "shared" with the audience) and are punished with death. Once the evil trait is released and threatens Susanna, it is discovered and slain.[39] This experience is intensified by the polarization of good and evil in this morality play as the personalities of Dr. Jekyll and Mr. Hyde are projected onto

[37] Pervo, "Aseneth and Her Sisters," 148. Despite the differences between the versions, both share one quality with the Greek novels: the heroine is erotic in spite of her intentions; her heart is innocent, but her body is provocative. In Greek novels, only an antagonistic and morally corrupt woman can be intentionally erotic. See Brigitte Egger, "Looking at Chariton's Callirhoe," in Morgan and Stoneman, eds., *Greek Fiction,* 39.

[38] *Sotah* 1:5. Pervo cautions against the use of this parallel because it cannot be dated as early as the narrative of *Susanna* ("Aseneth and Her Sisters," 148 n. 25), but the similarities are too close to ignore and the dates not that far apart. Note also that the image of the uncovering of the adulteress in a judicial setting already occurs at *Ezekiel* 16:35–38. We do not know in what way the legal provision was actually practiced when *Susanna* was written, but there is clearly a relation here between the legal tradition and the literary account. The social and cultural importance of this law can be seen in the fact that Helena, queen of Adiabene in the first century C.E., on converting to Judaism is said to have inscribed a tablet in Jerusalem bearing *Numbers* 5:12–31, the law of the suspected adulteress, on which the Mishnah *Sotah* passage and *Susanna* are based (Mishnah *Yoma* 3:10).

[39] Cf. in Chapter 1 the "unleashed" woman who is slain in Greek tragedy.

the characters: Susanna, the innocent heroine, and the evil elders, acting on their desires to possess her.

The voyeuristic male perspective in the story of Susanna and in visual representations of it has been analyzed by Margaret R. Miles.[40] She notes that the story of *Susanna* maintains the position of the status quo; there is no sense in which the social conditions that give rise to Susanna's vulnerability are ever questioned, and a conservative complacency, common also in bourgeois entertainments such as the Greek novel, pervades it. After all, the elders are only manipulating a system that would condemn a woman to ritual shame and death for the sin of adultery.[41] The underlying parameters of the legal situation are not just a happenstance of the story, something that it would be pointless to question; they are affirmed, and affirmed strongly. God sends a young advocate, Daniel, to ensure the inherent justice of the legal code. Later visual representations of Susanna continue to exploit her nakedness at the center of the painting, and her innocence, as a result, is compromised in the audience's perception, even by those artists, such as Rembrandt, who may fight against this. According to Miles, "In the visual mode, Susanna's nakedness inevitably contradicted her virtue." The artistic representations focus on Susanna's nude body on one hand and the contorted faces of the two elders on the other, "the Elders' intense erotic attraction . . . projected and displayed on Susanna's flesh." Although it is true that the visual image merges the elders' and the audience's perspectives, the literary medium of the original story allows for a more mixed response (a distinction that Miles also notes)[42] and, at the same time, for the investigation of a theme common to novelistic literature: a woman's thoughts. As in the Greek novels, eroticism is tempered with a bourgeois ethic of the containment of sexuality. At the same time that Susanna is caught in an erotic situation, the audience's point of view is brought into *her* perspective: "Susanna groaned aloud and said, 'I am trapped either way! If I do what they ask, it would be worse than death to me, yet if I do not, I will never escape your clutches! Yet it is better

---

[40] Margaret R. Miles, *Carnal Knowing: Female Nakedness and Religious Meaning in the Christian West* (Boston: Beacon, 1989), 121–24. See also, with a consideration of the differences between the Old Greek and Theodotionic versions of *Susanna,* Dunn, "Discriminations in the Comic Spirit."

[41] Men were also covered in adultery legislation, but men and women are not treated in all the relevant texts in the same way. The legal processes are not identical for men and women but construct two separate gender codes. It is this difference—and the way that it is realized in novelistic fiction—that is our main concern here.

[42] Miles, *Carnal Knowing,* 123.

for me to refuse and fall into your hands than to sin against the Lord' "
(vv. 22–23).

Whether such a perspective might indicate a female author—or perhaps a predominantly female audience—is difficult to determine. Certainly, this sort of reporting of female experience has been taken as evidence of a female readership in the Greek novels, and it would correspond with what we know of the readership of novelistic literature in the modern era. What can be noted with assurance is that the text of *Susanna,* unlike the visual depictions, includes within the audience's purview both the perspective of the elders and the perspective of Susanna.[43] This experience of sexuality is perhaps quintessentially "novelistic" in that it introduces the problematic of sexual desire into the framework of a bourgeois sensibility and resolves the tension favorably on the side of a traditional family morality, with, as Miles notes, no consideration of the underlying social and juridical situation that would place Susanna in such jeopardy.

Other evidences of a novelistic development in *Susanna* can be gleaned from a close reading of the text. The story of *Susanna* does not waste words, and it would be unwise to ignore even those that seem to be superfluous. The beginning description of the story, for example, is not indulgent—one might contrast it with *Esther*—but certain pieces of information here are important: "There was once in Babylon a man named Joakim, who was married to Susanna, the daughter of Hilkiah. She was very beautiful, and exceedingly reverent of the Lord. Her parents were righteous, and had taught their daughter according to the law of Moses. Joakim, who was a wealthy man, owned a beautiful garden adjoining his house, and all the Jews would come to visit him, because he was the most honored of them all." Joakim was rich, with a large and important estate, and Susanna, beautiful, to be sure, but also righteous, was instructed in the law of Moses by her parents; she is thus twice connected with respectability. The social position that she has achieved, in addition to her own life, is threatened in the story. Helmut Engel has observed that the changes reflected in the Theodotionic version highlight this. Whereas in the Old Greek Susanna is more of a

[43] The article by Bal, "The Elders and Susanna," came to my attention too late for me to use it extensively. She also emphasizes the double perspective on the voyeurism of the elders: "Depending on the episode, focalization (that is, the directing of the point of view) is now separated from, now coincides with, the voyeurism of the elders" (p. 10). She comes to conclusions similar to those of Miles regarding the visual representations, but she was evidently unaware of Miles's book.

moral exemplar, a "daughter of Judah," in the Theodotionic version she is subtly highlighted as an individual.[44] She is described and characterized more precisely, as is Daniel, who is almost her moral and romantic "mate" (even though she is already married). There is a slightly stronger emphasis on the wealth and status of Susanna's family and on how she is shamed before her servants and restored at the end to her family.

The story of *Susanna,* especially in the Theodotionic version, thus contributes several themes that would render the reader's perception of the whole more novelistic. First, there is the narration of male sexual tensions and the introduction of a beautiful, vulnerable female character, on whom the audience focuses its sympathy and its own sense of vulnerability. Second, there is a focus on the social shame that Susanna experiences in the presence of her husband, family, friends, and servants, that is, her household and extended family. The extended family would never qualify as a "novelistic" theme in the high period of Greek novels, but it is everpresent in the Jewish novels. This relation of the family to a notion of respectability and social position within the Jewish community is indicated also by the change in the setting for the trial—indeed, for all the action—in Theodotion's text from the synagogue to the estate of Joakim. We shall find that although the other additions can contribute to the creation of a more novelistic form, it is *Susanna* more than anything else that extends this possibility in Daniel.

Bel and the Dragon

Bel and the Dragon, like *Daniel* 1–6, is a court narrative, and its placement at the end of *Daniel* seems a logical way to extend the corpus as it had been extended several times before. *Bel and the Dragon* differs slightly in genre and origin from the rest of the legends of *Daniel.* It consists of two parts, each of which probably circulated independently.[45] In the first, the Persian king Cyrus is impressed with the vast quantities of food, wine, and oil offerings which the Babylonian god Bel evidently consumes inside the temple each day. The king points this out to Daniel and says, "Will you not now worship the living god?" Daniel, however,

---

[44] Engel, *Susanna-Erzählung,* 181–82, and Steussy, *Gardens in Babylon,* 142.

[45] Moore, *Daniel, Esther, and Jeremiah,* 121–25. It is entirely possible that the story actually consists of three parts and that the lion's den punishment scene at the end was added by the editor when the two stories of Daniel's clever and heroic actions were joined. Steussy (*Gardens of Babylon,* 55–99) treats the three parts of the story separately.

is not fooled, and he agrees to a test of the god. The seventy priests of Bel allow the king to place the food inside the temple and lock the door, sealing it with his ring. But before the doors are shut, Daniel sprinkles ashes over the floor. On the next day, when the king comes to break the seal and open the doors, Daniel shows him the footprints of men, women, and children in the ashes. The priests of Bel are summoned and reveal to the king a trapdoor by which they have entered the temple with their families each night to feast on the food left for Bel. The king orders their execution and allows Daniel to destroy the statue of Bel and its temple. In the second half, Cyrus points out to Daniel the great dragon worshipped by the Babylonians.[46] "Surely *this* is a living god!" says Cyrus. Daniel, however, gathers pitch, fat, and hair, cooks them into a cake, and feeds it to the dragon, which then swells up and bursts. The ingredients are not magical but everyday substances, which are presumed to swell up in the monster's stomach by their natural properties.

Bel and the Dragon plays cleverly with the irony of the common Jewish epithet "living God." Cyrus twice looks to the physical evidence for a god who is living—in fact, gorging—but Daniel exposes the foolishness of such notions, which the readers would readily attribute to pagan believers. The concrete aspect of the notion of a "living" God is anchored in the pagans' sensibilities to the mundane world, instead of being allowed to float upward in the direction that it is pointing. We shall note below clever and humorous uses of irony in *Judith,* but the particular ironic technique utilized here is paralleled also in two ancient masters of irony, Plato and John, the author of the fourth gospel. The technique involved is to juxtapose the sage's simple statement of the higher realities with the world's perverse insistence on misperceiving it on a mundane level. When Socrates is about to drink the hemlock, he asks the man who has borne him the cup, "Shall I make a libation? I understand that that is appropriate when one is about to make a journey from one place to another." "Oh no," replies the jailer, "I have made exactly the right amount to kill you" (*Phaedo* 117b). Likewise, when Jesus meets the woman at the well and offers her "living water," she points out to him that she does not have a pail (*John* 4:10–15; compare also 3:3–4).

[46] Whether it is a "dragon" or merely a large snake is not clear; the Greek word *drakon* is used in the Greek Bible for snakes and for mythological beasts. Some (e.g., Moore, *Daniel, Esther, and Jeremiah,* 141–42) would want to tie the *drakon* to the worship of a living animal, but this is hardly necessary. In light of the "beast" mythology in Babylonian tradition, where the story is set, "dragon" appears more likely.

In Plato and *John* these exchanges are the basis of a thoroughgoing contrast between understanding as the world understands and perceiving the clear, simple message of God. This theme is also enlarged in both authors to address the question, How is it possible that the wisest and most righteous man who ever lived could have come to be executed? Although this may be quite a development in sophistication beyond *Bel and the Dragon*, it is still built upon the same technique: the juxtaposition of the highest truths with the world's natural obtuseness. The audience, however, in each case is privileged to perceive things as they are really intended and can take great satisfaction in doing so.

The two stories in *Bel and the Dragon* are examples of the Jewish "idol parody narrative," in which the pagan's reverence for idols and sacred animals is exposed as baseless and superstitious by a brash Jewish protagonist. This lively genre was evidently a narrative expression of the same view that appears in poetic denunciations of idols in such texts as *Isaiah* 40:18–20, *Psalms* 115:4–8, and *Wisdom of Solomon* 13–15.[47] There may be broader literary parallels as well. C. P. Jones notes that two of Lucian's satires, "The Passing of Peregrinus" and "Alexander the False Prophet," can be considered "literature of exposure,"[48] in which the pretensions of popular charlatans are exposed for the literate audience, a device not unlike that used in *Bel and the Dragon*. We may see them and Lucian's satires on different ends of a class spectrum, but both are similar in displaying a rationalistic turn of mind harnessed to an entertaining purpose. Dorothy Sayers also noted that *Susanna* and *Bel and the Dragon* are both "detective stories"[49] (although it is more accurate to say that *Susanna* is a "courtroom drama"), and in both we find a brash young outsider who heroically uncovers the truth.

Bel and the Dragon would thus appear to add an element of humor to the *Daniel* corpus, but it would not be the only humorous episode. *Daniel* 3, as we noted above, is also humorous and satirical. The spirited debunking of the worship of idols in *Bel and the Dragon* is also, like *Daniel* 3, followed by threatening developments not found in the other

[47] Wolfgang Roth, " 'For Life, He Appeals to Death' (Wis 13:18): A Study of Old Testament Idol Parodies," *Catholic Biblical Quarterly* 37 (1975): 21–47. Another example of an idol parody narrative is found in Josephus, *Contra Apionem* 1.22.201–4. See also Wills, *Jew in the Court*, 131–34, and Steussy, *Gardens in Babylon*, 47, who notes that idol worship was probably not a real threat to Jewish religion but a foil to prove the reasonableness of Judaism.

[48] C. P. Jones, *Culture and Society in Lucian* (Cambridge: Harvard University Press, 1986), 148.

[49] According to Julian Symons, *Bloody Murder: From the Detective Story to the Crime Novel* (New York: Viking, 1985), 27.

idol parody narratives (and perhaps even inserted secondarily in the *Bel* tradition). The angry reaction of the Babylonians to the destruction of their cultus precipitates a court conflict, wherein Daniel is sentenced to be thrown into a den of lions. He remains in the den unharmed for seven days, but if that were not miracle enough, the prophet Habbakuk, who is far away in Judaea boiling soup, is whisked away, soup in hand, by an angel and transported to Daniel's side, where he offers up his pottage. The combination of the humor of the idol parody narrative with the mortal threat of the court conflict is difficult to reconcile, but we may understand it as a pious tendency similar to what seems to have occurred in the combination of stories in *Daniel* 1–6.

That in the new corpus of Greek *Daniel* the hero is sentenced to the lions' den twice, once in *Daniel* 6 and once here, has led some scholars to posit a common origin for the two stories. A confinement in a pit is, to be sure, quite common—compare Joseph or Ahikar—and as Niditch has noted, often marks a transformation for the character.[50] True enough, but there are no lions in those cases. The collocation of Daniel, court, king, and den of lions indicates that we are dealing here with variants of the same story. Duplicate narratives have been included in the corpus of Greek *Daniel,* a very common phenomenon in popular and oral transmission. We should not assume, however, that *Bel and the Dragon* is an altered and sensationalized version of *Daniel* 6 (as if *Daniel* 6 were not already sensationalized!). It is equally likely that the liveliness of *Bel and the Dragon* has given way to the more pious depiction of *Daniel* 6, and a reasonable hypothesis may explain the changes that were (according to this reconstruction) introduced into *Daniel* 6.[51] To begin with, although *Bel and the Dragon* contains some indications that it was part of the Daniel tradition, it was not necessarily originally composed for inclusion in the book of *Daniel* as we know it. Of the two versions of *Bel and the Dragon,* the Theodotionic continues a succession chronology parallel to but not in total agreement with it *Daniel* 1–6: Cyrus succeeds Astyages (the Mede), not Darius the Mede, as in *Daniel*

---

[50] Niditch, *Underdogs and Tricksters,* 103–4. A closer parallel to our text is also found in the Greek novels. Anthia is thrown into a pit with dogs (Xenophon 4.6). She survives, however, because her appointed executioner has fallen in love with her and regularly feeds the animals so that they will not devour her. He also feeds Anthia, much as Habbakuk feeds Daniel in *Bel and the Dragon.* Thus, the apparently disruptive and secondary nature of Habbakuk's intervention in *Bel and the Dragon* may actually have been part of a combination of motifs that had previously circulated together, though altered in *Bel and the Dragon* to take on the tone of a miracle.

[51] See also Wills, *Jew in the Court,* 134–38.

6. *Bel and the Dragon,* with a focus on Cyrus, would therefore come after *Daniel* 6 in temporal order. The less canonical Old Greek version of *Bel and the Dragon,* however, presents an earlier, even more independent narrative. It lacks the succession chronology entirely (the unnamed king is Babylonian), and Daniel is introduced in a way totally inappropriate for *Daniel* 1–6: he is "a priest, by the name of Daniel, son of Abal, who was a confidant of the king of Babylon." Daniel is introduced here as if for the first time, whereas in the Theodotionic version of *Bel* his story is merely taken up again. As was the case with *Susanna,* the Old Greek text of *Bel and the Dragon* thus contains compelling evidence of a relatively independent narrative, and the Theodotionic text, an episode edited for inclusion in the growing Danielic corpus. Furthermore, *Bel and the Dragon* is not simply independent of *Daniel* 6; it probably reflects an older version of the narrative. The motif of the king's ring used as a seal, common to both of the narratives, is much more logical in *Bel:* the king seals the doors of the temple of Bel after locking the food inside. The use of this motif in *Daniel* 6, however, where the stone, after it is placed over the lions' den, is "sealed" with the king's ring, is totally artificial. (Exactly how, one might ask, is a large stone over the opening of a pit "sealed" with a ring?)

It is still incumbent upon a reconstruction such as this to explain why such wholesale changes were introduced into the narrative of *Daniel* 6, if it ultimately derived from a story similar to *Bel and the Dragon.* The most fundamental difference between *Bel and the Dragon* and *Daniel* 6 is the prominence of the political structure of satrapies in the latter. These divisions of the worldwide Persian state, read back into the fictitious kingdom of Darius the Mede, were actually introduced by Darius of Persia. He only created twenty satrapies, however, and so the number one hundred and twenty is an exaggeration that likely betrays the same fun-loving attitude as does the introduction of "Darius the Mede" in the first place. The satrapies become the projection of the idealized state structure, and ruling over them becomes the prize to be attained. This attainment in the political realm is the new theme of *Daniel* 6 and the theme that has motivated the transformation of *Bel and the Dragon* (or its close relative).[52]

---

[52] The fact that *Bel and the Dragon* is more schematically structured than *Daniel* 6 does not militate against their being duplicate narratives but gives credence to the present reconstruction (contra Fenz, "Ein Drache in Babel," and Moore, *Daniel, Esther, and Jeremiah,* 147–49). The structure of *Bel and the Dragon* would be appropriate for an orally transmitted narrative, and this structure is precisely what would be lost as the story is altered in the direction of *Daniel*

Bel and the Dragon, despite being more humorous than *Daniel* 6, is not necessarily more novelistic. The humor has a home in the tradition of the idol parody narrative, which was as likely to be oral as written. *Bel and the Dragon* does, however, extend the framework in a biographical or aretalogical direction (that is, describing the great deeds of the protagonist), and, assuming that it appeared at the end of the Danielic corpus, it subordinates the apocalyptic visions to the interests of the narratives.[53] It certainly does not alter the complexion of the whole as much as *Susanna* does, with its interest in the domestic novel, but it does continue the narrative with another episode, and although it may appear clumsily added and in fact is, it also accomplishes a humble goal: the narrative "extension" required by the novelistic impulse.

The Stages of Greek *Daniel*

Greek *Daniel,* then, constitutes a new novel that came into existence sometime after the Maccabean Revolt. *Susanna* was likely the first chapter, introducing the young Daniel, and *Bel and the Dragon* was most likely added to the end, after the visions of chapters 7–12. The eroticism and courtroom theatrics of *Susanna* and the broadside farce of *Bel and the Dragon* surely tip the resultant document back in the direction of novelistic literature and also fiction. The "biographical novel" suggests itself as a category here; the life of the powerful sage, who has visions and is miraculously protected by God, is recounted in greater detail.[54] Such a category is not inappropriate for the whole, but the presence of *Susanna* here introduces some issues that point toward a more domestic novel. It is not just the plight of the beautiful, innocent maiden, which could arise in any folktale, it is also the nature of the setting: domestic relations within a respectable Jewish household, outside of the arena of important political events. Still, the potential for novelistic evolution was not fully explored here. Ultimately, despite the extension of the corpus as a whole to the length of a Jewish novel, the focus of the whole remained closer to a biographical interest, with many separate episodes, and the

---

6. The differences between the two narratives are not that great, once a reasonable hypothesis (such as above) is introduced to suggest why the differences were introduced.

[53] Steussy, *Gardens in Babylon,* 167.

[54] Hengel uses the term *aretalogical novella* (*Judaism and Hellenism* 2:24 n. 215), by which he means a biography that recounts the miraculous deeds of an extraordinary, even revered figure.

novelistic impulse was not carried through to lengthen one episode, *Susanna,* into a longer domestic drama of the size of *Esther* or *Judith.* The addition of *Susanna*—which by itself might have grown into a novel—certainly brings some of the issues of the novel into the ambit of the Daniel corpus, but Greek *Daniel* becomes a bourgeois entertainment not so much by the introduction of new techniques or extension of certain important scenes as by simple agglutination.

Summarizing the probable stages, then, which shift markedly at each turn, we see that *Daniel* 1–6 consists of separate court narratives, some originally oral, which are based on biblical and Persian models. They are, however, not simply strung together to form a larger corpus. The eschatological oracle against the king which has been taken over in *Daniel* 2 has provided an order for the succession of kings represented in the stories. The negative oracle has nevertheless been restrained by its inclusion in a typical court legend that contains a rather predictable happy ending; the oracle nevertheless conditions the ordering and identity of the kings in *Daniel* 1–6. In this collection there is an awareness of the negative oracle, but the stories are only in some cases negative toward Babylonian kings and accommodationist toward Median and Persian kings. The oppressed authors of *Daniel* 7–12, writing in a period of crisis, take up again the visionary genre, replaying the four-kingdom schema. Some years later, the genre of the whole is tipped back in the direction of entertainment by the addition of *Susanna* and *Bel and the Dragon.* At the risk of polarizing the options, then, it appears that there was a sort of seesaw pattern at play in the development of the Daniel tradition, by turns serious and comic. This "genre jumping" is a puzzling problem, although it happens often enough in the history of literature. It calls into question, however, any attempt to use a later layer as a key to understanding the reception of the previous one. We do not know whether the authors of any layer were intentionally rerouting the message of the previous tradition or simply imposing their new genre demands on its subconsciously.

The evolution of *Daniel* from a conglomeration of short, independently circulating narratives into a longer, novelistic work provides a fascinating reflection of the shift of Jewish narrative techniques from the Persian and early Hellenistic periods to the late Hellenistic period. The incremental nature of the process can only be called "evolutionary," not simply because it moves along a developmental path but also because it seems to have a goal, a growing impulse: the communication of the values of a literate Jewish middle class through a description of everyday reality. This goal is no different from that of all other novel-istic literature. The Great Leap Forward that Perry rightly insists upon for the large Greek novels has not occurred, but the popular audience's appetite for diverting, episodic reading matter is being provisionally met. And it is not coincidental that the length of Greek *Daniel* is now about the same as that of the other Jewish novels, the process of growth having provided *Daniel* with the optimal page range for the new Jewish market.

CHAPTER 3

Tobit as Tale
and Novel

.The *Book of Tobit* is a light novel that recounts the separate problems of the elder Tobit, the younger Sarah, and the intertwined solutions to their problems. Although like the Greek novels it concerns lovers, it is much shorter, and the sexual union of the lovers—or the obstacles that stand in the way of their sexual union—does not dominate the story. The union is not erotic, and it constitutes only one of the two resolutions of the narrative. The book has been received as a pleasant diversion, pious and uplifting, with many warm domestic scenes of Jewish Diaspora life strung on a fairy-tale plot line. As Jonas C. Greenfield characterizes it: "Religious and ritual matters such as the holidays, the giving of tithes, ritual purity, prayer towards Jerusalem (with hands uplifted) and almsgiving are skillfully used. These served to set the scene of the 'romance' and to make the Jewish reader feel at home." [1] Other modern scholars have gone further, seeing ennobling themes in its pages. Frank Zimmermann's commentary introduces the work thus: "Tobit contains the earliest Jewish source of the Golden Rule; a tender consideration for women; a stress on Jewish brotherhood; a strong sense of interfamily relationship and devotion; and illuminating sidelights on the etiquette of a bygone age. The deeply felt sympathy of the author for his characters, his sturdy belief in God's compassion, his call for loyalty to principle and ideals may still evoke from us a response, and from across the centuries, a salute of respect." [2] I feel downright perverse

---

[1] Jonas C. Greenfield, "Ahiqar in the Book of Tobit," in *De la Tôrah au Messie,* ed. Maurice Carrez, Joseph Doré, and Pierre Grelot (Paris: Desclée, 1981), 334.

[2] Zimmermann, *The Book of Tobit,* 1–2.

68

to suggest that the earliest readers of *Tobit* may have responded with laughter rather than a salute of respect, but such was probably the case, as we shall see. George Nickelsburg and Toni Craven detect humorous episodes within this work,[3] but they still underestimate the comic overtones. To be sure, *Tobit* is not a full-blown satire, and there are "serious" themes in it, but the work is guided by a persistent whimsy. The category to which *Tobit* belongs and, thus, the poetics it embodies force us to be wary of comparisons to more serious literature.

The story takes place at the time of the loss of the northern half of Israel to Assyria in the late eighth century B.C.E. Although probably written in the Diaspora of the postexilic period, it is set in the "first Diaspora," after the fall of the north. The characters are unknown to Jewish history, although Tobit is said to be related to Ahikar, an Assyrian courtier who was made famous in *The Story of Ahikar* and who, interestingly, is here taken to be an Israelite. The book begins by describing Tobit's activities in trying to give a decent burial to Jews who were part of the captivity community in Nineveh, capital of Assyria. (Technically, the corpses would be those of "Israelites" from northern Israel and not "Jews" or Judahites, but this distinction is lost on our author, who writes at a much later time and emphasizes "Jewish" identity.) This practice places Tobit in peril, because King Sennacherib has forbidden the burial of Jews. Tobit goes into hiding, but when Sennacherib is killed and his son Esarhaddon comes to reign, Ahikar, a kinsman of Tobit and a highly placed counselor in the royal court, intercedes for him and he is allowed to return.

The narrative thus far is very brief, relating a very dramatic story in only one chapter. The situation has returned to a state of calm, but this calm soon gives way to a new plot complication, the main concern of the book. Tobit is about to sit down to a lavish feast celebrating Pentecost (Shabuot, or the Feast of Weeks) when he finds that a Jew has just been killed and lies unburied. Tobit leaves his dinner untasted, proceeds to bury the Jew, and then returns and goes to sleep outdoors with his head uncovered. Droppings from a bird on the wall above fall onto his eyes, causing white patches to form that render him totally blind. For four years he remains in this condition, and his wife works at domestic chores. Once, when she is paid a bonus of a small goat, Tobit accuses her of having stolen it. She rebukes him strongly, and Tobit, disconsolate over what he perceives as unjust reproaches, prays to God that

---

[3] Nickelsburg, *Jewish Literature Between the Bible and the Mishnah*, 30–35; Craven, *Artistry and Faith in the Book of Judith*, 116 esp. n. 7.

he may die. At exactly the same time, in Ecbatana, capital of Media, a young Jewish woman named Sarah is reproached by her servant because, although she has been betrothed seven times, on each of the wedding nights the groom has been killed by the evil spirit Asmodaeus. Sarah then also prays that she be allowed to die rather than live with this stigma. Her prayer and Tobit's are heard in heaven, and the angel Raphael is sent to resolve both of their problems. While Tobit prepares to die, he sends his son Tobias to Media to retrieve a large sum of money that he had placed on deposit many years earlier with a relative. Tobias finds a man to guide him on his journey, and the reader is informed that this man is none other than the angel Raphael in human form. They travel together to Media, and on the way Raphael instructs Tobias to cut the entrails out of a fish they have caught, since the organs can be used to exorcise evil spirits and to remove white patches from the eyes. Raphael also convinces Tobias to stop along the way at Sarah's house and to become betrothed to her, since she is a relative and would make the perfect wife for him. Once there, the young Tobias is betrothed to Sarah, and on their wedding night he uses part of the entrails of the fish to drive away the evil spirit Asmodaeus. In the morning there is much rejoicing that Sarah is released from her curse and married to a most suitable young man.

After retrieving the money from Tobit's kinsman, Tobias, Raphael, and Sarah return to Nineveh. Tobias applies the fish gall to Tobit's eyes and peels off the scales. Tobit rejoices at regaining his sight but is even more overjoyed to hear that his son has made a successful marriage and has retrieved the money. Tobit and Tobias agree that the man who served as a guide in the journey should receive half of the deposited money, but when they approach Raphael with this offer, he reveals to them his true identity. Raphael then takes his farewell and ascends to heaven. Thus concludes the main narrative, but after it also appear Tobit's prayer of thanksgiving and his deathbed instructions for his son concerning the prophecy of the fall of Nineveh.

The book thus falls into three parts: the first adventure, in which Tobit narrowly escapes execution for burying the corpses of fellow Jews (chapter 1); the second, the bulk of the book, in which Tobit's and Sarah's plaints are answered by the intervention of the angel Raphael (chapters 2–12); and the third, which consists of prayers and a deathbed testament (chapters 13–14). These three parts indicate a lack of cohesion in the text, and other structural problems can be seen as well. The book begins, for instance, with Tobit recounting his story in the first person. From the moment that the narrative introduces Sarah's story at 3:7, however, there is a change to third-person narration. The book as it stands, then, is not unified in style. The first-person narration and the fact that the story line of the first chapter is so abbreviated suggest that the first part of the book was once separate from the rest of the present work. This may in fact be the case, although the first-person narration extends beyond chapter 1 into the beginning of the main line of the narrative (ending at 3:7), and this preamble intrigue is not totally unrelated to the story as a whole.[4] Also, the addition of prayers, sayings, and teachings not only is a problem at the end of Tobit but occurs elsewhere in the book as well. It is not clear whether the combination of separate narratives gives rise to these and other organizational problems; at any rate, the *Book of Tobit* retains the power to delight in spite of them. It combines well various subplots and devices and easily maintains the reader's attention. The main part of the book still has a clear and entertaining structure that is readily discernible and unaffected by the minor problems. We shall return to the question of sources and additions below.

As with all of the popular Jewish novels, the determination of authorship and provenance is difficult. Most of the theology of *Tobit* is unremarkable. The importance of Ecbatana and Media in the work points to an Eastern orientation, as do several other elements: the Persian name of the demon, Asmodaeus; the fact that he flees to Upper Egypt, exactly as the demon does in the Syrian *Hymn of the Pearl*,[5] and the concern for burial, which was more likely an issue in the East, where cremation was the standard ritual means of disposing of the dead. However, the geographical notice at the beginning of chapter 1, giving Tobit's genealogy and place of origin before the deportation of the northern tribes, has also been plumbed for revealing information about the real author's origins. It reads: "He . . . was carried away as a captive from Thisbe, which

---

[4] The problem of two kinds of narration is analogous to that of two languages (Hebrew and Aramaic) in the legends of *Daniel* 1–6 (see Chapter 2). In both cases, the switch occurs just after a new movement of the story is underway and appears to be prompted by an element of the story: in *Tobit*, the shift to a description of Sarah's plight (about which Tobit knows nothing) gives rise to third-person narration, and in *Daniel* 2, a quotation of Chaldaean courtiers in Aramaic shifts the entire narrative into that language until chapter 8.

[5] Geo Widengren, "Quelques rapports entre juifs et iraniens à l'époque des Parthes," Supplements to *Vetus Testamentum* 4 (1956): 197–241, esp. 215–16. He describes the importance of the eastern areas mentioned (p. 215 n. 7), noting that the satrapy of Media was the eastern border of the Parthians and that Median was adopted as the official language of the Parthians, while Ecbatana became their capital and the center of their resistance to the Roman invasions.

is south of Kedesh Naphtali, in Upper Galilee north of Hazor, but facing westward, north of Phogor." Thisbe and Phogor (or in Hebrew, Pe'or) have never been identified with certainty, but Kedesh and Hazor are correctly located in the tribal land of Naphtali. J. T. Milik ingeniously suggests that the variant readings of Thisbe found in the ancient texts, Thebes or Thibes, are actually Thebez, about ten miles northwest of Samaria.[6] This town appears in *Judges* 9:50 and *Second Samuel* 11:21, but more important for our purposes, it is a Samaritan area in the later period. Milik thinks that the *Book of Tobit* originated in an attempt to give an ideal projection of the Tobiad clan, a wealthy dynasty of landowners and entrepreneurs who were localized mainly in Samaria. The fact that Tobit's son is named Tobias, the family name of the Tobiad clan, increases the likelihood that this view is correct, and Tobit's own name may be a Graecized version of the family eponym.[7] Milik's central observation that this work was composed by or for members of the Tobiad family seems likely and will be taken here as an operating hypothesis. The emphasis on burial has prompted scholars to search for a time and a place where this might have been a concern, and Zimmermann plausibly suggests that *Tobit* was written during the reign of Antiochus IV Epiphanes, who prohibited the burial of his Jewish opponents (*Second Maccabees* 9:15).[8] As noted above, however, the burial motif, especially in a Persian environment, may reflect a more general ethnic friction.

The *Book of Tobit* entertains in spite of the best efforts of the reader to rise to a higher critical standard. If some Jewish novels can be compared with romances, this one can be compared with a modern "romantic comedy" in that a happy ending is so thoroughly guaranteed—there is never any tension—that our interest is focused solely on the various adventures and comic scenes that propel the work forward. The ominous threats to the protagonists' safety that mark the Greek romances are absent here. The interest here is not what will happen but how.

---

[6] J. T. Milik, "La patrie de Tobie," *Revue Biblique* 73 (1966): 522–30. It is also possible, however, that the present reading of Thisbe results from an assimilation to the more famous Tishbe of Gilead (in Greek, *Thisbe*), home of Elijah.

[7] Zimmermann, *Book of Tobit,* 44. We shall have reason to return to the Tobiad clan in Chapter 7. The Samaritan origin of this Tobiad family romance has, according to Milik, been intentionally obscured by the addition of place names from the tribal area of Naphtali. The more common area associated with the Tobiad family, however, perhaps as far back as the sixth century B.C.E., is Gilead, in the Transjordan, bordering Ammon. Inscriptions have been found in this area (Araq el-Amir) that refer to the Tobiad family. However, the Tobiads also maintained close business relations with Samaria. See B. Mazar, "The Tobiads," *Israel Exploration Journal* 7 (1957): 137–45, 229–38, esp. 140–45, 234.

[8] Zimmermann, *Book of Tobit,* 24.

When Tobit and Sarah make separate prayers to God, it is stated that the prayers of both have been heeded and Raphael is sent to cure both of their problems (3:16–17).[9] Even the names of some of the principal characters connote a happy outcome: Raphael means "God heals," Tobias means "God is good," Anna means "grace," Azariah means "God helps," and so on.

Folklore Parallels

Many of the plot elements of the work have been rightly compared with fairy-tale motifs.[10] Very similar to Tobit are numerous versions of the tale type called the Grateful Dead Man. In this common tale, a traveler ransoms a stranger's corpse by paying off the dead man's creditors, in order to give him a proper burial. Later on in his journey, he is joined by another traveler (the doppelgänger of the dead man), who urges him at one point to accept betrothal to a princess, even though several of her previous grooms have died on their wedding night. The man accepts, and when a dragon appears in her bedchamber on the wedding night, the stranger slays the dragon. Although the overall parallels are obvious, commentators have also noticed several seemingly trivial details in Tobit that can be explained by recourse to this and other folktale types. For instance, in the folktale the stranger insists that the hero divide anything he gains on their journey in half, even to the extent that in some versions the princess is cut in half. We recall that Tobit and Tobias offer Raphael *half* of their recovered money at the end of the narrative. Important differences between Tobit and the Grateful Dead Man have also been delineated, however. The role of the hero in our story is divided between two characters—Tobit, who buries dead people, and Tobias, who proceeds on the journey with Raphael—but as Vladimir Propp has

---

[9] Some Greek romances also intimate early on that the protagonists will ultimately be reunited. Graham Anderson (*Ancient Fiction: The Novel in the Greco-Roman World* [Totawa, N.J.: Barnes and Noble, 1984], 123, 144–48) has noted that Xenophon of Ephesus creates little tension in his novel and that the oracle at the beginning of Xenophon's romance (1.6) implies threats but then promises a happy ending.

[10] The most important recent treatments of this question would include Blenkinsopp, "Biographical Patterns in Biblical Narrative"; Milne, "Folktales and Fairy Tales"; Soll, "Tobit and Folklore Studies, with Emphasis on Propp's Morphology"; Zimmermann, *Book of Tobit*, 5–12; and Stith Thompson, *The Folktale* (Berkeley and Los Angeles: University of California Press, 1977), 50–52. Deselaers, *Das Buch Tobit*, 268–70, provides an excellent review of scholarship on Tobit as a tale.

shown, it is relatively common for the same role in a tale to be divided and assigned to two characters who operate in tandem.[11]

Other folk narratives and motifs have been adduced as parallels to Tobit, but one very suggestive folktale comparison, the Turkish tale "The Blind Padishah with Three Sons," has evidently been missed by the commentators.[12] In this tale, a rich man who has become blind dreams that his eyes can be cured with a handful of soil on which his horses have not trod. The two oldest sons try to find such soil, but in each case it turns out that the father, who with the aid of a magical horse has traveled far and wide, has ridden over the soil that they have presented. The youngest son, however, forces his mother to tell him how his father retrieves the magic horse and, with the horse now under his control, sets out on his search for the soil. The spot where the soil is found is beneath the head of a sleeping dragon; this same dragon, in fact, had scorched the father's eyes and made him blind. When the young man meets the dragon, he asks for a handful of soil, but the dragon insists that he will only give it to him if he can present to him a certain *khoja* girl, a Muslim priestess (a figure who only exists in folktales, not in actual Muslim practice). With the help of the horse, the young man does bring the *khoja* girl, and the dragon graciously gives him the soil and allows him to take the girl on his way. After other adventures, the young man returns to his father, cures his blindness, and marries the magical *khoja* girl.

The similarity with *Tobit* can be easily noted. In both a blind father sends a son on a crucial mission, and the son returns with a cure for the blindness. Destiny plays a role in both—divine providence in Tobit, kismet in "The Blind Padishah." In both the hero is accompanied by a magical companion—a horse in the Turkish tale, the angel Raphael in Tobit. The dragon in the Turkish tale, evidently infatuated with the *khoja* girl, is equivalent to Asmodaeus, who is attached to Sarah as a "demon lover." In both stories, the woman associated with the monster becomes the bride of the young man. To be sure, both stories have extra episodes, outside of this basic plot, that are not parallel, and their tone

[11] Propp, *The Morphology of the Folktale,* 79–83, esp. 81–82.

[12] Niditch ("Father-Son Folktale Patterns and Tyrant Typologies in Josephus' *Ant* 12:160–222") rightly adduces this parallel in regard to the *Tobiad Romance* (on which see Chapter 7) but does not note its significance for the study of *Tobit*. This folktale is found in Warren S. Walker and Ahmet E. Uysal, *Tales Alive in Turkey* (Cambridge: Harvard University Press, 1966), 10–24. "The Blind Padishah" is similar to tale type 301, "The Three Stolen Princesses," in the type index of Antti Aarne and Stith Thompson, *The Types of the Folktale,* 2d ed. (Helsinki: Suomalainen tiedeakatemia, 1964).

is often quite different. In Tobit the binding of Asmodaeus is a central crux in the story, whereas in "The Blind Padishah" the monster is not central and is not bound or destroyed (although there is a meeting with another monster who *is* slain).

In some ways this tale is much closer to the central story line of Tobit than is the Grateful Dead Man: the blindness of the father is parallel, as is the father sending his son on an adventurous quest that will cure his blindness. Previous commentators have been so struck with the burial theme in Tobit that the Grateful Dead Man tale type overwhelmed the discussion of folk parallels, but when Tobit is compared instead with "The Blind Padishah," the theme of burial appears to be tangential or perhaps even to have been added later to the main story line. One wonders, for instance, whether the blindness of the father might at one time in the oral prehistory of Tobit have been caused by the demon Asmodaeus, as in "The Blind Padishah," rather than as an ironic punishment for burying the dead.[13] By the same token, for scholars who compared Tobit closely with the Grateful Dead Man, the blindness of Tobit and the division of the protagonist's functions into two characters, father and son, were the tangential difficulties that had to be explained away.[14] In terms of folktale parallels, then, the *Book of Tobit* does not unequivocally reflect one tale type or the other, nor should we expect it to.[15] This should caution us against assuming that whatever lies outside of one tale type is an "external" influence or that the author has consciously adapted a traditional narrative to biblical paradigms at every turn.[16]

Furthermore, the accumulation and comparison of folk parallels should also not force upon us the assumption that Tobit is essentially an oral composition. Motifs common in oral tales can easily be utilized in composing a popular written work.[17] What is perhaps most fascinating about the comparison with folktales, however, is that although Tobit is rightly considered "talelike," it is worlds apart from these tales in many

[13] This possibility would be easier to entertain if the first episode of *Tobit* were not part of the original story; see below.

[14] It was further argued that these two "foreign" motifs must indicate the influence of the biblical patriarchal narratives, where the relation of father and son and the blindness of the father both figure. Compare the excellent, but I think in this respect incorrect, article by Lothar Ruppert, "Das Buch Tobias," esp. 111, 113.

[15] See especially the remarks of Soll, "Tobit and Folklore Studies," 39–41.

[16] See the discussion of this issue by Ruppert, "Buch Tobias," 114–15, and Deselaers, *Buch Tobit,* 292–308.

[17] Niditch points out that some writings, including many biblical narratives, make use of the same "traditional" (or "ethnopoetic") motifs and themes as oral narrative, but she does not presume that they are orally composed (*Underdogs and Tricksters,* xiii–xiv).

ways. The moaning of Tobit and Sarah, their *intertwined* fates and the morality play orchestrated by Raphael, the long prayers and proverbs collections, the unromanticized presence of the money—all these serve to attach Tobit more to a novelistic genre, that is, a "novelized" folktale.[18] Also, the folk motifs present in Tobit are not recounted in a linear narrative time line typical of folktales. The interest in the main narrative section is created by the intertwining of the two subplots, which gradually resolve into one. As Tomas Hägg has shown, the Greek romances, which are self-consciously literary compositions, often showed a great degree of experimentation with parallel subplots and nonlinear time lines.[19] Although *Tobit* does not exhibit the sophistication of the Greek romances in this regard, this section is composed with some artistry and with a light, almost antic, comic touch. The real focus for the author of *Tobit* is evidently not the details of plot but the intertwining of the two complications and resolutions. It is not a *hidden* working of God that lies at the core of the book but a *playful* working of God, and in this respect it can be contrasted with the Joseph story. The artifice of *Tobit* does, however, render the work involving and enjoyable, if hopelessly contrived.

Literary Themes and Structure of *Tobit*

Turning to a closer analysis of the literary structure of *Tobit,* we can begin with Nickelsburg's short but very helpful treatment of the parallel story lines.[20] He notes the parallel structures of the depictions of Tobit's and Sarah's problems:

---

[18] See Ruppert, "Buch Tobias," 111, 117, and Deselaers, *Buch Tobit*, 273–78 (including authors cited in n. 473).

[19] Hägg, *Narrative Technique in Ancient Greek Romances,* passim. This principle of a linear thread of narrative development is what Axel Olrik refers to as "the greatest law of folk tradition" ("Epic Laws of Folk Narrative," in *The Study of Folklore,* ed. Alan Dundes [Englewood Cliffs, N.J.: Prentice-Hall, 1965], 139). At first reading, it appears that "The Blind Padishah" contains such egregious violations of the "greatest law of folk tradition" that the composer would be in danger of being arrested. However, although this tale contains digressions—and digressions within digressions—it does not develop two *parallel* story lines. It does come tantalizingly close at points, for example, p. 17: "Now let us leave these people and go back to our hero, who is lying at the bottom of the well." Surely this is one of the greatest transitions in the history of narrative.

[20] Nickelsburg, *Jewish Literature,* 30–35, and "Stories of Biblical and Post-Biblical Times," in *Jewish Writings of the Second Temple Period,* ed. Michael Stone (Philadelphia: Fortress, 1984), 40–45.

Tobit's piety (2:1–7)	Sarah's innocence (presumed, 3:14)
Tobit's problem: blindness (2:9–10)	Sarah's problem: demon (3:8a)
Tobit reproached (2:14b)	Sarah reproached (3:7, 8b–9)
Tobit's prayer (3:1–6)	Sarah's prayer (3:10–15)

This information is presented carefully in the novel, with explicit markers to the reader that the lives of these two people are guided by the same providence: "At the same moment, the prayer of both was heard before the glory of God" (3:16), and "At the same time that Tobit returned from the courtyard into his house (after his prayer), Sarah, the daughter of Raguel, also came down from the upper room (after her prayer)" (3:17).

The intertwining of the two subplots is carefully orchestrated by God's angel all along. The trip that Tobit's blindness prompts brings Tobias into contact with Sarah; Sarah's need for a husband makes hosting Tobias an attractive venture for Sarah's father. The fish organs that Tobias has procured with Raphael's help heal them both. "Each problem," says Nickelsburg, "contains the germ of a solution for the other." [21] From the beginning, Tobit and Sarah have prayed for death as an end to their distress, but God foresees happiness for the two instead.

Nickelsburg also notes the humorous irony that underlies much of the narrative. Tobit has prayed for death (somewhat petulantly) and gives his son Tobias his last words of advice, which have as a strong theme that God will reward those who practice charity. This advice, of course, totally contradicts the facts of Tobit's own situation. Tobit has been a model Diaspora Jew, has risked his life to aid his countrymen, and has been blinded for his efforts. Ironic also is Tobit's dialogue with the angel Raphael: he demands to know the angel's lineage, which the angel, appearing as a human, is willing to falsify in order to satisfy Tobit. Tobit then sends Tobias on his way with Raphael and says that an angel will accompany him. Nickelsburg, while recognizing the humor of these passages, still attaches a fairly elevated interpretation to Tobit. The author, he says, "creates a portrait of a God who carefully orchestrates the events of history, working them to his own gracious ends." [22] We shall have reason to question whether all is as pious here as this judgment implies.

The main motif that ties together many of the subplot elements is the theme of family, specifically, the creating and maintaining of family

---

[21] Nickelsburg, *Jewish Literature*, 32.
[22] Ibid.

continuity in the Diaspora. At first sight the focus of family would appear to be solely on the arrangement of a union between the unfortunate Sarah and the marriageable Tobias, but on closer reading it becomes clear that the perspective is much more inclusive than that. First, marriage must be seen here in the context of alliances within the proper tribes and of people of high moral bearing. But more than that, it is clear that the network of relations among these characters creates an extended family that threatens to take over all of Assyria. Every one of the characters introduced, it should be noted (aside from the Assyrian kings), claims affiliation with the tribe of Naphtali and kinship with Tobit. Although Tobit exhorts his son to marry a woman from this tribe, in the narrative world of this novel it seems unlikely that Tobias could ever meet anyone who was not a relative. Sarah and her family and Gabael are all kinfolk. Ahikar, elsewhere a non-Jewish figure of legend, is here not only Jewish but a close relative of Tobit (1:22), as is Nadab, his nephew (11:18). Whereas in *The Story of Ahikar* Nadab is the villain, here he is another beloved cousin (*exadelphos*). Even Raphael, in his human guise, claims to be related (5:12). We are probably correct in seeing this theme in a whimsical way, for it becomes a *reductio ad absurdum.* Whenever one character greets another, it is always as "brother" or "sister"; in fact, the words *brother* and *sister* occur sixty-six times. They are used as polite greetings by people who are related (that is, by everyone in the novel) but also as nouns of address by Tobit to his wife (5:22), by Raguel to his wife (7:15), and by Tobias to Sarah (8:4; compare 7:12) as they are preparing to lie down to bed together for the first time.

We should note, of course, that the word for brother in Hebrew, *'aḥ,* and in Aramaic, *'aḥah,* is routinely extended to mean more distant relatives or fellow members of the same tribe. It could be argued that this usage of the term corresponds with the real intention of the *Book of Tobit:* the importance of marrying within the tribe. However, the pointed and continued use of the term in the narrative—sixty-six times!—calls for interpretation. The extended family network that envelops this novel places a very dutiful cast on the love between Tobias and Sarah. If we were to look here for parallels with the erotic themes in Greek romances, we would be disappointed. In the case of these two young protagonists, sexual love disappears almost completely, as it does, on the surface at least, in *Joseph and Aseneth.* Tobias and Sarah retire to their bedchamber after dinner, but the story is told with a reserve that is quite unlike the Greek novels. From *Tobit* 8:1–9:

When they had finished their eating and drinking, they wanted to go to bed. They led the young man away and took him to the bedchamber. . . . Tobias said to her, "Sister, let us arise and pray to our God, that he grant mercy and deliverance for us." She joined him and began to pray that they might obtain deliverance, and he prayed . . . , "Now I take this sister of mine not in illicit lust, but in truth. Grant that she and I obtain mercy and grow old together." They both said "Amen, Amen," and slept through the night.

Compare the wedding night from Xenophon's *Ephesian Tales* 1.9:

Both of them felt the same emotions and were unable to say anything to each other or to look at each other's eyes but lay at ease in sheer delight, shy, afraid, panting—and on fire. Their bodies trembled and their hearts quivered, their souls were agitated. . . . [She] kissed him all over his face, pressed all his hair to her own eyes, and took off all the garlands and joined his lips to hers in a kiss. . . . With this they relaxed in each other's arms and enjoyed the first fruits of Aphrodite; and there was ardent rivalry all night long, each trying to prove they loved the other more.

It is difficult to believe that the *Book of Tobit*'s reserve about the consummation of the wedding night could be attributed to the dread of the demon Asmodaeus. The lovers in Xenophon's novel also knowingly lived under the spectre of an ill omen. Besides, the release of the tension in *Tobit*—even though the tension has not been overwhelming—has come just before the bedroom scene; it only paves the way in the reader's mind for a joyous consummation of the wedding night, which has been denied to Sarah heretofore. The use of the terms *sister* and *brother,* which has been strange in its overuse, is even stranger here: "I take this sister of mine not in illicit lust but in truth." She was a "sister" before the marriage, since she was part of the extended family, but the implication here seems to be that the bond is sanctioned by marriage to knit two parts of the clan together. They are not indulging their lust but performing a sacred duty.[23] The function of this central scene in Tobit will be addressed below.

[23] The Greek novels would show no hesitation in describing the desire that the hero and heroine have for each other or in rendering a full account of the consummation in the wedding bed, but it is still true that the Greek romances retain a very strict notion of chastity for the protagonists *outside of these socially recognized bounds of marriage.* In the Greek romances, the protagonists are married early on, have a glorious wedding night, and *then* are separated for most of the course of the novel; they pine for each other, struggle to remain chaste, and are in general only allowed to have sex again when they are reunited at the end.

If we were to look for the second most commonly occurring leitmotif of this novel, after family relations, it would be burial. The word "to bury" (*thapto*) occurs eighteen times, "tomb" (*taphos*) six times. The novel begins with a very serious tone in connection with the motif of burial, recounting how Tobit is persecuted for trying to bury the remains of dead Jews, but there is a falling-off of seriousness after this point, and burial—Tobit's personal obsession—is soon treated in a more humorous way, with a touch of the sardonic. When Tobit prays to God that he be allowed to die, he decides to settle matters on earth by telling his son about money that is being held for him by his kinsman Gabael. Calling his son, he says "Bury me well." He then urges him to see to his mother and adds, "When she dies, bury her beside me in the same grave." We could grant Tobit this understandable concern, but the matter does not end here in the story; it is on everyone's mind. When Raphael suggests to Tobias that he marry Sarah, Tobias protests that since all her other betrothed have died, this marriage would bring his mother and father to their grave out of worry for him, and after all, they do not have another son to bury them (6:15).

If we are unsure whether this concern for proper burial has gotten a little out of hand, the ambiguity is soon resolved. Very early on the morning after Tobias and Sarah have retired to the bridal chamber, Raguel wastes no time in calling servants and digging Tobias's grave, on the presumption that he is already dead (8:9). When, however, he and his wife find that Tobias and Sarah are alive, they give an emotional thanksgiving to God and then hurriedly order the servants to fill in the grave before dawn comes and it is discovered (6:18).[24] Finally, when Tobit dies and the story comes to what may have been its original end (14:1), he at last achieves his goal and is buried nobly in Nineveh.

Although Zimmermann suggests that *Tobit* reflects a period when the burial of Jews was prohibited, that is, in the time of Antiochus IV Epiphanes, the lack of seriousness in the main body of the narrative in regard to this topic argues against it. But aside from its comic overtones, the leitmotif of burial still may reflect a thematic concern. In *Bel and the Dragon* 32 (Old Greek version), the topic also arises, where execution in the lions' den is considered a horrible death precisely because there will be no bones left for burial. This fear may arise for Jews living as an ethnic minority in the Persian Empire, where there was an abhorrence of burial. Among Zoroastrians, corpses were exposed to

---

[24] The comic ramifications of these actions are noted by Craven, *Artistry and Faith*, 116 n. 7.

scavenger birds, and then the bodies were burned. They perceived the burial of the bodies as a mixing with the material earth, not a release into a spiritual fire. The presence of a Persian demon in Tobit makes this interpretation even more likely.

These two central motifs of family building and burial come together at one point, possibly an intentional juxtaposition. At 6:15 (noted above), Tobias hesitates to consider marrying Sarah because, should he die, he has no brothers to bury his parents. This reason is his stated motive for fearing Sarah; he does not seem to fear his own death. Raphael replies, however: "Do you not remember the commandments of your father, how he commanded you to take a wife from your father's family? Now hear me well, brother, and do not take any heed of this demon, but marry Sarah. For I know that tonight she shall be given to you as your wife." It is possible that there is an intentional contrasting of burial and marriage in the novel as opposing concerns, that is, death and life. The satirizing tone of the novel regarding burial is perhaps met here with a positive answer: leave the dead to bury the dead; follow the exhortations of your father to take a kinswoman as wife to build up the family. Choose life! It is, after all, Tobit's *burial* arrangements that prompt him to send his son away to retrieve the money, and it is on this mission that the latter meets his wife. Tobias's decision, then, is a transvaluation of Tobit's agenda of burial preparations to an embrace of life's possibilities. Other novels that we are analyzing also contain a scene in which the protagonist must make a momentous decision. In *Esther* 4, for example, the narrative is intentially retarded and complicated by the dialogue of Mordecai and Esther through an intermediary, so that the audience can focus on Esther's need to commit herself to defending her people before the king.[25] Although relatively less tension inheres in Tobias's decision, it is still a necessary step for the narrative to move from negative to positive.

This romantic message is interesting partially because it is not particularly pious; it may even contradict the heavy-handed moralizing of chapter 1. It is certainly not so pious as to dampen the bent toward humor in this work. In addition to the humor found in the central leitmotifs of family and burial, we may note the tone of chapter 2 (which would begin the main narrative if chapter 1 were considered secondary). When it opens, Tobit is sitting down to the Feast of Weeks. With

---

[25] George W. E. Nickelsburg, "The Genre and Function of the Markan Passion Narrative," *Harvard Theological Review* 73 (1980): 153–84, esp. 157, and Chapter 4 for further discussion of *Esther* 4.

the smell of the food drifting up to his nostrils, he sends his son out to find a poor, pious Jew and says, "I will wait until you return." This extraordinary delayal of gratification seems farfetched,[26] but we find that he is rewarded for it by being blinded from bird droppings falling on his eyes. This development for such a pious man might be seen as a tragic contrast to the joyous occasion of the Festival of Weeks were it not for the scatological mode of God's dispensation.[27] At the time of *Tobit,* the Festival of Weeks was seen as a celebration of God's certain covenant; later, it commemorated the day on which Moses received the Torah from God. Tobit, however, receives bird feces. Tobit's Joblike plaint in chapter 3, begging for release from life after contracting cataracts (as a result of sitting under defecating birds, no less!), would also strike the reader as pure bathos were it to be taken seriously.[28] Though never quite as farcical as *Esther,* the tone of the main body of this novel is quite whimsical.

To be sure, other literary themes can be traced in *Tobit* that are treated positively and not satirically. Connected with Tobias's choice of marriage over burial preparations are the warm associations of the union itself. The extended network of family relations in *Tobit* is in the rest of the novel obsessively described, as a kinship unit within the tribe of Naphtali. The families of Tobias and Sarah that are united in marriage are already closely related descendants of a certain Gabael; other characters are more distant relations from within the tribe of Naphtali (*Tobit* 1:1).[29] Only in the bedroom scene is this perspective altered, when during his prayer Tobias moves beyond the tribe of Naphtali and compares their union to that of the primeval couple, Adam and Eve:

> You created Adam and made Eve his wife as a helpmate and support.
> From the two of them came all of the generations on earth.
> You said, "It is not good for man to be alone.
> Let us make for him a helpmate like himself."

[26] The invitation of Rab Huna for a poor person to join the feast, now associated with Passover (Zimmermann, *Book of Tobit,* 55), is similar but hardly constitutes such an unbelievable delay of the meal.

[27] Although it is true that bird droppings are used as a magical agent in some folktales, they generally have *curative* powers. In *Tobit,* the droppings effect a totally undeserved abuse, unless we invoke Oscar Wilde's moral observation that "no good deed will go unpunished." This statement, at any rate, would not be far from the humorous intent of the novel.

[28] Bow and Nickelsburg note that, although Tobit's prayer is paradigmatic for Israel (as opposed to Sarah's more individualistic prayer), he is actually whining and self-centered ("Patriarchy with a Twist," 128–30).

[29] Deselaers (*Buch Tobit,* 309–15) explains the kinship relations in detail.

And now I take this, my sister, not in illicit lust, but in truth.
Grant that she and I obtain mercy and grow old together.

(8:6–7)

For a brief moment, the two lovers are identified with the archetypal couple, the first "nuclear family"—an ancient motif in the blessings of Jewish weddings (*bKetubot* 8a). It is not just a fleeting association here; in the hubbub of the narrative, the couple is transported into prehistoric, mythical time, as the ideal mythical couple. The Greek romance focused on the unit of the married young lovers, elevating their status to the level of a sacred social institution. In this early Jewish novel, the young couple does not indulge their lust but subordinates it to their duty to create a proper family. The fantasies of the full realization of erotic bliss, which the Greek romance conveys, are not explored in Tobit, but a hope is expressed that the conjugal pair can re-create the divine sanction to be fruitful and multiply. Amy-Jill Levine has argued that the establishment of this union is depicted as a triumph of endogamous marriage over the threat to Jewish life in the Diaspora.[30] Traditional boundaries of Jerusalem/Exile, divine/demonic, male/female roles, and so on are broken as Tobit and Sarah descend into despair and ask to die. This process is reversed through the intervention of the angel Raphael, and stable marriages and extended family ties are reformed in the Diaspora. Genealogy, not geography, defines Israel. The "instability" of satire should not obscure the fact that a very strong, even mythical message is being presented here; the happy ending confirms the importance of conservative family structures.

Sources and Redaction in *Tobit*

We may return now to the question of the integrity of chapter 1 with the main narrative in chapters 2–12. Chapter 1 is a separate background narrative that relates the trouble that Tobit creates for himself by burying dead Jews during the reign of the Assyrian king Sennacherib. It is very different in several respects from the main narrative, and it is

---

[30] Levine, "Diaspora as Metaphor." Although some of Levine's observations concerning the boundary relationships may be overdrawn, her basic conclusions seem to me to be correct: "Women properly domiciled in an endogamous relationship become the means by which the threat of the Diaspora is eliminated. That territorial relations are displaced onto gender relations is reinforced by the manner in which hierarchical, value-laden gender differences structure the novella" (p. 105).

narrated in the first person, unlike most of the main story (the shift from first-person narration to third beginning with the introduction of Sarah's distress at 3:7). Several considerations at least raise the possibility that it derives from a different hand from the main narrative. To begin with, chapter 1 is more earnest on the issue of burial; we note, for example, that the strongest piece of evidence for burial to be connected with persecution is found in chapter 1 (especially 1:18). Other than a "remembrance" of the events of chapter 1 at 2:8, there is no further reference in the main narrative to the political offense of burying Jews, to the threat of the king or political powers, or to persecution. True, the king who has declared burial to be an offense is dead, but the tone of the two sections is quite different. The narrative in chapter 1 is much more similar to other stories of the persecution and vindication of the righteous person, such as the Joseph story of *Genesis* 37–50, some of the Daniel legends, and *Esther*,[31] in which a wise figure, often a courtier (or here, a court purchasing agent), is wrongly persecuted and suffers a fall from grace but is in time vindicated and restored to his former position. Such stories do not have to be deadly serious—compare *Daniel* 3 and the analysis above in Chapter 2—but in this case it is, especially when compared to the main story. The persecution/vindication story line in chapter 1 is also paralleled in the non-Jewish *Story of Ahikar,* and it is just at this point in *Tobit* that Ahikar is introduced. We must assume, with a number of scholars, that Ahikar is added secondarily,[32] the persecution/ vindication plot line may be as well.

Perhaps here the distinction between legends and tales, often used in folklore, is helpful.[33] Chapter 1 is a legend or, if it did not circulate separately, is at least legendlike. It venerates the wisdom and piety of the protagonist. Chapters 2–12 are more like a tale, whether they were oral

---

[31] George W. E. Nickelsburg, *Resurrection, Immortality, and Eternal Life in Intertestamental Judaism* (Cambridge: Harvard University Press, 1972), 48–58, and Wills, *Jew in the Court.* The influence of this Jewish thematic construct can also be found in the gospel passion narratives. See Nickelsburg, "Markan Passion." Another close parallel is the biographical legend in *Matthew* 1–2, where a similar flight from persecution occurs, as well as a return when the king dies.

[32] Lothar Ruppert, "Zur Funktion der Achikar-Notizen im Buch Tobias," *Biblische Zeitschrift* n.f. 20 (1976): 232–37; Ruppert, "Buch Tobias," 109–19; Deselaers, *Buch Tobit,* 24–25.

[33] William Bascom, "The Forms of Folklore: Prose Narratives," *Journal of American Folklore* 78 (1965): 3–20, and "Folklore," in *International Encyclopedia of the Social Sciences,* ed. David L. Sills, 17 vols. (New York: Macmillan, 1968), 5:497. The distinction between tales and legends that Bascom advances has been challenged as overly neat and content-oriented (rather than performance-oriented) for universal application in folklore studies, but it remains quite workable for a general separation of "talelike" and "legendlike" materials.

or written, and were probably not meant to be believed by the original audience. The fanciful world of folktales gives free reign to the providential guiding of people's fate and to the easy passage of angels and demons into and out of our midst. Those scholars who have suggested that *Tobit* reflects a mixture of characteristics of the tale and the legend[34] might have agreed that there is more of a clear distinction when the two parts are viewed separately.

Corresponding to this difference in the level of seriousness are several other divergences between the two sections. First, chapter 1 reflects a difference in tone with regard to Tobit's reaction to circumstances. In chapter 1 his reaction is presented in a few lines, with little emotion: "When I found out that the king knew about me and that I was being sought for execution, I became frightened and ran away. Then everything that I owned was confiscated—nothing was left to me. It was all placed in the royal treasury, except for Anna, my wife, and Tobias, my son." We do not get off so easily in chapters 2–12, and Tobit's prayers and complaints come to dominate the narrative in chapters 2 and 3. Second, the geographical associations of the two sections are different. As noted above, the beginning of chapter 1 portrays a Palestinian locale, which has perhaps been added to an originally Samaritan setting. Tobit is then deported to Assyria, but this is still part of "western" history. Chapters 2–12, however, are full of eastern references, from the Persian demon Asmodaeus to the main city, Ecbatana of Media, which has almost no role in the biblical books. Third, certain other issues are expressed in different ways in the two separate sections. Although the issues of almsgiving and showing mercy (*eleos* and *eleo*, derived from the same root in Greek) are common throughout Tobit, they are associated overwhelmingly with Tobit's actions in chapter 1 but with God's in chapters 2–12.[35] Fourth, dialogue as a narrative technique is utilized much more in 2–12 than in chapter 1.[36] Fifth, the important motifs of Judaism and Jerusalem are nowhere to be found in chaps. 2–12.

It is possible, of course, to provide a literary rationale for an intentional differentiation in style between the two sections. David McCracken also perceives a strong comic element in the main narrative

---

[34] Hermann Gunkel, *The Folktale in the Old Testament,* 89–90, 103–6.

[35] The exceptions in the latter section are mainly found in Tobit's sayings in the Vaticanus/ Alexandrinus version. Other exceptions are 2:14, 7:7, and 9:6; 12:8 (twice) and 12:9 (twice) are likely additions.

[36] The first person narration does not rule out dialogue—cf. chapter 2. It is really the time span of events in chapter 1 that makes dialogue unnecessary.

section and believes that it satirizes the self-righteous figure of Tobit.[37] This satire is begun in chapter 1 where we hear Tobit's voice speaking and are only given his perspective on events. Things are much more serious here, and his righteous acts are recounted by him in a straightforward account. The piety displayed, according to McCracken's reading, is a bit thick, however, and it is when we move from Tobit's perspective, in first-person narration, to the omniscient narration of chapter 3 that we are let in on the more satirical point of view. The first two chapters are thus a necessary preamble to the body of the story and are necessarily different; the seriousness with which Tobit's plight is invested there is not the author's evaluation but Tobit's own. McCracken's analysis does provide a plausible reason for some of the differences, but I am not convinced of his very intriguing suggestion. The switch from a pious tone to a satirical tone can be explained on this theory, but other differences cannot, or at least they cannot be explained as easily, especially the shift in geographical orientation from Nineveh and Jerusalem to Persia.[38] Although, on the basis of McCracken's argument, I would leave open the possibility that chapter 1 was composed by the same author as chapters 2–12, I deem it somewhat more likely that it arises from a different hand.

Many of the same questions arise with the end of *Tobit* (chapters 13 and 14), and it is much more difficult here to account for the divergences by literary arguments. The latter is a deathbed testament of Tobit to his son Tobias, in which he refers to the prophet Nahum and his denunciation of Assyria. Tobit goes to some length to assure Tobias that every word of the prediction of the fall of Assyria will come true. It is followed by further predictions of the fall of Israel, Samaria, and Jerusalem. The glorious rebuilding of the temple is foretold, as is the eventual conversion of the nations and the possession of the land of Israel by all Jews. Here again, the difference in tone, compared with that of chap-

[37] David McCracken, "Tobit and the Comedy of Perspective," presentation at the Society of Biblical Literature Annual Conference, November 22, 1993. McCracken notes an interesting modern parallel in Oliver Goldsmith's *The Vicar of Wakefield,* which satirizes the overly pious man even though the narrative is told through his words, in the first person.

[38] *Tobit* 1 is also, in my reading of it, purely straightforward in its perspective. It does not give any indication that an intentional overemphasis on piety is being introduced. Contrast, in this regard, Goldsmith's vicar, who in the opening lines reveals his (and the author's) character: "I was ever of opinion, that the honest man who married and brought up a large family, did more service than he who continued single and only talked of population. From this motive, I had scarce taken orders a year, before I began to think seriously of matrimony, and chose my wife, as she did her wedding gown, not for a fine glossy surface, but such qualities as would wear well."

ters 2–12, suggests that a redactor has added this testamentary ending and done it rather awkwardly. At first reading, it seems a wild flight of unmotivated prophetic utterances. The redactor of this chapter has evidently taken up a new interest and expressed it in the form of apocalyptic predictions. Zimmermann suggests that they were added after the Roman destruction of the Jewish temple in 69 C.E. [39] The predictions of the rebuilding of the temple, on the surface referring to the erection of a second temple, are more likely to be looking forward to the erection of a third temple, after the second has been destroyed. It is also said that Tobias and Sarah migrate to Ecbatana to live with her parents. This statement places that region in a very positive light: they lived happily ever after there and even watched over the destruction of Assyria by "Ahasuerus, king of Media." [40] Despite the inappropriateness of this designation—Ahasuerus was another spelling for Xerxes, king of Persia—it is possible that the positive depiction of Ecbatana and Media, especially as military powers, represents the eastern home of Diaspora Jews: the Parthian Empire. Ecbatana and the Median satrapy were the western front of the Parthian Empire against Roman military incursions, [41] and "Assyria" (the Roman province of Syria) would in that case represent the Roman Empire. Many Jews in the eastern Roman Empire viewed the Parthian Empire as a more favorable world power and even threw in with the Parthians in the border clashes with the Romans. [42] In such a context, naming the Roman Empire as enemy would be impossible, and so we should perhaps take "Assyria" as the evil empire.

One further discrepancy between *Tobit* 2–12 and 13–14 argues for separate authorship. In 14:10, Ahikar's nephew Nadab is a villain who has turned on his uncle, and this is, in fact, in complete agreement with the popular *Story of Ahikar*. In 11:19, however, this aspect of his character is ignored; Nadab is simply a beloved cousin. Although the discrepancy could be attributed to the fact that chapter 11 relates a part of the narra-

---

[39] Zimmermann, *Book of Tobit,* 24–27, 112. He also notes (pp. 133–35) that there is a late Aramaic version of Tobit that lacks chapters 13 and 14, but it is probably too late to bear on our argument. Soll's excellent introduction to a Proppian analysis of Tobit runs into some problems, I believe, where he subsumes the issues of chapters 2–12 to the Exile issue of chapters 1 and 13–14 ("Tobit and Folklore Studies," 50–52). His project would look quite different—and would be more consistent—if he analyzed the talelike section of chapters 2–12 by itself, but this would be begging the question of a possible explanation outlined above for the divergent tones of the three sections.

[40] On this and other historical blunders in the Jewish literature of this period, see Chapter 8.

[41] Widengren, "Quelques rapports," 215.

[42] See Neilson C. Debevoise, *A Political History of Parthia* (Chicago: University of Chicago Press, 1938), 93–95, 236, 242.

tive before Nadab's fall, it is more likely that the tradition of Nadab's villainy has simply been subordinated to the more romanticizing intention of chapters 2–12.[43]

Tobit as a Didactic Novel

The entire issue of additions and insertions in *Tobit* forces us also to reconsider the role of the long proverbs section in *Tobit* 4 and the common designation of the book as a didactic narrative or wisdom book.[44] This genre description derives from the combination of proverbial teachings with narrative. The sayings are presented as the instruction of a father to his son—typical in proverbs collections—and Raphael's closing words to Tobit are parallel. The narrative as a whole is often treated as if it were a vehicle for this teaching, or at least a parallel enactment of the sentiments found in the sayings. The incorporation of sayings material into a wisdom narrative is not unknown in the ancient Near East: *Ahikar*, the Egyptian *Instructions of Onkhsheshonq*, and *Matthew* and *Luke* all do this. But the nature of the sayings and the relation to the

---

[43] A different approach to the source criticism of Tobit has been proposed by Deselaers, *Buch Tobit*. He notes some of the same difficulties mentioned here, but rather than separating off the beginning and the ending to arrive at an earlier narrative, as I have suggested, he isolates numerous passages throughout Tobit as redactional, positing, indeed, several layers of redaction. For instance, in *Tobit* 6:14–15 (6:13–14 in English translations), Tobias at first fears the demon in respect to his own life; then he interjects, somewhat awkwardly, the concern that his parents will have no one left to bury them. Raphael's remonstrance to follow his father's command to seek a wife from his kin evidently responds to Tobias's fear for his safety and does not arise in response to the problem of burial. This indicates that the burial motif has been added (pp. 33–34), as it is elsewhere in *Tobit* according to Deselaers.

The core narrative he thus isolates has unity of tone and appears, in fact, quite plausible. There are certain places in the text where a much smoother narrative can be obtained by following his suggested excisions. In addition, in many cases we find that the clumsy clauses that are taken in his analysis to be additions also have recurrent themes, suggesting that the hypothetical redactor had a consistent agenda. At other points, however, his arguments appear overdrawn, and he excises passages from the core that are often considered necessary for the literary structure. He eliminates from the core, for example, Anna's reproach of Tobit (2:11–14) but retains that of Sarah's maids (3:7–9; see *Buch Tobit*, 26–27). The parallels between the two strands of the narrative posited by Nickelsburg (above, this chapter), however, require a reproach for *each* of the pious protagonists. My conclusions are clearly at odds with those of Deselaers, but it should be noted that the strongest objection that has been raised to his analysis is that it is carried out on the basis of the Vaticanus/Alexandrinus version, which, in order to propose a source analysis, would have to be the best and earliest text of Tobit. Evidence of the Aramaic fragments found at Qumran, however, strongly favor Sinaiticus.

[44] See Müller, "Die weisheitliche Lehrerzählung im Alten Testament und in seiner Umwelt," and the discussion of various genre classifications that have been advanced at Deselaers, *Buch Tobit*, 262–79.

narrative are not the same in the two principal ancient versions of *Tobit* that we possess. The Sinaiticus text (used in the New English Bible), considered by most scholars to be closer to the original,[45] gives a shorter recital of sayings by Tobit to his son. This shorter collection does not distract as much from the narrative situation, and the sayings have at least two interesting points of contact with the narrative—they replay the burial motif, and they emphasize that God rewards the just—both intentionally ironic contrasts with the narrative, where we find that Tobit has just been mischievously punished by God after Tobit's burial of a Jewish corpse. The other version of Tobit, however, the Vaticanus/Alexandrinus text (found in the Revised Standard Version of the Apocrypha),[46] includes a much larger collection of sayings, which has a very different relationship with the narrative. This collection of sayings can be divided into sections that address three topics: the importance of almsgiving, the importance of marriage with those of the same nation (or tribe), and assorted injunctions appropriate for the wealthy gentleman. The second of these sections relates to the narrative of chapters 2–12, but the first and third do not. What the first and third groups have in common—and what may motivate their inclusion in the Vaticanus/Alexandrinus version—is the promulgation of the values of the patronage system, an important part of the social economy of the ancient Near East in the Greco-Roman period. However exploitative the patron really was in Greco-Roman society, the language associated with the patron—and probably the self-concept as well—was that of guardian of the client. The benefactor has a noble virtue of beneficence for the poor, even if the resultant obligation and client relationship strips the recipient of economic independence.[47] If we consider again Milik's suggestion, mentioned above, that the social background of this book lies in the Tobiad family, many of whom were active patrons to a host of clients (Chapter 7), then we can easily see how such sayings would have been added to this narrative.

In the shorter Sinaiticus version of the sayings, therefore, the sayings

[45] Zimmermann, *Book of Tobit*, 39–42, 127–28; Pfeiffer, *History of New Testament Times*, 258–60. As noted above, the Qumran fragments of Tobit strongly indicate that the Sinaiticus version represents the older version.

[46] Some versions of the New English Bible place this version of the sayings in a long footnote. Though Zimmermann in general follows the Sinaiticus text of the narrative, when he comes to the sayings (*Book of Tobit*, 68–71), he finds them too abbreviated and inserts sayings from the longer version.

[47] Zimmermann, *Book of Tobit*, 28–29, calls Tobit's ethic "high-minded," but this pronouncement ignores the possible sociological background of these sayings. On the exploitative nature of the "patron as benefactor," see the discussions in Chapters 4 and 7 below.

function within the narrative; they are too short and too specific to the context to have a separate teaching value. They serve instead a narrative purpose: they help characterize the protagonist, and they emphasize the ironic contrasts of the story. To be sure, the overall course of events in *Tobit*—that the protagonist despairs but is finally rewarded with a happy life—can be considered a dramatization of the doctrine of divine rewards, but the humorous, even satirical tone of *Tobit* indicates that this moral will only be indirectly revealed. The moral perspective of the author is not to moralize over the just end of the good and the bad, and at any rate, our sympathies for Tobit as a suffering righteous man have long since been strained as a result of his insufferable character.

If chapters 2–12 do not constitute a wisdom book but are instead satirical, do they lack any serious purpose? Perhaps the whimsy of the talelike narrative camouflages deeper psychological functions. Mircea Eliade has observed that fairytales play out on the level of fantasy the same pattern as the ritual of initation: a separation from the security of the family; a liminal period of danger, vulnerability, and adventures; and a reintegration into a more secure family structure: "The tale takes up and continues 'initiation' on the level of the imaginary. If it represents an amusement or an escape, it does so only for the banalized consciousness [*conscience banalisée*], and particularly for that of modern man; in the deep psyche initiation scenarios preserve their seriousness and continue to transmit their message."[48] If we recall that the central point in *Tobit* is the bedroom scene of the young married couple, it becomes likely that the "information" imparted in the liminal state at the crux of the narrative consists of the image that stands outside of historical time: Adam and Eve. From this point on, all of the main characters are almost giddily happy, and the obsession with burial is reversed, as Raguel rushes to *cover* a grave. Although this happiness is checked to some extent in the narrative—there is a delay for Raphael to retrieve the money, and Tobit and Anna are forced to wait anxiously at the side of the road to see if their son will return—the audience knows that all is well. When the young couple does return, the happy ending is allowed to be consummated. The unrestrained rejoicing is reflected in the narrative at 11:16–17 by the overabundant use of the word "to bless" (*eulogeo*):

---

[48] Mircea Eliade, *Myth and Reality* (New York: Harper and Row, 1963), 202. The application of Eliade's theory to Tobit was introduced by Blenkinsopp, "Biographical Patterns in Biblical Narrative."

Tobit went out to the gate of Nineveh to meet his daughter-in-law, bless-ing God as he went. When the people of Nineveh saw him marching forth, with a brisk stride and no one at his side to guide him, they were as-tounded. Tobit declared before them all how God had shown mercy upon him and how He restored his sight. As Tobit approached Sarah, the wife of Tobias his son, he blessed her and said, "Welcome, daughter! Blessed be God who brought you to us, my daughter! Blessed be your father, and blessed be Tobias my son, and blessed be you, daughter! Welcome to your new home; enter in joy and blessing! Welcome, daughter!"

The conjugal couple that is established in chapter 8, likened to Adam and Eve, is here reintegrated into the patriarchal family structure, and the problems of both Tobit and Sarah have been triumphantly solved.

Tobit as Tale and Novel

In terms of the evolution of the *Book of Tobit,* one is tempted to say that an oral tale has evolved into a written novel. The plot motifs of *Tobit* lie closer to those typical of oral tales than do any of the other novels here studied. The book takes its style from the world of folk-lore, yet even the main body of the work does not appear to be simply a written transcription of an oral narrative. The interwoven plots of Tobit and Sarah; the digression concerning Tobit's wife, Anna; and the use of dialogue all argue for a partial adaptation to a written medium and the demands of the primitive novel. But traditional folk motifs can appear in popular written novels, and so we cannot assume that an oral tale actually circulated and was adapted over time to the written medium. It is necessary simply to acknowledge the two worlds represented in Tobit.

Beyond the question of this first stage of evolution, however, I have posited another kind of evolution, since it was argued that *Tobit* 13–14 was definitely added at some point to the novel of *Tobit* 2–12 and that *Tobit* 1 likely was as well. If such is the case, then we do not have to search far for the redactional themes that may have motivated the additions. Important themes found in chapters 1 and 13–14 but lacking in 2–12 include Jerusalem, piety, and persecution. The spirited novel of chapters 2–12 has become heavily laden with theological pretension. It is not just that weighty issues are paraded through; Tobit's entire character also changes as he takes on the role of exemplar. Chapter 1 presents a pious Jew who would always, under any circumstances, bury the body of a dead Jew; chapter 2 depicts a Jew who buries one corpse, is blinded by a seemingly capricious act of God, and reveals himself as a self-centered and insufferable curmudgeon. The function of the added chapters, in my accounting for the development of the book, is to create a wise and righteous hero of legend, like Daniel.[49] The *Book of Tobit* thus approaches a goal very similar to that of *Daniel;* humorous sources are harnessed to a didactic reediting, even though the sources in question in the two cases are quite different. The category of didactic or sapiential novel, used at times in the secondary literature,[50] seems in these final documents to be quite appropriate. Whether it applies to *Tobit* 2–12, however, is a different matter. The variety of purposes of novels have to be taken into consideration. Novels such as *Tobit* 2–12 entertain by creating an imaginary world, a comedy of divinely guided resolutions of unreal problems, which says to the reader, "Life is not like this (would that it were)." Didactic novels have a moral earnestness about them which indicates that, however elevated the exemplary figure may be, there is a crucial lesson the reader should take to heart: "Life is like this; go and do likewise."

Why, then, did *Tobit* 2–12 not strike the editors of chapters 1 and 13–14 as inappropriate material to be transformed into a didactic novel? This is precisely the same problem faced above in regard to *Daniel*. In that case, lighthearted and historically inaccurate source materials were wedded to the urgent message of the Endtime in the visions of *Daniel* 7–12. It is impossible to say what the later editors saw or did not see in the preexisting materials, but changes such as these were common enough to render this a quite plausible explanation of the stages of development in Tobit. We shall see in the next chapter that Greek *Esther* comes about in a similar way as well, and the issue will be taken up again in Chapter 8. At any rate, precisely these changes may have been responsible for ensuring that *Tobit* was preserved as sacred literature, since they alone make this possible.

---

[49] The comments here refer to the changes reflected in the Sinaiticus version. A further editing presumably occurred in the Vaticanus/Alexandrinus recension. Sze-Kar Wan has shown ("Report on the Different Recensions of the Book of Tobit," unpublished seminar paper, Harvard University, March 2, 1983) that the conclusions that can be drawn from the sum total of differences between Sinaiticus and Vaticanus/Alexandrinus are that the latter deletes references to Jewish practice and Jerusalem, shortens some of the dialogue and narrative description, and increases the sayings material.

[50] To be sure, *Daniel* 1–12, the canonical version in the Hebrew Bible, is more oriented to the apocalyptic visions, but the versions that existed before it and after it, *Daniel* 1–6 and Greek *Daniel,* both fit the category of didactic novel quite nicely.

Esther and Greek *Esther*

The *Book of Esther* as it appears in the Hebrew Bible (and thus in the Protestant canon as well) is, like *Daniel* 3 and 6, the apocryphal additions to *Daniel,* and the Joseph story of *Genesis,* a court narrative that follows the pattern of the "court conflict": a courtier in good standing, here Mordecai, suffers a fall from grace as a result of the machinations of another courtier, Haman, and, after an ordeal in which he is threatened with death, is vindicated and restored to a more secure position at the head of the court. This typical pattern of the court conflict, however, though adequate for the examples from the Daniel tradition, is only a skeleton of the longer narrative here, and the story as a whole is surprisingly complex. In the description just given, for example, only the male protagonist, Mordecai, was mentioned and not the female. In addition, instead of stressing the court, the story opens with a florid description of the opulence of the palace. Another plot line, parallel to the court conflict, is initiated: The favorite wife of King Ahasuerus's harem, Vashti, refuses to come before the guests of the king to display her beauty.[1] The king follows the advice of his best courtiers, renounces

---

[1] The Vashti episode is substantial, taking up all of chapter 1. Her refusal has prompted some feminists to see in her a kindred spirit—e.g., Elizabeth Cady Stanton, *The Woman's Bible* (New York: European, 1898), pt. 2, 86–87, and, more recently, Gendler, "The Vindication of Vashti." (This number of *Response* was published separately as *The Jewish Woman,* ed. Liz Koltun [Waltham: Jewish Educational Ventures, 1973].) Vashti's motives and reactions are not described, and the *Book of Esther* appears to ignore her bravery, positing instead a countermodel in Esther herself. Nevertheless, Michael V. Fox argues (*Character and Ideology in the Book of Esther,* 166–70) that the nature of Vashti's refusal—positive in the author's eyes—is indicated by the obtuseness of her opponents, the men of the court.

her, and begins an empirewide search for a new queen to reign in her place. Thus Esther enters the story; she comes before the king, wins his admiration, is made queen, and, from her new position, is able to save the Jews, who have become imperiled by Mordecai's action. Most of this lies outside of the Mordecai court conflict, and yet it is the drama that propels much of the narrative forward.

The version of *Esther* in the Hebrew Bible (hereafter "Hebrew *Esther*") is constructed throughout, then, as a double plot, marvelously interwoven, to be sure, but still progressing along two tracks. Mordecai's refusal to bow to Haman provokes in the latter a thirst for revenge that drives him to contrive two treacherous plans: he first convinces the king to proclaim an edict of persecution, not against Mordecai but against all the Jews of Persia. In addition, he also erects a gallows on which to hang Mordecai. The double threat will also find a double release from danger. The release from the latter danger begins in chapter 6, when the king finds that it was Mordecai who had earlier uncovered a plot against his life and saved him. For the former threat, there is a more involved resolution, not completed until chapter 9, when a new edict is proclaimed that allows the Jews to kill those who would have harmed them. The double threat-and-deliverance structure follows an *a-b-b-a* pattern: threat to Jews / threat to Mordecai / deliverance of Mordecai / deliverance of Jews, with chapter 6 (Mordecai honored before the king) as the crux of the reversal of action.[2] This structure only begins to describe the complexity, however, for the deliverance of the Jews, though completed in chapter 9, actually begins in chapter 4, with a dialogue between Mordecai and Esther. When Mordecai appears in the city square in sackcloth and ashes, Esther, in a pathetic gesture, sends clothes for him. When word returns from him that a decree has been written against the Jews, she responds that anyone who approaches the king unbidden risks death. Mordecai then reminds her of her identity: "Think not that in the king's palace you will escape any more than all the other

---

[2] Yehudah T. Radday, "Chiasm in Joshua, Judges, and Others," *Linguistica Biblica* 3 (1973): 6–13; cf. also Niditch, *Underdogs and Tricksters,* 130. My brief description of the narrative intentionally emphasizes the doubled, separable tracks of the plot, in opposition to those who argue for the unity and integrity of the work, e.g., Niditch, esp. 132, and Sasson, "Esther," 340. It must be granted, for instance, that although Mordecai is honored before the king in chapter 6, he is not delivered from danger until chapter 7, at the time that the plot against the Jews is uncovered. As I shall argue below, however, the two strands of source and redactional levels can often be separated in *Esther,* although they are now quite successfully and thoroughly interwoven. See also Wills, *The Jew in the Court of the Foreign King,* 153–91, for a more detailed argument concerning the structure of *Esther.*

Jews. For if you keep silence at such a time as this, relief and deliverance will rise for the Jews from another quarter, but you and your father's house will perish" (4:13–14). The words evidently affect Esther; she is now up to the task. She orders Mordecai to organize a general fast of the Jews, while she prepares to enter in before the king, and Mordecai now obeys her words.[3] This movement of the story in chapter 4, where both characters are prominent, is the most complex in the book, and the double plots are here most thoroughly integrated.

W. Lee Humphreys has grouped *Esther* with other court narratives as writings that describe and commend a "life-style for Diaspora."[4] *Esther, Daniel* 1–6, *Bel and the Dragon,* and other Jewish writings of this period focus on the precarious relationship of Jews to the pagan authorities and yet seem to conclude on a hopeful note of coexistence for Jews who remain true to the Jewish religion. Loyalty to Judaism thus becomes a central value for a Diaspora community, and it need not, as *Esther* shows, mean opposition to a gentile king. The Jewish Diaspora community, in fact, will prosper only when loyalty to Jews and to king are both upheld. Humphreys has presented a plausible explanation for the themes and social function of these short narratives, yet beneath the surface of *Esther* can be found many of the issues that arise in the study of ancient Jewish novels. It appears to be a trifling narrative, at times bombastic, yet surprisingly complex and artful. It strikes many readers as overly vengeful or even paranoid, yet it is optimistic about acceptance and coexistence. And what may be the most surprising and important contradiction is that the security of all the Jews of Persia is threatened on religious grounds and yet there is no mention of Jerusalem, nor of Jews in any other part of the world, nor of God.

Many artistic excesses and improbabilities can be found in this work. We note especially the preposterous fixing of a date far in advance for a riot to ensue (possible in nineteenth-century Russia, perhaps, but not likely in Persia), the pseudohistorical appeals to the "Book of the Chronicles of the Kings of Media and Persia" (10:2), the exaggerated revenge motif, in which the Jews slay 75,800 of those who wanted to do them harm (9:16), and the king's ultimate decision against Haman, prompted not because Esther has brought the king to his senses but because he thinks Haman is assaulting her while he himself steps out-

---

[3] Berg, *The Book of Esther,* 173–87, esp. 176–78; and Fox, *Character and Ideology,* 56–67, 196–204.

[4] Humphreys, "A Life-Style for Diaspora." See Chapter 2 and also Wills, *Jew in the Court,* passim.

side the room (7:5–8).[5] Although the modern reader may feel that he or she is simply suffering from misunderstandings of ancient literary conventions or of the proper context of the narrative, the artistic excesses and improbabilities in the work were probably intended. It was likely composed as a work of fiction—the readers would hardly have believed that there had really been a Jewish queen of Persia—but it has caused great discomfort to many later readers because of its "nationalist" spirit and bloodthirsty revenge. The discomfort that it has caused has not been so much to Jewish readers, who associate it with the wild party atmosphere of the Purim celebration, as to Christians, who see its spirit of revenge as a violation of the Christian ethic of love and nonretaliation. Luther's condemnation of it—"I am so hostile to [Second Maccabees] and to Esther that I could wish that they did not exist at all, for they Judaize too greatly and have much pagan impropriety"[6]— is echoed by many twentieth-century Christian scholars. Georg Fohrer calls Esther "the product of a nationalistic spirit . . . which has lost all understanding of the demands and obligations of Yahwism, especially in its prophetical form."[7] Bernhard W. Anderson, in what is perhaps the most quoted judgment of recent scholarship, says: "The story unveils the dark passions of the human heart: envy, hatred, fear, anger, vindictiveness, pride, all of which are fused into intense nationalism. . . . The church should recognize the book for what it is: a witness to the fact that Israel, in pride, either made nationalism a religion in complete indifference to God or presumptuously identified God's historical purpose with the preservation and glorification of the Jewish people."[8] Defenses of the book, primarily from Jewish scholars, bring the discussion back to the nature and genre of the original work, a work that does not fit well into doctrinal categories. It is seen by Jewish scholars through the

[5] Sasson, "Esther," 335. See also Gunkel, Esther, 50–53, and Greenstein, "A Jewish Reading of Esther." Fox's fine study is incorrect, I believe, in seeing the appeal to named court chronicles—and other aspects as well—as evidence of a pretense of historicity (Character and Ideology, 148–50).

[6] Martin Luther, Table Talk, trans. William Hazlitt (London: David Bogue, 1909), 11. Bickerman notes, however (Four Strange Books of the Bible, 212–13), that the context of Luther's statement is crucial. In Luther's view, the Book of Esther is simply found wanting in prefigurations of Christ.

[7] Georg Fohrer, Introduction to the Old Testament (Nashville: Abingdon, 1968), 255, quoted also by Clines, The Esther Scroll, 153–54.

[8] Bernhard W. Anderson, "The Place of the Book of Esther in the Christian Bible," Journal of Religion 30 (1950): 37–38. See also Otto Eissfeldt, The Old Testament: An Introduction (New York: Harper and Row, 1965), 511–12, and, to a milder degree, Robert H. Pfeiffer, Introduction to the Old Testament (New York: Harper and Brothers, 1941), 747.

lens of the Purim celebration, which even in an early period was a bois-terous festival of release. The nature of this festival tells us much about the Jewish interpretation of *Esther* and perhaps about the composition of the book as well. We find in the practice of Purim the same sort of ritually demarcated release as found in Halloween in the United States (though the latter is much milder) or Mardi Gras. The Talmudic trac-tate *bMegillah* 7b enjoins the participants at Purim to drink wine until they cannot distinguish between "Cursed be Haman" and "Blessed be Mordecai." The anthropologist McKim Marriott depicts a similar sort of festival which allows for an even wilder release of social tensions, the Indian festival of Holi.[9] There Marriott witnessed all social distinctions blurred or reversed as participants became increasingly inebriated on a hashish concoction. Wives beat husbands, low-caste villagers beat high-caste ones, the anthropologist himself was doused in buffalo urine—in short, it is an upheaval of liminal-period reversals and release. Purim is also such a ritual, if indulged in with somewhat less abandon, and the *Book of Esther* should perhaps be judged accordingly.

Even apart from its connection to Purim, its themes have been too harshly judged. Jon D. Levenson points out that the work is not, in fact, "nationalistic" or "anti-Gentile."[10] In regard to the first charge, the Jews in the *Book of Esther* do not mount a campaign to create a sepa-rate Jewish state or to return to Israel. In fact, Israel (or Judah) is not even mentioned, nor is the temple or anything at all having to do with mourning over the Exile of Jews to foreign lands. The Jews in this book want to live as citizens of Persia. Regarding the second charge, the book is actually remarkably *pro*-Gentile. The king is ultimately positive, the Jews live happily in a foreign land, and thousands of the people "con-vert" or "live as Jews", even if it is out of "fear of the Jews." Levenson and Jack M. Sasson both point out that the function of the revenge is a *literary* balance; it is a poetic justice that is part of the fairytalelike quality of the story, not an actual policy statement for Jewish civic leaders. The death of Haman and his family would have been considered appropri-ate justice in morally balanced stories in antiquity—one need look no further than the Daniel stories in Chapter 2 above. But although Leven-son and Sasson specifically mention the moral balance of the deaths of

---

[9] McKim Marriott, "The Feast of Love," in *Krishna: Myths, Rites, and Attitudes,* ed. Milton Singer (Honolulu: East-West Center Press, 1966), 200–212. Cf. also the emphasis of Mikhail Bakhtin (*Rabelais and His World* [Cambridge: MIT Press, 1968], esp. 7–21) on the role of carnival and reversals in European culture.

[10] Levenson, "The Scroll of Esther in Ecumenical Perspective."

Haman and his sons, they leave out of consideration the 75,800 others who are also killed (9:6, 15, 16).[11] "Balance," moral or otherwise, has been lost. Even if the ones killed were those who hated the Jews and were preparing to kill them, the typical narrative technique of a morally satisfying just punishment and just reward at the end has been blown sky-high. The tone here, as in many other places, can only be described as farce.

Date, Social Situation, and Theology

The dating of *Esther*, like the dating of most of the novels, is difficult, but a clear notion of provenance would be very helpful in determining the social world of the document. Two arguments for dating have won advocates among modern scholars, and both are intriguing for a literary discussion. The first is that *Esther* was written during the late Persian period, sometime after the events described but before the conquest of Alexander the Great. It is noteworthy that the *Book of Esther* never mentions Jerusalem or the temple and is obsessed with Persian court manners and power and with the security of the Jews of Persia. The work is oriented toward a proper "lifestyle for Diaspora," not toward party politics in Palestine.[12] It was the Diaspora book par excellence, yet with little consciousness of the Jews having been exiled, and it is still positive about Diaspora life in Persia. Because of the lack of Greek loan words, according to this argument, it was also likely composed before the Greek conquest, or about the fifth or fourth century B.C.E. The parallels with Persian narrative traditions of the court and of "palace intrigues" would lend support to this date.

[11] Levenson, "Scroll of Esther," 444; Sasson, "Esther," 341. On the interpretation of the exaggerated revenge, see also Gunkel, *Esther*, 50–52. Many scholars also make the correct observation that Mordecai, the descendant of Saul's tribe, is carrying out the extermination of Haman's family (descended from Agag), which Saul himself had failed to do under God's direct command (*First Samuel* 15). Although this gives a biblical basis for the execution of Haman's sons, it does not apply to the exaggerated revenge motif. The larger revenge motif is also seen as a defensive strategy against the large group of people who still pose a threat (cf. Fox, *The Redaction of the Books of Esther*, 111), but this is only true *within* the unreal narrative world of the story. Fictitious enemies have been created, not unlike the menacing Indians of American westerns, and an opportunity is afforded to crush them. Real enemies have certainly existed often enough in Jewish history and may indeed have existed in the world of the author, but here the situation and the justification are both contrived.

[12] Levenson, "Scroll of Esther," 444–45; Albert Baumgarten, "Scroll of Esther," in *Encyclopedia Judaica*, 14 vols. (Jerusalem: Keter, 1972), 12:1051–52.

Other scholars prefer a later date. The scene of revenge and forced conversions in *Esther* 9 is an anomaly in the history of Israel, and yet there is one place and period where such a scene would have seemed possible to the author and audience: the Judaean kingdom of the Hasmoneans, especially under John Hyrcanus (135–104 B.C.E.), one of the successors of the Maccabees.[13] After the Maccabean Revolt, the Hasmoneans wrested control of more and more of the surrounding regions, creating a Judaean empire larger than Solomon's. Enforcing a Mosaic constitution on the inhabitants, they converted large numbers of people at the point of a sword. The emphasis on conversion through "fear of the Jews" makes sense as Hasmonean royal propaganda, but is difficult to imagine under other circumstances. Further, it is not just the Jewish reaction to persecution that is an anomaly in ancient Jewish history; it is the religious persecution itself. Many textbooks on Jewish history will note that the proscription of Jewish practices by Antiochus IV Epiphanes in 165 B.C.E., which gave rise to the Maccabean Revolt, is one of the first *religious* persecutions in history.[14] Could the prospect of an empirewide persecution of the Jews have played a crucial role in a

---

[13] Pfeiffer, *Introduction to the Old Testament*, 742. Not all of Pfeiffer's arguments need be upheld to hold to a date under John Hyrcanus. Baumgarten objects, for example, to Pfeiffer's implied condemnation of Esther's vengefulness and his identification of the supposed spiritual aridity of *Esther* with that of John Hyrcanus, the "spiritually lowest" stage of the Hasmonean dynasty. These objections are quite valid but do not eliminate the possibility of resurrecting Pfeiffer's dating. Furthermore, Christians and Jews may both display theologically based motives in their interpretation of *Esther*. The *Book of Esther* has been considered an embarrassment by Christians, although it has not by Jews—*unless it was written during Hasmonean rule*, when its triumphalism would have been paralleled by real forced conversions carried out by the Hasmonean kings. Although the celebration of military revenge in later centuries by powerless European Jews may seem relatively innocent, such a celebration during the Hasmonean period does not.

The two suggestions for dating discussed here are the most likely but by no means the only possibilities. See also the discussion in Carey A. Moore, *Esther* (Garden City, N.Y.: Doubleday, 1971), lvi–lix.

[14] Cf., for example, Elias J. Bickerman, *The God of the Maccabees* (Leiden: Brill, 1979), 62; Tcherikover, *Hellenistic Civilization and the Jews*, 175, 183; and Shaye J. D. Cohen, *From the Maccabees to the Mishnah* (Philadelphia: Westminster, 1987), 30. There was a pogrom against the followers of Pythagoras in southern Italy in about 450 B.C.E. (Walter Burkert, *Greek Religion* [Cambridge: Harvard University Press, 1985], 303–4), but it was not a state policy. It could be argued that Haman's campaign against the Jews was not a "religious persecution" aimed at stamping out certain *practices*, as Antiochus IV Epiphanes imposed, but an attempt to kill all members of one group, regardless of whether they abandoned their practices or not. The latter would be akin to the slaughter of the Magi in Persia, as recounted by Herodotus 3.61–79. The account in Esther is mixed, however, referring to the extermination of both an ethnic group *and* its religious practices. The suppression of religious practices comes through very strongly and seems to presuppose the possibility of a suppression of practices.

novel if it had no reality in the popular consciousness? Possibly, but it does not seem likely. Furthermore, some of the perceived problems of a late Hasmonean date may evaporate if we consider the genre of *Esther*. The favorable view of the Gentile king has been seen as a difficulty for a Jewish state that was born in revolution from pagan rulers, but a *Persian* king, in a story set in the more remote past, could surely be judged sympathetically. After all, the Persians (or their successors, the Parthians) had aided the Hasmoneans. The focus on Persian customs and setting, to the exclusion of Jerusalem and Palestine, would appear to be a difficulty as well, but this may simply be a pretense of the novel genre. We note, for example, that some of the Greek novels have idealized ancient settings, which include the Persian court.[15] It is entirely possible that the *Esther* novel strives for an idealized fictional setting that is intentionally *separated* from its contemporary setting. The presence of Persian loan words thus becomes understandable, as does the absence of Greek: one group of terms was introduced intentionally, the other avoided. Either dating of the *Scroll of Esther* would have fascinating implications for its social function. An early dating would indicate a rousing palace intrigue in the tradition of the Persian courtly literature, and a late dating, a high-spirited celebration of Hasmonean victories. I believe the Hebrew *Scroll of Esther* as we have it is more likely to have fallen into the latter category, but below, in the investigation of possible sources, we shall see that at different stages it might, in fact, have been both.

The recent positive assessments by Jewish scholars have produced several attempts to affirm its theology, allowing interesting counterinterpretations to the Christian condemnations of its pages. Levenson concludes his objections to the latter by pointing up the unusual—in fact, unique—perspective of *Esther*. Paralleling in some ways the redemption of *Exodus, Esther* nevertheless differs in situating the hope of the future life of the Jews of Persia wholly in the Diaspora, with no necessary reliance on Jerusalem or the temple: "Thus, Esther brings the Diaspora into the great pattern of redemption history, without, however, insisting that it (the Diaspora) commit suicide in the process. Purim speaks to the existential situation of the Diaspora somewhat the way Passover speaks to Israel in their Land."[16]

---

[15] Chariton and Heliodorus make great use of the Persian court, in both cases projected onto a colorful ancient past. See Reardon's introduction to Chariton in Reardon, ed., *Collected Ancient Greek Novels*, 18.

[16] Levenson, "Scroll of Esther," 449. Also on the relation to *Exodus* see Bickerman, *Four Strange Books*, 211, and especially G. Gerleman, "Studien zu Esther: Stoff-Struktur-Stil-Sinn,"

Two recent studies would defend the literary qualities of the book and, by doing so, would also find the indirect expression of very positive theological concerns. Sandra Beth Berg begins her analysis by isolating motifs that appear constantly in the work, such as banquets, kingship, and issues of obedience and disobedience.[17] Alongside these constant motifs Berg finds several overarching themes of the narrative, especially power, loyalty to the Jewish community, and reversal. It is reversal, in fact, that structures the whole story: at 4:13–14, Esther reverses her role from passive to active, giving commands to Mordecai and deciding to go in before the king. By this action, she puts into motion a series of reversals of fortune, saving the Jews and unmasking and punishing Haman and his partisans. From observations such as these, Berg perceives a set of theological interests of the author. History is not random but guided by God. But unlike other scholars who see the book as pointing the way to God's rule of history—albeit indirectly, since God is never mentioned—Berg argues that the reversal is achieved through human agency. Reversal is not, as is often the case in the *Psalms,* a hoped-for result of God's grace. It results in this narrative from a correct human response, an active role that emphasizes Jewish solidarity.[18] Even Mordecai's enigmatic reference in 4:13–14 to "help from another quarter," which many scholars explain as an oblique reference to God, is taken by Berg to refer to Jewish help. Is Mordecai holding romantically to the hope of a Jewish solidarity that will ultimately vanquish Haman's designs? (Whether it is realistic or not is beside the point.) Berg does not deny the role of God in controlling events; she merely emphasizes that the reversal here requires *human* agency. It must be noted, however, that her arguments, as well as those of other scholars, for the hidden role of God call upon a fairly "serious" reading of Esther, and it may be more appropriate to see in this work a humorous satire or even a broadside farce.[19] As noted above, this work was probably in its ori-

---

Biblische Studien 48 (1966): 1–48, and *Esther* (Neukirchen-Vluyn: Neukirchener, 1970). Gerleman overemphasizes the reflections of *Exodus* in the text of *Esther;* see Moore's critique, "Esther Revisited: An Examination of Esther Studies over the Past Decade," in *Biblical and Related Studies Presented to Samuel Iwry,* ed. Ann Kort and Scott Morschauser (Winona Lake, Ind.: Eisenbrauns, 1985), 166, and his review of Gerleman, *Journal of Biblical Literature* 94 (1975): 293–96. Note below, however, that the Greek additions to *Esther* introduce more of an explicit *Exodus* theme.

[17] Berg, *Book of Esther.*

[18] Ibid., 173–87, esp. 176–78.

[19] In addition to Berg, note the strongly theological interpretation of Clines, *Esther Scroll,* 152–58, although it must be noted that Clines is more interested in a hypothetical *source* of

gins, or at an early stage, a *Purimspil,* that is, a reading for the Jewish festival of Purim, and this interpretation comports with the many wild improbabilities of the work. An *order* can be seen in the narrative, in that a series of events leads in a coherent way to a happy ending, but it is not a theology of history as much as a romance or farce. It is not so much a question of whether God is behind the outcome of events as of what theological conclusions are to be drawn. The more appropriate theological summation may be the command to drink wine. By focusing on the character of Esther in chapter 4 and the change she undergoes from passive to active, Berg also shifts the usual "center" of the story from chapter 6, where Haman's plot begins to unravel and the reversal of *outcomes* begins, to chapter 4, where the reversal of *responses* had already been inaugurated. Here Esther, in dialogue with Mordecai, begins to find herself and take on an active role in the salvation of the Jews, moving from taking orders from Mordecai to giving them. Despite the fact, therefore, that Mordecai figures in the more minor reversal of chapter 6, it is Esther's continued banquets and entreaties in chapters 4–7 that ultimately reverse the decrees.

Michael V. Fox's more detailed study of characterization in *Esther* comes to conclusions similar to Berg's on many points.[20] The role of Esther is central, her character clearly drawn for the audience as a person who moves through a series of reversals from passive—a subservient wife who replaces the upstart Vashti—to active, now one whose influence with the king can save the Jews. Fox also presses the satirical implications of Esther for undercutting the authority claims of the pagan state. By the end we see that the king and his courtiers are obtuse and malleable, and Mordecai and Esther can rise to positions of great influence.

The approaches of Berg and Fox have highlighted important literary qualities of *Esther*—literary patterns and structures in one case and characterization in the other—but one issue they only touch on should be noted in greater detail. Recent theories of narrative poetics have introduced the concept of "focalization" to account for the various means

---

Hebrew Esther, which may have been less farcical (see below). On a more comic interpretation, see Glendon E. Bryce, review of Berg, *Journal of Biblical Literature* 100 (1981): 276–77; Wills, *The Jew in the Court of the Foreign King,* 153–91; Sasson, "Esther," 339; Greenstein, "Jewish Reading;" Fox, *Character and Ideology,* esp. 25, 249, 253; Goldman, "Narrative and Ethical Ironies in Esther"; Jones, "Two Misconceptions about the Book of Esther," and Radday, "Esther with Humour."

[20] Fox, *Character and Ideology.*

of creating a "subject" in the text, a character whose perspective governs the reader's perception of events.[21] This concept is often, but not always, closely related to that of point of view or to the way the reader identifies with a protagonist, but focalization implies a more precise elucidation of how our perceptions are guided in a text, often shifting from one character's perspective to another's. Thus, Berg and Fox would see Esther as the focalizing subject in Hebrew *Esther,* but this is not unambiguously the case, since Mordecai also plays such a large role. Jack M. Sasson, for example, emphasizes Mordecai more as a fully fleshed-out character. Entering and exiting at crucial points, Mordecai is not the central figure on stage for the bulk of the story, but he is nevertheless, in Sasson's view, thoroughly revealed as a character cumulatively in each appearance: "Mordecai is played like a theme in a Sibelius symphony, with fragments of his personality occurring scattered in the early chapters; only after Haman's fall are they integrated into a full version to represent the writer's perfect image of a partisan Jew in a position of mastery."[22] Now, whether Sasson sees this "perfect image" as a focalizing subject is not clear, although he does make large claims for Mordecai's centrality to the narrative. Sasson sees Mordecai's overall authority among the Jews to be higher than Esther's. He asserts that the elevation of Esther is temporary, for the special purpose of acting on the Jews' behalf, and that she returns to Mordecai's control after her moment of triumph.[23] To be sure, the conclusion at 10:1–3 does sing the praises of Mordecai alone, but the relative authority of Mordecai and Esther, both with Jews and in the Persian king's palace, are mixed in chapters 8–10. We are also concerned with how this relates to the character's different functions in the story. Others may find Mordecai opaque as opposed to transparent, morally steadfast but thinly drawn as a character, and not at all capable of becoming the focalizing subject.[24]

[21] See the excellent introduction to this issue in Rimmon-Kenan, *Narrative Fiction,* 71–85, which is largely based on Gérard Genette, *Figures,* 3 vols. (Paris: Éditions du Seuil, 1968–72), 3:206–23. In American biblical criticism, the vaguer term *point of view* has often been used; see Berlin, *Poetics and the Interpretation of Biblical Narrative,* 50–51, and Brichto, *Toward a Grammar of Biblical Poetics,* 9–10. Largely on account of the discussion of focalization by Bal, *Narratology,* 100–115, biblical scholars have taken up the more subtle uses of this term; see, e.g., Funk, *The Poetics of Biblical Narrative,* 99–132.

[22] Sasson, "Esther," 338.

[23] Sasson, "Esther," 337.

[24] Fox, *Character and Ideology,* 178, 185–95, applies here Alter's analysis of the narrative reticence in the story of Saul and David (*The Art of Biblical Narrative,* 114–30). There the reticence comes in the descriptions of David's emotions, which are contrasted to the emotional out-

In regard to this and a number of other important questions, therefore, we find that there is a split decision among scholars: Is the *Scroll of Esther* to be dated in the Persian or the Hasmonean period? Is there a moral balance in the extreme revenge motif? Is chapter 4 the dramatic center of the work, or is chapter 6? Is Esther or Mordecai the focalizing subject of the narrative? It is possible that all of these questions can find some resolution in an approach that attributes some of these properties to a source and others to one or more redactional layers.

Variant Versions of *Esther* and Possible Sources in Hebrew *Esther*

If the various ancient versions of *Esther* and the possible sources within Hebrew *Esther* are taken into consideration, it becomes clear that we do not have one *Esther* but many. Through comparison of them we can reconstruct a hypothetical stemma of development that bears significantly on the question of the evolution of popular novels. Like many other popular literary works in the ancient world, *Esther* circulated in various versions. These different versions not only provide us with a view of how *Esther* changed and expanded but, through careful comparisons, may also allow us to reconstruct prior stages in the tradition that are no longer represented among the extant texts. The older books of the Bible, such as the five books of Moses or the early prophetic works of *Amos* and *Hosea,* are relatively stable in the ancient translations, whereas many of the later books—or the books that were edited at a later date—exhibit many discrepancies in the Greek translation, some of them very significant, as in the case of *Jeremiah* or *Proverbs* or of *Daniel* and *Tobit*. This is certainly true of *Esther,* which is known in a number of recensions.[25] Hebrew *Esther* is not so much a single, unique text as

---

bursts of Saul. Mordecai (like David) is opaque, whereas Haman (like Saul) is transparent. Regarding Mordecai, however, we must ask, Reticence in regard to what? The depth of the character's tragic dimension is simply not there. We may wonder whether the genre would even allow for the possibility in a character like Mordecai, but see Chapter 6 on the varied characterization of Joseph in *Testament of Joseph*.

[25] As noted in the introduction, for sake of brevity we shall omit from our present study the two main Latin versions, the two Aramaic targums of *Esther,* and various other witnesses to the ancient texts. The targums differ the most from Hebrew *Esther,* but they are likely from a later period than the one we are studying, and they are more interesting for the history of midrashic elaborations than for the rise of the Jewish novel. For introduction and translations, see Bernard Grossfeld, *The Two Targums of Esther* (Collegeville, Minn.: Liturgical Press, 1991).

it is a snapshot of a literary tradition in progress. It appears that *Esther* was rarely simply copied without being substantially rewritten in the process, an aspect of popular literature we noted in the Introduction. We take Hebrew *Esther* as our "main" version simply because it stands in the Jewish and Protestant canons and has received the larger share of attention from biblical scholars. The standard ancient Greek translation, which is the basis of the Greek Orthodox and Catholic biblical texts (referred to hereafter as "Greek *Esther*"), includes six substantial additions to the work: Mordecai's premonitory dream of the events that are about to happen and his discovery of a plot against the king, the king's letter ordering the massacre of the Jews, prayers of Mordecai and Esther, Esther's detailed entrance before the king, the king's letter rescinding his previous order, and a conclusion that interprets Mordecai's dream and draws the work to a close. The effect of these additions is to create a more exciting narrative at a number of points, to heighten the effect of the marvelous, and to emphasize the piety of Mordecai and Esther. God, never so much as mentioned in Hebrew *Esther,* is brought into the action through the prayers of Mordecai and Esther. These additions greatly alter the overall character of the work, but otherwise this version is a fairly faithful translation of Hebrew *Esther.*

There is another ancient Greek version of *Esther,* however, the so-called Greek A text, which, although it also contains the six apocryphal additions listed above, diverges widely over the course of the "core" narrative, especially from chapter 8 on. It thus differs from both Hebrew and canonical Greek *Esther.* It is possible, of course, that the difference can be attributed to the editor of Greek A, who altered the text of *Esther* drastically, but David J. A. Clines has argued (following an older suggestion of Charles C. Torrey) that an earlier version of *Esther* existed that ended in chapter 8. This text, now lost to us, was according to this theory fleshed out with two separate endings: the one now in the Hebrew Bible and the one now in Greek A.[26] A close analysis of the Greek A text reveals several interesting differences from Hebrew *Esther:* (1) the unalterability of the royal decree against the Jews in Hebrew *Esther* is lacking in Greek A, and it is this unalterability that keeps the threat to the Jews alive in Hebrew *Esther* chapter 9; (2) there is a literary integrity of the story without these elements; and (3) the clumsiness

---

[26] Clines, *Esther Scroll,* and Charles C. Torrey, "The Oldest Book of Esther," *Harvard Theological Review* 37 (1944): 1–40, reprinted in Moore, ed., *Studies in the Book of Esther.* Fox, *Redaction,* 17–34, provides a more exacting discussion of the arguments for considering the Greek A text as a witness to an older form of *Esther.*

of many of the transitions in chapter 8, both in Hebrew *Esther* and in Greek A, can be explained as the result of new material being inserted at the conclusion of the story. The references to God and religious practices, present in Greek A but not in Hebrew *Esther,* were, according to this theory, part of the source, systematically eliminated by the editor of the Hebrew version.[27] Greek A probably does reflect an older form of *Esther* than does the Hebrew version, but as Clines notes, it is likely not the precise version (even in a Hebrew original) that the editor of the Hebrew scroll had in possession. Rather, the *source* of Greek A is probably the *source* of Hebrew *Esther,* but Greek A as it now stands has evolved slightly, moving along a path separate from Hebrew *Esther.* Elsewhere I have proposed another means of reconstructing this proto-*Esther* and arrived at a reconstruction similar to Clines's in many respects (though with some significant differences as well).[28] The fact that the arguments used in each case are so different, while the conclusions are often similar, serves to strengthen the case that some such source existed as the source behind both Hebrew *Esther* and Greek A.

The starting point for my reconstruction was the observation that much of the narrative in *Esther* is expansive or repetitive. Although it is possible that this simply reflects the mixed style of a single author or that two or more narratives were interwoven (as several scholars have suggested), it is also possible that the expansiveness and duplication in many cases arose from a broad reediting of a single, more economical telling of the story. In chapters 1 and 2, for example, important plot elements are related in relatively few verses, but interspersed throughout are long descriptions of the pomp and elegant surroundings of the Persian palace, as well as the lengthy deliberations of the characters at court. One might wonder whether the expansive descriptions were the result of a later editing. Although this division between an economical story and an expansive editing may appear to be arbitrary, it can be supported by a linguistic observation: the economical story thus isolated is written in a different Hebrew style from the embellishments. During the centuries after the Babylonian Exile (sixth century B.C.E.), Hebrew developed a number of significant changes that have been catalogued by scholars. When the hypothetical source and the embellishments are thus considered separately, the latter exhibit many of these changes, whereas

[27] Clines, *Esther Scroll,* esp. 71–114.
[28] Wills, *Jew in the Court,* 153–72.

the former is written in a style more typical of classical Hebrew.[29] The partial agreement of the Greek A text with this hypothetical reconstruction offers some corroboration as well.

These two studies together, therefore, give strong evidence that a shorter, more economical version of the Esther story circulated (hereafter "*Esther Source*"), although its exact contours cannot be determined. The character of this source can best be seen by contrasting it to the charming excesses of the embellishments found in Hebrew *Esther*. *Esther Source* can be described both by what it does have—the narrative elements that are retained in the reconstruction—and what it lacks in relation to Hebrew *Esther*. Among the latter are

1. The floridly extravagant descriptions of the court (chapter 1)
2. The edict protecting the domestic sovereignty of husbands (1:16–22)
3. The detailed preparations of the women of the harem (2:12–15)
4. References to the empirewide import of the edicts (3:12–15; 4:3, 8; 8:9–14)
5. The duplications of banquets (5:4–6)
6. Haman undone when he falls on Esther's settee (7:7–8)
7. The exaggerated revenge motif (9:6–12, 16–19)
8. The institution of Purim (3:7, 8:15–17; 9:20–32)

The last element may be the most surprising, but if the reconstruction is correct, the source is propelled by a narrative interest oriented toward

---

[29] The main linguistic indicators of different sources are, first, the predominance of converted verbs in the source (whereas in the embellishments one finds a much higher percentage of unconverted verbs, often with subject-verb word order) and, second, the use of pronominal suffixes on finite verbs in the source passages (but not in the embellishments). Other indicators are also listed in the extended treatment in Wills, *Jew in the Court*, 157–70. The indicators of late biblical Hebrew have been identified by Robert Polzin, *Late Biblical Hebrew: Toward an Historic Typology of Biblical Hebrew Prose* (Missoula: Scholars, 1976); see also Avi Hurvitz, "The Date of the Prose-Tale of Job Linguistically Considered," *Harvard Theological Review* 67 (1974): 17–34, and Lawrence M. Wills and Andrew Wilson, "Literary Sources of the Temple Scroll," *Harvard Theological Review* 75 (1982): 275–88. Although the indicators are rightly divided into early and late aspects of the Hebrew language, they likely coexisted for several centuries, and in fact the source, which mainly evidences early forms, contains some late elements as well, just as the redactional level attests some early elements. For instance, pronominal suffixes on finite verbs, associated with the source layer, are actually a late manifestation of biblical Hebrew. It should be noted that since Polzin did not consider the division of *Esther* into source and redactional layers, he concluded in his analysis that *Esther* was composed in a mixed Hebrew style, containing both early and late elements, as did Hans Striedl, "Untersuchung zur Syntax und Stilistik des hebräischen Buches Esther," *Zeitschrift für die alttestamentliche Wissenschaft* 55 (1937): 73–108.

neither a justification for Purim nor a liturgical reading for the festival. It may even predate that holiday. The source also affords much less of a role for Esther. In view of the increase in the number of female characters in Jewish prose of this period, an expansion of the role of Esther in Hebrew *Esther,* above and beyond that found in the source, should not surprise us.[30] The comparison of this reconstruction with Hebrew *Esther* also allows us to posit important changes in the latter, where it reorients the audience's attention to different parts of the narrative. In Hebrew *Esther,* for example, Esther delays in expressing her request to King Ahasuerus, retarding the action with a series of banquets, and the denouement in which Haman is unmasked (chapter 7) is also expanded. This represents quite a shift in emphasis from the hypothetical source. The presentation of the crucial plot elements involving Mordecai in chapters 3 and 6—the very backbone of the court conflict between Mordecai and Haman—is foreshortened and relegated to the background so that something else might be brought into the foreground, the interweaving of Esther's role and the climax and denouement of chapters 4, 5, 7, and 8.

Other source theories have also been proffered over the years but lack the supporting evidence offered by a comparison with Greek A or the corroboration of linguistic data. Some scholars suggest that totally separate Esther and Mordecai stories once were utilized as sources but are now hopelessly intertwined.[31] In the case of the Esther subplot, it is difficult to imagine a separate Esther narrative without importing a good deal of the action that now involves Mordecai as well. Esther *reacts* to the predicament created by her proud cousin. It is altogether different with Mordecai, however. If one selects out all verses that deal with the plot line concerning the conflict of Mordecai and Haman, omitting all the references to Esther and her subplot, a very plausible "Mordecai Source" can be obtained, which is fascinating for the discussion of the early history of the Esther tradition.[32] Since it is "prenovelistic" and perhaps

---

[30] Fox notes (*Character and Ideology,* 261, 272) that Esther has a stronger role in Hebrew *Esther* than in either Greek A or canonical Greek *Esther.* His own hypothetical reconstruction of the source of Greek A (*Redaction,* 125), like Clines's (*Esther Scroll,* 30) and my own, does not have any reference to Purim.

[31] Cazelles, "Notes sur la composition du rouleau d'Esther"; Jürgen Christian Lebram, "Purimfest und Estherbuch," *Vetus Testamentum* 22 (1972): 208–22; and Bickerman, *Four Strange Books,* 171–88. See also the discussion in Moore, *Esther,* l–liii; Wills, *Jew in the Court,* 154–55, 172–81; and especially that of Fox, *Redaction,* 97–114.

[32] This proposed Mordecai/Haman source is reconstructed in Wills, *Jew in the Court,* 172–81. There I perhaps do not make it clear enough that I intended the reconstruction as a suggestion of the *outlines* of a narrative and not as a verbatim account.

originally oral, it will only be discussed here in passing. The Mordecai/
Haman story would have been a short court narrative (as reconstructed,
about the size of the legends in *Daniel* 1–6) that demonstrated the folly
of Haman's petulance and reaffirmed the ultimate justice of the court in
vindicating Mordecai for his earlier denunciation of the two conspira-
tors, Bigthan and Teresh. Such narratives were common—we saw that
Daniel 3 and 6, for example, were very similar—and expressed a set of
strongly held moral beliefs in the Persian-ruled countries. But far from
placing Mordecai at the center of the account or making his character
the focalizing subject of the audience's perceptions, it is told almost entirely from *Haman's* point of view. We are placed inside the mind of a
man who loses control. The Mordecai/Haman source is in some ways
very similar to a Persian-era narrative from Egypt, *Onkhsheshonq*,[33] and
this story is also a "wisdom" tale told from the fool's perspective, documenting his obtuseness and its consequences. The next step according
to our reconstruction, the *Esther Source*, could be seen, as Bickerman
suggests, as simply the addition of a "palace intrigue"—also typical of
Persian-era literature—which has been ingeniously interwoven into the
narrative.[34] This type of story would also have been known as far back

[33] Cf. Wills, *Jew in the Court*, esp. 172–91, and for a translation of *Onkhsheshonq*, see Miriam
Lichtheim, *Ancient Egyptian Literature*, 3 vols. (Berkeley and Los Angeles: University of California Press, 1973–1980), 3:159–84. Fox argues (*Redaction*, 98–99) that since both the Mordecai
and Esther sections have parallels to the Joseph story, they were not likely composed separately. This argument loses its force, however, if the existence of a separate Esther story is not
being advocated. The parallels to Joseph could have begun with the Mordecai/Haman story,
only to be increased with the addition of each layer. Note also that the parallels may derive as
much from the *genre* of courtly advancement as from the Joseph narrative per se. See Niditch
and Doran, "The Success Story of the Wise Courtier."

[34] The kind of "palace intrigues" that we find in Greek accounts of the Persian court, such
as Ctesias's *Persika*, may have influenced *Esther*, even if actual sources were not taken over
for the composition of the present book. See Gunkel, *Esther*, 115; Roland de Vaux, *Ancient
Israel* (New York: McGraw-Hill, 1961), 516; Bickerman, *Four Strange Books*, 182–84, and especially now the evidence for Estherlike palace intrigues found at Qumran: Milik, "Les modèles
araméens du livre d'Esther dans la grotte 4 de Qumrân." These narratives are usually called
"harem intrigues," but I have preferred "palace intrigues" because, although they are not without an erotic aspect, they should not be confused with erotic adventures such as those in *A
Thousand and One Nights*. That other motifs in *Esther* also have parallels in ancient literature
suggests that the author may have incorporated older popular narratives. The defeat of female
prerogatives in the Vashti episode of chapter 1 has been rightly compared with the story of
Candaules, king of Lydia, and his wife in Herodotus 1.8–13, and the empirewide scurging of
a religious minority is found in the revenge on the Magi in Herodotus 3.61–79. These may
indicate influences from roughly contemporary narrative traditions but not sources as such.
Niditch does not focus on these sorts of particular influences as much as on the general folk-
loristic narrative style of Esther, and she denies the possibility of isolating sources (*Underdogs
and Tricksters*, 132).

as Herodotus or Ctesias (fifth and fourth centuries B.C.E.), and yet in
this example there are adaptations that indicate a new move in the direction of popular literature, exemplifying the novelistic impulse. In
particular, a woman character is introduced in a role that is somewhat
domesticated when compared to the palace intrigues. Esther is a "com-
moner," interested less in kingship or dynasty than in her relationship
with her adopted father, Mordecai, her real father's family (4:14); and,
by extension, all Jews in Persia. Furthermore, the psychological dimension of the danger is emphasized as Esther must come to grips with her
own role and is exhorted in this direction by Mordecai in a scene that is
already beginning to focus on interior emotion.

Some of the thematic differences among the *Mordecai/Haman Source*,
the *Esther Source* (which, recall, includes the *Mordecai/Haman Source*),
and Hebrew *Esther* (which, in turn, includes the *Esther Source*) allow
us now to propose answers to the scholarly quandaries posed above.
Concerning the date of composition, the earliest layers of *Esther* may
derive from as far back as the early part of the Persian period (fifth
century B.C.E.), but Hebrew *Esther* was probably composed during the
Hasmonean period (late second century B.C.E.). Concerning a moral
balance in the execution of the enemies, there is a fairytalelike balance
in the execution of Haman and his family in the two early layers of
Esther but not in Hebrew *Esther,* where the revenge takes on an exaggerated character. In respect to the dramatic center of the book, chapter 6
is the center of the *Mordecai/Haman Source* but is no longer the dramatic
center in the *Esther Source* or Hebrew *Esther,* where the interchange of
Mordecai and Esther in chapter 4 becomes the new center. Furthermore,
Mordecai is an important dramatic character in the source layers, but
his position as the focalizing subject is mixed; he often loses it to Haman
or to Esther as we move through the layers. And if, as Sasson argues,
authority is restored to Mordecai at the end of Hebrew *Esther,* it is only
after Esther has become the central focalizing subject in the body of the
narrative. It is through her eyes, for example, that we see Mordecai in
chapter 4 walking about dressed in sackcloth and ashes. It is *her* confusion in this chapter and then her resolution to act that are experienced
by the audience, whereas Mordecai is heard as an external party.

As far as novelistic developments are concerned, *Esther Source* and
Hebrew *Esther* seem primitive, and yet there may be more that can be
said about the novelistic achievement of the latter. Berg's analysis of the
structure of Hebrew *Esther* emphasized a unity of purpose in the work,
explaining all parts of it in terms of the guiding themes of decision,

loyalty to Jews, and human responsibility. It is possible, however, to fracture this unity somewhat by analyzing the characterization at play here. Fox's study of characterization in Esther emphasized the different human makeup that is communicated for each main character, and this should be examined more closely. Mikhail Bakhtin, for example, develops further than other theorists the notion of multiple focalizations of a text (although he uses different terminology).[35] Focalization, to Bakhtin, is not just the bits and pieces of information that are described in a novel from a particular character's vantage point. He speaks instead of the "zone" that each character inhabits, the different characters' "voices" that are introduced into a novel, and how they enter into dialogue with one another: "A character in a novel always has . . . a zone of his own, his own sphere of influence on the authorial context surrounding him, a sphere that extends . . . beyond the boundaries of the direct discourse alloted him. . . . Every discourse has its own selfish and biased proprietor; there are no words with meanings shared by all, no words 'belonging to no one.' "[36] Bakhtin outlines how each character comes to dominate the perspective of his or her "zone." In Turgenev's *Fathers and Sons,* a rich landowner, Pavel Petrovich, is described as having a collar that is striped, "as is correct for morning wear." Now, Turgenev himself does not care whether a striped collar is correct for morning wear, and neither does the reader. They are, in fact, both somewhat contemptuous of the bourgeois pretensions of the man and are collaboratively engaged in satirizing him and his class. It is the character alone, Pavel Petrovich, who cares whether the collar is appropriate or not. We are encroaching on *his* zone, where *his* perspectives rule. Each character presents to the reader a different voice, and the narrator too can complicate the dialogue with one or more voices. The result is a dialogue of voices, which is for Bakhtin the essence of the novel (as opposed to other, single-voiced genres). The elements of irony, parody, and satire are central in this process, since they celebrate the multitude of voices in dialogue and contribute the proper themes for the novel genre. Bakhtin can, as a result, argue for a revolutionary definition of the novel as a form that takes an arch, parodic perspective on reality by presenting and interrelating various voices.

Bakhtin was not romantic about the ease with which this goal could be achieved. He expresses disappointment that the Greek novels never

[35] Bakhtin, *The Dialogic Imagination.*
[36] Ibid., 320, 401.

managed to explore the potentialities of a fully realized dialogue of characters. He never (to my knowledge) turned to ancient Jewish literature, however, and he only rarely mentions early Christian literature. Hebrew *Esther,* more than any of the other novels addressed here, reflects just such a diversity of voices. It is probable, to be sure, that some of the distinct voices in Hebrew *Esther* originally derived from the sources outlined above.[37] Nevertheless, the editor of Hebrew *Esther* appears to have an ingenious ability to control the voices of the past and to orchestrate, with new embellishments, a dialogue of voices that makes use of many of the effects of irony and parody that Bakhtin posits for the high novel.

We begin with the character of Ahasuerus, king of Persia, and Vashti, his queen, in *Esther* 1. In an earlier work I proposed the following as a reconstruction of the *Esther Source* version of chapter 1:

> In the days when King Ahasuerus sat on the throne of his kingdom, which was in Susa the capital, he made a banquet for all his princes and ministers. When the king was feeling merry with wine, he commanded the courtiers who served before him to bring Vashti the queen in to the king, wearing her royal crown, to show the people and the princes her beauty, for she was very beautiful. But Queen Vashti refused to come at the king's command which came by way of the courtiers, and the king became very angry. Then the king said to the wise men who knew the times: "According to law, what should be done to Queen Vashti, since she did not obey the command of King Ahasuerus, which came by way of the courtiers?"[38]

A simple text with a unitary style; whether or not it represents the source of Hebrew *Esther* chapter 1, clearly the latter is totally different.

[37] A reading of Bakhtin's views on variant voices within a text might lead one to assume that he would oppose source criticism as a misinterpretation of the inconsistencies of a text, inconsistencies that can even be found in works by a single author. However, Bakhtin appears to be silent on the subject, and my own view is that he would be neutral. The dialogue of voices that is created by a novelist is a precious achievement, not common in world literature; it is limited to novels and closely related genres and is not to be equated with the mere juxtaposition of multiple voices (which may or may not be "in dialogue") that source criticism might propose for texts of any genre, either novelistic or nonnovelistic. Bakhtin simply does not seem interested in ancient texts that can be demonstrated to have multiple authors. (His remarks on the Greek novels are found in *Dialogic Imagination,* esp. 111–29.)

[38] Wills, *Jew in the Court,* 159–60. Recall that the evidence for proposing a more economical source is not just succinctness, which would be a weak argument indeed. The reconstruction of a source is based, to be sure, on literary considerations, such as doublets and rough transitions, but also on the indicators of later Hebrew style in the parts attributed to the redactor and, in some cases, on agreements with Greek A.

Ahasuerus, first of all, is introduced pompously, indeed humorously: "In the days of Ahasuerus, the Ahasuerus who reigned from India to Ethiopia over one hundred and twenty-seven provinces, in those days when Ahasuerus sat on his royal throne in Susa the capital, in the third year of his reign he gave a banquet for all of his princes and servants" (1:1–2). The pomp but also the bounteous festival atmosphere of the Persian court are emphasized: "There were white cotton curtains and blue hangings caught up with cords of fine linen and purple to silver rings and marble pillars, and also couches of gold and silver on a mosaic pavement of porphyry, marble, mother-of-pearl, and precious stones. Drinks were served in golden goblets, goblets of different kinds, and the royal wine was lavished according to the bounty of the king" (1:6–7). The hyperbole in the descriptions seen here is found in almost every verse, from the lists of those present to the prescriptions for imbibing. There is a "voice" in these embellishments that is consistent. It is Ahasuerus' voice, but it is more than just his. It is the voice of the court, the harem, the people, the festival, the "court-in-festival."[39] It is the riches of the Persian Empire. Even the drapery "speaks."

Another voice, that of Ahasuerus' queen, Vashti, is also introduced but entirely by contrasts and silences: "Queen Vashti also gave a banquet for the women in the palace, which belonged to King Ahasuerus" (1:9). The difference in style could not be greater. Although she is spoken *about* by others and ordered about, she never speaks, and she is described by the narrator only once more: "But Queen Vashti refused to come at the king's command conveyed by the eunuchs" (1:12). The voice of Vashti is that she has no voice; it is a characterization by silence. The simplicity of her zone indicates that she is not susceptible to this festival atmosphere. She alone in the entire nobility refuses to come. Her refusal creates a crisis in the first voice, the court-in-festival: "Then the king said to the wise men who knew the times—for this was the king's procedure toward all who were versed in law and judgment, the men next to him being Carshena, Shethar, Admatha, Tarshish, Meres, Marsena, and Memucan, the seven princes of Persia and Media, who saw the king's face, and sat first in the kingdom—'According to the law, what is to be done to Queen Vashti?'" (1:13–15) This voice is described again with ludicrous overkill, but when Vashti is expelled, her presence,

---

[39] See Bakhtin, *Rabelais*, 10–16, on the inclusion of all citizens in carnival festivities. The initiation of everyone into an all-encompassing social ritual is crucial to the carnival, and if the festivities in *Esther* 1 are to be understood as one, then the import of Vashti's refusal becomes clearer.

her voice, is once again perceived through silences: "After these things, when the anger of King Ahasuerus had abated, he remembered Vashti and what she had done and what had been decreed against her" (2:1). Vashti, an important character in Esther, does not utter a single word and is only mentioned by the narrator in three short notices. Yet her role is seen in contrast to the overstatement of life at court. Furthermore, since the actions of the court figures in chapter 1, according to Fox, border on buffoonery, her character by comparison takes on the aura of a simple integrity.[40] Whether she is meant to be heroic or simply outside of the carnival atmosphere of the court is not clear, but this reading reverses the common view that Vashti's haughtiness is viewed by the author as a negative foil to Esther's compliance.

The festival now over, the voice of the court-in-festival recedes, and the voices of others are introduced, notably Mordecai, Esther, Haman, Haman's wife Zeresh, and Ahasuerus. The same sort of analysis of voices could be carried through with each of the voices described both distinctively and in dialogue. As in Bakhtin's modern examples, it is the way that the characters are described, in addition to what they say, that gives them voice. Haman, for example, in the course of the book reveals himself increasingly as one who, because of his seething hatred for one rival, Mordecai, has lost control and is doomed to fall, while Mordecai speaks relatively seldom (except in the crucial chapter 4) but is at the center of many dramatic scenes, a silent moral exemplar. The repressed anger of Haman and the impassive rigidity of Mordecai are both revealed in their first central scene together:

And all the king's servants who were at the king's gate bowed down and did obeisance to Haman; for the king had so commanded concerning him. But Mordecai did not bow down or do obeisance. Then the king's servants who were at the king's gate said to Mordecai, "Why do you transgress the king's command?" And when they spoke to him day after day and he would not listen to them, they told Haman, in order to see whether Mordecai's words would avail; for he had told them that he was a Jew. And when Haman saw that Mordecai did not bow down or do obeisance to him, Haman was filled with fury. But he disdained to lay hands on Mordecai alone. (3:2–6)

[40] Fox, *Character and Ideology*, 164–70. Much of the discussion that follows, on characters' voices in Esther, is indebted to Fox's perceptive discussion. Note that the two "voices" here, Vashti and the court-in-festival, are found in the source and redaction layers, respectively, that I outlined above. Although I believe the voices were introduced by different hands, they are now in dialogue, in the sense that the reader perceives the whole as a novel in the making, with ironic distinctions of characters—distinctions realized through narrative style.

Esther is depicted as a developing character who changes—in one scene—from a timid, withdrawn figure to one who is bold and assertive, giving commands to Mordecai and her people. Later, after Haman has been undone by her testimony, she must also halt the destructive decree the king had promulgated on Haman's advice: "Then Esther spoke again to the king; she fell at his feet and besought him with tears to avert the evil design of Haman the Agagite and the plot which he had devised against the Jews" (8:3). Esther now moves easily and confidently to make important petitions to the king, and her manner is most to be contrasted with Mordecai's. Except at 4:13–14, where Mordecai is convincing Esther to stand up for her people, Mordecai does not speak directly once! Significantly, it is in this same scene that Esther speaks directly for the first time (4:11).[41]

It is a pity that Bakhtin never turned his attention to the *Scroll of Esther*. Fox's discussion of the various characterizations and the way they are related to each other certainly comes very close to what Bakhtin was addressing, but it has as yet to be placed in a broad enough generic context. Bakhtin would take the layering of voices and the dialogue between them as the essence of a novel, a generic category for *Esther* that Fox rejects.[42] The fact that Hebrew *Esther* is caught up in a festival atmosphere and may have originated as a reading for a carnival of release and reversal would only strengthen Bakhtin's judgment that *this* was a novel! But it is also true that Bakhtin's theory, suggestive as it is, isolates only a particular novelistic ethos and not a universal characteristic of novels. Some of his favorite examples are not novels, and many classic novels are never mentioned, presumably because they are not sufficiently multivoiced.[43] Hebrew *Esther,* though advanced in Bakhtin's scale of literary achievement, remains ambiguous as to its moment in the evolution of the novelistic tradition. When we consider the further developments in the additions in Greek *Esther,* however, we find a fuller engagement of more conventional novelistic flourishes, even if the polyphony of voices is flattened.

[41] The latter observation is found in White, "Esther," 169–70, the former in Fox, *Character and Ideology,* 191–95. Fox is quite correct about Mordecai's "reserve" but perhaps still underestimates the extent to which it is a deliberate contrasting of styles with Esther's. He does rightly note (p. 169) that Vashti and Mordecai are alike in being taciturn.

[42] See Fox, *Character and Ideology,* 144–45, where genre definitions are clearly presented and discussed but in a way very different from my own and with very different conclusions. Put simply, Fox compares *Esther* to Ctesias and presumably (without naming them) the Greek novels, and he notes their differences. However, he does not address the larger generic question of the relation of all of these to the developing streams of novelistic writings, especially the indigenous novels.

[43] Todorov, *Mikhail Bakhtin,* 85–86.

Additions to *Esther* in the Greek Versions

Our consideration of the possible sources of Hebrew *Esther* serves to emphasize the process of creation of a primitive novel or of the novelistic experiments which might give rise to a novel, but the next phase in the evolutionary schema of the Esther tradition is not dependent on conjecture; it is based on the later additions that were inserted into the text of *Esther* and are now found interspersed in the two Greek versions. Although the two Greek versions differed in regard to their "core" narrative, allowing us to utilize one of them, Greek A, as an aid in reconstructing a source, in regard to the additions they are nearly identical. The six additions (traditionally identified with the letters A–F) consist of

A. Mordecai's symbolic dream of what is about to occur;
B. Text of Artaxerxes' (Ahasuerus's) decree of extermination;
C. Mordecai's and Esther's prayers;
D. Esther's audience before King Artaxerxes;
E. Text of Artaxerxes' decree rescinding previous decree;
F. Mordecai's interpretation of his dream and conclusion.

The additions accomplish many things in the new version of the story of Esther, beyond the most obvious, which is to invoke the name of God explicitly and piously. We shall consider the additions individually, noting especially the changes they introduce that bear on the literary question.

The first addition is placed at the beginning of the story, before the action of Hebrew *Esther*. After an identification of Mordecai by lineage (a common emphasis of the period; compare *Tobit, Judith,* and *Matthew* 1 and *Luke* 3), Greek *Esther* begins with a flourish of mock-apocalyptic. Mordecai dreams that two great dragons arise and prepare to fight. The righteous nation trembles as the world is filled with gloom and foreboding, but the people of the righteous nation pray to God, and a tiny stream appears, which grows to a mighty river. The gloom disappears and the sun returns, exalting the lowly and humbling those previously held in honor. The dream differs from apocalyptic visions of contemporary Jewish literature. It is short, and the symbols do not cover a whole range of history; even though they are not explained at this point, they clearly pertain to a limited number of historical figures and serve a literary function that the reader would perceive as related to the narrative that is coming. It is an artificial apocalypse that does not arise out of the rich ancient Near Eastern visionary traditions. It gives notice of the rousing adventures to come and serves the same function as do dreams and oracles in Greek novels. In Xenophon's *An Ephesian Tale* (1.6), for instance, an oracle at the beginning of the novel predicts both the harrowing adventures of the protagonists and their ultimate happiness. Several of the Greek novels, in fact, contain dreams or oracles in a similar position at the beginning of the story, to foreshadow the dangers and, in some cases, to predict a happy resolution as well.[44] A difficult question raised by the additions, which already asserts itself in addition A, is, Who is now the main character? Esther came to dominate Hebrew *Esther,* but here Mordecai is introduced first and will appear to take the greater role. It is a very complicated matter, however, for both Hebrew and Greek *Esther,* since in both cases the two protagonists take on *different* roles. We shall return to this question below.

The next addition is B, the text of Artaxerxes' decree to annihilate the Jews, which Haman has essentially planted. Although the Greek of most of the additions appears to be a coarse "translation Greek" that adheres closely to its Semitic language original, the text of Artaxerxes' decree and the corresponding rescinding decree at the end are both composed in a much better Greek, definitely not translated from a Semitic language.[45] They are, in fact, quite pretentiously and rhetorically composed in perhaps the highest-level Greek in the entire Greek Bible. It is likely that these two additions were composed in the sophisticated Greek city of Alexandria in Egypt (note also the colophon of the final addition). One sentence will suffice to capture the tone of the first decree: "Since I (Artaxerxes) have come to rule over many nations and subdued the entire world, I have resolved—not invoking the full power of my authority, but exhibiting throughout a kinder and gentler spirit—

---

[44] In addition to Xenophon, see *Leucippe and Clitophon* 1.3, *Daphnis and Chloe* 1.7, and *An Ethiopian Story* 1.18. On the mock-apocalyptic in addition A, see Fox, *Redaction,* 129–30. Fox's interpretation of the additions is in general quite correct, I believe, though he discusses their *theological* meaning more than their *literary* function: "The purpose of the interpretation [of the dream, which comes in addition F] is not to give a message about the future, but to *give meaning to the past* [italics his] by setting it in the context of a higher reality." True, but this is also the case for prophecies and oracles in Greek novels. We must think about these themes both as theology and as the wish fulfillments of popular entertainments.

[45] In addition to having been composed in Greek, these two additions are also the only ones to which Josephus does not refer in his *Antiquities.* These two pieces of evidence might be used to suggest that they were late and not yet added to Josephus's text. However, it has been plausibly argued that Josephus would have good reason to omit them: they do not solicit the good opinion of Gentiles, which his book was attempting to do. See Moore, *Esther,* 154, 166.

to insure that my subjects can lead their lives in every way untroubled by cares and hardships, to promote harmonious social relations throughout the kingdom, to guarantee freedom of travel to the edges of its borders, and to restore the peace that is the hope of all people." (13:2) Here we have before us one sentence, quite long, constructed with typically Greek subordinate clauses and utilizing as well a very rhetorical gesture, the magnanimous disavowal of one's authority, which could otherwise be imposed. As noted in Chapter 1, the literary letter is a device at home in the novels, for instance, in the *Alexander Romance,* and there too it is sometimes written in a better Greek than is the rest of the work.[46] Here the decree appears to perform a similar function. One could argue that elevated diction is used because it is the language of the king, but this is not a sufficient explanation. Many kings in the Bible speak and write in monosyllables. The reason, rather, seems to lie in the new issues of additions B and E, which both utilize this more sophisticated rhetoric.

The content of the decree sets up a very painful situation for Jews, which had been stated somewhat differently in Hebrew *Esther.* Haman's justification for the persecution of all the Jews of Persia presents standard anti-Jewish arguments in both Hebrew *Esther* and the Greek addition, but there is a development between the two texts that probably mirrors the refinements in anti-Jewish propaganda of the period. In Hebrew *Esther* Haman states that Jewish law keeps its adherents separate (and presumably antisocial) and opposed to the king's laws (3:8).[47] In the Greek addition B, however, the author skilfully states the position of Haman (reflected in the king's decree) in even greater detail, so skilfully, in fact, that it becomes almost credible. Haman is known to the king for his loyalty and "unshakable good will" and has advised the king that his policy of bringing peace and harmony to the empire is hampered only by the obstinacy of the Jews: "Since we understand that this nation alone stands in constant opposition to all people, rejecting established laws in favor of a strange and foreign way of life, and is contemptuous of our administration, to the extent that they have committed the worst sorts of evils in order to keep the harmony of our kingdom from becoming a reality" (13:5). The utopian scheme of the king of Persia, aided in every way by Haman, is much more positively stated than in Hebrew *Esther* and is held up as a goal to which every

---

[46] This quality of the *Alexander Romance* was pointed out to me by Gregory Nagy of Harvard University.

[47] See the very subtle analysis of Fox, *Character and Ideology,* 47–51.

reasonable person would strive to attain, and yet, as in Hebrew *Esther,* the laws of Jews necessarily press them to oppose it. Jews are contrary and hostile to the good order that all other people universally desire. In addition, in the next few lines of the decree several new themes are introduced, specifically, that Jews possess a "strange and foreign way of life" and that they commit nefarious acts to disrupt the present harmony. A strong array of charges, couched in a very eloquent critique of religious particularism—the list is probably not original, however, but is identical to the typical list of anti-Jewish calumnies that were current in Egypt in the Greco-Roman period. Although many of the pagan authors who comment on Judaism in the ancient world were positive or mixed in their regard for Judaism, there is one period and location in which pagan views become consistently negative. The Greek authors writing in Egypt in the first century B.C.E. to the first century C.E. pass on a series of unrelievedly negative attitudes about Jews and uniformly mention their obstinacy and antisocial hostility (themes beginning to be expressed in Hebrew *Esther*) but also their origins in a foreign superstition and their crimes against humanity (which are lacking in Hebrew *Esther* but find full flower in this addition).[48]

The question here, of course, is whether the author of this addition is so convincing in creating a foil because he or she is in reality ambivalent about the position of a particularist ethnic minority in a stridently universalistic society. Excellent Greek is used here to express an ideal that had been attractive for generations: conforming to the one universal standard of the *oikoumene* ("entire civilized world"). Philo, a roughly contemporary Jewish philosopher residing in Alexandria, chided some of his coreligionists for considering their tradition a philosophy, while they ignored the particular outward observances of the Jews (*Migration of Abraham* 89–93). One wonders also whether there is a parallel between the ambivalence of Jewish social life in Alexandria and in, for example, nineteenth-century Europe. The latter has been well researched and its negative effects given a name, "Jewish self-hatred." In Europe, Jews who were active in urban society were caught between the demand for civilized behavior as an Enlightenment ideal and loyalty to Jewish tradition. As Sander L. Gilman explains, "Self-hatred arises when the mirages of stereotypes are confused with realities in the world, when

[48] References to Jews by ancient authors have been collected by Menahem Stern, *Greek and Latin Authors on Jews and Judaism,* 2 vols. (Jerusalem: Israel Academy of Sciences and Humanities, 1974, 1981). This material has been analyzed and interpreted by John Gager, *The Origins of Anti-Semitism* (New York: Oxford University Press, 1983), 35–115.

the desire for acceptance forces the acknowledgement of one's difference."[49] Scholars of modern Jewish self-hatred focus on the linguistic
dual world of Jews, that is, their sense of having a second, hidden language in society.[50] To be sure, Jews in Egypt may often have been ignorant of Hebrew (as were many Jews in nineteenth-century Germany),
but the emphasis on the nature of language as reflective of the ambivalence seems equally applicable to our ancient example. The fact that
the decree was written in a sophisticated, rhetorical Greek indicates an
ability to control the medium of the civilized language. Furthermore,
the ambivalence that surfaces here will be resolved in the counterdecree
of addition E. In a sense, the two decree additions are the natural culmination of the theme that was constant in the court narratives for several
centuries: Jews can excel and ultimately succeed in pagan culture. Here,
however, the success may come at the price of an uneasy awareness of
differences and embarrassment over religious particularism.

Each expansion of the Esther tradition created a more complicated
and potentially fragmented narrative, but in Greek *Esther* the experien-
tial center of the work is in additions C and D, the prayers of Mordecai
and Esther and Esther's audience before the king. One of the effects
of the additions is therefore to move—once again—the "center" of the
book, first from *Esther* 6 (*Mordecai/Haman Source*) to *Esther* 4 (*Esther
Source* and Hebrew *Esther*) and now to these additions (Greek *Esther*).
Addition C, the prayers, serves to represent more explicitly the piety
of the two protagonists.[51] The insertion of prayers is quite common in
the literature of this period; we found it above in the Greek translation
of *Daniel* 3, where the long *Prayer of Azariah and the Song of the Three
Young Men* is added, and other examples were given there. It was also
noted there that the use of prayers to reveal inner piety was already
increasing in Jewish texts in the early postexilic period. Such a tendency is consistent with the development of internalizing psychology
in the Hellenistic period and the depiction of emotion; thus we have a
number of converging influences on the prayers in this addition. The
Greek novels include a number of eloquent prayers to the gods that

[49] Sander L. Gilman, *Jewish Self-Hatred* (Baltimore: Johns Hopkins University Press, 1986),
4. See also John Murray Cuddihy, *The Ordeal of Civility: Freud, Marx, Lévi-Strauss, and the Jewish
Struggle with Modernity,* 2d ed. (Boston: Beacon, 1987).

[50] In addition to Gilman, see Salo Wittmayer Baron, *A Social and Religious History of the Jews,*
16 vols. (New York: Columbia University Press, 1952–1976), 7:8–10, and Paul Wexler, "Jewish
Interlinguistics: Facts and Conceptual Framework," *Language* 57 (1981): 99–149.

[51] For all their differences, the two targumim to Esther are interesting in also including
prayers for the protagonists at this point.

reveal inner piety (compare Heliodorus 8.9), but this same function is more likely to be communicated in prayers of separated lovers to each other (for example, Chariton 2.11). Although the alternative version of Greek *Esther,* Greek A, was described above as attesting an *earlier* version of the Esther story, it also contains some novelistic touches that are lacking in Hebrew *Esther,* specifically, the inclusion of Mordecai's internal psychological and emotional states (8:16). Mordecai's revelations about his own motivation in not bowing before Haman constitute an important indicator of the transition from oral story-telling techniques to novelistic concerns.[52]

The separate prayers of Mordecai and Esther strike a number of different chords, and it is important to remember that they have different narrative and character-revealing functions. Mordecai's prayer begins as a resounding hymn of praise to an all-powerful God whom no one can resist. Mordecai informs the God "who knows all things" why he had not bowed before Haman. It is of course we, the audience, who are being informed that Mordecai would be willing to "kiss the souls of Haman's feet" if it would save Israel and that he did not bow because he could not "set human glory above the glory of God." Parallels can be drawn here with the contemporary Jewish martyr accounts of *Second Maccabees* 6–7, where Jews are given opportunities to save other Jews but refuse to cheat God of the divine glory. The symbolic acts—bowing to Haman, on the one hand, or eating pork, on the other—suddenly assume immense importance, in the latter case understandably so. Antiochus IV Epiphanes had, in fact, imposed just such tests in the persecution of the Jewish religion that gave rise to the Maccabean Revolt.

Esther's prayer is quite different. As is often the case in the Jewish novels of this period, the tribulations of the heroine are explored fully, as a reflection of the audience's sense of vulnerability. Unlike Mordecai, Esther, "having been gripped with a deathly anxiety, took refuge in the Lord." Where Mordecai's prayer begins in broad, universal theological assertions, her prayer contains a more personal appeal to God: "Help me, I who am all alone, and have no helper but you, for my life is in mortal danger" (14:3–4).[53] Her beauty, long emphasized and only made more spectacular through the use of the world's most expensive cos-

---

[52] See chapters 1 and 3. Text and translation of the Greek A text is found in Clines, *Esther Scroll.*

[53] Recall from Chapter 3 that Bow and Nickelsburg ("Patriarchy With a Twist," 128) detected precisely this distinction between public and personal petitions in regard to Tobit's and Sarah's prayers.

metics, must be stripped away. Simply taking off her beautiful robes and jewelry and putting on garments of mourning will not do; she must undergo a profound psychological experience of self-abnegation. Before she prays, she must take off her beautiful royal garments, put on clothes of mourning, and smear ashes and dung on her head instead of her perfumes: "She thoroughly humbled her body; every part, in whose adornment she had once taken such delight, she now covered with her tangled hair." In the Hebrew version it is Mordecai alone who rends his clothes and puts on sackcloth and ashes (4:1), and although he is carrying out an act of ritual mourning, he does not debase himself as Esther here is said to do. The debasing of her beautiful garments, her perfume, her head, her body, her hair—in other words, every part of her that the reader would likely associate with her sexuality—is all the more striking in comparison with the following chapter, where she reverses this entire process in order to beautify herself to enter into the king's presence. As we shall see in Chapter 5, Judith, who lived in a state of ritual mourning for her dead husband far beyond what was required, also adorned herself to appear before the pagan king. In both cases the woman has a "true" identity in ritual mourning, even debased in terms of her sexuality, but also a "false" persona that she presents to the pagan king: beautiful, erotic, sexual. In *Esther,* however, the implications of this debasing of the woman's sexuality is carried further. In her prayer but not in Mordecai's, the background history of the Jews' predicament is given: "But now we have sinned before thee, and thou hast handed us over into the hands of our enemies, because we glorified their gods." Her state of sexual debasement is penance for past sins. The reader sees a hero in Mordecai but a penitent in Esther. Mordecai intones the rulership of God, while Esther humbles herself so that the reader can experience a pious self-abnegation and penitence through her.

Her prayer has contained a plea for God's help in delivering the Jews from their oppressors, but it ends on a note of her own vulnerability: "Save me from my fear!" Prayers of all sorts appear increasingly in the Jewish literature of the postexilic period, but the personal concerns of Esther indicate clear parallels to the novelistic literature of the period. "Let this be the undoing of all things—fear, danger, anxiety, hope, love," says the hero of Heliodorus's novel (2.1). The centrality of emotions, even the surfeit of emotions, marks both the Greek novels and the Jewish novels. Esther's prayer scene, where her inner and true self is revealed, is a fount of emotions turning to God in vulnerability and penitence. Just as Mordecai informed the God who knows all things of the motive of his upright act, so Esther informs the God who knows all things that she "abhorred the bed of the uncircumcised and of every foreigner." But "abhor" is an ambiguous word. Did she *reject* and *refuse* the bed of the uncircumcised, or did her "public self" have sex with the king? It is certainly implied that she did, but the God who knows all things presumably knows this as well. At any rate, she abhors her crown, which she consigns to her public self: "I abhor the sign of my nobility, which I wear upon my head on the days when I appear in public. I abhor it like a menstruous rag, and I do not wear it on those days when I am at leisure." Her "inner self" has had no joy except in the worship of God. In one thing only does she merge her inner and outer self: she refuses to eat at the king's table or drink the wine offered to gods; that is, she remains kosher.

The extent of the separation of roles for Esther and Mordecai is much greater in these additions than in Hebrew *Esther,* and it raises again the question posed in Chapter 1: Is the psychological introspection and penance explored in the "debased" scene of Esther a foreshadowing of Jewish and Christian asceticism? Christianity, by retaining the additions, also kept at its disposal a theological affirmation of a wide separation of the true, inner self from the morally questionable public self. Not all movements and periods within Christianity could be so characterized, but it was a fundamental principle that was widely influential. Judaism ultimately rejected both the additions (more perhaps because they were not known in a Semitic language) and the psychological dualism they imply.

Addition D describes the reappearance of Esther's public self, but it is a public self with a mission. We see here further narrative touches that are paralleled in Greek novels. Esther has prayed for three days and, at the end of this period, takes off all of her clothes of mourning and dresses once again in her beautiful garments—simply "royal garments" in Hebrew *Esther*—just as Judith and Aseneth will beautify themselves after their scenes of mourning. Dressing in new garments has obvious significance as a symbol of transformation and has many parallels in ritual, such as the new garment of Christian baptism,[54] or in the symbolic world of the Gnostic *Hymn of the Pearl,* where a new knowledge and identity is symbolized by new garments. Another parallel example that is quite useful for our purposes is that of Heliodorus's *Ethiopian*

---

[54] Margaret R. Miles, *Carnal Knowing: Female Nakedness and Religious Meaning in the Christian West* (Boston: Beacon, 1989), 24–52, esp. 36, 40.

Story 10.9–11. Here the hero and the heroine, Theagenes and Charikleia, must undergo a test of chastity, which is to step onto a gridiron that scorches the feet of anyone who is not chaste: "[Charikleia] produced, from a little pouch she was carrying, her Delphic robe, woven with gold thread and embroidered with rays, and put it on. She let her hair fall free, ran forward like one possessed, and sprang onto the gridiron, where she stood for some time without taking any hurt. . . . In her magnificent robe she seemed more like an image of a goddess than a mortal woman." The robe marks Charikleia's special status when her chastity has been tested, much as did Aseneth's bridal gown (see Chapter 6), but Esther's clothes are perhaps more ambiguous. Charikleia's robe marks her pure and true identity, whereas Esther's beautiful garments mark her public identity. Her pure and true identity is more marked by the garments of mourning and ashes and the dung in her hair. The same irony is present in Judith: her beautiful garments are her *false* identity; her mourning garments are her chaste and *true* identity. Yet Esther and Judith both take on their beautiful garments of false identity for a mission, and, in a sense, they are marching forth for God. Despite the different interpretations placed on the significance of the robes, the Greek novels and the Jewish novels utilize the new garments for a symbol of identity, and both also tie it to chastity, even if the Jewish examples will explore this relationship with various ironic permutations.

The ironies of Esther's characterization in the additions do not end there but are pressed further. In addition C, she has just prayed for help from God, specifically to give her courage to speak in order to change Artaxerxes' heart (14:13; cf. 14:19, 15:2). But no sooner does she enter the king's chambers than she faints at his awesome splendor! We see this surprising irony used elsewhere in novelistic literature of the period. In *Acts of the Apostles* 18:9–10, Paul is told by God not to fear in Corinth, because no harm would come to him, although two verses later he is set upon by opposing Jews. In both *Acts* and *Esther,* what appears on the surface as an abandonment of divine aid works ultimately to a providential end. The full force of this irony in Esther has actually been building. Mordecai and Esther have both emphasized the power of words. Mordecai asks God not to destroy "the mouth of those who praise thee." Esther says the evil partisans of Haman "have placed their hands upon the hands of their idols and vowed to destroy what thy mouth has ordained . . . , to muzzle the mouths of those who praise thee . . . , and to open the mouths of the nations to sing the praises of their vain gods." The open mouth for Esther appears to be more an instrument of her "inner self" for the praise of God. Her beauty and de-mure femininity suffice as instruments of her public self, with no need to rely on persuasive words whatsoever:

> Resplendent in appearance, . . . she took her two maids with her. On one she leaned gracefully for support, while the other trailed behind her, carrying her train. Blushing in the full bloom of her beauty, her face seemed bright and cheerful, as though she were basking in her love's af-fection; within, however, her heart was frozen with fear. . . . The king lifted his face, flushed with the power of his bearing, and glared at her in anger. The queen in turn swooned, turning pale and faint, and collapsed upon the maid at her side. God then changed the spirit of the king to gentleness; he sprang from his throne in alarm and took her in his arms until she came to.

Esther's prayer for the courage to speak appears now to be answered. Artaxerxes embraces her and says, "I am your brother. . . . Speak to me." She responds, "You appeared to me, lord, like an angel of God, and I was stricken to my heart with fear of your splendor." Before she can address the king with her petition, however, she faints again. The addi-tion concludes here, and the story continues with the text of *Esther* 5:3, in which Esther (now revived) makes a request for the king and Haman to come to her banquet. In addition to the wrenching prayer of Esther, therefore, the additions have also added the theme of Esther's exquisite sensibilities when she approaches the king. The difference from Hebrew *Esther* is significant. There she dresses in *royal* garments and *stands;* in the additions she dresses in *beautiful* garments and *faints*.[55] Although I noted in the Introduction the parallels between this heroine and the Gothic heroine of a later century, here I would point out the more contempora-neous literary similarities that can be found in the Greek novels. When Chariton's heroine, Callirhoe, now a slave, comes before the nobleman Dionysius to make an impassioned plea (2.5), her reactions are similar to Esther's:

> Callirhoe blushed and bowed her head. "This is the first time," she said in a low voice, "that I have ever been sold. . . ." "I told you she wasn't a slave," said [Dionysius], "and in fact I predict that she will turn out to be of noble birth. Tell me everything, lady; first, your name." "Callirhoe,"

---

[55] Fox notes the significance of the Hebrew Bible presentation of Esther's new show of strength (*Character and Ideology*, 67–68, 261, 264).

she said—Dionysius liked her very name—and then she fell silent. Dionysius persisted in questioning her. "Sir," she said, "please do not make me talk about what has happened to me. What happened before is a dream, a fable. Now I am what I have come to be—a slave and a foreigner." As she spoke, tears ran down her cheeks, though she tried to avoid attention. Dionysius too was moved to tears, and so were all those present.

The heroine of the Jewish novel, as well as that of the Greek novel, is recognized for her beauty and modesty but not (at this point, at any rate) for her speaking ability. The nobleman in each example reacts positively, drawing the heroine under his wing. The character of the king in Greek *Esther,* in fact, has evolved remarkably; no longer a drunken and fickle monarch as in Hebrew *Esther,* he has become an imposing, awe-inspiring presence whose heart is touched by God, and in the process his disposition becomes that of a benevolent protector. His words to Esther that he is now her "brother" (15:9) would appear strange, but we have seen this expression in *Tobit* and will also see it again in *Joseph and Aseneth.* It is often used of a husband, as the word *sister* is often used for a wife, and in the Jewish novels it seems to be a blanket term for family relationships that can apply equally to the nuclear family or to the extended family. In the Jewish novels it is always a warm, affective term that cements the bonds of the family. Its use here then raises more acutely the problem of Esther's marriage to a Gentile. She has just stated in her prayer that she abhorred her marriage bed, yet the king here is moved to a positive relationship with her. The novelistic effects here—especially considering the parallel with Chariton above—have perhaps overwhelmed the logical considerations of the plot, but it is also possible that the two additions (that is, the prayers and the appearance before the king) derive from two different hands representing divergent points of view.

We now turn to the fifth addition, addition E, which is the text of the counteredict rescinding the judgment of the first. Its style is as elevated as that of addition B. In addition to canceling the order of the first decree, it contains a number of remarkable points. Artaxerxes essentially lays blame for his destructive policy against the Jews on the guile of Haman, who had betrayed the trust that the king had placed in him. He states that Mordecai had in fact been "our savior and perpetual benefactor," an important use of language that should not escape our attention. Savior and benefactor (*soter* and *euergetes*) were very public terms for the role of the patron of a city, common in inscriptions and the public language of the Greek and Roman cities. The role of the patron is played up a great deal in other Jewish novelistic literature, particularly the historical novels (see Chapter 7). For now, we can simply note that the grandiose tone of addition E is matched with a very high-minded and weighty role for Mordecai. Furthermore, the calumnies against the Jews that were so impressively presented in the first decree are here countered, resolving the problem of allowing the charges to hang so threateningly—and convincingly—before the reader: "Now we find that the Jews, who were consigned to total destruction by this thoroughly scurrilous villain, are guilty of no crime whatsoever but live their lives governed by most righteous laws, being children of the mighty, the living God Most High, who has maintained our kingdom in its perfect harmony, both for our ancestors and for ourselves" (16:15–16).

The only legal basis for the response to the anti-Jewish charges is the Roman legal principle that, in the event of riots, the state should find against the party that instigated the violence,[56] but this law is not invoked here at all. The former accusations are not actually rebutted but are simply seen to be misguided. Jewish law is not evidence of misanthropy or a contrary lifestyle but constitutes a set of "most righteous laws," which, all appearances notwithstanding, are not particularistic at all; they are the inspiration of "the mighty, the living God Most High," and all social harmony rests on God's guidance.

Also remarkable in the counterdecree is the insistence that Haman was a Macedonian (that is, a Greek) and not a Persian (16:10). We need not worry that this fact might have antagonized the Greeks in Egypt; they would not likely have been reading *Esther*. It does, however, underline a common view among Jews in the Greco-Roman world that the countries to the east, especially Persia and its successor states, are probably more accommodating. The natural alliances that sometimes grew up between the western Jews and the eastern nations, not least during the periods of Jewish rebellions, is probably reflected here.

The last addition, F, is placed at the end of the story and provides a new conclusion. Now Mordecai remembers the awesome dream he had at the beginning of the narrative (addition A) and realizes that each symbol stands for one of the characters of the recent events: the spring that becomes a great river is Esther, the two dragons are Haman and Mordecai, the nations are the ones who try to destroy the Jews, and

---

[56] Robert F. Stoops, Jr., "Riot and Assembly: The Social Context of Acts 19:23–41," *Journal of Biblical Literature* 108 (1989): 79–80.

the one nation that calls out to God is Israel. The tone of triumph, certainly not lacking in Hebrew *Esther,* is nevertheless expressed a bit differently: "The Lord performed great signs and wonders, which have never been wrought among the other nations. For this reason he made two lots, one for the people of God and one for the nations. These two lots came at a day and hour of decision for God among all the nations, and God remembered his people and judged in favor of his inheritance" (10:9b–11).

The effect of the additions throughout has not been to make the story more miraculous or manipulative in its effects but to render it more pious, to tone down some of its excesses. The same is true here. The sense of triumph is unrestrained in Hebrew *Esther,* yet here and elsewhere in the additions, a moral message is conveyed that tries to bring the entire narrative under the rubric of one theme: "This is Israel, who cried out to God and were saved" (10:9).[57] In regard to the question of the focalizing subject, however, in Greek *Esther* Mordecai reasserts himself to some extent, where his subjectivity dominates several of the additions: he has a premonitory dream at the beginning of all the events that will transpire, and he interprets their meaning at the end of the narrative. Perhaps because the additions have been composed by different hands, they present a rather extreme oscillation of point of view: Mordecai and Esther alternate as exclusive focalizing subjects of the narrative.[58]

The Development of an *Esther* Novel

At this point we can now consider the versions of the Esther/Mordecai narratives in the order of their development. At the top of the proposed stemma was the oldest form of the story, the *Mordecai/Haman*

[57] See Fox, *Redaction,* 130.

[58] The alternation of focalizing subjects is not impossible within a text written by a single author, but the extent of the shifting points of view in the Esther tradition, from Haman to Esther to Mordecai and back again, is quite unusual and is attributable, I believe, to different hands at work over a long process. However, for an opposing perspective, see Berlin, *Poetics,* esp. 43–55, on multiple points of view in biblical narrative. If focalization is broken down into the many different perceptions or perspectives of a scene, then almost every character can become a focalizing subject, but only for minute amounts of time, and for our purposes it becomes trivial. Bakhtin is referring to this process when he says that every character inhabits a "zone"—but we are more interested here in establishing a *protagonist,* the focalizing subject who is not just perceiving but also making moral decisions.

court conflict, which was tightly constructed around the opposite fortunes of a wise courtier, Mordecai, and a foolish one, Haman, wherein one rises at court as the other falls and one falls as the other rises. It was similar in genre and length—to the extent that the length can be determined—to other court narratives of the Persian period, and it likely circulated at first without any novelistic embellishments. This narrative was then expanded by the addition of a female character, Esther, who provides a counterpart within the palace to Mordecai within the court, and a subplot that extends the threat from Mordecai to all the Jews of Persia. Though greatly expanded beyond the *Mordecai/Haman* story, this version still lacks many of the embellishments of Hebrew *Esther,* as well as the motif of the Purim celebration. This document, which I termed *Esther Source,* is thus closer to the palace intrigues that were common in Persian tradition. Other than the addition of a female character, which palace intrigues and even biblical literature allowed for, there is little at this level that would be characterized as novelistic. Although this stage, like the one before it, is only hypothetical, in this case a Greek version of *Esther,* the Greek A text, is similar at many points, suggesting that they are roughly parallel stages in the development of the Esther tradition.

The next stage is the *Scroll of Esther* in the Hebrew canon. The changes in the narrative at this stage vis-à-vis *Esther Source* are quite dramatic, involving the introduction of the Purim festival, the court descriptions, the exaggerated revenge, and the turn to a farcical tone, but it is not clear whether these changes can be classified as "novelistic." Niditch, for example, points out that Hebrew *Esther* is peopled with characters from the indexes of folk literature,[59] and this is true, but the question here is, How are they rendered? Niditch recognizes in the mixed style of *Esther* an occasional literary treatment of folk themes; I would emphasize this more strongly. If we begin, as we did in the Introduction, with the one criterion that seems to dominate novelistic literature, the surfeit of emotions, then Hebrew *Esther* appears perched on a breakthrough into the new genre. Haman's emotions are certainly displayed (chapters 3 and 6), but they were present in the earliest stages of the *Mordecai/Haman Source* and are not in themselves sufficient. What is key is the exploration of the emotions of the protagonists, especially insofar as they express the sympathies of the audience to the character's vulnerability. This is what we find in the character of Esther in chapter 4. The emotional turmoil is presented in a rudimentary form, but it heralds a significant

---

[59] Niditch, *Underdogs and Tricksters,* 127–35.

change in the character. What might have been one-dimensional characters are sometimes drawn in with greater depth: the development of Esther's resolve, the malleability of King Ahasuerus, the continuing self-delusion of Haman. We can perhaps sense here an experiment in novelistic writing and the new core around which the other elaborations constellate. Furthermore, the interweaving of various distinct voices, all in dialogue, which Bakhtin posits as the sine qua non of the novel, is present in Hebrew *Esther,* and the carnival atmosphere and parodic intent of the work only solidify this connection.

Greek *Esther* proceeds to add novelistic embellishments of a different sort. Mordecai's dream now inaugurates the narrative with a tone of magic and high adventure, and the king's edict places a stylized Greek pronouncement before the reader's eyes.[60] The woman character is now unquestionably brought forward as a focus of the audience's vulnerability, and her inner emotional states, now more extreme, are described fully. She is possessed of romanticized femininity and sensibilities, especially in her vision of the great Persian king, and her gentleness and God's guiding hand ultimately allow her to reverse the chain of threatening events. The experience of reading this version, specifically the surfeit of emotions, is identical to that of the Greek novels. It is precisely this latter connection, however, that indicates a falling-off of the novelistic spirit Bakhtin would have championed. The Greek novel, for Bakhtin, flirted with novelistic experimentation but depended too throughly on plot contrivances to motivate the narrative, and characterization and the interplay of voices collapsed. Other modern critics also note this unfortunate predominance of plot over character.[61] Most of the additions to *Esther* likewise undercut the bold experiments of Hebrew *Esther;* the former are more novelistic in some respects but reduce the interrelation of the characters' voices: characters have visions, pray, faint, and so on, but the relationship of voices is lost to these more dramatic effects. We find fewer instances of the artistic manipulation of style, that is, the distancing of the reportage from the author's own

[60] The tendency to attribute either historicizing or pious motives to the redactors is often, I believe, incorrect. Moore asserts that the purpose of the decrees is to provide a note of greater authenticity (*Daniel, Esther, and Jeremiah,* 153). Rather, the literary effect is probably a stronger motive for including it, if "authenticity" is desired at all. Likewise, Fox depicts the editing of Greek A as a dialogue between a redactor and an "authoritative" text, canonical Greek *Esther* (*Redaction,* 93). It was not likely that the question of the authority of the texts arose at this early stage. The versions were merely competing editions on the popular market.

[61] Scholes and Kellogg, *The Nature of Narrative,* 99.

perspective. Only in the rhetorically composed anti-Jewish decree and its refutation in the counterdecree (additions B and E) do the additions provoke reflection in the reader on the interplay of voices. And these two additions, we should recall, were written by a different author from the others.

The very rich Esther tradition can thus be described as a stream of development, with the latter stages reflecting an increasing number of novelistic adaptations—granting, of course, that we probably possess only a partial sampling of the versions that circulated in ancient times. It would be methodologically naive to suppose that novelistic developments proceed in neat, easily observed steps; the experimentation of popular novelistic forms is much too chaotic for that. The stages of the Esther tradition that we examine here, whether hypothetical sources or texts that actually exist, are merely the points in the line of development that have survived as grist for our discussion. There is much that is chaotic among them, and yet the overall direction of the Esther tradition clearly reflects a development or evolution. The parallels to the Greek novels indicate the common purposes of the two corpora of texts, but the discussion need not be limited to comparisons with the literary techniques of the Greek novels; we should also observe the birth of the novel in the myriad independent or indigenous experiments of the Esther tradition, which in some cases, as in Hebrew *Esther,* may represent important developments in narrative art.

CHAPTER 5

The *Judith* Novel

The story of Judith and her decapitation of the Assyrian general Holofernes is well known in Western religion, art, and culture, but few realize that this famous climactic scene is only a brief moment in what is actually a more lengthy work. *Judith* is, for example, twice as long as *Esther* and half again as long as *Tobit*. Because the story is quite long-winded about establishing the final dramatic situation, many commentators who admire the artistry of the second half of the story deprecate the first. A. E. Cowley set the tone for subsequent literary-critical opinion: "The book is thus about equally divided between introduction and story proper. The former is no doubt somewhat out of proportion, and the author dwells at rather unnecessary length on the military details. In spite of these defects of composition, the literary excellence of the work is universally recognized even through the uncomely disguise of the Greek translation."[1] Toni Craven has shown, however, that the overall design of the author was missed by Cowley and others and that a large array of literary parallels and catchphrases in parts 1 and 2 create a carefully composed diptych of studied contrasts.[2] Chapters 1–7 depict the campaigns of Nebuchadnezzar, incorrectly depicted as king of Assyria, and his general Holofernes as they close in on Judaea and the Jewish town of Bethulia. Chapters 8–12 introduce Judith as the one who will save her town and all of Judaea by a bold plan. The two halves

---

[1] A. E. Cowley in *Apocrypha and Pseudepigrapha of the Old Testament*, ed. R. H. Charles, 2 vols. (Oxford: Clarendon, 1913), 1:242–43.

[2] Craven, *Artistry and Faith in the Book of Judith*.

of the work reflect a descent/ascent pattern characterized by opposites. The first half focuses on male non-Jews who are caught up in military campaigns. The foreign armies are approaching Judaea and imposing a stranglehold on outlying Jewish villages. In the second, Judith—a Jewish woman, whose name means "Jewess"—enters the scene and saves the day single-handedly. "Once Judith takes the stage in chapter 8," says Craven, "she shares it with others but surrenders it to no one."[3] Though Holofernes and Judith are the opposites whom we see, each stands for a higher figure: Holofernes for Nebuchadnezzar, Judith for God. Thus, overarching the many smaller opposites in parts 1 and 2 is the one grand contrast: Who is to be worshipped as a god, Nebuchadnezzar or the god of the Jews?

The patterning that Craven has detected in the work consists of more than just paired contrasts found in the two halves. Contrasts and parallels within each half are also arranged in a carefully plotted pattern of matched pairs:[4]

First half
A. Campaign against disobedient nations; the people surrender (2:14–3:10)
B. Israel is "greatly terrified"; Joakim prepares for war (4:1–15)
C. Holofernes talks with Achior; Achior is expelled (5:1–6:11)
C.′ Achior is received in Bethulia; Achior talks with the people (6:12–21)
B.′ Holofernes prepares for war; Israel is "greatly terrified" (7:1–5)
A.′ Campaign against Bethulia; the people want to surrender (7:6–32)
Second half
A. Introduction of Judith (8:1–8)
B. Judith plans to save Israel (8:9–10:9a)
C. Judith and her maid leave Bethulia (10:9b–10)
D. Judith overcomes Holofernes (10:11–13:10a)

C.′ Judith and her maid return to Bethulia (13:10b–11)
B.′ Judith plans the destruction of Israel's enemy (13:12–16:20)
A.′ Conclusion about Judith (16:21–25)

Despite the fact that a careful literary strategy is indicated on the author's part, the artistic achievement should not be judged solely in terms of such structural patterns. Rather than artfully bringing forth more

[3] Ibid., 62.
[4] Ibid., 60–63.

profound human issues, they may appear somewhat contrived (as is the irony at times) and artistically limited. The exuberance of *Judith* is hardly bound by such patterns, however, and the literary achievement perhaps resides elsewhere, as we shall see.

The genre of the first half of *Judith* appears at first to be history, modeled on the histories of the earlier biblical books, but it is actually truer to the novel genre, with self-mocking historicizing pretensions. The length, first of all, seemingly out of all proportion to the "main" part of the story, alerts us to the play of some literary motive other than historical reconstruction of the past. The construction of the first sentence, in fact, with a long and bombastic relative clause, serves to frame with great fanfare a personage, Arphaxad, whose only role is to be defeated by a *greater* personage (who never really existed), Nebuchadnezzar of Assyria:

> In the twelfth year of the reign of Nebuchadnezzar, who ruled the Assyrians from his capital in Nineveh, Arphaxad was reigning over the Medes from Ecbatana—it was he who erected a great wall around Ecbatana, made of hewn stones, each five feet thick and nine feet long, the wall constructed from them being a hundred feet high and seventy-five feet thick, and the towers, placed at the city gates, each standing a hundred and fifty feet high and ninety feet thick at the base, while the gates of the city were a hundred feet high and sixty feet wide, allowing his battalions to march forth with his infantry in full formation—so it was during that time that King Nebuchadnezzar made war against King Arphaxad in the great plain along the border of Ragau.

Craven goes on to catalog all of the historical absurdities in this section and rightly notes that the reader would have seen in it the stage setting for a fanciful work of fiction.[5] The pseudohistoriography of this section is paralleled as well by the pretensions of geographical details:

> They marched from Nineveh three days to the plain of Bektileth, making camp near there at the mountain north of Upper Cilicia. Holofernes then proceeded into the hill country with his entire army of infantry, cavalry, and chariots, totally destroyed Put and Lud, and plundered the people of Rassis and the Ishmaelites from the edge of the desert, south of the land of the Cheleans. Following the Euphrates and proceeding through Mesopotamia, he laid waste all the fortified cities along the Wadi Abron

[5] Ibid., 65–74.

as far as the sea, and from there he marched to Cilicia and occupied that region, destroying all those who came out to meet him. (2:21–25)

Some of the geographical sites are unknown (Bektileth, Rassis) or incorrectly described (the distance from Nineveh to Upper Cilicia cannot be traversed in three days). The geographical details are thus as fanciful as the historical, and the lists of nations in Judith are probably intended to be as comical as they sound to modern readers. A similar list of nations occurs in the *Alexander Romance* with similar effect, when Nectanebos, the last king of Egypt, hears that his country has been invaded: "It is not just one nation that is advancing upon us but millions of people. Advancing on us are Indians, Nokimaians, Oxydrakai, Iberians, Kauchones, Lelapes, Bosporoi, Bastranoi, Azanoi, Chalybes, and all the other great nations of the East, armies of innumerable warriors advancing against Egypt" (1.2). This list is particularly interesting for our purposes because the exaggerated tone is the same and also because the same military invasion may have inspired both this author and the author of *Judith*. The *Alexander Romance* is referring to the attack of Artaxerxes III Ochus of Persia, who made two major expeditions against the West in 350 and 343 B.C.E. It is likely that the author of *Judith* also writes with a historical memory of this invasion, because the names of two of the generals under Artaxerxes' command, Holofernes and Bagoas, also appear in the book of *Judith*.[6]

The impression that one usually takes from the first seven chapters is that they are totally taken up with the military conquests of Nebuchadnezzar and Holofernes, which gradually choke off all hope of rescue for the Jews. These chapters, however, are actually mostly talk, and they reveal on closer analysis just how the illusion of the biblical history genre is maintained in the service of a well-wrought novel. Chapter 1 certainly establishes the sweeping drama and threat of the expansions of Nebuchadnezzar's reign, but all the military expeditions that follow are seen to be motivated by a dramatic consideration: the nations have ignored Nebuchadnezzar's summons to join him in war against Arphaxad, and the great king's fury has been ignited against them. The entire "history" that follows is caused by the dramatic reverberations of Nebuchadnezzar's fury (a theme encountered already in *Daniel* 1–6, albeit with a different "Nebuchadnezzar"). Chapter 2 focuses on the

---

[6] Pfeiffer, *History of New Testament Times*, 294; Nickelsburg, *Jewish Literature Between the Bible and the Mishnah*, 108.

palace discussions of how Nebuchadnezzar's plan of revenge will be enacted, and the impending threat is now represented indirectly: threatening decrees, marshaling of troops, long marches, and only *then* battles, which are actually described very briefly and in summary fashion. The clouds of dust rising from Nebuchadnezzar's expeditionary forces are described more prominently than the actual scenes of battle. Though all of the other nations sue for peace and accept Nebuchadnezzar's rule with celebration (*Judith* 3), the Jews gather in consternation and prepare for siege. The ensuing calamity creates a grim resolve in the Jewish people; their fasting and prostration consume most of chapter 4, but the unrestrained, even exaggerated description is probably not meant to be taken wholly seriously. Surely a humorous tone is indicated by the fact that all the characters, including the children, are clothed in sackcloth, as are the cattle (4:10).[7]

Chapter 5 slows the narrative exposition of the campaigns even further as Holofernes asks the Moabites, the Ammonites, and the Canaanites who these Jews are. Once again we find stylized, dramatic scenes and orchestrated parallels and contrasts to the last half of the story. The Moabites, Ammonites, and Canaanites are all hated enemies in Israelite history and have been chosen here to represent the nations who have gone over to Nebuchadnezzar's side. The Ammonite leader Achior is then introduced, borrowed from the ancient Near Eastern tradition of the wise courtier Ahikar, who figures also in *Tobit*.[8] Achior recounts Israelite salvation history and becomes a spokesperson for a position that will be expressed again by Judith at 11:9-15: if the Jews are loyal to their god, they are invincible. He is wise—his name was associated with the *Story of Ahikar*—but this wisdom is not attributed to him directly; it is shown by the course of his actions. After forthrightly describing the power of the Jews and their god to Holofernes, he is banished to Bethulia, the city of the Israelites, where he converts to Judaism (14:5-10). Israel is thus glorified in his mouth, and he is the only *active* character on the Jewish side other than Judith. There is an obvious irony in the fact that he, a non-Jew, speaks up for Israel and is more steadfast than the Jewish males. As a male alter ego, he is something like Barak, who aids Deborah in *Judges* 4.[9] Most interesting, however, is the fact that

---

[7] Craven, *Artistry and Faith,* 115-16. The covering of animals with sackcloth at *Jonah* 3:8 was probably perceived as humorous as well.

[8] On Achior in *Judith* as Ahikar, see Haag, *Studien zum Buch Judith,* 32-33, and Henri Cazelles, "Le personnage d'Achior dans le livre de Judith," *Recherches de Science Religieuse* 39 (1951): 125-37. On Ahikar in *Tobit,* see Chapter 3.

[9] White, "In the Steps of Jael and Deborah," 10.

his dialogue with Holofernes is subject to the same kind of irony as Judith's exchange with Holofernes a few chapters later. He prefaces his account of who the Israelites are by saying that no lie shall pass from his lips (5:5). This statement is not ironic, but it is in almost the same words that Judith will later utter to Holofernes (11:5), and *she* will be lying.[10] The irony is completed when Holofernes rejects Achior's advice and banishes him to the camp of the Israelites: "You will not see my face again until I take vengeance on this race of people who came out of Egypt!" (6:5) Indeed, the reader of *Judith* will find that Achior does see Holofernes' face again, but only after it has been severed from the rest of his body. As the noose is tightening around the Jewish village of Bethulia near the end of the first half, geographical details are once again paraded out, forming an *inclusio* for the overture to Judith's story:

> The army of the Ammonites set out with five thousand Assyrians and pitched camp in the valley; from there they seized the springs and wells belonging to the Israelites. Then the Edomites and the Ammonites went up and pitched camp in the hill country opposite Dothan and sent some of their troops to the south and to the north in the direction of Acraba, near Chusi on the Wadi Mochmur. The rest of the Assyrian army encamped in the plain, covering the face of the earth. Their tents and supply train were spread out about them in one vast encampment, for the size of the army was huge. (7:16–18)

Contrary, then, to the former consensus, the first half does provide a crucial function in the book. A number of very important narrative themes are developed, albeit slowly. In the second half we find the response to this portentous threat. Whereas the first half involves a sweeping movement of vast numbers of troops and peoples across much of the then-known world, the second is precisely focused on the hill town of Bethulia and the plain below it. The shift is abrupt but effective. Judith is introduced and described as a widow of extraordinary beauty and piety. She condemns the elders of Bethulia for giving up hope and preparing to capitulate to Holofernes, and she sets about her plan to save the city. As in the other novels, here too the heroine engages in the acts of ritual grief and mourning. She puts ashes on her head and uncovers the sackcloth that she was already wearing in mourning for her dead husband (or perhaps takes it off; the Greek is not clear). She prays fervently to God and then proceeds to bathe and make herself up in her

---

[10] Craven, *Artistry and Faith*, 54, 95.

most beautiful clothes and finest makeup, in order to "bewitch the eyes of as many men as might see her." (10:4) Thus, as in Greek *Esther,* there is a scene of private piety and transformation as she leaves her former state (mourning for her husband), ritually defiles herself with ashes, and then reenters the world of the living "dressed to kill." The admiration of her beauty is on everyone's lips, and as these observations reach a crescendo, Judith makes one last bow to God and orders the gates to be opened. The scene is described with an almost cinematic eye:[11] "Judith and her maid went out, and as they proceeded, the men of the city watched her closely until she had descended the mountain and passed out of sight" (10:10).

Her encounter with Holofernes is described with a deceptively deft hand. The pacing is quite controlled as she instantaneously arrives at the camp, only to be ushered around for two and a half chapters to allow everyone to react to her beauty. When she finally attains her audience with Holofernes, her dialogue is laced with irony. Judith addresses Holofernes with fawning and flattering words, but the audience understands her real meaning: "And if you follow the advice of your servant, God will accomplish a great deed through you; my lord will not fail in his plan." (11:6) Holofernes understands "my lord" as referring to Nebuchadnezzar (or possibly to himself), but in Judith's private conspiracy with the audience, it refers to God. Holofernes is duped by her flattery and verbally plays into her hands a few verses later, unknowingly predicting his own end: "God has done well in sending you from your people so that control may fall into our hands, for death will be the lot of those who ridicule my lord." The irony extends beyond simple plays on words, however, and is ubiquitous in the climactic section. Considerable interest is maintained by the disparity between Holofernes' designs on Judith and what the audience knows will happen. He is trembling with excitement, thinking he is about to perform his manly duty (12:16), but six verses later he has passed out on his bed, impotent and defenseless. Six verses beyond that, he is dead. The decapitation itself is quick and bloodless:

> Stepping up to Holofernes' bedpost, she took down the sword hanging beside his head, and turning toward him, she lifted his head by the hair. "O Lord God of Israel," she prayed, "give me strength!" Then she

---

[11] Alonso-Schökel, *Narrative Structures in the Book of Judith,* 7. Hägg notes this same cinematic quality in Heliodorus (*Novel in Antiquity,* 55–56).

struck him twice in the neck with all her might, severing his head from him. She then rolled his body off the bed and took the curtain from its poles. Pausing but a moment, she stepped outside and handed the head of Holofernes to her maid, who placed it in her food pouch. The two of them then proceeded out, as if to pray, just as they had done in the past. (13:6–10)

After she has decapitated Holofernes and returned to her village, the frightened Assyrians are sent scurrying by the emboldened Jewish warriors, and peace and order is restored to the land. Judith frees her handmaiden, retires from all contact with society, and lives out her days in confinement on her estate, as if she has taken on the life of a cloistered nun. Like *Joseph and Aseneth,* this narrative suggests a certain relationship to the ascetic life, but the only ascetic Jews that we know of from this period would not seem to fit this document. The Essenes at Qumran were sectarian and anti-Jerusalem, but *Judith* is strongly pro-Jerusalem (9:1, 15:8–9, 16:18–19). The Therapeutae, a group of communitarian Jews who lived in the Egyptian desert, would not likely have had much interest in such a militaristic and pro-Jerusalem rally to arms. It is possible, however, that asceticism is not just a practice of a small elite who withdraw from society but an ideal whose implications can be contemplated by desert practitioners and comfortable urban Jews alike.[12] Asceticism is a state of mind and a worldview that came to have an overarching role in Greco-Roman culture. As such, asceticism may exist in a purely idealized, fictional context. This "narrative asceticism" may be reflected in the world of Jewish novels and in the world of Greek novels as well. We shall return to this question in Chapters 6 and 8.

Biblical Allusions in *Judith*

The *Book of Judith* is a rich tapestry of biblical traditions and allusions, all interwoven so smoothly as to betray no seam. Many scholars have traced the biblical parallels;[13] I will not repeat this process here in

---

[12] The many issues that revolve around asceticism cannot be resolved in this chapter or even in this book. In regard to the important recent article by Fraade, "Ascetical Aspects of Ancient Judaism," I would note here that I am not simply trying to broaden the range of what should be considered ascetical *practices* but would focus on *ideals* as well, ideals that may not have had any correlation in actual practice.

[13] Dubarle, *Judith,* 1:137–62; Haag, *Studien zum Buch Judith,* 118–24; and Nickelsburg, *Jewish Literature,* 106–7.

full but instead focus on some of the most important examples. The central, overwhelming image of the *Book of Judith,* the decapitation of Holofernes, is paralleled very closely by Jael's assassination of Sisera, the general of the Canaanite king, in *Judges* 4–5. *Judges* 4 and 5 are actually a prose narration and a poetic narration of the same event. In the prose narration, Deborah, a prophet and judge, exhorts Barak to take the field against Sisera. Sisera's army is routed, but Sisera himself runs to the tent of Jael, the wife of Heber the Kenite, and seeks refuge. She admits him, offers him milk, and covers him with a rug. When he falls asleep, she takes a tent peg and drives it through his temple.

The direct parallel is the execution of the general of the mighty foreign power by a woman using a blow to the head,[14] but other parallels can be drawn between the characters of Deborah and Judith. Deborah, not Jael, controls the course of events and, acting in faithful trust in God, admonishes Barak to go to war. This role is very similar to Judith's, and the admonishing of Barak can be compared to Judith's urgent address to the elders of Bethulia. The list of lesser motifs paralleled in the two narratives can be drawn out and is sufficiently long to indicate that the author of *Judith* is probably making conscious use of the story as found in *Judges.*[15] *Judith* emphasizes gender roles and reversals more than do *Judges* 4 and 5, but the same ironies are certainly present in both.

The next most important biblical tradition being played upon in *Judith* is *Genesis* 34, the revenge of Simeon and Levi for the rape of their sister, Dinah. Judith refers explicitly to this incident when she prays for courage to perform likewise (9:2–4), and Judith's lineage is also traced through Simeon's children (8:1) and thus by extension through him back to Jacob. The resonances between the two passages are fascinating. In *Genesis* 34, Dinah, the daughter of Jacob, is raped by Shechem, a Canaanite, who nevertheless appeals to his father to arrange a marriage between them. Jacob restrains himself until his sons return, and though incensed, they institute a great deception. Their condition for intermarriage between the groups, they say, is that every male of the Canaanite city be circumcised. All the males agree and are circumcised, but while they are still sore, Simeon and Levi sneak into the city, slay all the males, and take Dinah back to their land. In the *Book of Judith,* the heroine calls upon God to grant her the vengeance God granted to Simeon for the

---

[14] The motif of the humiliating death at the hand of a woman is found also at *Judges* 9:50–55 and is perhaps implied at *Second Samuel* 20:14–22.

[15] White, "Jael and Deborah."

rape of Dinah, emphasizing the degradation of Dinah and the extent of the vengeance and capture of booty, including wives and children. Both *Judith*'s retelling of the story and *Genesis* 34 focus on the gathering of the males to avenge the family honor. Although Simeon's and Levi's slaughter is questioned in *Genesis* 34 and condemned outright in *Genesis* 49:5–7, it is seen as a positive example here, as elsewhere in postbiblical Jewish tradition.[16] Although the deceit of Judith is often compared to the ruses of biblical women such as Rebecca (*Genesis* 27) and Tamar (*Genesis* 38),[17] it is actually closer in some respects to this story of the sons of Jacob. Here it is stated that they dealt deceptively with the enemy (34:13), and the violence and revenge are similar. Judith rightly adduces this precedent for a violent response to aggression. Although Judith notes that she is but a widow, figuratively it is Israel who has been raped, and she will act as the avenging male clan member.

Date and Place of Composition

As with many of the novels here under study, reconstructing the time and place of writing is difficult. Many scholars have tried to associate the campaigns depicted in the first half with historical campaigns, but this goal becomes ephemeral when the historical personages in the story are presented so cavalierly. The chief royal power is given an impossible title: "Nebuchadnezzar, king of Assyria." Nebuchadnezzar was king of the Neo-Babylonian Empire, which succeeded the Assyrian Empire as a major world power in the late seventh century B.C.E. Furthermore, *Judith* 4:3 states that the Jews have returned from captivity and the temple has been resanctified; the resanctification postdates both the Assyrians and Nebuchadnezzar. Holofernes and Bagoas, as noted, are names found in the lists of generals involved in the campaign of the Persian king Artaxerxes III Ochus against Phoenicia and the Jews in 353 B.C.E., but as Nickelsburg and others suggest,[18] traditions from the

---

[16] Morton S. Enslin and Solomon Zeitlin, *The Book of Judith* (Leiden: Brill, 1972), 122. We note especially that in *Joseph and Aseneth,* Simeon's violent spirit is not condemned, although it is nevertheless controlled by Levi's wiser counsel. Dubarle notes (*Judith,* 140) that *Jubilees* 30, in recounting the same story, agrees with Judith in blaming all the foreigners, not just Shechem.

[17] Dubarle, *Judith,* 140–42. On the motif of the deceptive woman in biblical tradition, see Chapter 1 above.

[18] Nickelsburg, *Jewish Literature,* 108–9; Pfeiffer, *History of New Testament Times,* 292–95; and Enslin and Zeitlin, *Book of Judith,* 28–30.

Persian era have likely been adapted in a story written in the Maccabean period, around the middle of the second century B.C.E. "Nebuchadnezzar, king of Assyria," in that case would make sense as a cipher for "Antiochus, king of Syria" or for any of the belligerent Syrian kings after the Maccabean Revolt, since both Nebuchadnezzar and the Syrian kings were arch-foes of Judah and since Assyria is likely taken to represent Syria, as it does elsewhere. The evidence that strengthens a Maccabean dating is found in the campaign of Nicanor, a general sent by the Syrian king Demetrius I to dethrone Judas Maccabaeus. When Judas defeated Nicanor and killed him, he beheaded him and displayed his head in Jerusalem (*First Maccabees* 7:47). The reconsecration of the temple and vessels, so out of place in *Judith,* is now seen to evoke the similar reconsecration recounted in *First Maccabees* 4:36–51. These similarities certainly indicate that Judith is playing on the memories of victory over this invading general. If a date in the Maccabean period is accepted, then *Judith* depicts the "Jewess" turning the tables on Holofernes—read Nicanor—in a celebration of national victory.

History of Interpretation and Feminist Analysis

Recent feminist analysis of Judith has been very successful in adumbrating the sexual undertones of the novel, but there has not been agreement on a most important question: To what extent does the work project a "feminist" consciousness? The fact that Judith behaves "like a man" has intrigued many. Patricia Montley points out the androgynous nature of Judith, but it is an androgyny unlike that of most mythological androgynes; she is not composed of male and female attributes simultaneously but moves from one to the other and back again.[19] Judith, in fact, begins and ends in a reclusive, chaste state that would seem at first to be neither male nor female as she withdraws from normal gender roles.[20] In the course of the narrative, she passes through a traditional male role in upbraiding the weak-willed citizenry, then a traditional female role in seducing Holofernes, and then once again a male role in decapitating him. Her final state is closest to a female role, devoted to the memory of her dead husband. Montley sees this as a positive depiction of Judith's role: "In her marvelous androgyny, Judith embodies yet

[19] Montley, "Judith in the Fine Arts." Her article is summarized in Moore, *Judith,* 65.
[20] Cf., for example, the chastity of Aseneth before she encounters Joseph; see Chapter 6.

somehow transcends the male/female dichotomy. To this extent, she is a heroine who rises above the sexism of her author's culture."[21] Others— for example, Nickelsburg and Elisabeth Schüssler Fiorenza—would see at least implicit in Judith a symbol of a woman's potential power.[22]

Two folklorists, however, Mary P. Coote and Alan Dundes, relate the narrative of Judith to the common tale type described by Antti Aarne and Stith Thompson as the Faithful Wife (type 888).[23] The tales that reflect this type usually involve a chaste wife whose husband has been captured by a mythical beast or foreign army. The wife must disguise herself as a man to rescue her husband and secure the safety of her people. The same narrative pattern can be found both in epic versions and in tales. Although Judith's husband is dead, she is symbolically married to Israel (hence her name "Jewess"), and it is Israel that is captive. Rather than disguising herself as a man, Judith dresses in her finest and most provocative clothes and jewelry and proceeds to "act the man." Coote joins others who would question the feminism of this projection: "It is often patriarchal societies, where male and female roles are sharply distinguished and women have a passive role, that in fantasy produce myths of a female savior."[24]

The depiction of Judith's unusual character, which has elicited such strong and contrasting reactions in the West, must be seen in the light of projections of women in imaginative narrative. Folktales often contain strong and positive depictions of women, characterizations that bear no relation to the ways that women really live their lives. This phenomenon has been noted in a very interesting way in Warren S. Walker's and Ahmet E. Uysal's study of contemporary oral traditions in Turkey.[25] In the tales they have collected, there is often a *"khoja* girl," with spiritual or magical qualities, who is a Muslim priestess, a role forbidden to women in Islam. "Occasionally in folktales," they suggest, "there is a toying with the notion of a female religious leader in Islam, an idea characterized by the same attraction-repulsion syndrome that informed the

21 Montley, "Judith," 40.

22 Nickelsburg, *Jewish Literature*, 108, and Schüssler Fiorenza, *Bread Not Stone: The Challenge of Feminist Biblical Interpretation* (Boston: Beacon, 1985), 148. Craven (*Artistry and Faith*, 121) seems to be intrigued by the possibility but hesitates at a clear endorsement.

23 Their responses are found in Alonso-Schökel, *Narrative Structures*, 21–29. Antti Aarne and Stith Thompson, *The Types of the Folktale*, 2d ed.) Helsinki: Suomalainen tiedeakatemia, 1964).

24 Coote in Alonso-Schökel, *Narrative Structures*, 26.

25 Warren S. Walker and Ahmet E. Uysal, *Tales Alive in Turkey* (Cambridge: Harvard University Press, 1966), 260.

Pope Joan legend in the West." One might suspect—and, indeed, it has been suggested—that these Turkish tales were transmitted by women, and reflected a wish fulfillment that resulted from restricted roles, but the Turkish tales were actually collected by the authors among men who were sitting in coffeehouses.[26] It is more plausible to posit for Judith a similar "attraction-repulsion syndrome" that can be played out in male fantasy life.

This is not to suggest that the gender construction is simple and without ambiguity. Amy-Jill Levine describes the process of this novel as the deliberate confusion and reversal of categories.[27] Judith, a surpassingly beautiful woman, is separated from normal family relations by the fact that she is a widow. Yet she is not simply in mourning; she has extended the usual period of mourning to three and a half years, and thus, despite her beauty, she is more separated from normal female social roles than is necessary—and by choice. Her separation extends to her praying alone on her roof but at times that coincide with the prayers offered by the priests in the temple in Jerusalem. "Close to the deity in spirit and in physical location," notes Levine, "she is removed from the people both religiously and spatially."[28] She stands up among her people and rebukes the male leaders, critiques their theology, and eventually moves single-handedly out of the city into the enemy camp to slay their leader. The constant reversals at every step subvert the proper role for woman in society, but after this liminal-period reversal of roles, is stability returned in the form of patriarchal order? Levine appears ambivalent: "All that remains of the intrusion of Judith's otherness into the public realm is her 'fame' (16:23). That is, her deed becomes incorporated into public memory and public discourse, and it is thereby controlled. Yet each time her story is told, this woman who represented the community as well as exceeded that representation, will both reinforce and challenge Bethulia's—and the reader's—gender-determined ideology."[29] Closely related to the theme of reversals is Judith's inability to reintegrate into society: "Only by remaining unique and apart can Judith be tolerated, domesticated, and even treasured by Israelite society."[30] Here we may perceive a typical heroic paradigm in which the protagonist, who can perceive the danger to his or her people and save them from formi-

26 Walker and Uysal, *Tales Alive in Turkey,* 2.
27 Levine, "Sacrifice and Salvation."
28 Ibid., 22.
29 Ibid., 28.
30 Ibid., 24.

dable enemies, is never truly able to integrate into society and must pass away on the other side of danger, unable to participate in the society's celebration of the return of peace.

The provocative ambiguities in the text also elicit a trenchant feminist analysis by a literary critic, Mary Jacobus.[31] She focuses mainly on important historical perceptions of Judith. The central image of the *Book of Judith*—a beautiful seductress who tempts a great general, gets him drunk, and then chops off his head—proved much more unsettling in the modern period than it had earlier. Freud, in particular, focused on the story as a classic enactment of castration anxiety on the part of Holofernes and penis envy and the virginity taboo on the part of Judith. Freud was strongly influenced by Friedrich Hebbel's tragedy *Judith,* which was typical of a late European understanding of Judith. Hebbel's (and thus Freud's) retelling of the story of Judith includes several important changes from the Apocryphal book. First, Judith was not just a chaste widow, as in the ancient version, but was, in fact, a *virgin* and a widow, since her husband, Manasseh, was possessed on their wedding night with a strange anxiety and never consummated their marriage before his death. Second, rather than remaining a cool-headed manipulator of events, in Hebbel's version she was first *raped* by Holofernes, and her gruesome deed is as much an act of psychosexual revenge— and a wild attempt to compensate for the female's inadequacy, which springs from penis envy—as it is political or religious. Jacobus analyzes paintings of the decapitation scene from the sixteenth century on which display a variety of views of Holofernes' state at death. One, Horace Vernet's *Judith and Holofernes,* shows Holofernes asleep and fulfilled, content in his drunken state *and* evidently sated in his indulgence of his sexual appetites with Judith; another, Michelangelo Caravaggio's *Judith and Holofernes,* seems to take the perspective of Holofernes, where at the moment of death he looks not upon the beautiful Judith but on Judith's old, severe handmaiden, as if to suggest that this is Judith as she really is. In Hebbel's play and Freud's rendition of the narrative, Judith's heroic gesture is viewed uneasily, even as a threat, while Holofernes' perspective becomes more and more identified with that of the audience.

Jacobus also notes a bizarre sidelight on Hebbel's and Freud's interpretation in the recent rediscovery of a woman artist of the same period as Caravaggio, Artemisia Gentileschi, who *was* raped at the age of eigh-

---

[31] Jacobus, "Judith, Holofernes, and the Phallic Woman."

teen and who later painted similar paintings of both Jael's killing of Sisera and Judith's killing of Holofernes. The slayer in both cases resembles the artist herself, and it is not difficult to perceive a sense of revenge and psychological resolution in the stony, determined faces of the young women in these paintings. Gentileschi's artistic "revenge," however, does not in any way invalidate Jacobus's central observation: Freud, following Hebbel, *invented* a scenario in which the saving of Israel from a foreign enemy was subordinated to a sexual relationship between two people that could only be played out in rape and revenge.[32] The fact that this recast scenario is realized in the art of an actual rape survivor, who works out a sort of psychological resolution in her paintings, merely serves to emphasize once again the potential in Judith for a continuous turnabout in gender roles. The book, as Levine noted, has an eerie ability to set off a chain of surprisingly deep and complex psychosexual reactions that defy explanation and compartmentalization. Seen in comparison to these later interpreters, the character of Judith in the Apocryphal book seems naively ebullient and heroic, the "triumph of morality and innocence over force," as Jacobus describes it.[33] Putting aside, however, the fascinating modern transformation of Judith, we must still ask what the roles of the "castration" scene and the "phallic woman" are in the earlier period. A female wish fulfillment perhaps springs to mind, but Jacobus also notes that acting out the drama of castration can reassure the *male* psyche that the phallus is potent and remains in possession: "Representations of the phallic woman protect the viewer against doubts about his masculinity. Making her (Judith) like a man conserves the small boy's narcissism, his belief in the universal power of his phallus. . . . Becoming phallic, Judith embodies a fantasized creative potency."[34]

A similar debate can be traced in regard to Judith's mirror narrative, Jael's assassination of Sisera in *Judges* 4–5. The arguments are so similar, in fact, that it is helpful to consider their applicability to *Judith*. Susan Niditch has brought Freud's categories to bear on a discussion of *Judges* 4–5 and notes the sexual undertones in regard to that scene.[35] Citing Robert Alter's depiction of *Judges* 5 as a parody of the rape of captured women and an "aggressively phallic" assassination, she asserts that Jael

[32] This invention is quite ironic, of course, in light of Freud's theory that women who recounted stories of being sexually abused as children were fantasizing the experiences.
[33] Jacobus, "Judith," 118.
[34] Ibid., 127–28.
[35] Niditch, "Eroticism and Death in the Tale of Jael."

becomes the aggressor, raper, and despoiler: "A man is not rendered womanish by another man, but is despoiled by a woman. He, in a pose to make love [Sisera lies between her legs], is felled by her."[36] Niditch also considers whether female power and castration here may reflect a male concern, "a man's fear of both death and his own sexuality, his insecurities, a male fantasy of Eros become Thanatos [death]."[37] She questions Jo Ann Hackett's characterization of *Judges* 5 as a "very female piece of literature"[38] but still allows an opening for a positive feminist reading of *Judges* 5: "One is not suggesting that women become men-slayers in some simple-minded reading, but rather that the tale is rich in images of directed action, self-assertion, and consciousness on the part of the underdog. The archetype expressing on many levels male anxieties can thus become a powerfully charged model for all marginals, in particular women."[39]

Despite the fascinating parallels between *Judith* and *Judges* 4–5, we must take full cognizance of the differences as well. The reversal in *Judges* is portrayed as a directive of the Lord, a turn of events that could not have been manipulated by human power alone and that is convincingly presented as a cause for unexpected joy and thanksgiving. In *Judith,* the outcome is much more mechanically handled. There is no real experience of doubt or contingency on the part of the reader, all of Judith's protests to the contrary notwithstanding (8:11–17). Correspondingly, it is interesting to note that in *Judges* Sisera is killed by Jael only after he is already defeated. He collapses on the floor of Jael's tent a defeated man, defeated on the field through the commands of a woman and now begging to be comforted by another woman, who will drive a stake through his head with a caress. The irony here communicates a poignance that borders on tragedy, compounded even further in the poetic version of *Judges* 5. There we find a sudden change of scene to the room of Sisera's mother as she, ignorant of the fate that has befallen her son, speculates as to what booty he has taken that has delayed his return so long. In *Judith,* however, Holofernes is no tragic figure, and Judith, striding out

---

[36] Niditch, "Eroticism and Death," 51. Alter's works are *Art and the Nature of Biblical Poetry* (New York: Basic, 1985), 43–49, and "From Line to Story in Biblical Verse," *Poetics Today* 4 (1983): 129–37.

[37] Niditch, "Eroticism and Death," 51–52.

[38] Hackett, "In the Days of Jael," 32–33. Hackett's characterization could more appropriately be applied to *Ruth,* but in her defense, *Judges* 5 is "a poem whose entire focus is the lives of women." Deborah, Jael, and Sisera's mother dominate the poem, even though they may be male projections.

[39] Hackett, "In the Days of Jael," 53.

to the plain, is stylistically presented as someone who does not need God in her plans. This point is, interestingly, one at which *Judith* differs from the other novels. In both *Esther* and *Judith,* a woman is relied upon to save the Jewish people, but unlike Esther, Judith is implacable and invulnerable and knows what she will do. The buffeting of the protagonists that characterizes the Greek and Jewish novels is not present. It could be argued that she is merely a strong, independent woman, a literary character we are not used to seeing. She is strong, however, in a way few male heroes are. They have faults and shades of gray; she is more like the holy man of legend or, ironically, the trickster—always in control.

There is also something more to the sexual imagery than has been described before, that has remained subliminal even to those investigators who have gone looking for it. The "phallic woman" and symbolic castration of Holofernes are not the full extent of the sexual imagery. In the ancient world, the ideology of hierarchy that prevailed in male/ female relations was also accompanied by the notion that the male role in sexual intercourse—penetration—was considered honorable, while the female role—to be penetrated—was considered a part of women's lower status.[40] Homosexuality, for example, when criticized, was not condemned equally for all involved. It was generally considered more humiliating for a male to be penetrated than to penetrate, whereas for a woman to assume a dominant role, rather than a passive "female" role, with another woman was considered an even more monstrous aberration of sexual boundaries. Even where homosexuality was accepted in principle, hierarchical distinctions based on active versus passive roles were imposed. This distinct valuation of the penetrator and the penetrated comes to play in Judith. Alan Dundes points out that the reversal of Judith and Holofernes is not only depicted in the decapitation scene; it has been prepared for us all along. The name of Judith's mountain town is Bethulia, which, as many commentators note, may mean "virgin" or "young woman." The pass to this town is narrow, and it is this pass that Holofernes is attempting to penetrate. The sexual imagery is obvious, and as Dundes puts it, "Judith penetrates Holofernes' camp rather than Holofernes penetrating [the Jews'] city."[41]

[40] Bernadette Brooten, "Paul's Views on the Nature of Women and Female Homoeroticism," in *Immaculate and Powerful: The Female in Sacred Image and Social Reality,* ed. Clarissa Atkinson, Constance H. Buchanan, and Margaret R. Miles (Boston: Beacon, 1985), 61–87, esp. 67–68, 73, 78–79.
[41] Dundes in Alonso-Schökel, *Narrative Structures,* 28.

This interpretation seems inescapable, but it still focuses only on the phallic imagery. Even with the abundance of studies of gender roles and symbols, both feminist and Freudian, we are still much more apt to see phallic symbols than vagina symbols, yet the author of Judith has designed a depiction of reversals that includes both. It is sometimes the case that a tent is not a tent. The care and attention that is taken in *Judith* to describe Holofernes' tent suggests that there is here a clever manipulation of images to convey to the reader—whether consciously or unconsciously—that the tent is Holofernes' vagina. The tent is introduced innocuously enough at 10:20, when Judith is first led to meet Holofernes, but no sooner do we enter into it than our attention is also fixed on the mosquito net: "Holofernes was resting on his bed, inside a mosquito net that was woven with purple and gold threads, interspersed with emeralds and precious stones" (10:21). The luxurious nature of the net stands out as a curious detail. While the tent appears to represent Holofernes' vagina, the mosquito net in particular may represent his hymen. As we compare the other references to the tent and the net, this appears more likely. To begin with, it is interesting that Holofernes chooses to come out of this inner chamber into the front part of the tent to meet Judith, as if to preserve, for the moment, his inner sanctum. When Judith next reverses her feminine role to become a phallic woman, entering the inner chamber with the drunken Holofernes and cutting off his head, we find that once again the netting comes into play: "She rolled his body off the bed and took down the mosquito net from its poles. A moment later, she went out and handed over the head of Holofernes to her maid, who placed it in her food bag" (13:9). She has taken two trophies with her back to Bethulia, the head and the mosquito net. "Here is the head of Holofernes, commander-in-chief of the Assyrians!" she says upon arrival back in Bethulia. "And here with it is the mosquito net, beneath which he lay in a drunken stupor. The Lord has struck him down by the hand of a woman!" (13:15) At 15:11 Judith is awarded Holofernes' tent as booty, and at 16:19 she presents the net at the Jerusalem temple as a votive offering. The quasi-legal aspect of this last act in particular calls to mind the "tokens of virginity" (*bethulim*) in Israelite and Jewish law, whereby a young woman could be proved to be a virgin (*Deuteronomy* 22:13–21). It is Holofernes' tokens of virginity which Judith has placed before the priests.

The theme of reversal is clear, but is the net really a symbol of Holofernes' hymen and not merely of his riches and position? It could also be read as a countertrophy, being in the reader's mind equivalent to the temple curtain that Antiochus IV Epiphanes confiscated during the Maccabean Revolt (*First Maccabees* 1:22). The latter is conceivable but does not rule out the possibility of a second symbolic meaning. That the net is mentioned so often and in such detail, that it is identified with Holofernes' bed and inner sanctum, that it is closely associated with his beheading, and that it comes to stand as Judith's main trophy all argue for attaching to it a deeper significance in this psychosexual drama. The reversal is here made complete. Judith has not only castrated Holofernes; she has penetrated him, robbing him of his virginity, and has taken the "tokens of virginity" as a trophy fit for a triumphant man. The net–as–hymen renders the "manning" of Judith and the "unmanning" of Holofernes balanced symbols. The reversal that dominates this work is a male fantasy, the violent castration and penetration of an enemy, made all the more provocative and satirical by being carried out by a beautiful siren. The book is also driven from first to last by a military theme, the conquest of an enemy, and, like the dramatic situation in *Susanna,* can give rise to "permissible erotica." Scholars have noted a recurrent connection between images of sex and military slaughter in a number of ancient cultures,[42] and an overarching military justification for erotic play in art is not hard to find today. On entering Harvard University's Widener Library, one is confronted by a huge painting by John Singer Sargent dedicated to the American soldiers who died in World War I, with the inscription, "Happy those who with a glowing faith in one embrace clasped Death and Victory." A soldier is holding an obscured figure of Death in one arm, but in the other arm, dominating the viewer's perspective, he clutches a mostly nude female figure of Victory. His mouth is open, reaching for her breast. In his hand, which is placed near her vagina, he holds a bloody bayonet. If *Judith* was written after the Maccabean Revolt (as was likely the case), then it bears the same temporal and psychological relationship to its past as the Harvard painting does to its own: they both utilize permissible erotica to identify the sexual experience and a recent military victory. One may also invoke here a common tenet of feminist analysis of pornography: sexual violence directed against men may be closely related to sexual violence directed against women. If the male "viewer" witnesses a woman raped and murdered or a man castrated and murdered, the effect amounts to the same thing. It is a response to a desire for violence and power, not

---

[42] Niditch, "Eroticism and Death," 43; Emily Vermeule, *Aspects of Death in Early Greek Art and Poetry* (Berkeley and Los Angeles: University of California Press, 1979), 101–3, 145–78.

a sexual urge. Judith is pornographic, by a definition that takes a blending of sex and violence to be pornography, and is not "anti-male." It is, rather, typical of male visions of the exhilaration of sexual violence.

Perhaps the ethos of the narrative world of *Judith* can also be placed in perspective by comparing it to *Ruth*. The *Book of Ruth* has been seen by Elena Pardes (among others) as genuinely feminist. Rather than depicting a rivalrous relationship of women, such as Rachel and Leah in *Genesis,* who only have important roles in relation to their husband, the *Book of Ruth* foregrounds the otherwise secluded, women's concerns, and affirms the relationship between Ruth and Naomi: "The Book of Ruth offers an antithetical 'completion' of the limited representation of female bonding in Genesis. . . . The Book of Ruth is the only biblical text in which the word 'love' is used to define a relationship between two women. And once such love is represented, an intriguing rewriting of Genesis takes place."[43] The tendencies of modern feminist novels certainly follow in the same pattern. It would be a utopian fantasy for women to demolish the patriarchal structures that determine their lives; this outcome rarely occurs in their novels. One finds instead a strong underlying theme of the necessity for women to relate to each other. Women characters either discover each other and, in moments of understated triumph, affirm the importance of their relationship, as in Louisa May Alcott's *Work* or Alice Walker's *The Color Purple,* or fall into despair because they are isolated from each other and have only men's perspectives on the world, as in George Eliot's *The Mill on the Floss* or Charlotte Perkins Gilman's *The Yellow Wallpaper.*[44] The attempt to see a "women's relationship" between Judith and her female slave[45] must be judged a misinterpretation. This slave is never named, never speaks, fulfills unimportant narrative functions at Judith's whim; even when Judith frees her, she disappears without a personality. This slave is a nonperson. This slave is a slave.

It becomes questionable, then, whether the figure of Judith could be held up as a feminist heroine who somehow managed to survive the

[43] Pardes, *Countertraditions in the Bible,* 100–102. See also Trible, *God and the Rhetoric of Sexuality,* 195–96, but note also that Naomi is actually favored as the "true subject" of most of the narrative (so Bal, *Lethal Love,* 77–79).

[44] See, for example, Sandra M. Gilbert and Susan Gubar, *Madwoman in the Attic: The Woman Writer in Nineteenth-Century Literary Imagination* (New Haven: Yale University Press, 1979).

[45] Craven, *Artistry and Faith,* 121. The lady's favorite slave is a common narrative motif, occurring in *Joseph and Aseneth* 10.4 and Chariton 1.4; see Christoph Burchard, "Joseph and Aseneth," *Old Testament Pseudepigrapha,* ed. James H. Charlesworth, 2 vols. (Garden City, N.Y.: Doubleday, 1983), 2:215 note j.

patriarchal canonizing process, as some would seem to hold. Whether Judith *can* be reconciled with a feminist ethic is not the question. The question is, does Judith reflect a male projection or a female projection? Judith clearly reverses every socially determined aspect of feminine respectability as she comes out of mourning to beautify herself, move with cunning into the enemy's camp, lie and tempt Holofernes with her beauty, kill him by chopping off his head, and return and exhibit the head as one of the spoils of war, in the process rebuking the flaccid men of Bethulia who had despaired of success. It is true that the reversals, ironies, and broad satire appear to place accepted social rules in a shimmering, unsettled state. One wonders, however, whether it is the sheer enthusiasm of the satire, the joie de vivre that appears liberating. Judith invites the description "phallic woman" and seems to wear it with a pride that triumphs over the murmerings of male or female critics. Ultimately, however, the genie is returned to her bottle, for once she is done with her mission, she retreats to a very chaste and withdrawn position. Society has no room for her.

Moral Evaluation of Judith's Character

Aside from Freud, a host of other critics have evaluated Judith's character negatively. Criticisms have arisen concerning her lying, her sexual provocativeness, and her violence. It is interesting that her lying to Holofernes has elicited some of the harshest disapproval. An interesting representative of Victorian sensibilities is the nineteenth-century English biblical scholar Edwin Cone Bissell:

> The character of Judith . . . is not simply objectionable from a literary point of view, but even more from a moral stand-point. . . . Her way is strewn with deception from first to last, and yet she is represented as taking God into her counsels and as having his special blessing in her enterprise. . . . Indeed, her entire proceeding makes upon us the impression that she would have been willing even to have yielded up her body to this lascivious Assyrian for the sake of accomplishing her purpose. That God by his providence interposed to prevent such a crime, cannot relieve her of the odium attaching to her conduct.[46]

[46] Edwin Cone Bissell, *The Apocrypha of the Old Testament* (New York: Scribner's, 1880), 162–63 (quoted in Moore, *Judith*, 64–65).

Somewhat more muted is the criticism of certain modern scholars, for example, Wayne Shumaker, who, although he does not find Judith quite so reprehensible, does object to her lying to attain her ends. Dundes, in response to Shumaker, comes to her defense by pointing out that Judith is simply a typical trickster.[47] The appeal to the trickster category, however, does not fully explain people's strong reaction. Her dishonesty is partially criticized because of a common category mistake by which all sacred literature, including warrior literature, is "churchified"; that is, it is subordinated to the uses of an institutionalized ethic that cringes at the prospect that such a moral gambit—lying to a foreign tyrant to save one's people—might become universalized to lying to one's priest, minister, rabbi, or neighbor. But other figures lie in the Bible, including the patriarchs, and in the next chapter we shall see that Joseph lies piously over and over in *Testament of Joseph*. The moral problem here is that a pious woman lies while flaunting her sexuality. She prostitutes herself in order to castrate her would-be client.

The discomfort with Judith's use of violence is apparently also common among Christians in the modern West but does not go back earlier than about 1600. In the early centuries of the Christian era, Judith was assimilated in Christian art as a type of the praying Virgin or the church or as a figure who tramples Satan and harrows Hell. She was sometimes grouped with other violent women, such as Jael and even Queen Tomyris, who beheaded Cyrus the Great, but Judith's depiction does not reflect any anxiety or ambivalence.[48] The figure of Judith herself remained removed and unreal, separated from real sexual images and thus protected. The new sculptures and paintings that appear in about 1600, however, differ significantly. Violent depictions of the decapitation were created, especially that by Caravaggio (mentioned above), and Judith became a threatening character to artist and viewer. Contemporary with Caravaggio's violent Judith is a painting by Christofano Allori which depicts Holofernes in the likeness of the artist himself, while his faithless lover had evidently become the model of a cool Judith.[49]

[47] Schumaker and Dundes in Alonso-Schökel, *Narrative Structure*, 33, 51.

[48] In the *Speculum humanae salvationis* ("Mirror of Human Salvation"), written in 1324 by a Dominican monk, Judith, Jael, and Queen Tomyris appear together as figures of the victory of the Virgin Mary over Satan. See Robert W. Berger, "Rubens's 'Queen Tomyris with the Head of Cyrus,'" *Bulletin of the Museum of Fine Arts, Boston* 77 (1979): 4–35.

[49] Nira Stone, "Judith and Holofernes." The varied perceptions of Judith in western history would be a fruitful area for further research. I am told by Jan Ziolkowski of Harvard University that Judith's popularity among Germanic peoples in the church may reflect their desire for a martial savior figure. He also points out that the ambivalences about Judith co-

The discomfort with Judith on several levels evidently lies in the fact that she is no longer an unreal or distanced figure but has entered into our homes. In the modern era, audiences (at least male audiences) have come to see her relationship with Holofernes as evocative of their own personal relations—and quite threatening. It is perhaps in comparison with this modern anxiety that the ancient novel seems to liberate the female character from social constraints; the ancient author expresses no ambivalences about her potency.

Conclusion

In this chapter I have ventured further from questions of poetics and purely formal aspects of this novel and spent more time with the feminist and psychological aspects. *Judith* necessitates this approach. We return, however, to questions of the relation of genre and poetics. It is not surprising that the *Book of Judith* has long been compared to ancient romances. The classicist Ulrich von Wilamowitz made this connection, and from the point of view of ancient Near Eastern studies, Ruth Stiehl and Franz Altheim seconded his observation.[50] Why was *Judith* accorded this classification earlier than, say, *Esther?* Clearly the erotic element in *Judith* is felt much more intensely, especially since the possibility, even the threat, of a sexual encounter is broached explicitly. The mingling of sex and violence could hardly be more charged than here. Yet this is only part of the answer. The *Book of Judith,* pious as it is, pushes a further distance from the patterns of "sacred literature" and develops certain novelistic techniques of great importance. We saw in Chapter 2 that *Daniel* achieves its novelistic extension by combining episodes that originally circulated independently and that *Tobit* and *Esther* have likely been expanded over time by the addition of subplots. *Judith,* however, the longest of these novels, has an unusual integrity of composition. Although *Judith* reflects a fairly simple plot line, as opposed to *Tobit* (which fairly brims over with engaging plot), the one climactic scene in

---

incide approximately with the gynecocratic controversy in England and should perhaps be seen as related.

[50] Ulrich von Wilamowitz in Wilamowitz et al., *Die griechische und lateinische Literatur und Sprache,* 3d ed. (Leipzig: Teubner, 1912), 189; Ruth Stiehl and Franz Altheim, *Die aramäische Sprache unter den Achaimeniden* (Frankfurt am Main: Vittorio Klostermann, 1963), 200. See also Weimar, "Formen frühjudischer Literatur," 130, and Zenger, "Der Juditroman als Traditionsmodell des Jahweglaubens."

Judith is prepared for dramatically, with a vast historical movement and a cast of thousands, and is followed by a measured release of tension and a satisfactory resolution. The author extended the story not by duplicating plot elements or adding episodes but by drawing out the experience of a single, linear progression of rising and falling action, through the use of a stirring historical setting, description, and dialogue. Overdone as the story sometimes is, this very extension of a single plot line nevertheless constitutes a remarkable literary achievement we should in no way take for granted.

Aristotle had earlier asserted (*Poetics* 1450b–52b) that narrative should consist of a unitary, integrated, linear plot line composed of rising action and tension, a climax with a reversal of fortunes (*peripeteia*), and falling action. This pattern was only realized, however, in the Greek tragedies that Aristotle had before him. The Greek and Roman novels in some cases achieve the length of modern novels, but only by such primitive means as duplicating episodes and resorting to parallel, intertwined plots.[51] They therefore could not achieve the effect of a single, elongated expansion of rising action, climax, and falling action but were essentially episodic. Walter Ong identifies Aristotle's ideal narrative pattern as a concomitant of literate culture, as opposed to oral culture, but only achieved in prose in the modern period.[52] The goal—and the great achievement of the modern novel—is to create a huge expanse of narrative that is essentially *one* episode, with an integrated beginning, middle, and end. It is analogous to the expansion of inner space and the creation of a vaulted interior in the construction of Gothic cathedrals through the use of flying buttresses. When the supports for the roof were thus moved from the interior to the exterior, the cathedral acquired a unitary interior vision of huge dimensions, in place of the cramped, repetitive, and broken space which existed before. The Greek and Roman novels do not achieve a "vaulted narrative," but *Judith* seems to possess a sense of this ideal—primitive, to be sure, but if followed to its culmination it is the major literary achievement of literate culture. What we see in our laboratory of the Jewish novels is the transition from oral materials and techniques, through a series of literary experiments, to wholly literary effects. From *Daniel*, a "novel by agglutination," to *Tobit*, to *Esther*, to *Judith* is a march in the direction of popular literary technique. *Joseph*

---

[51] See the detailed analysis of Hägg, *Narrative Technique in Ancient Greek Romances.*

[52] Ong, *Orality and Literacy,* 142–44. It is partially this expansiveness, along with the all-encompassing realism of the modern novel, that prompts Georg Lukács to call this genre the "epic of a world that has been abandoned by God" (*The Theory of the Novel,* 88).

and Aseneth, though complicated by mystical digressions, will mirror some of the achievements of *Judith.* This is not to suggest that *Judith* somehow attains the level of internal expansion of the modern novels. It is much too short for that comparison. But the *technique* is being manipulated, and the very artificiality of *Judith,* its bloated rhetoric and contrived matched pairs in the two halves of the book, so easy to disdain from our vantage point, are actually some of the means by which the author is able to extend the reader's engagement over many pages without resorting to repeatable episodes. The bombastic style and contrived effects constitute a primitive flying buttress that allows for the creation of a vaulted narrative.

If the extension of a single plot line to novelistic length is the main technical concern of the author of *Judith,* is there a sense in which we can specify the main thematic? Is it a parable of God's dealing with the Jewish people (Ernst Haag) or a new rendering of the folktale theme of male and female reversal (Coote, Dundes, and Levine)? We would expect there to be a correlation between the technical means of the author and the major theme, and such is evidently the case. It would be simplistic to try to reduce any literary work to one "main" theme, as if others are superficial or even excluded, but at the same time, it remains a valid question as to what the principal motive force (or forces) behind a work of art is, what makes it compelling to its audience. The motive force behind the *Book of Judith* is the reversal of weak and strong, male and female, but with a further development that differentiates it from many other examples, especially Jael and Sisera in *Judges* 4 and 5. In *Judges,* Sisera is a great leader who is already fallen, defeated in battle by the forces led by Deborah, and comes before the reader as a tragic figure. We are moved by fear and pity as we witness, in the prose version, an evocation of a sexual reversal when Sisera lies between Jael's legs and, in the poetic version, Sisera's mother hauntingly awaiting the victorious return of her son, who will presumably be sated with both booty and women. The separation of the "victor" character into three agents (Deborah, Barak, and Jael) and the separation of the victory itself from the fall of the enemy both allow for a differentiated examination of the roles and the process of defeat and victory. The *Book of Judith,* on the other hand, concentrates the victor in one character, and there is no differentiation between the exaltation of victory and the fall of the enemy. A more unitary view of triumphalism pervades the work. Some scholars have insisted that Judith champions the victory of the weak over the strong.[53] There is no tension built up, however, around the heroine's (and the audience's) sense of vulnerability, as there is in *Esther* or *Susanna;* from the reader's perspective, the vanquishing of the enemy is guaranteed by the invulnerability of the protagonist. This is not just the invulnerability typical of the trickster in trickster tales or the holy man or woman in saints' legends. Those are short narratives known to us mainly through collections of episodes, which have in one case an entertaining and satirical function and in the other a hortatory one. *Judith* moves beyond oral culture usages to a new potentiality only available in literate culture: the author enlarges an episode of reversal and deliverance into one great triumph. It is a victory for all time, with propagandistic value far beyond what the collection of episodes could have provided.

[53] Alonso-Schökel, *Narrative Structures,* 52.

CHAPTER 6

Joseph and Aseneth
and the Joseph Tradition

One of the most intriguing aspects of a study of Jewish popular literature is the high number of novelistic retellings of the Joseph story that are known from the Greco-Roman period. Although it was common for different versions of the same novel to circulate (as in the case of *Esther* or *Tobit*), with the Joseph tradition we find that totally separate narrative traditions were created, all based on the biblical narrative but having little relation to one another. The general pattern of these narratives is that of midrash, or the interpretation and application of some aspect of the biblical text,[1] but each of the stories at hand focuses on a different part of the episodic *Genesis* narrative. The situation is perhaps analogous to the traditions about Daniel, except that the individual Joseph narratives are much longer and more ambitious and ultimately partake of a wider variety of literary genres.

The inspiration for these retellings, the Joseph story of *Genesis,* has often been called "novelistic" and is in many ways similar to the novelistic literature of a later period. In his 1917 commentary on *Genesis,* Hermann Gunkel had already observed that the Joseph story stood apart from the rest of the biblical sagas because of its greater length and more descriptive style.[2] Narrative details are present that would not likely

---

[1] See most recently Kugel, *In Potiphar's House;* Hartman and Budick, eds., *Midrash and Literature;* and Stern, *Parables in Midrash.*

[2] Hermann Gunkel, *Genesis,* 4th ed. (Göttingen: Vandenhoeck & Ruprecht, 1917), liii–lv. Note also the remarks by Kugel, *In Potiphar's House,* 13–14, and Niditch, *Underdogs and Tricksters,* 123–24. Von Rad considered it a *Novelle* rather than a *Sage* ("Biblische Joseph-Erzählung

have been included in the sagas, such as Joseph's washing at *Genesis* 41:14 or the dialogue between Joseph and Potiphar's wife at 39:6–18. The narrative is also greatly drawn out in relation to the other sagas, partly by the intertwining of two separate sources (usually attributed to the J and E epic sources) but much more by adroitly utilized retardation techniques, as in 40:23, where the butler forgets about Joseph's abilities and delays his elevation, or the two separate trips of the brothers down to Egypt (*Genesis* 42–44).[3] There is further the inclusion of complicating episodes. The attempted seduction by the wife of Potiphar, existing only in the strand attributed to J, is an extended subplot, unnecessary to the overall scheme of fall and rise but serving to reroute the story and draw out Joseph's progression from servitude to power. When this digression and the various trips of the brothers are all brought into the story structure, we have the effect of a succession of narrative panels, each of which is significantly long and involving.

The Joseph narrative can be differentiated from the patriarchal sagas not only by length but also by the manner in which the emotions of the characters are depicted. The question, of course, is not whether emotions are depicted but how. Novelistic writings in all cultures tend to treat the strong emotions of the protagonists openly and directly and are often accused of manipulating the emotions of the audience. To draw a contrast from outside of the Pentateuch, we note that the rape of Tamar in *Second Samuel* 13 plays on a series of intensely emotional situations but without raising the level of the diction or the description of the characters' feelings, aside from reporting that they exist. The experience of reading this scene is not necessarily less emotional from the reader's point of view, but it is presented in a restrained and suggestive way. The reader must supply the experience of the emotions, which are simply not developed in the text. Figures in classical Greek drama or classical Hebrew literature could show emotion in situations of "tragic" proportions, but emotions displayed in other circumstances, for instance, upon being reconciled to one's siblings, would not have taken on cli-

---

und Joseph-Roman") but evidently in the sense of a separate, entertaining story that is not part of a saga cycle in the sense of a German *Roman* (novel).

[3] On plot retardation in the Joseph story, see Niehoff, *The Figure of Joseph in Post-Biblical Jewish Literature*, 17–21. In noting quite minor examples of retardation, Niehoff fails to mention what is probably the most impressive example in the entire Hebrew Bible: the delay of the denouement of the Joseph story while the brothers return to their father and come back again to Egypt.

mactic significance, as they do in the Joseph story. We may compare, for example, the terser and more matter-of-fact report of the emotions displayed by Jacob and Esau upon their moving reconciliation (*Genesis* 33). The Joseph narrative focuses, more than anything else, on the emotions involved in the relationships between Joseph and his brothers.[4] This section of the story is the longest, and it is the part of the narrative that has been most retarded for effect. In Joseph the interest has shifted from the difficulty of coexistence (as in the Jacob and Esau saga material) to the ultimate necessity of coexistence and the emotional and affective bonds that would bind the brothers together. It is the kind of domestic issue that becomes the stuff of novelistic treatments.[5] In some periods of the ancient world, as is the case in the modern period as well, emotion should perhaps be seen as a value of the private life (though not necessarily hidden), especially when it concerns love relationships and the relationships of the family. The Joseph story thus shares this value with the novelistic literature of any period.

The conclusion would seem to be that the Joseph story of *Genesis* is much like the other novels—it is even about the same length—and yet it is usually dated many centuries earlier. Some scholars have argued for a much later date for the Joseph story, and because of its import for the present study, this possibility must be considered. Its usual dating in the early monarchic period (with the other patriarchal sagas) is generally based on the ascription of its two strands to the J and E epics. This assumption, however, is not without its challengers. George W. Coats and John Van Seters deny the necessity of positing two intertwined sources, the latter scholar insisting that the dating of the story (and the Pentateuch as a whole) can be brought down to the exilic period, the sixth century B.C.E.[6] Others, such as Donald B. Redford, would posit two layers in the narrative but not attribute them to the older

---

[4] Errol McGuire overstates the centrality of the father-son relationship in the Joseph story ("The Joseph Story: A Tale of Son and Father," in *Images of Man and God: Old Testament Short Stories in Literary Focus,* ed. Burke O. Long [Sheffield: Almond Press, 1981], 9–25). The father-son relationship is crucial for the genealogical thread that unites the Joseph story to the rest of the Pentateuchal narrative—and thus the narrative begins and ends with this theme—but the emphasis that now lies at the heart of the Joseph story is on the brothers.

[5] Other traits of the Joseph narrative, such as its lack of a direct and personal role for God as a character and its psychologizing, have been considered evidence of a provenance within the wisdom traditions of ancient Israel (so von Rad, "The Joseph Narrative and Ancient Wisdom"), but they may equally be related to novelistic concerns.

[6] George W. Coats, *From Canaan to Egypt: Structure and Theological Context for the Joseph Story* (Washington, D.C.: Catholic Biblical Association of America, 1976); John Van Seters, *In Search of History* (New Haven: Yale University Press, 1983).

J and E epics. As a result, Redford, like Van Seters, sees no need to date the Joseph story earlier than the sixth century.[7] Even some confirmed pentateuchal source critics allow for uncertainties when approaching the Joseph story. Frank Moore Cross, for example, has expressed some question about the neat division of the Joseph story into sources, the attribution of the parts to J and E, or the dating of either part.[8] If the Joseph story were thus loosened from its moorings in J and E, how late would it be possible to date it? It was certainly present in the Pentateuch when it was translated into Greek in about the third century B.C.E., but beyond that, the date may be relatively open. On the one hand, it retains an important function within the pentateuchal sagas, sharing many parallel themes with the Jacob cycle.[9] These would indicate an early date. On the other hand, the Joseph story is a court narrative, like *Esther, Daniel,* and other postexilic writings that may betray a Persian influence.[10] From this we derive very broad early and late limits for the work, from about the eleventh to the fourth century B.C.E. This introduces a very intriguing possibility for the study of the Jewish novel, since it effectively adds another exemplar to the same general historical epoch. However, something of a historical gap still remains. The Joseph story is a full-blown novel, and considering the necessary period of development (especially if it was composed, as I believe, of two strands), it would preexist the other novels by a good two centuries. This gap is not impossible, since the early terminus for the origins of the genre are unclear, but the Joseph story is more developed in a novelistic direction than extant Persian-era literature. Despite the fact that a very late dating would place the Joseph story closer to an era associated with the rise of novelistic experiments in the Hellenistic period, it does not place it close enough to make more than a strained connection.

The novelistic nature of the Joseph story, however, does not require

---

[7] Redford, *A Study of the Biblical Story of Joseph (Genesis 37–50),* 251–53.

[8] Frank Moore Cross, "The Epic Traditions of Early Israel: Epic Narrative and the Reconstruction of Early Israelite Institutions," in *The Poet and the Historian,* ed. Richard Elliott Friedman (Chico, Calif.: Scholars, 1983), 13–39.

[9] Coats, *From Canaan to Egypt,* passim, and Niditch, *Underdogs and Tricksters,* 93–125.

[10] Helmut Koester has in conversation pressed the possibility of a late date for the Joseph story, based on the similarity in style to Persian and Greek narratives, and these similarities are significant. The similarity with the court narrative *genre,* however, is perhaps more illusory than real. Although the Joseph story has been routinely compared to the later court narratives, as indeed I have done in *The Jew in the Court of the Foreign King* (esp. 39–74), the particular nuance of the latter—the drama of the wise courtier caught between king and other courtiers—is lacking.

us to search out a late date. The "novelistic impulse" can and does arise in different historical periods. It is just as likely that the Joseph story, whether or not the two strands are attributed to J and E, reflects an early attestation of the novelistic impulse, a development perhaps of the Solomonic Enlightenment of the tenth century or of slightly later court literature. Although I have entertained the possibility that the Joseph narrative is late, so that we may explore the significance of such a dating for the other novels, my own opinion is that it is indeed of early date and is composed of strands of the J and E narrative. It is, in my reading, more novelistic than the rest of the patriarchal narrative, but this is likely because the different parts of the biblical material have been edited and reworked by different hands; some parts now exhibit more distance from the original oral epics of J and E, some less. In the transition of the pentateuchal narrative from the oral epics, now lost to us, to written prose, the Joseph narrative came to reflect a more novelistic approach in both its J and E versions, but it was still associated with what we refer to as the J and E narratives.

For the purposes of discussion, then, we shall leave the biblical story of Joseph behind as an early novelistic narrative that lies before our present time frame. By the Greco-Roman period, at any rate, a new body of Joseph narratives are attested, indicating that Joseph must have been one of the most popular of the patriarchs for midrashic embellishment. Early Christians made surprisingly few references to him, but for Jews he appears to have been one of the most important figures.[11] He was not always conceived of as a perfectly pious figure in rabbinic literature, but in the period under study here, he is always a positive moral exemplar. Lengthy narrative versions of the Joseph story can be found in *Joseph and Aseneth*, *Testament of Joseph*, Josephus, Philo, and Artapanus.

---

[11] Early Christian literature and art do not reflect a great deal of interest in Joseph, although there is intriguing evidence of the depiction of Joseph and Aseneth in early Egyptian Christianity; see Gary Vikan, "Joseph Iconography on Coptic Textiles," *Gesta* 18 (1979): 99–108, and Claudia Nauerth, "Joseph," *The Coptic Encyclopedia*, 8 vols. (New York: Macmillan, 1991), 2:387–88. On the Byzantine-era Joseph tradition, see Alexander Kazhdan and John H. Lowden, "Joseph," *Oxford Dictionary of Byzantium*, 3 vols. (New York: Oxford University Press, 1991), 2:1072–73. Rabbinic midrashim have a tradition of an all-too-human Joseph, depicted with a series of faults. In some traditions he cooperates with Potiphar's wife, thus providing a moral reason that God would allow him to be placed in prison. In some, he treats his brothers who are sons of the handmaids Zilpah and Bilhah as slaves (a criticism that will be interesting below in relation to the *Testament of Joseph*), and in others, he is arrogant and vain. See Kugel, *In Potiphar's House*, 94–98, and Niehoff, *Figure of Joseph*. The latter trait, we note, is attributed to Aseneth in our literature but not to Joseph. Daniel, as we recall from Chapter 2, was also viewed negatively in rabbinic literature for remaining too friendly with Nebuchadnezzar.

The rabbinic midrashim and the targums also involve many interesting embellishments that may represent early traditions, contemporary with the novelistic literature analyzed here, but the embellishments themselves rarely attain the length that would qualify as novelistic. Here I will limit the discussion to the earlier, longer narratives.

Testament of Joseph

The *Testament of Joseph* is part of the *Testaments of the Twelve Patriarchs,* a Jewish document from about the turn of the era that has been supplemented at points and transmitted by Christians. The narrative sections we are examining are wholly Jewish.[12] The document presents the last words of each of the twelve sons of Jacob to their children. The deathbed speeches are hortatory, emphasizing mainly the danger of sexual sin, but the *Testament of Joseph,* unlike the others, contains a narrative as its sermon illustration.[13] This narrative, told by Joseph in the first person as he recounts some of the dramatic episodes of his life, can be divided into two parts. The first, 1.4–10.4, details the succession of attempts by the wife of Potiphar to seduce him and how he resisted; the second, 10.5–18.4, concerns the sale of Joseph by his brothers to Ishmaelite traders.[14] Even a superficial reading indicates a disjuncture between the two halves; the second narrates events that precede the first in the *Genesis* narrative. In addition, other discrepancies between the two sections can be detected that render it very likely that they were composed by separate hands. The two halves illustrate different virtues and themes: self-control (*sophrosune*) in the first and patient endurance (*makrothumia* and *hypomone*) in the second. They also present a different portrait of Joseph: strong, active, and pious in the first half; weak, taciturn and apathetic in the second.[15] The midrashic techniques that are

---

[12] Marinus de Jonge has opposed the main trend of scholars and argued that large parts of the *Testaments* are Christian (*The Testaments of the Twelve Patriarchs: A Study of Their Text, Composition, and Origin* [Assen: Van Gorcum, 1953]), but the consensus of scholars is that they are mainly Jewish, and certainly the sections under discussion here betray no sign of Christian redaction.

[13] The English translation is that of Howard Clark Kee, "Testaments of the Twelve Patriarchs" found in *Old Testament Pseudepigrapha*, ed. James H. Charlesworth, 2 vols. (Garden City, N.Y.: Doubleday, 1985), 1:219–25.

[14] Chapters 19 and 20 contain a dream vision and the testamentary conclusion, which will not be of concern to us here because they tell us little about the narrative sections.

[15] Becker, *Untersuchungen zur Entstehungsgeschichte der Testamente der zwölf Patriarchen,* 241; Braun, *History and Romance in Graeco-Oriental Literature,* 47–48, where other arguments are also

utilized in the two sections are also different. The first narrative merely
enumerates trials of Joseph by Potiphar's wife that are not specified in
the short text of *Genesis* 39:10. The latter simply reads, "And although
she spoke to Joseph day after day, he would not listen to her, to lie with
her or to be with her." In *Testament of Joseph* 1.4–10.4, these trials, ten in
number, are likely arranged in a salutary manner, similar to the ten trials
of Abraham, which we find elsewhere in the Jewish literature of this
period.[16] The second narrative, however, is relatively freer of the biblical
text, creating scenes that are nowhere mentioned there and that in fact
contradict the biblical version. The emphasis of this second narrative is
that Joseph refused to tell anyone that he was actually a free man taken
captive and enslaved, whereas in *Genesis* 40:15 he states openly that he
was "stolen out of the land of the Hebrews."[17]

It will be very important to observe the literary qualities of the two
sections. It has been noted that the first contains many typical motifs of
the Greek novels. First and foremost, the attention paid to the attempted
seductions of Joseph by Potiphar's wife reflects influence of the Greek
Phaedra legend, depicted in Euripides' *Hippolytus,* which was widely attested and copied in the Greco-Roman period and which spawned many
similar scenes in Greek novels. The *Genesis* account (39:6–12) merely
states, without providing further details, that Potiphar's wife repeated
her overtures to him, but the *Testament of Joseph* develops the psychological profile of the seductress into a stereotyped scene: "Many times she
sent messengers to me saying, 'Acquiesce in fulfilling my desire, and I
will release you from the fetters and liberate you from the darkness.' . . .
For when I had been with her in her house, she would bare her arms
and thighs so that I might lie with her" (9.1, 5). Her pleas to him are
put in many forms: threats, promises, begging. She offers to kill her
husband so that she and Joseph can rule his estate together. Similar pleas
are placed also before the heroes of the novels, such as Manto's before
Habrocomes (Xenophon, 2.5.2), or Demaenete's and Arsace's before
Knemon (Heliodorus, 1.10, 7.20, 25).[18] But beyond the presence of the
Phaedra motif, there are many other parallels with the Greek novels,

---

presented. Some would deny the need to divide the text at all. See especially Hollander,
"The Ethical Character of the Patriarch Joseph"; and Kee, "Testaments," in Charlesworth,
Pseudepigrapha, 1:819 n. 1a.

[16] Pervo, "The Testament of Joseph and Greek Romance," 18. See *Jubilees* 17–19 and *Mishnah
Abot* 5.3 on the ten trials of Abraham.

[17] Nickelsburg, "Introduction," in *Studies on the Testament of Joseph,* 6.

[18] Braun, *History and Romance,* 48.

such as the threat of suicide, the languishing in prison, the poison intrigue, the lovesickness that not only makes the woman pine for Joseph but deludes her into thinking that Joseph loves her, and the dramatic contest in general of a woman driven by lust and a beautiful young man who defends his chastity.[19] The readiness with which Joseph turns to weeping (3.6, 6.3) is also evidence of a key characteristic of novelistic literature noted above—an easy display of intense emotional states.

The unity of this narrative, along with these parallels to typical romance motifs, suggests to Jürgen Becker that this section of the narrative circulated separately and has been inserted at this point.[20] Martin Braun, on the other hand, argues that the first section is the one that is the more closely related to the other *Testaments*—in that it, like them, is concerned with sexual ethics—and is especially close to *Testament of Reuben*.[21] The theme of patient endurance, which dominates in the second section, in turn is paralleled not in the other *Testaments* but in Philo, *On Joseph*, 41.247–50, and therefore it is this section that must have been inserted. The weight of the evidence probably falls on the side of Becker, however, since the first narrative appears to have disrupted the theme of envy of the brothers that may have at one time connected 1.3 and 10.5. This question, to be sure, cannot be answered with certainty, and for our purposes, it is subordinate to a more important question: What is the genre of each section, regardless of its order of inclusion? Fortunately, the answer to this question is not difficult to discern. By dividing this testament where we have (10.5), we find that each part corresponds to a common homily structure to which I have referred elsewhere as the "word of exhortation."[22] Many Jewish and Christian writings contemporary with the *Testaments* contain what appear to be sermonic addresses, displaying a common form. First, they present a set of exempla for the listener—episodes from the past, philosophical

[19] Becker, *Untersuchungen*, 236–37; Braun, *History and Romance*, 46–93; Pervo, "Testament of Joseph," 15–28.

[20] Becker, *Untersuchungen*, 230.

[21] Braun, *History and Romance*, 47–48. His evidence is equivocal. *Testament of Reuben* 4.8–10 refers to Joseph in a way similar to the first section of *Testament of Joseph*, but it interrupts the discussion in that work and could easily have been added as an editorial layer when the first Joseph section was added in its present location. In addition, the second section of *Testament of Joseph* has its parallels in the other writings as well, for example, *Testament of Simeon*, which is also concerned with Joseph and envy.

[22] Lawrence M. Wills, "The Form of the Sermon in Hellenistic Judaism and Early Christianity," *Harvard Theological Review* 77 (1984): 277–99. See also Pervo, "Testament of Joseph," Becker, *Untersuchungen*, 230, and Collins, *Between Athens and Jerusalem*, 158–61. It was noted above in Chapter 2 that the Old Greek text of *Susanna* also partakes of this form.

arguments, or biblical quotations. Second, they draw a conclusion from this data that reveals a connecting theme in the actions of the past or in a series of biblical quotations. Third, they apply this conclusion to the listener, exhorting that person to righteous action in the future. In the case of *Testament of Joseph,* the many attempts of Potiphar's wife to seduce Joseph, and his self-control, constitute the exempla. The conclusion drawn about these exempla is found at 10.1: "So you see, my children, how great are the things that patience and prayer with fasting accomplish." The exhortation follows at 10.2–4 (although it is stated rhetorically as a condition): "You also, if you pursue self-control and purity . . . , the Lord will dwell among you, because he loves self-control."

The second section of *Testament of Joseph* also reflects this pattern: 10.5–16.5 are the exempla, this time on another theme, that of Joseph's endurance (*makrothumia*). The conclusion is at 17.1: "So you see, my children, how many things I endured in order not to bring my brothers into disgrace . . . ," and the exhortation is at 17.2: "You, therefore, love one another and in patient endurance conceal one another's shortcomings." As in many of the other examples of this sermon type, the exhortation flows into new disquisition that combines further indicatives and imperatives (17.3–18.4). Despite the disjointed nature of the writing, therefore, it could be argued that the bulk of it was composed at one time, as a sermon illustrating two separate virtues, chastity and endurance. This explanation of the disjuncture has in fact been offered before.[23] However, it is equally true that the word of exhortation form was quite common, and sermonic topoi were transmitted and recombined often, allowing for the possibility that these two halves attained their present form independently. The distinctive literary tones of the two, coupled with the fact that 10.5 can follow upon 1.3, indicate that the two word of exhortation cycles found here were not composed at the same time but were merely edited together, and other considerations below will bear this out. The outward form of the two halves, then, is sermonic and not indicative of novels, but the extent to which the

---

[23] Kolenkow, "The Narratives of the TJ [*sic*] and the Organization of the Testaments of the XII Patriarchs," 37–46, and Hollander, "Ethical Character," 47–104, both in Nickelsburg, ed., *Studies on the Testament of Joseph.* It is also indeed common for sermons of the word of exhortation type to consist of a longer address, composed of a series of repeated cycles of exempla/ conclusion/exhortation. The ending of the last cycle of the word of exhortation has likely been disturbed by the addition of the dream vision of chapter 19, and chapter 20 constitutes the conclusion of the testament, parallel to the others in the collection but of little concern to us here.

internalized psychology of the period is played out in these narratives has suggested to Elias Bickerman that the entire hortatory collection of the *Testaments of the Twelve Patriarchs* is moving in the direction of a "primitive historical novel" that was read, not preached, by Jews in the Diaspora.[24] He notes especially the typically Hellenistic analysis of internal emotional states. It is conceivable that the *Testaments of the Twelve Patriarchs* as a whole was shifting its literary function to become a popular novelistic work, and in the case of the *Testament of Joseph,* this seems especially likely. It reflects the novelistic impulse at play in transforming two sermonic topoi into popular literature.

We should not, of course, think of these two artistic forms, sermon and novel, as being irreconcilably different. The psychological interplay between liturgical and literary forms is precisely what constitutes the *Testaments.* The first section of the *Testament of Joseph* enacts in a series of narrative vignettes the ten trials of Joseph, in a manner similar to the listing of ten trials of Abraham as found in the contemporary literature. The narrative sequence is not logical as it stands, in that actions are either unmotivated or apparently out of sequential order. Potiphar's wife's attempts, for instance, to insinuate herself into Joseph's affections by pretending to love him as a mother at 3.7–8 appear comical after she has just propositioned him so shamelessly in the previous verses. The actions are not intended as a narrative of the course of events; rather, they are illustrations of her typical, recurring behavior.[25] The emotional responses of Joseph regarding his trials are "typical" also. They are the actions found in the psalms of a person in distress, the so-called psalms of individual lament, such as *Psalms* 22, 34, 69, 109, and 118. The emotional distress of the individual in these psalms is expressed through images of praying, weeping, wearing sackcloth, fasting, and self-humiliation, precisely what Joseph does at several points.[26] Although these actions are ostensibly in response to some external threat, both in the psalms and in *Testament of Joseph,* one is probably not far wrong to assume it is part of a penitential piety that has internalized external strife, as in Greek *Daniel* and Greek *Esther.*

The individual motifs that are paralleled in Greek novels have been emphasized sufficiently by Braun and Pervo, but also striking is the atmosphere created. An unusual intensity is evoked in both halves, and the second half—where there are fewer obvious parallels to the Greek

[24] Bickerman, *The Jews in the Greek Age,* 210.
[25] Pervo, "Testament of Joseph."
[26] Hollander, "Ethical Character," 60–68.

novels—has claustrophobic tone that is quite realistic in the novelistic sense; that is, the actions of normal human beings play out issues of potentially tragic significance. The virtue that the story illustrates is Joseph's love for his brothers, which is so great that he is determined to remain silent and not divulge that they had kidnapped him and sold him, a free man and a son of a great and righteous man, to the Ishmaelites. A certain ironic poignance is built up as the story progresses, since everyone recognizes Joseph's true identity, even as he himself denies it with greater and greater inner turmoil. From his appearance, for example, the Ishmaelites suspect that he is no slave[27] and leave him with a merchant for temporary safekeeping. The wife of Pentephris (that is, Potiphar) hears about him and, upon her arrival with her husband, convinces the latter to free this man who has been unjustly sold as a slave. Her protestations are particularly ironic since the audience knows that she is correct—he has been unjustly enslaved—but they also know how wicked are her true designs. When the merchant and Joseph are brought before Pentephris and beaten, Joseph maintains again that he is truly a slave of the Ishmaelites who had deposited him with the merchant. He remains in bonds, even though Pentephris's wife protests that he is really a free man. When the Ishmaelites return, however, they tell him that they have learned that he was a free man, the son of Jacob, who was mourning for him, and they demand to know why he had misled them. Once again Joseph, though internally stricken, retains his outward composure and maintains that he is a slave, to protect his brothers: "When I heard this my inner being was dissolved and my heart melted, and I wanted to weep very much, but I restrained myself so as not to bring disgrace on my brothers. So I said to them, 'I know nothing; I am a slave' " (15.3). They, for their part, do not believe him, and with the merchant they beseech him to tell Pentephris once again that he was a slave purchased legally. After negotiations, they then sell him to the eunuch of Pentephris's wife.

It is at this point, however, that Joseph's restraint, which has effectively grown through repetition, takes on even greater proportions. The eunuch paid a great sum for Joseph but not as great as the figure with which Pentephris's wife had entrusted him. He had secretly pocketed

---

[27] This motif, we may note even in this second half, is reminiscent of the Greek novels. In addition, the parallels to the interrogations of Jesus in the gospel passion narratives should not go unnoticed. Nickelsburg has pointed out ("Introduction," 11–12) that the combination of a *narrative* of the persecuted righteous person with references to the *Psalms* of the persecuted righteous person is common to *Testament of Joseph* and the gospels.

the difference, but even here, Joseph remains silent: "Although I knew the facts, I kept quiet in order not to bring the eunuch under disgrace" (16.5). The passivity or, to put it positively, the "patient endurance" (*makrothumia*), which Joseph exhibits to protect his brothers is here even extended to an unscrupulous eunuch of an official's depraved wife. This would seem to go beyond the sort of self-sacrifice that would normally be required, and generalized beyond the family. Perhaps it is not a clearly thought out humanitarian ethic that is being advocated here but an exercise in hyperbole, an extreme example that drives home a deeply held attitude. And hyperbole, when examined in the light of day, often becomes absurd, but it is here held together by a superb narrative and ironic logic. In each of the episodes the characters whom Joseph meets are depicted as increasingly corrupt, and he descends further and further into a moral quagmire in which he can maintain his moral identity only by covering for his brothers' sin—that is, by lying—more fervently: Joseph is led away by the innocent Ishmaelites and insists he is a slave to protect his brothers. Pentephris's wife, who is morally tainted by her designs on Joseph, enters the scene, but Joseph still maintains that he is a slave. The Ishmaelites then return, and although they now know the truth about his background and are no longer innocent, they bluntly ask him to cover for *them*. Finally, the unjust steward of Pentephris's wife cheats her in the process of purchasing Joseph for her lustful pleasures, but Joseph covers for him as well. The narrative is actually quite skillful in leading to this point and surprisingly realistic in rendering the inner tribulations of a person who in this context appears ordinary and unheroic.[28] The fact that the actions are not clearly motivated and are, in fact, unbelievable—not to mention in direct contradiction to the account in *Genesis* on which it is based—hardly matters. In this pious narrative world, it works. The second story retains a more coherent narrative progression than does the first, even though it recounts the moral resolve of a protagonist who becomes increasingly mired in what we would call a pathological and self-destructive passivity.[29] Joseph is an "enabler" of his brothers' cruelty.

[28] It is entirely possible that the heroic conclusion in chapter 18, in which Joseph is likened in stature to Jacob, is not the original conclusion to 10.5–17.8 but is rather a continuation of the ending of the first story. Despite some key terms that are also in the second story (and may have been added at the time of combination), chapter 18 continues with some of the terms and themes of the first part of *Testament of Joseph*.

[29] The passivity of the hero of the novel is recognized as a general trait by Lukács (*The Theory of the Novel*, 89–90), and is tied to the interiorizing perspective, on which see below, this chapter.

So ends the narrative per se, but the sermon is next drawn to a typical conclusion and exhortation (of which the narrative constituted the ex-ampla), and the focus of this narrative is brought to bear on the family ethic. The true recipients of this generosity of spirit, we are told in the next line, are the brothers:

> So you see, my children, how many things I endured in order not to bring my brothers into disgrace. You, therefore, love one another and in patient endurance conceal one another's shortcomings. God is delighted by harmony among brothers and by the intention of a kind heart that takes pleasure in goodness. . . . I did not permit (my brothers) to be troubled by the slightest matter, and everything I had under my control I gave to them. Their sons were mine, and mine were as their servants; their life was as my life, and every pain of theirs was my pain; every ailment of theirs was my sickness; their wish was my wish. (17.1–7)

One wonders if this obsession with self-sacrifice for the family is related to *Tobit*'s attention to this issue. The organization of Jewish social life in the Diaspora appears to have been guided by an abiding concern for keeping the extended family together and properly oriented. This is per-haps the social reality that acquired narrative realization in the second half of *Testament of Joseph*. The realism and psychological intensity are similar to what we might find in a modern novel, where the psychol-ogy of the characters is dissected, especially in regard to their values to determine how they will fit into the social structure.

Joseph and Aseneth

Joseph and Aseneth is the final novel that we come to and, in many ways, the most "evolved." Its title was actually added in the modern period on the analogy of the titles of most of the Greek novels, and, as Ross Kraemer has pointed out, *The Marriage and Conversion of Aseneth* actually fits the emphasis of the present text better.[30] Usually dated to

---

[30] Kraemer, *Her Share of the Blessings*. Once again, however, the question of the evolution of the work enters in, and the focus may have shifted over time. The strong emphasis on Aseneth's conversion experience may be a secondary addition to an older work, as I attempt to show below.

I have used here Christoph Burchard's text of *Joseph and Aseneth* ("Ein vorläufiger grie-chischer Text von Joseph und Aseneth," *Dielheimer Blätter zum Alten Testament* 14 [1979]:2–53) but *not* his translation (found in Charlesworth, ed., *Pseudepigrapha*, 2:177–248), which is much

the first century C.E., it begins by recounting the meeting of Aseneth and Joseph when the latter, now prime minister of all Egypt, comes to inspect the plantation of Aseneth's father, Pentephres (here not the same as Potiphar, despite the use of this name for Potiphar in *Testament of Joseph*). Aseneth's parents want to betrothe her to Joseph, but she scorns him as a foreigner who is beneath her. Upon finally seeing him, however, she is struck to the heart and chastises herself for having uttered harsh words about him. Joseph, for his part, is wary of all women—because they try to seduce him—until, that is, he hears that Aseneth is not only a virgin but has never been seen by a man until he himself had caught a glimpse of her. He thus agrees with her father to marry her. Before the marriage can be consummated, however, Aseneth must put away her idols and convert to the worship of the one true God. This conversion, indeed, is the major action of the book. Aseneth retires to her bedroom, throws away her idols, and commences a week of agonizing soul-searching, fasting, prayer, and penance, culminating in the appearance of an angelic "Man from Heaven" with whom she shares a mysterious communal meal. At the end of the seven days, Joseph is reunited with her, and they are married before Pharaoh.

This constitutes the first half of the novel, every step of which is laden with symbolic significance. The allegorical or mystical elements introduced into the text at times break the bounds of the narrative, forcing the reader to look constantly beyond the story for external referents. Aseneth, for example, has not just spurned her other suitors; she hates all men and, as noted, has never even been seen by a man. Her refuge is her tower, consisting of ten rooms where she is attended by seven virgins born on the same night as she. At this point such details could simply be considered fanciful hyperbole, intended to convey a sense of wonder and riches beyond imagination. Soon, however, the symbolic elements begin to consume the narrative. The court of her family's house is surrounded by a high wall with four gates, each guarded by eighteen strong men. Beautiful fruit trees, with fruit ripe for harvest, fill the courtyard. A spring within the court empties into a cistern, which in turn overflows to create a stream running through the court-

---

too literal. It should be noted, however, that although it has been commonly accepted that Burchard's text is a better reconstruction of the original than Philonenko's (*Joseph et Aséneth*), Kraemer questions this assumption. In addition, she notes (pp. 110–12) that there are serious issues at stake here: Burchard's text is more androcentric than Philonenko's. I have chosen here to proceed with the text of Burchard, but the entire question of the text criticism of this novel is being taken up by Kraemer, as is the question of dating and provenance.

yard, providing water to all the trees. The symbols thus go beyond rich, suggestive detail to full-blown allegory, but there is no attempt to provide a key for the reader to interpret them. When Joseph arrives, for example, he enters by the gate to the east, with great fanfare, dressed in royal garb but with an extra detail: he holds an olive branch dripping with oil.

Aseneth's long repentance scene is carried out in several movements, each of which contains a long prayer (chapters 10–13; compare 6.1–8). First, she takes off her rich garments and puts on a black tunic of mourning; then she throws all of her idols and rich jewelry out of her north window to the street below, where beggars live. Girding herself with sackcloth and sprinkling ashes upon her head, she begins a week-long ordeal of repentance: "She spread the ashes over the floor and struck her breast with both hands over and over, and, weeping bitterly, she lay down in the ashes. All night long she lamented loudly, moaning and weeping until dawn." Gestures of mourning—black tunic, sackcloth, ashes sprinkled on the head—here become indicative of dying to the life of idol worship, but they also indicate debasement and purging as the extent of her self-castigation is pushed further and further:

> Spent and exhausted from the fasting of the seven days, Aseneth was able to lift her head but a bit from the floor and ashes where she was lying. She slowly rose to her knees, placing her hand upon the floor for support, but her head still hung down, and her hair was matted with ashes. Clasping her hands together, she shook her head from side to side and struck her chest with her hands, her head drooping down against her chest, as her face flooded over with tears. She groaned loudly and pulled at her hair, sprinkling ashes again over her head.

A similar kind of rending of the hair—and of the heart as well—can be found in Greek novels (compare Xenophon 1.4, Chariton 3.10), but there the internal suffering is always over something external, usually the loss of the loved one, and the despair over the impossibility of reunion. In *Joseph and Aseneth* the internalizing has become an end in itself; in other words, at issue is the *inward* transformation of the protagonist, and the despair results from the conviction on Aseneth's part that she could never be worthy. The concentration on the interior life of the protagonist, which Georg Lukács considered a hallmark of the novel,[31] is carried to an extreme in *Joseph and Aseneth*.

The intensity of the long night's conversion ritual is the most riveting

---

[31] Lukács, *Theory of the Novel,* 66, 88–90, 118–19.

aspect of the novel, and it inevitably gives rise to all sorts of interpretations of mystical theology. Victor Aptowitzer sees the characters as referring to proselytism, with Joseph standing for Israel, Aseneth the "true proselyte," Pharaoh and others as "Godfearers," that is, Gentile sympathizers of Judaism, and so on.[32] Others, such as Marc Philonenko, have noted the solar and astral imagery, which would associate Joseph with the sun, Aseneth with the moon, and the seven virgins with the seven planets.[33] The meal that Aseneth and the angel share has perhaps attracted the most attention, since it is similar to the eucharistic meal of the New Testament. There are references in *Joseph and Aseneth* to the "bread of life," the "cup of immortality," and the "ointment of incorruptibility." These appear in the formulaic language of a ritual (15.5) and, since they have nothing to do with the narrative development, may have been adapted from a cultic ritual.[34] But added to these sacraments is a new element, a honeycomb, which is not introduced with formulaic language: "Extending his right hand, the man broke a piece off of the comb and took a bite from it, then with his hand put the rest in Aseneth's mouth and said, 'Eat,' and she ate. . . . With his right hand the man touched the comb where he had broken it, and it was immediately restored and filled out as it had been" (16.15–16). From the broken honeycomb there proceeds a vast swarm of varicolored bees. The formulaic language concerning bread, wine, and oil no longer seems to be the principal focus. Aseneth never consumes these elements, but only the honeycomb and the bees that come out of it remain at the center of the description. The bees, surely to be considered a curious feature by the modern reader, are crucial to the allegorical reading; some wear golden diadems, and others circle about her mouth and make a new honeycomb like the one the Man from Heaven has broken (16.18–20). Their presence in the symbolic world of the narrative may derive from the fact that the Egyptian goddess Neith is associated with the bee, and the name Aseneth in fact means "consecrated to Neith." The honeycomb and the bees likely represent the key to the message of immortality that is present in the other sacraments as well.[35] Some of the other

[32] Aptowitzer, "Asenath, the Wife of Joseph." See also Nickelsburg, *Jewish Literature Between the Bible and the Mishnah,* 262.

[33] Philonenko, *Joseph et Aséneth,* 79–83, and "Joseph and Aseneth."

[34] K. G. Kuhn, "The Lord's Supper and the Communal Meal at Qumran," in *The Scrolls and the New Testament,* ed. Krister Stendahl (New York: Harper, 1957), 75–76, and G. D. Kilpatrick, "The Last Supper," *Expository Times* 64 (1952–53): 4–8.

[35] On Neith: Philonenko, *Joseph et Aséneth,* 61–79; on the significance of the honeycomb in the context of the meal: Collins, *Between Athens and Jerusalem,* 215–16; Philonenko, *Joseph et Aséneth,* 96; Burchard, *Untersuchungen zu Joseph und Aseneth,* 129–30.

symbolic levels that are likely operative in this section of the novel are indicated by the curious colors that are associated with the bees. They are "white as snow, with wings shimmering of purple, violet, scarlet, and linen interwoven with gold threads" (16.18). This combination of colors is identical to the colors of the priestly ephod or mantle in *Exodus* 28:5: "They [the priests] shall receive the gold and violet and purple and scarlet cloth and the fine white linen."[36] Why the bees are represented with these colors is not clear, but it is typical of the ambitious symbol making with which this section is invested.

The communion of Aseneth with the "Man from Heaven," the culmination of her week of penance and preparation, has erotic overtones: "And Aseneth stretched out her right hand and placed it upon his knees, and said to him, 'I beg you, Lord, sit for a while upon this bed, for it is pure and undefiled; neither man nor woman has ever sat upon it'" (15:14). The erotic union of the hero and heroine, normally a central part of the Greek novel, has been denied Aseneth and Joseph. They have both been extraordinarily chaste, but though now betrothed, they are separated again while Joseph proceeds about Egypt, storing grain for the seven years of famine, and Aseneth completes her conversion process. We wonder at this point whether they will continue to be celibate; the value of celibacy appears to overwhelm this genre usually devoted to romantic love, and the ancient reader may have questioned whether it should ever be fulfilled. The entry of the Man from Heaven becomes as a result even more charged. Is he a symbolic substitute for the sexual union one expects between Aseneth and Joseph? Early Christian apocryphal acts often sublimate the sexuality of the chaste heroine into a quasi-erotic relation with an apostle. Thecla, for example, in *Acts of Paul and Thecla,* is more than once thrown together with Paul in an inten-

---

[36] Suggested by Cynthia Baker in an unpublished seminar paper at Harvard Divinity School, 1986. The Greek version of *Exodus* and *Joseph and Aseneth* use identical terms. Aseneth's other jewels, sashes, and accoutrements are also reminiscent of the priestly accessories, and we note too that the court compound of her parents' estate is similar to the temple compound and that Aseneth's new name, City of Refuge, may be symbolic of Jerusalem. This is not to go as far as U. Fischer, however (*Eschatologie und Jenseitserwartung im Hellenistischen Diasporajudentum* [Berlin: de Gruyter, 1978], 115–23), who sees in Aseneth a symbol of the *heavenly* Jerusalem. See the refutation of this more extreme position by Burchard in Charlesworth, ed., *Pseudepigrapha*, 2:189. Coming to my attention too late to be incorporated here is the work of Gideon Bohak, who is completing a doctoral dissertation at Princeton University. There he argues that the equation of the estate to the temple is key to the interpretation of the whole of *Joseph and Aseneth* and that the document is in fact written as a justification for the building of Onias's temple at Heliopolis, the very site of Aseneth's family estate. I find his thesis very compelling and look forward to the publication of his results.

tionally "compromising" position. Kraemer refers to this quasi-sexual relation of the chaste heroine to the apostle as "erotic substitution" and notes that celibate Christian women are sometimes said to be married to the "true man."[37] Thus the Man from Heaven is an example of an erotic substitute, just as Joseph is almost an erotic substitute himself. The relationship of such a depiction to asceticism will be addressed below.

The second part of the novel operates on a more mundane plane. Upon the completion of Aseneth's conversion process, she and Joseph are married by Pharaoh, and they travel to meet Joseph's father, Jacob. They are blessed by Jacob and honored by Simeon and Levi, Joseph's brothers who are sons of Leah. Pharaoh's son has also seen Aseneth and is struck by her beauty. He lays a plot first before Simeon and Levi to kill Joseph while he himself will attempt to kill his own father, so that he might take Aseneth as bride and usurp the throne in one stroke, but they refuse to join him. The prince, however, thereupon turns to Dan and Gad, sons of the maidservants Zilpah and Bilhah, who envy Joseph, and they agree to kill him and allow Pharaoh's son to take Aseneth for himself. Taking advantage of a temporary separation of the newlywed couple, they prepare an ambush for Aseneth, but Joseph's brothers who are sons of Rachel and Leah intervene and save her, killing all of the troops who were under the command of their brothers, along with Pharaoh's son. Before they can dispatch the brothers who had tried to kill her, however, Aseneth intercedes and counsels mercy, bringing an end to the bloodshed. The story concludes with Pharaoh, grieving for his dead son, leaving his throne to Joseph as he too succumbs and dies.

The ostensible point of departure for this entire narrative is a single reference in *Genesis* to Joseph's marriage to Aseneth: "And Pharaoh called Joseph's name Zaphenathpaneah; and he gave him in marriage Aseneth, the daughter of Potiphera priest of On" (41:25). Other than this one reference, then, the story that this novel unfolds is not based on the biblical text at all. Certain details in the story will show some relationship with the *Genesis* account, but the narrative is a long episode that lies outside the biblical version of the story. One verse here inspires a very long narrative indeed. The story is essentially a "free" narrative that actually has more in common with motifs from Greek novels: the surpassing beauty of the young hero and heroine, her being struck with "lovesickness" upon first seeing him, the jealous rival and the "brig-

---

[37] Kraemer, "The Conversion of Women to Ascetic Forms of Christianity," 303–4. The symbolism is not unlike that of the marriage of Catholic nuns to the church.

ands" (Dan and Gad, the sons of the maidservants), and the chastity of the two lovers.[38] The love story that is the theme of the first half and the adventure story of the jilted lover in the second both convey at times an authentic sense of the Greek novel. Furthermore, Aseneth's conversion, on first inspection very Jewish in its content, imposes very little of Jewish *observance,* focusing only on monotheism. Burchard points out the similarities to the initiation of Lucius in Apuleius's *Golden Ass,* adding that Aseneth could almost be Lucius's sister![39] *Joseph and Aseneth* clearly contains more substantive and structural parallels to Greek novels than do the other novels.

At the same time, there are distinct ways in which the special perspective of Jewish piety enters in. Joseph insists on maintaining his chastity in the presence of Aseneth, not when he is separated from her against his will, as would be the case in the Greek novels. She must undergo a special transformation before they can be joined together, but this transformation is an obstacle to love that would not be present in Greek novels. In short, the *extent* to which divine sanction and revelation enter into the story also distinguishes this novel from the Greek novels.[40] If the relationship between the protagonists reflects the ideal social relations of the audience, then *Joseph and Aseneth* appears suspended between Jewish and Greek culture. Particularly intriguing is the theory that *Joseph and Aseneth* was composed and used by the Therapeutae, an ascetic group of Jews in Egypt whom Philo describes in *On the Contemplative Life,* and there are many parallels to suggest this idea. Our document, like Philo's account of the Therapeutae, emphasizes praying toward the east at the rising of the sun, the value of self-control, and the importance of sacred numbers. Furthermore, Philo's description of the members leaving behind their families to join the monastic group would create the emotional sense of separation and abandonment that is present in Aseneth's hymns, even though in the narrative she is not abandoned by her family.[41] Opposition to this theory has generally cen-

---

[38] Philonenko, *Joseph et Aséneth,* 43–48, and "Joseph and Aseneth," 10:223; West, "Joseph and Asenath"; Burchard, *Der dreizehnte Zeuge,* 59–86, esp. 81–86.

[39] Burchard, *Dreizehnte Zeuge,* 83; see also Kee, "The Socio-Cultural Setting of Joseph and Asenath," and Shaye J. D. Cohen, "Crossing the Boundary and Becoming a Jew," *Harvard Theological Review* 82 (1989): 13–33.

[40] Burchard, *Dreizehnte Zeuge,* 85; Philonenko, *Joseph et Aséneth,* 44.

[41] M. Delcor, "Un roman d'amour d'origine thérapeute: Le Livre de Joseph et Asénath," *Bulletin de Littérature Ecclésiastique* 63 (1962): 21–23. See also Kee, "The Socio-Religious Setting and Aims of Joseph and Asenath," 187–88, and "Socio-Cultural Setting"; Kraemer, "Monastic Jewish Women in Greco-Roman Egypt," 361–62.

tered on the contradictions between Aseneth's lifestyle and the lifestyle of the Therapeutae, since she only temporarily renounces her riches and sexual involvements and ultimately resides in wealth, marries Joseph, and has children.[42] These objections, however, presume a one-to-one correspondence between elements of the narrative and aspects of the social world of the author and readers. We must look at the general ethos or, perhaps more precisely, the romanticized ethos of the work, especially of those sections where the allegorical character of Aseneth's conversion is contained. In these the reader notes that virginity and self-control are highly prized. The marriage of Joseph and Aseneth is also so thoroughly symbolic that it no longer rises up as a model of the nuclear family. They are part of an ancient past, the patriarch and matriarch of Egyptian Judaism, and their participation in sexual reproduction—and even wealth and luxury—were necessary for the future life of Jews. Thus, the Therapeutae could have interpreted the novel on two levels, an ancient paradigm and a contemporary ascetic ideal.

As we have seen in the previous chapters, the Jewish novels do not evolve from a single primitive genre of "pre-novel" but derive from different story structures. *Joseph and Aseneth* is not like *Esther* and *Daniel,* which developed from court narratives, or like *Tobit,* which has close folk parallels. Its own origins can perhaps be discerned, however, if we analyze its various parts separately. Most attention is naturally focused on the first half of the novel (chapters 1–21), where the dramatic self-examination of Aseneth occurs, along with her meeting with the Man from Heaven and all of the enigmatic symbols. The second half (chapters 22–29) is quite different, and had it survived without the first half, it would never have prompted any speculation in the direction of Jewish mysticism. The second half is an adventurous melodrama provoked by jealousy of Joseph, first on the part of Pharaoh's son, who has also loved Aseneth, and then on the part of Joseph's half brothers who are sons of the maidservants Bilhah and Zilpah. There is actually very little reference in the second half to the conversion interlude of the first (note only 23:10), and the differences between the two sections are in fact quite marked.[43] To begin with, the second section is set in various locations, mostly outdoors, and this change of scene grants some relief to the reader after so much time spent in the claustrophobic quarters of Aseneth's suite. The second half also balances the presence of the dramatic

---

[42] In addition to the works of Kee cited above, see also Randall D. Chesnutt, "Conversion in Joseph and Aseneth," 21–24, 243–49.

[43] Burchard, "The Present State of Research on Joseph and Aseneth," 35–36.

personae among Joseph, Aseneth, Pharaoh, Pharaoh's son, several of the brothers acting independently, and hundreds and hundreds of soldiers. Thus we have a wealth of characters and a wealth of scenery held together by a quickly moving plot. Finally, the second half contains no allegorizing symbolism.

Richard Pervo suggests that the second part could derive from a source,[44] but my suggestion here will be slightly different, that the mystical union theme of the first half, with its attendant symbolism, has been introduced into a more typical Jewish novel, which actually begins with chapter 1. Here the story is introduced without a hint of allegory,[45] and all the seeds of the later adventurous plot are present: the role of Joseph as Pharaoh's emissary, the rich man Pentephres and his exceedingly beautiful daughter Aseneth, and the pining of Pharaoh's oldest son for Aseneth. The next few chapters are apparently mixed between original narrative and allegorization, but one can hypothesize that part of an older narrative is still present. Chapter 2 introduces elements of the allegorical layer: the separate tower; the ten chambers of Aseneth's suite and their belongings; the seven virgins who wait on Aseneth, who were all born on the same night as she, and who had never talked with a male; the court and court garden; the windows; and the bed on which only Aseneth had ever lain. After these symbolic elements are introduced, however, we may have something like the original narrative, altered at several points in keeping with the later redaction. Aseneth is told by her parents that she is to be betrothed to Joseph. She reacts petulantly, reviling him because of his humble origins and his ignominious imprisonment. When word comes that Joseph has arrived, however, she runs to her upper room to see him, whereupon she is immediately struck to the heart and is overcome with remorse for her earlier words. Here also we see evidence that an older, unallegorized narrative has been edited, for Aseneth's ascent of the stairs, where the reader fairly rushes to look out the window with her, is interrupted at 5.3 by material of a plodding but symbolic nature, which totally disrupts the otherwise diverting, fairy-tale-like story. Joseph's horses, clothes, and accoutrements are described with an eye toward their mystical significance. These details are not the description of opulence for storybook effect; they are much too laden with external meanings for that. A further indication that this material has been added is the disjunction that occurs when the

---

[44] Pervo, "Joseph and Aseneth and the Greek Novel," 178.

[45] Aseneth's similarity to Hebrew women is a foreshadowing of her coming conversion, but it is not necessarily part of the deeper allegory that suffuses chapters 2–21.

older narrative resumes. The mystical section concludes (5:7) by saying that Joseph *got down from his chariot* and extended his right hand to Aseneth's parents, but in the next verse (6:1) the older narrative apparently continues: Aseneth sees Joseph *on his chariot* and is struck to the heart. Aseneth's first prayer of repentance, which follows—short, dramatic, related to the narrative—could also be part of such an older narrative, although the later prayers, much more allegorical, could not.

And so one could continue in this manner, noting a division in the work between the original narrative and symbolic additions throughout this section. The hypothetical earlier narrative would be quite in keeping with the second half of the work. Rather than the common division between the first and second halves of the work, we would have an early layer, which begins in chapter 1 and continues to the end, and a layer of allegorical additions, which are concentrated in a few early chapters but bestow their cast on the entire first half. The earlier layer is a more typical adventure story—or even a romance—of Joseph and Aseneth, which treats them both about equally, while the allegorical layer turns intensely inward, rendering the inner turmoil of Aseneth's conversion as the central experience of the book. In the introduction I suggested that various genres of popular literature of this period must be distinguished, and there it was especially noted that among the indigenous works we may distinguish national hero romances, like *Ninus, Sesonchosis, Petubastis,* and Artapanus's *Moses Romance,* from novels, as treated in the previous chapters, and also from historical novels, such as *Third Maccabees,* the *Tobiad Romance,* and *The Royal Family of Adiabene,* which will be described more fully in chapter seven. The latter division may not apply uniformly outside of Jewish and Christian literature, but for our purposes it has proved helpful.

If the separation of *Joseph and Aseneth* into two layers is accurate, then, the earlier level appears to be a national hero romance. It concerns not one hero, however, but the true family of Jacob: Joseph, his brothers by the free women Rachel and Leah, and now also the convert Aseneth, whom Jacob has fully accepted (chapter 22). These characters appear as ideal or even divinely empowered figures from the ancient past, just as do the leading figures in *Ninus, Sesonchosis, Petubastis,* and the *Moses Romance.*[46] The relationship with the Pharaoh is not adversarial, as it is in most national hero romances, but that with Pharaoh's rightful heir,

---

[46] As interesting as Artapanus's fragments on Joseph are, he does not seem to invest as much importance in Joseph as he does in Moses.

his firstborn son, is, and the net effect is much the same; that is, there is a struggle over political dynasty. The entire beginning appears to be setting the stage for a fairly typical romance intrigue. Although Joseph has been named the king's vizier, upon his arrival at the house of Pente-phres, Aseneth spurns him and despises the shepherd from the land of Canaan. One is reminded partly of the *Ninus* romance, where too a bar-rier lies between the joining in marriage of the hero and heroine. In *Joseph and Aseneth,* however, the barrier is typically Jewish: the condem-nations she utters reflect the kinds of opprobrium that Jews sensed in the minds of the Gentiles, a theme paralleled in Greek *Esther.*

The allegorical layer focuses much more intensely on Aseneth, but the romantic love motif is attenuated, overwhelmed by the interest in asceticism and conversion. Thus the second layer is in this respect not more like a Greek novel but less; most of the parallels to the Greek novel that have been noted would occur in the early layer, not the late. The second layer is, however, more like a Jewish novel, where we have seen in general an attenuation of romantic love and a great emphasis on a woman's penance. The writing is opened up in the early chapters to attend, in excruciating detail, to the emotional turmoil of the heroine in respect to her sinfulness. This focus "domesticates" the narrative in a literal sense, bringing it into the home, and turns the attention to the woman character. Not surprisingly, the scene in which she is the princi-pal character is a self-abasement ritual of mourning and cleansing, this time in its longest, probably latest, and most extreme form. This scene may coincide, of course, with some unknown ritual of initiation, but even if it does not, we find an unexpected touchstone for comparison: the *Golden Ass* of Apuleius, where the action of the novel culminates in a mystery initiation and a conversion to Isis worship.[47]

Most of the attention of scholars is understandably focused on the allegorical layer, where such unusual symbols reside. The intensity of the narrative and the inwardness of Aseneth's experience, along with the impenetrability of the symbols, often call to mind Gnostic texts, although most scholars would minimize such a connection.[48] Still, there is a quality about this layer that should be considered in this regard. When the text of *Joseph and Aseneth* is divided, as here, into two layers, it becomes all the more clear how predominant is the notion of identity in

---

[47] Kee, "Socio-Cultural Setting."

[48] Compare, however, the suggestive comments of Dieter Georgi, *Weisheit Salomos* (Güter-sloh: Gütersloher Verlagshaus Gerd Mohn, 1980), 394.

the later layer. Although Aseneth suffers through her realization of her idolatry, she ultimately becomes a true worshipper of God. A Gnostic text would insist that she would have to realize her "true" identity, that is, the identity that had actually been hers from primordial times (compare again the *Hymn of the Pearl*), and in *Joseph and Aseneth* the obsession with her identity, her conscious distinction from the "strangers" who are kept outside the gate, reflects a similar concern of the age. Note also that, as another piece of evidence that there are two layers in the document, this particular attitude toward the strangers is not reflected in the base narrative. At 5.6 (allegorical layer), all of the "strangers" are locked *out* of the courtyard, whereas at 7.1 (original narrative), when Joseph is inside Pentephres's house, he insists on eating separately from the Egyptians of the household. The latter makes sense as a romanticized (and probably unrealistic) notion of Joseph's exaggerated kosher practices, but it does not jibe with the notion of the later layer, which sees the compound of Pentephres's house as a haven, with "strangers" outside.[49]

There is yet a further implication of separating the narrative into two layers. The original narrative contains interesting parallels to the second part of *Testament of Joseph*. The brothers' envy of Joseph is central to both (although in *Joseph and Aseneth* only some of the brothers are jealous) and is an extended-family issue, a common theme in the other Jewish novels. Both also contain passages promulgating an ethic of nonretaliation, rare in Jewish texts of this period, though not unknown.[50] It is interesting that these two sections are also the only parts of the Joseph traditions mentioned above which seem to delight in a *narrative* connection of events. The second layer of *Joseph and Aseneth* is less concerned with narrative integrity than is the national hero romance from which it sprang. One difference, however, between the early layer of *Joseph and Aseneth* and the second narrative of *Testament of Joseph* is the level of idealization: the former thoroughly romanticizes the true family of Jacob, whereas the latter experiments with realism.

What this comparison indicates is that *Testament of Joseph* and *Joseph and*

---

[49] Another allegorical reading could harmonize these two by saying that Pentephres's family represent God-fearers, whereas those outside represent pagans (so Aptowitzer), but this reading has justifiably not won converts. Aside from historical problems about the actual existence of a recognized class of "God-fearers," it is too mundane a division for such elevated mystical symbolism.

[50] See Krister Stendahl, "Hate, Non-Retaliation, and Love: 1QS x, 17–20 and Rom. 12:19–21," *Harvard Theological Review* 55 (1962): 343–55.

Aseneth, as well as other Joseph traditions, can be considered examples of a broad Joseph novelistic tradition. We probably possess only a fraction of the popular writings that must have circulated about him, his wife, and his family. The two works here studied can each be analyzed into two separate layers, and the four witnesses to the tradition thus adduced exhibit different kinds of engagement of the novelistic impulse. They may in some cases reflect much longer renderings now lost to history. Kugel has suggested that during this period there existed various midrashic derivations and expansions of the biblical Joseph story that were part of one oral tradition of midrashic interpretation.[51] The existence of this oral tradition is hypothesized from the parallel treatment of certain motifs in different sources, which can best be explained by the supposition of a fairly coherent body of oral tradition that sought especially to interpret certain difficulties and peculiarities of the *Genesis* account. His evidence is convincing in general, but *Joseph and Aseneth* appears to have much less relation to the biblical text than do the other Joseph narrative traditions, and this text and others (for example, Artapanus on Moses) may test the limits of the midrashic explanation. Even in *Joseph and Aseneth,* however, there are influences of the biblical text, for as Kugel has shown, the motif of Aseneth looking down to behold Joseph may be inspired by part of Jacob's blessing of Joseph in *Genesis* 49:22.[52] Kugel thus provides a much needed corrective to the view that diverse narratives were legendary traditions essentially unrelated to the biblical text.[53] Still, at the very point where the "novel" genre enters into the picture, we are perhaps further from the influences of the biblical text, adrift in large currents of the narrative tradition that are more free-form. These currents flow in that province of the narrative tradition that is written, rather than oral, and intended for popular, middle-class consumption. The two cultures, oral and written, which Walter Ong describes so well,[54] coexisted at this period, but their narrative approaches diverged. Kugel notes also, for example (pp. 6–7), the tendency of midrashic exegesis to retain a sense of the past in the face of

---

[51] Kugel, *In Potiphar's House,* passim, but see especially 264–68.

[52] Kugel, *In Potiphar's House,* 84–89. Kugel considers unusual readings of this difficult verse in the Hebrew to postulate a connection with various narrative motifs, but he is partly supported by the fact that his readings are also attested in early translations. It should be noted that if the normal rendering is taken—"Joseph is a fruitful bough" or a "son of fruitfulness" (as in the Old Greek)—then other connections to *Joseph and Aseneth* can be seen, namely, the motif of fruit trees and fruitfulness, which is common in the work.

[53] Cf. his remarks (p. 9 n. 2) about Louis Ginsberg's mammoth treatment of Jewish narrative traditions, *The Legends of the Jews* (Philadelphia: Jewish Publication Society, 1909–1938).

[54] Ong, *Orality and Literacy;* see also Chapters 1 and 8.

the temptation of Greco-Roman culture. The novels perhaps represent those Jews who were, to some extent, giving in to temptation. But perhaps *for this reason,* the issue of Jewish identity, of boundary formation and boundary maintenance, is even more pressing and explicit in the novels than in the midrashim and Aramaic translations (targumim).

To sum up, the fragments that we now have can be described in the following way. The first part of *Testament of Joseph,* the detailed treatment of the many attempts of Potiphar's wife to seduce Joseph, was seen to contain many motifs parallel to the Greek novelistic tradition, but the narrative was not coherent; rather, it was a listing of episodes organized as a series of trials for the ordeal of the hero. It was evidently organized in this way to serve as the content or exempla of a sermon, and these exempla were followed by a conclusion and an exhortation, a pattern found elsewhere in the *Testament of the Twelve Patriarchs* and in contemporary Judaism and early Christianity. Although it has been noted how often in the novels there is a scene of a woman's internal anguish and self-mortification, the first half of *Testament of Joseph* places this psychological experience in the context of a man's anguish, a man who invokes motifs from the psalms tradition of a person in distress. This portrayal lies, perhaps significantly, in the larger context of the hortatory testaments of the twelve sons of Jacob, which consistently condemn the wiles of women.[55] The second part of *Testament of Joseph,* the description of Joseph's silence about the sin of his brothers, was likewise part of a sermon with a similar form, but in this case the narrative was more coherent and compelling, laced with the irony that Joseph must lie again and again, to increasingly unscrupulous interlocutors, to maintain the integrity of his brothers' reputation. No longer of heroic proportions, Joseph here is quite passive. One might speculate that the story reflects a semignostic disengagement from the real world, such as has been associated with texts like the *Wisdom of Solomon*'s description of the righteous man,[56] but in addition, one notes a new element in the novelistic literature we have analyzed: psychological realism. Like the modern novel, and, according to Erich Auerbach, the Christian gospels,[57] there is an exploration of the psychological tensions and suffering of ordinary people (or people depicted in an ordinary way).

---

[55] When the Jewish novelistic impulse is carried through more thoroughly, however, to the point of the creation of actual novels, a woman character comes to the fore to convey this same experience, condemning not women in general but the sin in herself.

[56] See, e.g., Georgi, *Weisheit Salomos,* 394.

[57] See Chapter 1 above. Bickerman, *Jews in the Greek Age,* 204–10, also emphasizes the psychological interest of the *Testaments,* which he rightly connects to a similar interest among Greeks of the period.

Joseph and Aseneth should not be divided into a first half and a second half, as it is by many scholars, but into an early and late layer. The love-and-adventure story associated with the second half actually begins in chapter 1 but is then overwhelmed in most of the intervening chapters by the introduction of a symbolic conversion story. The genre of the base story, which treats both Joseph and Aseneth, is that of the national hero romance. The second layer then focuses on the intense self-examination of Aseneth in the conversion process and on the heavenly visitation she experiences as a result. This focus is greatly expanded beyond the other women's "identity crisis" scenes that we have found in most of the other novels, and although it may apepar extreme, it is a logical conclusion of the prior developments of the novel: an exploration of women's inner experience not unlike that found in the novels of other ages. Whereas all the Joseph traditions that we have here examined bear some resemblance to popular novelistic literature, this final version of *Joseph and Aseneth* is the only one that can actually be called a novel. Like the other Jewish novels, it seems to have less interest in the love-and-adventure plot elements of the Greek novel, even though these are present in the base narrative. They are certainly not expunged, though they are often transformed: "He extended his hands and called Aseneth with the look in his eyes, and Aseneth extended her hands and ran to Joseph and fell upon his chest. Joseph held her in his arms, and after they had clung to each other for a time, their spirits revived. Joseph kissed Aseneth and gave her the spirit of life, then kissed her again and gave her the spirit of wisdom, and kissed her a third time and gave her the spirit of truth" (19:10–11). The romantic interest has been spiritualized, especially in the central account of Aseneth's seven-day ordeal. There the late layer has moved to suspend the reader in a position of utmost vulnerability and precariousness, an experience not of Jewish triumphalism (as in the base narrative) but of extreme ambivalence and personal anxiety. In this respect, then, we are reminded of Greek *Esther* and perhaps also of other "literature of vulnerability," such as the *Gospel of John* and Gnosticism.[58]

---

[58] Lukács describes the alienation of the novel hero from the world in a way that often sounds gnostic (*Theory of the Novel*, 88–89): "The novel is the epic of a world that has been abandoned by God. . . . Interiority is the product of the antagonistic duality of soul and the world. . . . The novel tells of the adventure of interiority; the content of the novel is the story of the soul that goes to find itself, that seeks adventures in order to be proved and tested by them, and, by proving itself, to find its own essence." On the parallels between the sense of alienation in the Greek novel and in gnosticism, see Terry Comito, "Exile and Return in the Greek Romances," *Arion*, n.s., 2 (1975): 58–80.

CHAPTER 7

Jewish Historical Novels

Having concluded our closer analysis of the individual novels, we would profit at this point from a further consideration of the relation of the novels proper to the historical novels, that is, to the novelistic renderings of what were viewed as actual historical events from the recent past. As noted in the introduction, *historical novel* is often used to refer to a work of fiction that makes use of a historical personage or setting, rather than to history that is told with novelistic flourishes. One is clearly fiction; the other is considered history, if poor history. By *historical novel* I am referring to the latter only. These works could be assimilated to the history category as, say, "novelistic histories" or "popular histories," but I am convinced that, despite their assumption of a historical referent for the action, they are more closely associated with the other novels. Among those treated here are the *Tobiad Romance* and *The Royal Family of Adiabene* from Josephus and *Second* and *Third Maccabees*.[1] They are of the same genre as the Christian historical novels, *Acts of the Apostles* and the apocryphal acts, and bear some resemblances to such Greek works as the *Alexander Romance* or Xenophon's *Cyropaedia* and the indigenous novelistic literature from the eastern Mediterranean, such as *Ninus and Semiramis,* the *Sesostris* and *Petubastis* traditions, and others (see Introduction). A cross-cultural study of these works is very much in need but cannot be taken up here.

---

[1] I have excluded from the present analysis of Jewish historical novels the *Moses Romance* of Artapanus and also his shorter treatments of Abraham and Joseph. Their combination of retold biblical history and national hero romance does not render them uninteresting, but does set them somewhat apart from the historical novels.

The criteria by which historical novels are distinguished from novels indicate also the closeness of the two genres. Historical novels, for example, have the all-important commitment to emotional experience that was characteristic of the Greek and Jewish novels. This is one of the traits that makes them "novelistic." It is not a sufficient similarity, however, to warrant merging the two genres. The historical novels have chosen real subjects from the recent past who are of some import to Jewish (or Christian) history. Jean Radford's short definition of the novel, "a non-mimetic prose narrative focusing on emotion,"[2] serves here as a way of differentiating this separate but related genre. The historical novels are more mimetic than the novels because they are trying to recount the realia of the past. This criterion should be considered carefully, however. The historical novels may, in fact, be more miraculous than the novels. Hebrew *Esther* and *Judith*, for example, do not contain any explicitly supernatural manifestations, but *Royal Family of Adiabene* and *Acts of the Apostles* do. Miracle is hardly a criterion of fiction for a pious people in the Greco-Roman period, despite the almost overwhelming need of modern readers to equate miracle with fiction. Miracle is, to be sure, an aspect of "bad" history in the minds of some of the best Greek and Latin authors, but it is considered history nonetheless. For the Jewish audience, the criterion of fiction is more Whose story is being told? Is the narrative concerned with a real personage from the recent past or a lesser or invented figure from the distant past? Nevertheless, the question might naturally arise of whether the experience of reading a novel and a historical novel is in some cases the same. The *Tobiad Romance* and *Royal Family of Adiabene* both shy away from pure emotionalism (perhaps under Josephus's special care as an editor), but what of *Second* and *Third Maccabees*? The experience of threat, distress, and ultimate deliverance is as strong here as in the novels. We must simply posit here that these works appear to be attempting to communicate the events as they actually occurred in the recent past, and, as novelistic as they are, they do not place before the reader a "fiction," an invented account for entertainment and edification.

To be sure, such a neat division as that advocated here is not without its problems. Although Josephus, a historian with educated Greco-Roman standards of historical writing—he was later referred to by Jerome as the "Jewish Livy"[3]—includes the *Tobiad Romance* and *Royal*

---

[2] Radford, "Introduction," in idem, ed., *The Progress of Romance*, 8.
[3] Shaye J. D. Cohen, "Sosates the Jewish Homer," *Harvard Theological Review* 74 (1981): 391–96.

Family of Adiabene in his *Antiquities* as historical writing, in the same work he also incorporates *Esther* (with most of the Greek additions) and *Daniel* (without the Greek additions.) Should this fact press us to merge the genres or, even more radically, to conclude that they should both be merged with biblical history, with which *Antiquities* is largely taken up? Such a conclusion does not seem necessary. Two factors apparently influence Josephus in his use of these texts. First, I have posited in the introduction that Jewish literature, rather than strictly separating fact and fiction as Greek authors did, distinguished biblical history— or what might have been viewed by Jews as simply "ancient history"— from other literature. The gradual canonization of various parts of the Bible was a lengthy and ambiguous process (the place of *Esther,* for instance, would be debated), but in *Esther* and *Daniel* Josephus is making use of what were *to him* authoritative texts covering a much earlier period, that is, the sixth and fifth centuries B.C.E. He was not likely reading them as comic episodes but as chapters in biblical history. Second, Josephus's moralizing tendencies can often harmonize and even homogenize the texts before him. In his retelling of history, *Esther* and *Daniel* are used as *moral* stories of God's providence.[4] God's providence is a favorite theme of Josephus in this work, and these texts, though originally novels, would serve for moral instruction as well as any other part of Jewish history. (We shall return to this issue in the final chapter.)

Tobiad Romance

The Jewish novels that we have dealt with frustrate the historian because the connections with identifiable social realities are so tenuous that we can rarely date the documents with assurance or say for certain in what part of the Jewish world they were produced. The suggestions above for *Tobit,* for example, are just suggestions, and the only reason they are not shouted out of court is that there is no evidence that can be brought forth to recommend an alternative hypothesis. And so it is with many of the other novels as well: their provenance can only be guessed at. Such is not the case with most of the historical novels. Corresponding to the *Tobit* novel and likely also a product of the Tobiad family, there is a historical novel concerning the same family, the *Tobiad*

---

[4] *Antiquities* 11.6.11 §268, 10.11.7 §277–80. See Feldman, "Hellenizations in Josephus' Version of Esther," 165–66.

Romance, which does have concrete historical references. It refers explicitly to the same family dynasty that may have produced *Tobit.* If these two works do derive from the same wealthy dynasty, it is surprising that they appear to have very little in common between them.

In *Antiquities* 12.4.1–11 (§154–236), Josephus apparently incorporates an older account of two of the principal figures of this family into his universal history of Judaism. He has evidently changed the treatment very little; the narrative can be easily separated from the surrounding history, the style is simpler and brisker than Josephus's usual style, and the point of view is transparently prejudiced in favor of one wing of the Tobiad family, a group that Josephus would have no ostensible reason to defend. It is difficult to try to reconstruct what the overall scope of the original narrative might have been, but it now recounts the rise of two important Tobiads, Joseph and his son Hyrcanus,[5] who lived from the mid–third century to the very beginning of the second century B.C.E. The account is reverential of the protagonists,[6] even aretalogical (recounting the virtues of the heroes), but the protagonists are still less heroic and more realistic than Moses in Artapanus's national hero romance. It has correctly been noted by Martin Hengel that the closest parallel in Jewish and Christian popular literature is *Acts of the Apostles,* but he incorrectly assigns both *Tobiad Romance* and *Acts of the Apostles* to the category of "historical monograph," a subgenre of ancient history writing, to defend the historical value of the latter.[7] Their genre is historical novel, although this is not necessarily a statement about their historical reliability. Historical inaccuracies can be found in both *Tobiad Romance* and *Acts of the Apostles,* but some reliable information is conceded to be present here by even the most cynical of scholars.

What Josephus has preserved of the original can be summarized thus: The young man Joseph of the Tobiad family is disturbed that his uncle, the high priest Onias II, has been dilatory in his payments of taxes he

[5] It is difficult to keep straight the names of the figures of this period, especially when so many of the names encountered here are papponyms, i.e., names of grandfathers that are given to grandchildren, thus creating the constant repetition of the same name. Another confusion is caused here as well by the fact that a much more famous Hyrcanus, John Hyrcanus, appears on the scene in Jewish history a century later. The two are of no relation.

[6] Contra Smith, *Palestinian Parties and Politics That Shaped the Old Testament,* 150, 263 n. 8, who believes that the original text was a *chronique scandaleuse,* altered and toned down by Josephus.

[7] Hengel, *Acts and the History of Earliest Christianity,* 36–37. Hengel prefers a genre term that exists in the ancient world, and in general this is to be commended. However, many, if not most, popular genres function quite productively in society without genre names. In modern popular culture, for example, *film noir* movies were created by American directors for two decades before French critics gave them their characteristic genre designation in the 1960s.

has gathered to King Ptolemy of Egypt, and his delay will result in the king's punishment of Judaea. Joseph thus maneuvers himself into a position where he can obtain the right to farm the taxes of the region, a privilege granted by Hellenistic kings to the highest bidder. Joseph wins the bid to become the tax farmer for Judaea through cunning and a show of wit before the king. According to the author, the citizens then welcome Joseph's ascendancy to the role of tax farmer, since he will secure their safety with King Prolemy. He then proceeds to solidify his position by executing the leading citizens of one city who refuse to pay the king's taxes to him. As difficult as it may be for the modern reader to accept, we actually have before us hero legends concerning tax farmers, as if we were reading the Robin Hood legend told from the Sheriff of Nottingham's perspective.[8] There is no doubt that Joseph's aplomb in executing the tax resistors is viewed with admiration.

The narrative then shifts its attention from Joseph to his son Hyrcanus, whose birth is accompanied by special signs. Joseph falls in love with a pagan woman, but his brother tricks him while drunk into sleeping with his niece, who becomes pregnant with Hyrcanus. Here we have an interesting parallel to the patriarchal saga of Jacob and Laban (*Genesis* 29), and we are later told (§190) that Hyrcanus exhibited such extraordinary intelligence as a child that his brothers were jealous and tried to kill him, an obvious parallel to the Joseph story.[9] The latter parallel is especially significant, since both Tobiads, Joseph and Hyrcanus, are, like the biblical Joseph, entering into the favor of the great patron, the king of Egypt. This goal, however, runs counter to the desires of many Jews, including Joseph's own stepbrothers, who would prefer to cultivate relations with the Seleucid kings to the north. Unfortunately, Josephus appears to break off his source somewhat abruptly. Joseph's death is recounted, but Hyrcanus's fight with his brothers is only summarily told, and his last years flash past in a blur. When the Ptolemaic kings wane and the Seleucid kings take control of Judaea, Hyrcanus is also at loose ends. He kills himself—a surprise to the reader, considering the tone of the novel as a whole, but a reason for this conclusion is suggested below.

[8] Lest we bracket this work off, however, from all other novelistic literature on moral grounds, we should recall that in *Genesis* 47 Joseph takes advantage of a famine to turn the residents of Egypt into debt slaves. See Robert B. Coote and David Robert Ord, *The Bible's First History* (Philadelphia: Fortress, 1989), 185.

[9] See especially Niditch, "Father-Son Folktale Patterns and Tyrant Typologies in Josephus' *Ant* 12:160–222."

The story is mainly a series of adventures, told in a spirited and entertaining way, that demonstrate the pluck and cleverness of a successful father-and-son team in rising to economic importance.[10] The Tobiads Joseph and Hyrcanus arise as entrepreneur-adventurers with a brashness and swagger that is almost endearing, even in the face of their moral atrocities. The key to understanding their role in society is the whole relationship of patron and client that existed in the Greco-Roman world.[11] This is the social world that pervades every line of the *Tobiad Romance:* in the large hierarchical network of ownership and indebtedness, almost every individual was a client to some more powerful patron and a patron to some more humble client. Although relationships of hierarchical and exploitative indebtedness exist in all societies, in the Greco-Roman world (and in many other societies as well) they were accepted and institutionalized in a way that is not true in avowedly democratic capitalism. The structures of obligation in the Greco-Roman world, therefore, became much more reified, and language of benevolence and largesse was commonly used to describe patrons or to address them. This pyramid of power relationships is glorified in the *Tobiad Romance,* with Ptolemy as the greatest patron at the top and the mass of Jews as clients at the bottom. And where there are patrons and clients there are also brokers, those entrepreneurs who go between the lofty patrons and the myriad clients. The broker by necessity be-

---

[10] Precedents, of course, for a series of legends of cleverness and derring-do, connected into a historical narrative, would be parts of Herodotus's *Histories* and Xenophon's *Cyropaedia.* The latter case is especially interesting, since it is Cyrus's patronage (cemented through his gift giving) that is often emphasized.

[11] There is a large literature on the patron-client relationship in the ancient world and in cross-cultural perspective; there is also a growing literature on the patronage system in ancient Judaism and early Christianity. Historians include A. R. Hands, *Charities and Social Aid in Greece and Rome under the Early Empire* (London: Thames and Hudson, 1968); Richard Saller, *Personal Patronage under the Early Empire* (New York: Cambridge, 1982); Paul Veyne, *Bread and Circuses: Historical Sociology and Political Pluralism* (London: Penguin, 1992); Erich S. Gruen, *The Hellenistic World and the Coming of Rome,* 2 vols. (Berkeley and Los Angeles: University of California Press, 1984), 158–200; and Jérôme Carcopino, *Daily Life in Ancient Rome* (New Haven: Yale University Press, 1940), 171–73. Sociological studies include Jeremy Boissevain, *Friends of Friends: Networks, Manipulators, and Coalitions* (Oxford: Blackwell, 1979), and S. N. Eisenstadt and L. Roniger, eds., *Patrons, Clients, and Friends: Interpersonal Relations and the Structure of Trust in Society* (New York: Cambridge, 1984). Studies of patronage specifically related to ancient Judaism and early Christianity are J. H. Elliott, "Patronage and Clientism in Early Christian Society," *Foundations and Facets Forum* 3 (1987): 39–48; Halvor Moxnes, *The Economy of the Kingdom* (Philadelphia: Fortress, 1988), 36–47; Frederick Danker, *Benefactor: Epigraphical Studies of a Graeco-Roman and New Testament Semantic Field* (St. Louis: Clayton, 1982); and Bruce J. Malina, "Patron and Client: The Analogy behind Synoptic Theology," *Foundations and Facets Forum* 4 (1988): 2–20.

comes a patron to the clients and a client to the patron; as a result, terms associated with patrons often adhere to brokers as well. Joseph and Hyrcanus arose as brokers who mediated the patron-client relationship between Judaea and the Ptolemaic kings and queens in Alexandria and savored the role. The patronage system is supported by the bloated terminology of generosity, loyalty, and benevolence, and scholars on the subject often point out the exploitative reality that is typical of patronage. This discrepancy between the idealized depiction of the benefactor and the harsh reality of the economic plundering is evident at every turn in the *Tobiad Romance*. It also provides an explanation for why the narrative concludes with Hyrcanus's suicide when the Ptolemaic kings begin to wane. It is probably not overinterpreting to suggest that without a great patron, Hyrcanus could no longer fulfill his role as broker. The position that he and his father had gained and filled with such glee had been stripped from him.

From the very beginning we are made well aware of whom to admire and whom to detest. We are to admire, first of all, Joseph: "Though still young, on account of his reverence and foresight he enjoyed a reputation for uprightness among the citizens of Jerusalem" (§160). We are to detest his opponent Onias II, who was "petty and a slave to his own greed" (§162). We learn later that there are others to admire (Hyrcanus) and to detest (Hyrcanus's half brothers) and soon find that all moral valuations of people, except for the universal and unreserved reverence for the Ptolemaic kings, are applied to one wing or the other of the Tobiad family. Other shadings of praise and blame are introduced to characterize the two parties. Joseph, despite his "poor" background (§170), rises as a result of his "urbane wit" (*eutrapelia*; §§173, 214), a highly valued trait in Greek and Roman society, equivalent to Latin *urbanitas*. Hyrcanus's half brothers, on the other hand, are rustic and uncouth (§197). This document appears to represent a lively record of a bitter family feud. In this we see a parallel to *Tobit* but with quite a loss of a warm, romantic, family ethic. In *Tobit* blood was thicker than water; in the *Tobiad Romance* family members are the cause of much bloodletting.

The single-minded focus of Joseph and Hyrcanus on obtaining the good will of the Egyptian king has led some to question whether the author was Jewish, but this can hardly be doubted.[12] The relations of

---

12 Tcherikover (*Hellenistic Civilization and the Jews*, 140–41) considers but rejects this possibility.

these two Tobiads to the Jews in Judaea is clearly the thread that holds the entire narrative together. Other figures, even the king and queen, are scarcely described as characters but only laugh at the Tobiads' wit and cleverness or approve their plans; they serve merely as backdrop to the real drama. The line of thought that is carefully laid, however, is the relation of the Jews in Judaea to Joseph and Hyrcanus. Although there are clearly some "bad Jews" in this romance—most of Joseph's and Hyrcanus's kinfolk, in fact—the Jewish people *as a whole* acclaim these two as heroes. Onias II had endangered the Jews by withholding the payment of tribute to Ptolemy, but Joseph stepped to the fore and procured Onias's permission to act as envoy. He then called together the assembly of the people of Jerusalem, comforted them, and said that he would represent them to Ptolemy. They, for their part, thanked him gladly. The idealizing perspective of the author can be seen time and time again, but even the subtle points should not escape our attention. The will of the people acclaiming Joseph is couched in constitutional terms; they are referred to as "the populace" (*to plethos*).[13] Joseph's efforts had an immediate effect; the envoy sent by Ptolemy is highly impressed with this young man, and the basis for Joseph's role as broker has been established. He goes to Ptolemy to ask that the sins of the people be excused and is referred to as their "protector" (*prostates*), a term for patron.[14]

Despite the large number of historical personages and references in the narrative, an exact provenance has eluded scholars. Jonathan Goldstein has proposed that the author of the *Tobiad Romance* was Onias IV, great-grandson of Onias II, who resided in Egypt after being excluded from serving as high priest in Jerusalem.[15] Onias established a Jewish temple in Egypt and, according to Goldstein, would have had a motive in glorifying the legitimate dynasty of high priests, the Oniads, after an illegitimate dynasty had profaned the Jerusalem temple. Two problems militate against accepting this interesting hypothesis. First, as John Collins has noted,[16] Onias II is portrayed very negatively in this

---

[13] In this sort of context it is likely meant to signify the legitimate voice of the people as a whole in terms of the constitution of a city. The language at §165 is crucial: "The population bestowed their thanks upon him" (*to plethos eucharistei . . .*); it is typical of a dedication to a patron.

[14] The difficulties that have been encountered in trying to render this as a technical term for a political or priestly office are dissolved if we see it as a social and economic term for the patron–client relationship. Cf. also *Second Maccabees* 3:4.

[15] Goldstein, "Tales of the Tobiads."

[16] Collins, *Between Athens and Jerusalem*, 74–75.

narrative; we are thus on weak ground in suggesting that *this* is the key social category for the author. Furthermore, the geographic interest is not exclusively on Egypt but on Jerusalem and the cities of Samaria as well. Tcherikover even goes so far as to conclude that Transjordan must be the provenance of the author, since the details in the description of the Tobiad stronghold in that region are accurate.[17] It is important, however, to keep in mind the many geographical locales that are described in the work. Although it can be hypothesized that this writing arose among a particular family, the Tobiads, it is likely the case that a more precise provenance will be impossible to ascertain.[18] The last events described are around the turn of the second century B.C.E.; *Tobiad Romance* was probably written sometime in the second century B.C.E.

Second Maccabees

Second Maccabees, according to its unnamed author (2:23), is an abridgement of a five-book history, which is now lost to us, by Jason of Cyrene. We cannot say anything definitive about Jason's history, except that it was relatively long (though still considerably shorter than Josephus's twenty-book *Antiquities*). One thing we can say, however, about the abridgement is that it collapses the large history down to the size required for consumption as a historical novel. *First Maccabees* is nearly as long as the biblical historical books, but *Second Maccabees* (minus the introductory letters) is only slightly longer than *Judith*. Although *Second Maccabees* covers much of the same history as *First Maccabees,* it is different in several crucial ways. *First Maccabees* recounts the heroism of the entire Hasmonean family, who came to rule after their successful revolt against the Seleucid rulers, whereas *Second Maccabees* focuses on some of the events leading up to the revolt and then only on one of the Hasmonean brothers, Judas. *First Maccabees* glorifies the reconstitution of a new "Israelite" state—the idealized term "Israelite," rather than

---

17 Tcherikover, *Hellenistic Civilization,* 141–42.

18 By chance, there also exist several other sources on the Tobiad family, both literary and archaeological, which cannot be examined here. Evidence about this family has been derived from, in addition to *Tobit* and the *Tobiad Romance,* the Zenon papyri and the site of the Tobiad estate at Araq-el-amir. On the Zenon papyri and the Tobiads, see Tcherikover, *Hellenistic Civilization,* 126–42. On Araq-el-Emir, see C. C. McCown, "The Araq el Emir and the Tobiads," *Biblical Archaeologist* 20 (1957): 63–76, and Otto Plöger, "Hyrkan im Ostjordanland," *Zeitschrift des deutschen Palästina-Vereins* 71 (1955): 70–81. *Second Maccabees* may also figure in a reconstruction of this family, on which see below, this chapter.

"Jewish," is often used—through a historiography that copies biblical history; *Second Maccabees* promulgates a holiday (the defeat of Nicanor, 15:28–36) and is less concerned with the Hasmonean state per se. *Second Maccabees* contains a heightened presence of the miraculous and a tendency toward rousing entertainment lacking in *First Maccabees*. Moses Hadas speaks generally about the combination of the qualities of entertainment and historiography found in *Second Maccabees:* "The program of Hellenistic historiography could not be more succinctly expressed than by the words (of the preface) *psychagogia* (pleasure), *eukopia* (ease), and *opheleia* (edification)—with the inevitable concomitant of indifference to historical fact."[19]

Of the various genre classifications that have been assigned to *Second Maccabees,* most have emphasized what we might today call sensationalism, noting that this is a typical element of Hellenistic historiography. It has been labeled "pathetic history," "tragic history," or "rhetorical history," under the assumption that a clearly recognizable subgenre of history writing existed which corresponded to these names.[20] Ancient authors, writing derisively, often commented on certain unsophisticated historians who employed miraculous interventions and manipulative emotional effects, but it is by no means clear that a separate subgenre was being referred to, other than what a Polybius or a Cicero would consider bad history. Scholars who have advocated tragic or pathetic history as a category were also forced to admit that, aside from fragments, only one example of their subgenre is now extant: *Second Maccabees.*

In Robert Doran's critique of this dependence on an unsubstantiated ancient genre, he characterizes *Second Maccabees* as a specimen of "temple propaganda," that is, a writing that describes an epiphany of a god in defense of the sanctity of the god's temple precincts, a common topos in contemporary pagan literature. Doran is quick to point out—and rightly so—that this topos does not in itself constitute a *genre.* The genre of *Second Maccabees,* in his mind, is a rather unspecified form of popular historiography that happens to emphasize the "temple propaganda" theme.[21] I would agree with Doran's assessment in general but would aver that the genre of *Second Maccabees* should be specified further as historical novel. In distinction from *First Maccabees, Second Maccabees*

---

[19] Hadas, *Hellenistic Culture* (New York: Norton, 1959), 126–27.

[20] Advocates of "pathetic history" have included Elias J. Bickerman, *The God of the Maccabees* (Leiden: Brill, 1979), 95–96, and Goldstein, *1 Maccabees,* 34 (but cf. his later statement, *2 Maccabees,* 20–21). Doran critiques this usage in *Temple Propaganda,* 84–104.

[21] Doran, *Temple Propaganda,* esp. 104.

contains more of the typical thematic concerns of late Hellenistic novel-istic writing: miracles, visions, men and women in rending displays of penitence, and, above all, emotion. It meets the criteria set out above for a historical novel, that is, a prose narrative that presents a supposedly true account of important historical figures of the recent past, utilizing typical novelistic means.

In addition to considering *Second Maccabees* as a whole a historical novel, we should also consider whether certain sections may have been taken from an earlier work (presumably separate from Jason of Cyrene's history) that focused on the high priest Onias III, as several scholars have suggested. As chapter 3 opens, the high priest Onias III is introduced and described in extremely glowing terms: "For a period, the holy city of Jerusalem thrived in uninterrupted peace, and the laws were observed most faithfully, on account of the piety of the high priest Onias and his hatred of vice. Even the kings of the other nations honored this place, bestowing the finest gifts upon it; Seleucus himself, king of Asia, paid out from his own revenues the funds necessary for the maintenance of the sacrificial worship" (3:1–3). This transparently propagandistic en-comium calls to mind the similar tone in the descriptions of the Tobiad Joseph in the *Tobiad Romance*. The social type that Joseph represented was broker, a role he played with great zeal and success, to judge from the story. Onias III is also portrayed as a broker, and the fact that his leadership role in the temple is directly linked to the Syrian king's great gifts indicates that he, too, is successful. The ancient reader would rec-ognize the advantages of having Onias III as intermediator to the Syrian king, and when the relation is threatened later, Onias also figures at one point as intermediator with God to right the situation. Recall also that in the *Tobiad Romance,* Onias II was supplanted by Joseph because, though he occupied the position of high priest, he was performing his role as broker so poorly.[22]

---

[22] His leanings may very well have been with the Seleucid king, as some of his offspring were, and thus it is the pro-Ptolemaic author who depicts him as inept and quite unconcerned. Onias III, however, is depicted in *Second Maccabees* 3 as an effective broker with the Seleucid king, but this role may reflect his sense of *Realpolitik;* he himself was probably more sym-pathetic to the Ptolemies. Onias III's opponent in *Second Maccabees,* Simon, was none other than the Tobiad Joseph's son, but though he had come into his father's office of magistrate of the temple, he was one of the sons who had opposed his half brother Hyrcanus (incorrectly called son, not grandson, of Tobias in *Second Maccabees*). Very likely, the shift from Egyptian to Syrian hegemony over Palestine placed Simon in office. The split in the Tobiad family be-tween Egyptian and Syrian sympathizers is depicted in our sources as interfamily personality clashes.

In *Second Maccabees,* Simon informs King Seleucus that Onias III has secreted away in the temple treasury a large amount of unreported money, and the king's general Heliodorus is dispatched to Jerusalem to confiscate it. Heliodorus makes inquiries of Onias concerning these allegations, and Onias's response casts him in a very innocent light: in the temple were the deposits of widows and orphans and money of the nobleman Hyrcanus; Simon, says Onias, has unscrupulously falsified the case. Onias appeals to Heliodorus to cancel the impious plan to seize the temple funds, but the latter refuses and arranges a day to carry out his orders.

From the beginning of chapter 3 (which is actually the beginning of the narrative, since chapters 1 and 2 are introductory) to the point we have just recounted (3:14a), the style is uniformly focused on Onias, his role and esteem as the patron of Jews, and those who would do him ill. There is a shift, however, at this point from a focus on Onias and his opponents to the inclusion of the populace as a whole and the depiction of the temple as a sacred precinct protected by God. From 3:14b–23, the priests (plural) and the populace are in consternation and take center stage from Onias. Onias has been quite cool and restrained up till now, as he will be again later, but in this section he is so wrought up that he looks stricken (3:16–17, 21). Although Doran characterizes the book as a whole as "temple propaganda," I would prefer to see this theme as one that comes and goes as a result of the interweaving of two narratives. The section 3:14b–23 is temple propaganda, which emphasizes the people's reaction to the threatened violation of the temple, but the first section, 3:1–14a, was more concerned with the person of Onias III. The temple was mentioned in this earlier section, but from 3:14b on the narrative suddenly explodes with emotional reactions to the danger to it: "Throngs of people poured out of their houses and rushed together to make a supplication, because the temple was about to fall into shame" (3:18). God here intervenes for *all* the people, not just Onias (as will occur below), and responds to their collective prayer.

As Heliodorus enters the temple, he is scourged thoroughly by two separate apparitions, which emphasize different details. Just as a distinction in style was observed above between 3:1–14a and 3:14b–23, the double apparition alerts us to the possibility that here also we may detect two levels in the text: "There appeared before them a beautifully caparisoned horse, mounted by a rider of horrifying appearance. Charging at Heliodorus, the horse reared up and attacked him with its front hooves. The rider was wearing gold armor. There also appeared to Heliodorus

two young men with incredible strength, beautiful to behold and wearing dazzling attire, who stood on either side of him and scourged him
relentlessly, striking him time and time again" (3:25–26). In the ac-
companying description, we find that the horse and rider are visible to
all, and the bodyguards are left powerless. The two men, on the other
hand, are evidently only visible to Heliodorus, and the bodyguards are
unaffected.[23] When the two young men have had their effect on Heliodorus, the events that follow also move in two separate directions. First
there is a general thanksgiving by all the people: "The citizens began to
praise the Lord, who had chosen to single out this place for special protection, and the temple, which only a short time earlier was filled with
fear and tribulation, now overflowed with joy and celebration, because
the Lord Almighty had appeared" (3:30). This seems to be a resolution
and a happy ending to the threat of disaster, but next we move into a
second scene of deliverance, which retains a sense of danger. It focuses
not on the people or the temple but on the person of Onias. Some of
Heliodorus's companions hastily beg Onias to pray to the Most High
and so spare the life of their general, who is now lying at the very point
of death. The high priest Onias, fearing that the Seleucid king might
suspect the Jews of attacking Heliodorus, brings a sacrifice for the man's
recovery. As the high priest is making the expiation, the same young
men, dressed as before, again appear to Heliodorus and say: "Be very
grateful to Onias the high priest; it was on his account that the Lord has
spared your life" (3:33). One resolution thus concerns the thanksgiving
by all the people for the protection of the temple, the other Onias alone.
He once again arises as the single heroic figure, now a broker of God's
power who saves Heliodorus as a concern for his clients, the citizens of
Jerusalem, not the temple. We can now also understand an ideological
basis of the earlier statement (3:10) that Onias was guarding the deposits
of widows and orphans: the property, specifically the money, of the
people is what Onias brokers and protects, understood (as is typical of
patronage systems) as a great benevolence on his part. Although "the
people" appear in both sections, in the first (the temple section) they are
the subject of the action, in the second the object of Onias's concern.
When the two ghostly figures command Heliodorus to thank Onias, it
is because God had spared Heliodorus on account of Onias (3:33), not
the temple.

Throughout this section, it is possible to separate two versions of

[23] Goldstein, *2 Maccabees*, 211.

every incident, one focusing on Onias as broker of God's patronage (through which Onias becomes a patron of the people), the other on the sanctity of the temple. At 3:35–36, for example, the Onias-as-broker version of the incident at the temple seems to find its conclusion: "After taking leave of Onias, Heliodorus marched his troops back to the king. There he bore witness to all concerning the mighty acts of the supreme God, performed before his very eyes." As *Second Maccabees* 3 now reads, however, 3:37–40 extend the conclusion and return to the temple propaganda motif: "And when the king asked him what sort of man he should send to Jerusalem on the next occasion, Heliodorus replied: 'If you have any enemy, or if there is any traitor plotting against your government, by all means *that* is the place where you should send him. He will return to you soundly whipped—if he survives at all—for surrounding the temple is truly the power of God. The one who takes his habitation in heaven also watches over it and defends it." Goldstein and Elias Bickerman have suggested source theories for *Second Maccabees* 3 that begin to explain some of the doublets noted here, but the opposition to their theories suggests that a clearer and more convincing demarcation of sources is necessary.[24] This is what I have tried to provide. Goldstein's theory was introduced above: in connection with *Tobiad Romance* sections of the *Tobiad Romance* and the pro-Onias sections of *Second Maccabees* were part of one work written by the same author, specifically Onias IV, who departed from Jerusalem and established a temple at Leontopolis in Egypt. Problems with this theory were noted there. Similarities exist between these two works, but these similarities are not close enough to be derived from a uniform authorial intent. Goldstein's approach to *Second Maccabees* 3 in particular raises other problems. His differentiation of two sources attributes to the Onias sections a position opposed to the Jerusalem temple; the temple is protected by God *only* because Onias is there, and the piety of Onias was all that was protecting the temple.[25] More likely, the lack of emphasis on the temple in these sections is simply Onias-as-broker chutzpah, told in a way that is as much for entertainment as polemic. Two threads *are* in *Second Maccabees* at this point, but they are not diametrically opposed on a political plain

---

[24] Goldstein, "Tales"; Bickerman, "Héliodore au Temple de Jérusalem." Opposition includes Doran, *Temple Propaganda*, 17–19, and Collins, *Between Athens and Jerusalem*, 76.

[25] Goldstein, *1 Maccabees*, 57–58; see also Goldstein, *2 Maccabees*, 13–15, 35–37. This reading allows Goldstein to associate this view with the anti-Jerusalem perspective of Onias III's son, Onias IV. Cf. Doran, *Temple Propaganda*, 17–18, who argues against Goldstein but does not successfully prove unity of the text.

as Goldstein would suggest, and the one that focuses on Onias III is
not likely by the author of the *Tobiad Romance*. This division of the text
into two levels need not require two separate *sources*, however. It is just
as likely that, whereas the Onias-as-broker level was an independent
source,[26] the verses that can be characterized as temple propaganda are
redactional; this theme runs throughout *Second Maccabees*, as Doran has
correctly noted, and is most likely the primary concern of the redactor
of the whole.

Bickerman focuses more precisely than does Goldstein on the doublets in *Second Maccabees* 3. Although he makes his divisions between
possible sources in a way different from what I have suggested, his
observations are fascinating.[27] The source that depicts Heliodorus's
scourge as a warrior on horseback utilizes a Greek conception of a
"Macedonian gentleman," quite foreign to ancient Hebraic imagery, a
"Greek artistic representation of the horseman routing the enemy. . . .
The combination, however, is clumsy, because the contents do not
match the form."[28] In the other version, two young men in magnificent attire scourge Heliodorus and are apparently visible only to him.
Being beaten by an invisible scourge is a common folk theme. This second apparition may have been connected with the Onias-as-broker level
above. It is likened by Bickerman to other Jewish works of interest to
us: *Daniel* 1–6, *Bel and the Dragon,* and *Third Maccabees*. In all these works,
as here, the foreign king proclaims the God of the Jews as the most
powerful. The kings do not convert but acclaim God as the highest in
the pantheon, "perfectly in keeping with the ethos of pantheism."[29] Just
as most of the parallels listed by Bickerman were Daniel legends, here
we may posit a tradition of Onias legends. They both venerate the hero
as a true servant of God. We might imagine that in the source Onias
succeeds at brokering benefits from the foreign king or from God, calling down the power of God at critical times. Heliodorus is humbled
by the power of God in the same way that Nebuchadnezzar is, espe-

---

[26] Presumably used by Jason of Cyrene, the main source for *Second Maccabees,* or perhaps
by the redactor of the abridgement.

[27] Bickerman, "Héliodore," 172–74. His source divisions are 3:24–25, 27–28, 30 (source A),
and 3:26, 29, 31–36 (source B). Bickerman leans heavily on the use of certain words in each
of the sections, but Doran (*Temple Propaganda,* 20–21) rightly considers this a weak argument.
Some of Doran's counterarguments to Bickerman are rendered moot by my slightly different
division.

[28] Bickerman, "Héliodore," 179.

[29] Ibid., 180–87, esp. 184. Bickerman also notes that the title for God in this section is
"Most High," *hypsistos,* common in these sorts of writings.

cially in *Daniel* 3. Heliodorus's thanksgiving and witness are similar to
Nebuchadnezzar's, and the titles for God that appear in the Onias level
of *Second Maccabees* 3 (but *not* in the temple level!), "the Most High"
(*hypsistos*) and "the great God" (*megistos theos*), are quite common in the
Danielic legends.

As we look ahead into *Second Maccabees* 4, we see further evidence
of the use of an Onias-as-broker source. The focus of the story is now
strictly on the level of an Onias family romance. The evil cousin Simon
is back, now slandering Onias, alleging that he had incited Heliodorus.
Simon also begins to make new external alliances. Onias's response calls
forth a cascade of virtuous and heroic titles from the narrator, all of
which emphasize Onias's role as effective broker with the Syrian king:
"Simon dared to accuse as an instigator of a conspiracy a man who
was the very benefactor [*euergetes*] of the city, a protector of his fellow
Jews, and a pious observer of the laws. . . . Onias did not appear before the king as an accuser of his fellow citizens but as one concerned
for their welfare, both singly and as a nation" (4:2b, 5b). Doran, arguing against separate sources, insists that Onias's positive attributes here
only arise by way of contrast with the evil Simon, but this can hardly be
true. The propaganda of this level of *Second Maccabees* is emphatically to
the effect that Onias is the one true protector and patron of the Jewish
people. Many of the words used of Onias are in fact the standard terms
for patron, especially benefactor.[30] The genre of the Onias-as-broker
source may have been a cycle of legends (as in *Daniel* 1–6), or it may
have already been connected into a novel, one not unlike the broker
novel of the *Tobiad Romance*. One slight difference is that whereas Joseph
and Hyrcanus in *Tobiad Romance* are clearly brokers for the Ptolemaic
king, Onias III is first a broker for the Seleucid king and second a broker for God. Onias himself appears to be pro-Ptolemaic, considering
his positive relationship with Hyrcanus, but this is passed over quickly
in the perspective of the author. Rather, Onias's brother Jason usurps
the office of the high priest through corruption (*Second Maccabees* 4:7–
8), and Onias is left dangling in the narrative.[31] Jason is described as a
villain and is supplanted in turn by a worse villain, Menelaus, brother

[30] Although it may hardly be probative, it is also interesting that the emphasis in *Second
Maccabees* shifts away from this sort of family propaganda at exactly the same point where the
narrative begins to parallel *Second Maccabees*.
[31] In Josephus's account of events, Onias III dies without incident (*Antiquities* 12.5.1 §237),
and his office is assigned by the Syrian king Antiochus IV Epiphanes to Onias's brother Jason.

of the Simon who had so vexed Onias.[32] Onias resurfaces, however, at *Second Maccabees* 4:33, protesting Menelaus's reprehensible practices as high priest. When Menelaus sends his foreign ally, Andronicus, to kill Onias, the latter takes refuge in a sanctuary. Onias is lured out of the sanctuary and murdered and, as a result, becomes a martyr of the cause. The fact that the sanctuary is a temple to Apollo and Artemis is not presented as shocking, no matter how much it may surprise the modern reader. The known facts may have necessitated this honesty, but the narrator does not appear to perceive this as a problem, even though Onias has just been described as a "zealot for the law." Certainly, it is more at home in an Onias-as-broker source than in the large section of *Second Maccabees* that extols the glory of the Jerusalem temple.

Near the end of *Second Maccabees,* Onias appears once again in a vision to Judas Maccabaeus. He is described as a model of virtue and modesty, but he is also a heavenly master of ceremonies: he introduces Jeremiah, who hands Judas a golden sword, signifying that it is permissible for the Maccabean warriors to fight on the Sabbath (15:12–16).[33] It is conceivable that these two traditions about Onias—his death at the hands of Andronicus and his reappearance from the dead to Judas Maccabeus— are part of the source postulated above for 3:1–4:6. If so, then we may detect a narrative pattern here that is paralleled by the Christian gospels and in the Greek tradition of the hero: virtuous and heroic deeds of a revered person, unjust execution, and reappearance.[34] It thus remains a fascinating possibility that a lost novel, specifically a historical novel parallel in theme to the gospels, lies just beneath the surface of this text, in addition to the historical novel that is *Second Maccabees* as a whole.

Third Maccabees

Third Maccabees actually has nothing to do with the Maccabees themselves, although similar themes can be found in several works of this

---

[32] According to Josephus (*Antiquities* 12.5.1 §238), Menelaus is the brother of Onias III and Jason, not of Simon. Jason is exiled to Ammon, presumably to the family estate of the Tobiads, which Hyrcanus had come to occupy, and is therefore associated at this later period in his life with the pro-Egyptian party.

[33] This dream vision, which is told to justify an important shift in practice, is closely paralleled in *Acts* 10, where Peter is told in a vision that the Christian mission can now legitimately include Gentiles.

[34] See, for example, Nagy, *The Best of the Achaeans,* and Moses Hadas and Morton Smith, *Heroes and Gods: Spiritual Biographies in Antiquity* (London: Routledge and Kegan Paul, 1965).

202 The Jewish Novel in the Ancient World

period, and the situation of persecution and deliverance would tie it to the ethos of the other Maccabean literature. It is an account of an incident of persecution of the Jews in Egypt, which supposedly occurred under Ptolemy IV Philopator (222–203 B.C.E.).[35] The narrative of *Third Maccabees* begins abruptly, so much so that it may be necessary to assume that some of the introduction is missing: "When Philopator learned from those who had returned that Antiochus now controlled the regions that he himself had formerly held . . ." In addition, some of the characters paraded out in 2:25 as "aforementioned" have in fact not been mentioned before. Scholars have considered the work a compound work, written perhaps over an extended period from the beginning to the end of the first century B.C.E. Though not long, it consists of two separate episodes that are related by the theme of God's protection in times of oppression. The first, 1:1–2:24, recounts the circumstances surrounding Ptolemy IV Philopator's first bout of hybris, when he decides that he must see the inner sanctum of the temple in Jerusalem. This is forbidden, he is told, to anyone except the high priest and even to him except at the prescribed time. Ptolemy, however, ignores the pleas of the Jewish leaders not to enter, setting the city into a turmoil. The priests and citizens pour into the temple and the streets, wailing and begging God not to allow the temple to be defiled. Even the women leave their secluded preserves within their homes to run through the city, their hair strewn with dust and ashes. The sanctity of the temple and the threat of its violation is continually emphasized, as is the devotion of the people to protect it. The inflated rhetoric of the whole work, sometimes identified, as in *Second Maccabees,* with "pathetic history," is hardly to be outdone in this section: "For it seemed that not only the people but the very walls, the entire building itself, cried out, for indeed all would have chosen death over the violation of the holy place" (1:29).

The tone here is quite like those parts of *Second Maccabees* associated with temple propaganda. There, however, the temple propaganda theme was evidently interwoven with verses from a source that emphasized the high priest Onias's role as patron of the people. Here, in *Third Maccabees,* the high priest does not upstage the temple. To be sure, he steps forward and plays an important role, but he is not the central agent of salvation, any more than is the elder Eleazar a few chapters later. The high priest is simply the highest official associated with the temple;

[35] Although Josephus (*Against Apion* 2.53–56) records a similar incident under Ptolemy VIII Euergetes (145–117 B.C.E.).

no special patronage language is used, and there is no evidence that his presence here derives from another source. God's response is also similar to that in the temple propaganda section of *Second Maccabees:* Ptolemy is soundly scourged upon entering the temple, chastised violently, and nearly killed, but is then pulled from the temple by his bodyguards.

In *Second Maccabees,* this process was sufficient to bring about the repentance of the main antagonist (Heliodorus), but in *Third Maccabees,* it merely sets the stage for the next encounter. The second major episode does not resonate at all with the temple propaganda theme of the first but addresses instead issues of Diaspora relations in Egypt. Although the temple/Diaspora distinction is appropriate for a narrative that deals first with Jerusalem and then with Egypt, the vast difference in the concerns of the rhetoric is remarkable.[36] The urgent prayers of the second part, rather than reverberating in the stones of the temple as above, resound in the land itself where the Jews are located: "And when the Jews beheld all this, they cried out to heaven with so great a voice that even the surrounding valleys resounded, creating an uncontrollable terror in the armed guard" (6:17). In the second episode, Ptolemy has recovered from his first chastisement, only to propound a greater calumny. He promulgates an edict requiring that all Jews sacrifice to Dionysus and receive the mark of initiation, or else face death. The edict is communicated by letter to the provinces, where a feast is held by the local peoples, as the Jews fall into wailing and mourning. The latter are gathered to Alexandria and herded into a hippodrome, where Ptolemy has corralled five hundred elephants to set loose upon them. Although Ptolemy has given instructions that the elephants are to be driven into a frenzy by being fed liberal amounts of frankincense and unmixed wine, God causes him to oversleep, requiring the mass execution to be postponed until the following day. The next day, God intervenes again, this time causing Ptolemy to lose all memory of his intentions toward the Jews. His memory eventually returns, however, and on the third day, the punishment is once again to be carried out. On this occasion God sends two fearsome angels, who terrify the beasts and send them crashing over the soldiers who had led them in. Upon seeing this, Ptolemy

---

[36] See Nickelsburg, *Jewish Literature Between the Bible and the Mishnah,* 169–72; Hadas, *The Third and Fourth Book of Maccabees,* 10–11; and Tcherikover, "The Third Book of Maccabees as a Historical Source of Augustus' Time," 6–8, for arguments for separate origins for the two sections. The fact that the first episode bears a literary resemblance to *Second Maccabees* 3 and the second to a tradition in Josephus regarding a different Ptolemy tends to corroborate the division of the text into two traditions.

repents of his evil plan and restores the Jews to their property. He proclaims another edict, rescinding the first and confirming the value of the Jews to the state.

The highly rhetorical, flowery style of *Third Maccabees* seems appropriate for the ludicrous machinations of the plot.[37] The dastardly designs of Ptolemy—exciting the elephants' fury with frankincense and wine—are as laughable as the particular methods God utilizes to undo him: causing him to oversleep one day and to forget his original plan the next. These are obvious devices to retard and sensationalize the plot, but they do not create anything resembling tension. One may find it hard to believe that the miracles could have been taken seriously and the whole work received as anything but fiction, but we should understand these miracles in the same way as those in the Christian historical novels, the apocryphal acts, where beasts are foiled and even speak, bedbugs march out of a house at the command of an apostle, and so forth. It is not fiction but history with power; the experience of faith overrides any serious consideration of believability. What is unusual about this historical novel is that God appears as such an active character, an antagonist of Ptolemy's. Simon the high priest and the elder Eleazar can pray, but there is really no agent in the narrative on the Jewish side, other than God. The odd plot constructions serve, therefore, to press another issue, which is that God can make fun of the pagan king. The pagan king has become a buffoon, but it is a pity that the satire is so poorly executed. Not only is *Third Maccabees* leaden when compared with *Esther* or *Daniel;* there is also no attempt whatsoever to provide a transition or a plausible recognition on Ptolemy's part when he is suddenly faced with the power of God. The text merely says: "The king's anger was changed to pity, and he began to weep for all the evil things he had devised" (6:22). He then turns to berate his officials for participating in the planned torture of loyal citizens. The dramatic transformations here are even thinner than is normally the case in popular entertainments.

Third Maccabees bears some striking similarities to *Esther,* in both tone and substance. The misguided plan to abolish the Jews; the two edicts of the king, the second rescinding the first, which give cause for grief or celebration; and the intervention of God (explicit in Greek *Esther,*

---

[37] See the remarks of Hadas, *Third and Fourth Book of Maccabees*, 14–15, and *Hellenistic Culture,* 127–29. The pretentiousness of the style is also reflected in the constant desire of the author to choose rare or unknown words. Over one hundred words are not found in the Greek Bible, and fourteen are not found elsewhere in Greek literature! See Pfeiffer, *History of New Testament Times,* 205.

not in Hebrew *Esther*) are apparent. In addition, in *Third Maccabees* as well as in *Esther,* the Jews, in celebration of their deliverance, ask the king to allow them an opportunity to take revenge without restraint. But whereas in *Esther* they seek and are granted permission to defend themselves against the non-Jewish enemies who would have attacked them, in *Third Maccabees* they ask permission to execute *Jews* who had consented to worship idols. The king grants this strange request, convinced by their argument that Jews who would violate their own laws would also not have remained good citizens of the realm. The revenge motif of *Esther* is thus played out here also but with a different target group. If one assumes, however, that Jewish identity is the issue that underlies the literary strategy of each work, then the shift in focus is not so difficult to comprehend. *Esther* intends by its literary strategy to create a community that has a self-conception of separateness. This process is, in anthropological terms, "boundary formation," the drawing of a line of demarcation around one's own social group. The author of *Third Maccabees* presumes this boundary but perceives a threat to it in the form of assimilation, a very real possibility in Alexandria. The author therefore attempts to stigmatize and objectify the "weaker" Jews and is concerned with "boundary maintenance."[38] The weak-willed Jews, those who would assimilate under the pressure of pagan society, are threatening enough to the author to be executed in the narrative. Scholars are rarely confronted with such clear specimens of the two categories, boundary formation and boundary maintenance, but the corollary of this clarity is that as the social worlds of the authors come more sharply into focus and become more "real," the historical and political circumstances involved become more ephemeral. *Third Maccabees* may perhaps describe some historical occurrence (whereas *Esther* likely does not), but it has been refracted through a very thick lens.

In addition to parallels to *Esther,* there are also similarities to other Jewish writings of the period, especially *The Letter of Aristeas,* but parallels of motifs notwithstanding, the genre of *Third Maccabees* is best described as historical novel. Considerations of the genre of "pathetic history," mentioned in connection with *Second Maccabees,* are not ruled

[38] See Bruce J. Malina, *Christian Origins and Cultural Anthropology* (Atlanta: John Knox Press, 1986), 38–39, and along the same lines (though without anthropological terminology), Pervo, *Profit with Delight,* 119–21. Tcherikover ("Third Book of Maccabees," 21) and Nickelsburg (*Jewish Literature,* 169) maintain that the work is anti-Gentile, but Collins (*Between Athens and Jerusalem,* 108) is correct in pointing out that the narrative effects a rapprochement with the Gentile king, as do *Daniel* and *Esther.*

out, but this term likely refers only to an emotional and overblown style loathed by sober critics.[39] It is the association with the other works in this chapter that defines the status of *Third Maccabees* as a historical novel.

The Royal Family of Adiabene

The Royal Family of Adiabene is a title of convenience that we may apply to a section of Josephus's *Antiquities* (20.2.1–4.1 §17–96) that is likely derived from an independent source.[40] It recounts the fortunes of the royal family of the small kingdom of Adiabene during the first century C.E. (that is, shortly before Josephus wrote his work). Adiabene was one of the Hellenized nation-states, along with Armenia and Commagene, that arose in the east with the breakup of Greek rule. The account begins with the marriage of King Monobazus and his sister, Helena. She becomes pregnant, and when the king, lying in bed, places his hand on her womb, he hears a voice telling him to withdraw it to let the baby within lie undisturbed. The common motif of the divinely sanctioned birth of the hero is here reflected, and we are told that it is "foreordained by God that this infant would be blessed with both an auspicious beginning and a happy end." The child who is born, Izates, becomes the center of the ensuing narrative.

When the brothers of Izates become intensely jealous of him on account of his father's favoritism, the king ships him off to live temporarily with a neighboring king, whose daughter, Symmacho, the young man marries. While there, Izates meets a Jewish merchant, Ananias, who has taught the royal women of the kingdom to worship God according to the Jewish tradition, and he eventually convinces Izates as well. When, therefore, Monobazus dies and Queen Helena summons Izates back to Adiabene to assume the throne, Ananias accompanies him as well. As it happens, Izates' mother, Queen Helena, had in the meantime also converted to Judaism, and Izates decides that it is time to be

[39] On the parallels to *Third Maccabees,* see Hadas, *Third and Fourth Book of Maccabees,* 6–15. He is correct in emphasizing the parallels to Greek romances rather than history writing; I have simply specified the category further by separating historical novels from novels proper. On *Third Maccabees* as "pathetic history," see Nickelsburg, *Jewish Literature,* 169.

[40] Other than short descriptions in general handbooks on Jewish literature, there is very little written on this section of Josephus, but note Geo Widengren, "Quelques rapports entre juifs et iraniens à l'époque des Parthes," Supplements to *Vetus Testamentum* 4 (1957): 197–241; Neusner, "The Conversion of Adiabene to Judaism"; and Schiffman, "The Conversion of the Royal House of Adiabene in Josephus and Rabbinic Sources."

circumcised. Helena and Ananias fear, however, that the citizens will rebel if he openly converts and is circumcised, and they convince him to continue reverence for the one God while forgoing circumcision. Soon another Jew passes through the court, Eleazar, who is more observant, and citing the Biblical law before them, he insists to Izates that worshipping God properly entails circumcision and the outward observance of the law. Although Queen Helena and Ananias are stricken with fear when they hear this, circumstances soon arise that allow Izates to become circumcised and yet remain on the throne.[41] Artabanus, the king of the neighboring Parthians, flees his country when a conspiracy is initiated against him and is received warmly by Izates. Though Artabanus has now been deposed, Izates intervenes with the new ruler of the Parthians to effect a peaceful repatriation of the deposed king. On another occasion, Izates intervenes once again to prevent Parthia from foolishly going to war against Rome. Because Izates is able on two occasions to become benefactor to the mighty neighboring country of Parthia, he receives the gratitude of its citizens. When those in the royal family who have not converted to Judaism see what great things Izates has accomplished, they convert also.

Nevertheless, this esteem within the palace is not matched by a similar regard among the people. The leading citizens of Adiabene will not stand for a wholesale conversion of the royal family to Judaism, and they enter into a conspiracy with Abias, king of the Arabs, and agree that if he will attack, they will abandon Izates on the battlefield. Although their plan is carried out, Izates still manages to win a decisive victory, defeating Abias, and he executes the traitorous leaders. Still other citizens, however, enter into another conspiracy with the new Parthian king, Vologeses, who has a much greater army. When Izates takes to the field, he places himself in God's hands. The next day, Vologeses receives word that Parthia has been invaded by nomads and quickly departs. The narrative is concluded after this: Izates dies after a happy life; his brother, now also a convert to Judaism, assumes the throne; and his mother dies soon after and is buried along with Izates in Jerusalem.

In many respects, the narrative is like the *Tobiad Romance*. The account treats an important Jewish family of the recent past, glorifying

---

[41] I am omitting a section of the account that concerns Queen Helena's pilgrimage to Jerusalem and her benefaction to the poor during a famine. It appears to disrupt the narrative and is also paralleled at Mishnah *Nazir* 3:6; it is likely an independent tradition about this important family of Jewish converts. Where Josephus once again takes up this motif at the end of the *Adiabene* section, it also appears to be added secondarily.

the exploits of one or two central figures. This text differs mainly in being more pious in tone. The ideology of patronage, so constant in the *Tobiad Romance,* may lie behind this text as well: it is Izates' benefaction to Artabanus that turns the tide to Izates within his own kingdom. We may even term these two novels, along with the possible Onias-as-broker source of *Second Maccabees* 3–4, as "patron novels." *The Royal Family of Adiabene* also affirms that God guided Izates' fortune and that converting to Judaism was the source of his strength, even when many of his own citizens opposed it.[42]

This historical novel is often utilized for the reconstruction of Jewish missionary practices, as well it should be,[43] but even the historical novels have a "novelistic" reflection of social norms and ideals. The "message" of *Adiabene* is not so much about missionary practices as about Jewish identity. A pagan king comes to revere God according to Jewish tradition, but will he have the courage to be circumcised and proclaim his Judaism openly? This thematic problem is not unlike *Esther,* where identification with Jews is the psychological tension, even if outward observance is not there an issue. However, it is also like *Third Maccabees* in objectifying and condemning any reverence for Judaism that lacks outward observances.[44] One wonders, then, to what extent even the "historical" novel manipulates the historical figures to create, for literary and rhetorical effect, a tension and its resolution. The first missionary presents a pleasing message, a worship of the one true God without outward manifestation, but this message is challenged and finally overcome by the demand of the second missionary, who sees the necessity in Judaism of openly observing the law, as in *Third Maccabees.* This freedom with historical traditions is manifested in the other Jewish and Christian historical novels. One of the closest parallels, in fact, may be found in the *Acts of the Apostles,* a Christian historical novel that is roughly contemporary. We note, first of all, that the second Jewish missionary, Eleazar, finds Izates reading the law of Moses and adjures him to do what is commanded in it. In *Acts* 8 the missionary Philip meets an Ethiopian eunuch reading Isaiah and likewise counsels him to convert to Christianity on the basis of what he is reading. It has also

[42] It is certainly true that the great "benefactions" to Parthia, especially the diplomacy of opposing a war with Rome, can easily be seen as enlightened self-interest, but this view may be Josephus's own editorializing. Championing the cause of Rome and the folly of open opposition is a constant theme of his writings.

[43] See, e.g., Collins, *Between Athens and Jerusalem,* 164–68.

[44] Philo also condemns those Jews who would contemplate the eternal truths of their religion without participating in the outward observances (*Migration of Abraham* 89–93).

not escaped scholarly notice that the two Jewish missionaries, one liberal in his interpretation of requirements and one strict, are vaguely like
Peter and Paul.[45] The parallel of *Acts* could be pressed further. Scholars
have focused on the *historical* parallel of Ananias and Eleazar, liberal and
conservative missionaries, with Peter and Paul, to the detriment of the
literary parallel. One might assume that since *Acts* concerns missionary
activity, it is about boundary formation, that is, increasing the number
of Christians and identifying their separateness from pagan and Jewish
society. The message, however, as in *Royal Family of Adiabene,* may be
directed at those who are already converted. In each case the reader of
the historical novel is left to conclude that the "incorrect" view was supplanted by the "correct" view. The author of *Acts* probably intended to
reinforce an already existing boundary between Jews and Christians.[46]
The foregoing analysis of *Royal Family of Adiabene* and of *Acts* points up a
possible line of investigation in popular Jewish and Christian literature
(and, indeed, in popular literature in general), which is to discern in the
texts a "morphology of values," that is, to determine the ways in which
strongly held values are arrayed in opposition to each other, only to be
resolved ultimately into a benign happy ending. The ideological message of the text is thus communicated in a set of structural or syntactic
relationships that are not unlike the relationships of plot elements that
Vladimir Propp detects in fairy tales (see Chapters 1 and 8 of this book).
Approached in this way, the concrete "facts" of a historical novel are
seen to be malleable and vague, with an uncertain relation to the real
social world of the author and audience, whereas the values arrayed in
binary oppositions are much more dependable guides to the symbolic
universe of the text. The historical novels appear to be particularly ame-

[45] W. D. Davies, *Paul and Rabbinic Judaism* (London: S.P.C.K., 1948), 133 n.1. There are
also parallels with rabbinic figures, e.g., Shammai and Hillel, or Rabbi Joshua and Rabbi
Eliezer (*Yebamot* 46a). See J. Klausner, *From Jesus to Paul* (Boston: Beacon, 1943), 39–40; B. J.
Bamberger, *Proselytism in the Talmudic Period* (Cincinnati: Hebrew Union College Press, 1939),
48–51. Parallel traditions concerning the royal family of Adiabene are also found in rabbinic
literature, for example, *Genesis Rabbah* 46:10, Mishnah *Nazir* 3:6 and *Yoma* 3:10, and in the
Babylonian Talmud *Baba Bathra* 11a, *Sukkah* 2b, and *Menahot* 32b.

[46] Some scholars on *Acts* posit an early author who is looking ahead to future missionary
successes and is not particularly anti-Jewish, but I am more convinced by those who date
Acts to a later period (second century) and who envision an author who is looking *back* on a
romanticized period of early Christian missionary activity, which was supposedly troubled
by Jewish resistance. For the author of *Acts,* the boundary maintenance comes not in insisting
that Jews and Christians are separate—that would be boundary formation—but in insisting
that Jews were the ones who broke off relations. See most recently Jack T. Sanders, *The Jews
in Luke-Acts* (Philadelphia: Fortress, 1987), and Wills, "The Depiction of the Jews in Acts."

nable to this sort of analysis, consisting as they do of a series of value oppositions. Indeed, this tendency of historical novels can be invoked as one of the criteria of defining the subgenre.[47]

One more aspect of this narrative—indeed, of all the historical novels—must also demand our attention. The novels proper contain scenes of the female protagonist's debasement and prayer, which are clear focuses of the dramatic action. Several of the historical novels contain similar scenes but with important differences. In *Royal Family of Adiabene,* for instance, when Izates is beset by the Parthian king Vologeses, he refuses to capitulate, and we are told:

> He threw himself upon the ground and befouled his head with ashes and then fasted, together with his wife and children, calling upon God all the while: "Surely it is not for nothing, O Lord and Master, that I have been allowed to taste of your bounty and have come to consider you truly as the first and only Lord of all things. Come, be my defender and ally; protect me from my enemies, not only for my sake, but because they now dare to challenge your power." Izates thus lamented loudly, through tears and moans, and God heard his cry. On that very night, Vologeses received letters bearing the news that a large army of Dahae and Sakae had invaded and begun to lay waste to Parthia. (§89–91)

The penitential prayer and ritual of mourning is here enacted by a man (his wife and children are present but not rendered dramatically). Novels proper, certainly in their later stages, only depict women in this role, but the historical novels depict men or, as in *Second* and *Third Maccabees,* the citizenry as a whole in central scenes of penitence. Women sometimes appear, often with a sexually charged connotation, as when the normally secluded young women rush into the streets in ritual protest, their beautiful locks covered with dust and ashes (*Second Maccabees* 3:19–20; *Third Maccabees* 1:19, 4:6) They are part of the body of Jews, however, not individuals as they would be in the other novels. The psychological function appears different as well. In the historical novels, the emotional display and the prayer is brief and external and is followed immediately by God's response. The focus, in fact, is really on God's actions as the dramatic movement in the narrative. There is a

[47] In the debate among New Testament scholars over whether *Acts* is more like a history or a novel, it seems clear to me now that it belongs in this middle category of historical novel, not least because of its use of this technique of the binary opposition of values, specifically, Jewish opposition to the Christian mission and the resulting expansions. See Sanders, *Jews in Luke-Acts,* and Wills, "Depiction of the Jews."

strong manipulation of emotional reactions and pathos but little exploration of internal or individual emotional states. In the novels proper,
however, the ritual debasement and prayer is generally part of an intense psychological experience, which is felt by the female character and
in turn by the audience as well. The interest of the narrative in the novel
has been redirected, at least for a time, from the external events to the
inner state of the protagonist. God does intervene in the narrative events
at the conclusion of the prayer, but this intervention seems less important in the experience of reading the novel than the protagonist's shift
in identity from a voluptuous woman tainted with sin to a thoroughly
scourged and penitent partner of God. Once again, we are at a loss to
determine whether this is purely a statement about women and female
psychology—a construction of gender in respect to the nature of the
female psyche in its innermost recesses—or an appeal to the "feminine"
side of all readers, an exploration of bourgeois vulnerability that is examined in the person of a female protagonist. Surely it is possible that
both psychological experiences are at work in the novels.

CHAPTER 8

The Analysis of Genre and the Poetics of the Jewish Novel

Despite the difficulties in defining all of the formal characteristics of the Jewish novel, the general outlines of a hermeneutical model of the genre emerge fairly clearly. Although great differences are found in the narrative frames—largely attributable to the diverse backgrounds of the story materials—an attitude or "mode" can be discerned that is analogous in some respects to the Greek novel and to the popular written narratives of other ethnic groups. The Jewish novels are highly entertaining prose narratives, of roughly the same length, that tell the dramatic adventures of named but non-"canonical" individuals of the ancient past.[1] The shift toward more typical, less heroic protagonists is paralleled in the Greek novels and, as I noted in the Introduction, is characteristic of the modern novel as well, where the quite revolutionary focus on named but otherwise unknown individuals created an art form of everyday reality.[2] Like novels cross-culturally, the Jewish novels manipulate the written medium, utilizing such techniques as description, dialogue, and psychological introspection. The focus can be on broad social events—for example, the threat of the destruction of the Jews of Persia or of Bethulia and Jerusalem—but the social network in which the protagonists are situated is always the extended family. It further appears that the novels were read as fictions; that is, neither the author nor the audience presumed any referent in past events.

---

[1] As noted in Chapter 1, a shift occurs in *Joseph and Aseneth* from a focus on a canonical protagonist (Joseph) to a figure who is nothing more than a name in the canon (Aseneth).
[2] Ian Watt, *The Rise of the Novel*, 9–30.

I have posited a history of the Jewish novel that is roughly parallel, but lies partially prior, to the Greek novel, and the reflection of each that can be found in the other should be pressed as far as possible. Since the Jewish novels can in some cases be dated earlier than most of the Greek novels, they may be used to illuminate the early history of Greek novelistic literature. The Jewish novels lack some of the salient characteristics of the Greek—the lengthy recounting of adventures, travel, romantic love—yet they are interesting nevertheless for an analysis of the development of the novel, since they share some of the same ethos. They are rousing fictions that evoke strong emotional responses, and they also demonstrate a number of ways that shorter legendary materials were expanded to appeal to a new literate audience.

The emotion that is central to all ancient novelistic literature is not found simply in the depiction of a series of characters exhibiting love, fear, hatred, and so on; it is in the very fabric of the narrative. As the heroine says to the hero near the end of Heliodorus's *Ethiopian Story:* "The fact that we are so beset by one misfortune coming directly after another and subject to such various and excessive torments suggests that we are under heaven's curse and the victims of divine malevolence— unless it is the divinity's way of working miracles to plunge us deep in despair and then deliver us from the abyss!" (8.10). This last line could equally well describe the workings of the Jewish novel. Within the overarching category of novelistic literature in the ancient world, we do not find a set of themes that would tie them all together, not even the favorite themes of love and travel. There is a single ethos, however, that characterizes the broad group of writings: they consist of prose narratives that exploit new literate-culture techniques to entertain by manipulating emotion, that is, Jean Radford's "non-mimetic prose narrative focusing on emotion."

The Greek novels harness this broad conception of a genre to a particular theme, the adventures of a young, idealized conjugal couple and the threats to their chastity and perfect union; correspondingly, the central experience of the Greek novel is a recovery of identity in a rootless society. Jewish novels can equally be said to explore the theme of identity, but that identity is defined and communicated very differently, as is also the case in the novelistic writings of other indigenous cultures. The Jewish novels focus less on the importance of the mating of the conjugal couple and more on the extended family relationships and loyalty among Jews, although this focus too begins to change in *Joseph and Aseneth,* the last of the novels. Over time they increasingly emphasize the woman's scene of repentance, a theme found elsewhere in postexilic Judaism but here embodied by a vulnerable figure whose experience is transparent to everyone.[3]

Some of the differences among the novels arise from the diverse nature of the source materials. *Daniel* and *Tobit* may be derived from Persian narrative models, probably oral, whereas the later narratives, *Judith* and *Joseph and Aseneth,* do not reflect oral models directly but appear to result from a fully literate composition. Walter Ong has described the transformation of thinking and communication that is involved in this change from predominantly oral to predominantly literate culture,[4] and although this distinction should not become overly schematized, the literate culture developments are reflected in the development of Jewish novels. Many of the new themes of novelistic literature are precisely the concerns of literate culture, especially introspectivity and the creation of a "vaulted narrative," the extension of a single climactic plot line into an elongated reading experience, without recourse to separable episodes or repetitions.[5] Although I argued in Chapter 1 that popular novelistic literature exists as a midpoint between oral and high literary culture, it is fundamentally a literate-culture product, not a transcribed oral composition. It is composed by a writing author, in a literate environment, for an audience that consumes it in a way comparable to the way that other literate-culture writings were consumed (even if this involved a group reading or performance).

The early stages of the Jewish novels are likely only one step removed from oral performance. *Daniel* 1–6 is a collection of most likely oral legends, and *Tobit* is a literary rendering of common folk motifs. Their lack of conformity to literary-culture criteria can be seen in the way they have incorporated insertions without smoothing over the transitions. I have argued that *Daniel, Tobit,* and *Esther* (even Hebrew *Esther*) are all composite and that the "seams" are easily recognized. Other scholars have denied the composite nature of these writings, on the grounds that the supposed seams should be considered part of a compositional strategy of one author. No editor, it is argued, could be *that* oblivious

---

[3] It is not unrelated to the use of weak members of society in the earliest martyrdom accounts. An old man, a mother, and her seven sons are chosen as the role models in *Second Maccabees* 6–7, perhaps to show that their strength to witness to the ideals of Judaism was not based on physical strength but could be emulated by everyone.

[4] Ong, *Orality and Literacy.*

[5] Ibid., 69, 105, 153–54, 141–47. On vaulted narrative, see chapter 5. Ong uses the term "Freytag's pyramid," rather than vaulted narrative, to describe the same thing: a narrative that has a rising line of action, a climax with a *peripeteia* or reversal, and a falling line of action or denouement.

to the need for a smooth transition; the seams must reflect an intentional poetics whose rules are not precisely the same as our own. Rough seams, however, are only an inconcinnity in *literary* culture. Those who can read and write but who live in a predominantly oral culture occupy a special role in the history of literacy and of literature. "Scribal culture," an important and valid category for the study of the ancient Near East and elsewhere, is not usually literate culture. Scribal culture is usually the subculture of literate professionals in an illiterate society who reflect so-called craft literacy. Their drive to eliminate clumsy transitions and repetitions was probably less exercised than that of, say, the letter writers of eighteenth-century England who were part of an emerging literate culture (mentioned in Chapter 1), whom Samuel Richardson addressed in his guidebooks. Scribes in oral culture are often content to conflate texts and insertions without being overly concerned for transitions and narrative flow. The "story line," in the mind of a scribe in such a culture exists above and outside of the text and is undisturbed by infelicitous editing.[6] The recent transition in our own society from literary media to film and video suggests an analogous situation. During the 1940s and 1950s, World War II movies often incorporated newsreel footage of actual fighting, creating abrupt visual transitions. Such "seams" could no longer be perpetrated on an audience raised on television, and they were avoided in later films. Similarly, the last novels in our series, *Judith* and *Joseph and Aseneth,* do not betray telltale seams, and the mystical material that has evidently been added to the latter is not easily separated out verse by verse.

Although the Greco-Roman (and Jewish) worlds with which we are concerned were hardly fully literate when compared with other periods in world history, the literacy rate was probably quite high.[7] The reader-

---

[6] The possibility in general of a "story line" existing outside of a text or performance is entertained by scholars utilizing various methods. On the biblical prophet legends, see Alexander Rofé, "The Classification of the Prophetical Stories," *Journal of Biblical Literature* 89 (1970): 427–40, and, among literary critics, Rimmon-Kenan, *Narrative Fiction,* 6–8; Bal, *Narratology,* 11–48; and Gérard Genette, *Figures III* (Paris: Seuil, 1972), 71–76. The latter, for example, distinguishes between *histoire* (what I have called story line), *récit* (the text as it appears before the reader), and *narration* (the process by which a persona is created who narrates the story). Bal modifies Genette's divisions, using slightly different terminology.

On documenting examples of conflation in ancient texts that leave visible seams, see Jeffrey Tigay, ed., *Empirical Models for Biblical Criticism* (Philadelphia: University of Pennsylvania Press, 1985).

[7] The Greek language had become what Ong and others call a "grapholect," a widely disseminated medium for both oral and written discourse, which had developed a vocabulary and a syntactic complexity sufficient for literate-culture applications. See also E. D. Hirsch, Jr., *The Philosophy of Composition* (Chicago: University of Chicago, 1977), 43–48. Aramaic and

ship of Jewish novels would have been restricted to an educated class, but it was likely not as elite a grouping as that of the Greek and Roman novels, and the simple Greek of *Joseph and Aseneth* indicates the potential of a more democratized audience for the Jewish novel. The separate achievements of Hebrew *Esther, Judith,* or *Joseph and Aseneth* indicate the direction of Jewish literary culture and reflect the full engagement of new techniques to appeal to a literate audience, treatments in miniature of what we might associate with modern novels. It is carried out somewhat differently in the various novels, as if the same obsession were finding its partial and imperfect realization in the hands of a number of artists, but nowhere in the ancient world will we find a better series of controls and test cases for studying the transition from oral to literary culture and the rise of the novelistic impulse.

The Analysis of Genre and the Poetics of the Jewish Novel

In the Introduction, approaches to genre were divided into those that focus on semantic elements of a text and those that focus on syntactic relationships of the elements present. Semantic elements might consist of, on a superficial level, setting, characters, tone, and so on or, on a deeper level, themes such as endurance for epic, or love as identity in the Greek novel. Syntactic or morphological approaches, on the other hand, focus not on the individual elements, whether superficial or profound, but on the relations between separate elements. The elements themselves in such a definition are found to be variable and less intrinsically significant, except insofar as they relate to each other. Vladimir Propp suggests, for example, that the wide variety of Russian fairy tales can be reduced to a small group of structural relationships.[8] In many different tales we might find "lack" and "lack liquidated" as interrelated aspects of the plot, or "interdiction" and "interdiction violated." Furthermore, the interrelated plot elements would always occur in the same sequence, whereas the characters who act out these scenarios or the places where the stories are set are of less importance in determining genre than

---

Hebrew, the original languages of most of the novels, were also close to becoming grapholects in their own right, but it is significant that some of the more novelistic developments in the Jewish novels were composed in Greek, i.e., *Joseph and Aseneth* and some of the additions to *Esther.*

[8] Propp, *The Morphology of the Folktale.*

the structural relationships involved. Both semantic and syntactic approaches have continued to emphasize the importance of genre for our reading of a text and have in general been positive about the possibility of defining the criteria by which genres are identified.[9] Whereas semantic studies can look to any aspect of a text as a clue or code of its proper genre, syntactic studies claim access to an underlying core of relations and oppositions. I would propose that genre studies not be limited exclusively either to semantic or syntactic definitions. It would certainly be a mistake to assume, as some do, that semantic definitions are more superficial and structural analyses more attuned to the deep, constitutive core of a genre. Awareness of both semantic and syntactic codes is crucial to genre literacy. It is possible to delineate both semantic and syntactic descriptions of a genre, as Rick Altman has done,[10] but they must be set out separately and in order and only then interrelated. By reexamining certain aspects of the foregoing study of the Jewish novel, this same method can be applied here.

The semantic approach, followed through most of this book, will be reviewed first. The interrelationship of the members of the genre of Jewish novel is indicated by, among other things, two semantic elements that can be highlighted for special consideration: the "historical blunder" and the "woman's scene of self-debasement and regeneration."

The Significance of the Historical Blunder

There is an English jump-rope song that goes "Nebuchadnezzar, king of the Jews / Bought his wife a pair of shoes." The audacious and fun-loving attitude that lies behind this bold alteration of history is somewhat analogous to the disregard for historical facts in the novels. English children have doubtless been unaware of the inaccuracy, preferring instead to focus on the rhythmic bounce of the cadence, but the similar inaccuracies found in the novels were probably engaged in knowingly, part of the contract between author and audience in the consumption of popular literature. The rise of historical writing in pre-exilic Israel represented such a remarkable achievement that it becomes difficult to reconcile it with the later popular writings. The author of

[9] In addition to works included in the introduction, see Todorov, "Introduction," in *The Fantastic;* and Hawkes, *Structuralism and Semiotics.*

[10] Rick Altman, *The American Film Musical* (Bloomington: Indiana University Press, 1987), 95–102. On the relation of Altman's theories to literary criticism, see Chapter 1.

Daniel thought nothing of including what to us appear as egregious errors, such as Belshazzar losing the Babylonian kingdom to "Darius the Mede," [11] nor did the author of *Judith* balk at introducing the character "Nebuchadnezzar, king of the Assyrians."

Furthermore, it is not merely the *fact* of history writing in ancient Israel that is so remarkable; it is also its demanding moral purpose. The very phrase *Deuteronomistic history* (the name given to the older strand of the Former Prophets: *Joshua, Judges, First* and *Second Samuel,* and *First* and *Second Kings*) is coupled with *Deuteronomistic theology,* that is, the view that God condemns in history those who do not abide in the revealed laws. It is all the more striking, therefore, when alongside this shocking historical inaccuracy we also often find an equally shocking gap in the moral reckoning of history, for in Daniel there remains a surprisingly positive attitude toward Nebuchadnezzar. If one wanted to search for an archtypical villain in ancient Jewish history, one could hardly do better than Nebuchadnezzar—Morton Enslin referred to him as the "archvillain of all time," the "all-wicked king." [12] If the impression made upon the modern reader is that *Daniel* 1–6 condemns Nebuchadnezzar outright, it is influenced by the tradition about Nebuchadnezzar more in keeping with the oracles against Babylon in *Isaiah* and *Jeremiah.* [13] Surely one would expect consistency in depicting such a tyrant, especially one who was so destructive of Jews and Jewish institutions. The historical blunders that appear in *Daniel* and the other novels—not minor inaccuracies but wild flights of mock history—doubtless arise from the nature of the genre as a source of amusement and correspond to a similar tendency in Greek novelistic literature. [14] The humor or satire may vary from the romantic or whimsical (*Tobit*) to the farcical (*Esther*), but it seems in every case to be related to the creation of imagined worlds, that is, fiction. The historical blunders do not result from gaps in the au-

[11] Commentaries on *Daniel* will, of course, try to account for this discrepancy with the known facts by suggesting the actual identity of the historical personage who is "intended" in Darius the Mede or by noting that a Median king is required at this point in the succession of kingdoms because of the older oracle in *Daniel* 2. As I noted in Chapter 2, however, we are still left with a historical absurdity.

[12] Enslin and Zeitlin, *The Book of Judith,* (Leiden: Brill, 1972), 58–59.

[13] To be sure, the interpretation of Nebuchadnezzar's character was not totally consistent in ancient Judaism. Jeremiah appears on the surface to be ambivalent, but see John Bright, *Jeremiah* (Garden City, N.Y.: Doubleday, 1965), 201–3, 210–12 (on chapters 27–29) and 339–60 (on chapters 50–51), and A. Malamat, "Jeremiah and the Last Two Kings of Judah," *Palestine Exploration Quarterly* 83 (1951): 81–87. The third- or second-century author of *Apocryphal (First) Baruch* seems more accommodationist, although Babylon may be a cipher for some other kingdom.

[14] Winkler, *Auctor & Actor,* 280.

thors' knowledge but are an expected part of the experience of reading fiction.

The other Jewish novels appear as well to play with willful historical inaccuracies. *Tobit* begins with a historical setting that comports fairly well with the known succession of Assyrian kings (with the exception of a minor confusion of Shalmaneser for Sargon), but the author soon transforms Ahikar the Assyrian court counselor into Ahikar the Israelite; more striking is that at *Tobit* 14:15 Tobit is said to have lived long enough to see the destruction of Nineveh, capital of Assyria, by Nebuchadnezzar and Asueros (Ahasuerus, or Xerxes), king of Media. Nebuchadnezzar's father, Nabopolassar, and Cyaxeres, king of Media, actually captured Nineveh in 612 B.C.E. The substitution of Nebuchadnezzar for Nabopolassar here is understandable—it even occurs in some modern commentaries—but transforming a famous king of Persia, Xerxes, into a Median king and then compounding the blunder by placing him at the scene of the fall of Nineveh in Assyria is quite a different matter.[15] The spanning of centuries and recombination of monarchies contradict the sense of history that would have been known to literate Jews.

Judith, like *Daniel* and *Esther,* begins in a style that is typical of royal chronicles—"In the twelfth year of the reign of Nebuchadnezzar . . ."—but immediately the other shoe falls: ". . . who reigned over the Assyrians from his capital, Nineveh. . . ." The two most destructive powers in ancient Jewish history, Babylonia and Assyria, are here merged. A temptation to find some semblance of historical verisimilitude is inspired elsewhere in *Judith,* and we noted that Holofernes and Bagoas are two names associated with a military expedition of the Persian king Artaxerxes III Ochus into the West in about 350 B.C.E. This dating at least makes sense of the postexilic situation that is presupposed in 4:3 and 5:19. But the Great Error remains: Nebuchadnezzar, king of the Assyrians! Ernst Haag could argue that this error was all part of a grand parabolic and eschatological reading of history: the historical opponents are really to be understood as the metahistorical enemy of God, gathering to themselves all of the attributes of real and mythological opponents of God and the Jews in Biblical history: "The pagan world powers are no longer to be found in a real, historical realm, but in an ideal, metahistorical realm."[16] Other, perhaps more plausible ex-

---

[15] Zimmermann solves the interpretive problem of this blunder by correcting the names of the kings, with no textual warrant, on the assumption that the original text must have contained the correct kings (*The Book of Tobit,* 123).

[16] Haag, *Studien zum Buch Judith,* 78. On difficulties with Haag's involved hermeneutic of *Judith,* see the review by Frank Zimmermann, *Journal of Biblical Literature* 82 (1963): 343–44.

planations could be given for the Great Error, such as that Assyria is a cipher for Syria, that is, the recently defeated Seleucids,[17] but in any case we would have to ask how it is permissible to make over an important figure from history.

The book of *Esther,* probably also fictitious (that is, not bad history but a story without a referent in past events), nevertheless creates a certain degree of verisimilitude in its depiction of the Persian court. The king in question, Ahasuerus (Xerxes), was, as noted above, a Persian king who resided half the year in Susa. *Esther,* then, does not present the ancient or modern reader with impossible successions of kings, as do *Daniel, Tobit,* and *Judith.* Yet we find here a patently unhistorical situation: the queen of Persia is Jewish. As in *Tobit* and *Daniel,* Jews are found in the highest offices in the court, but here the "office" is the queenship, and it is in a dynasty not as far removed in the past as was the case with *Daniel* and *Tobit.* Would Jews in the third and second centuries B.C.E. have considered this possible? More likely, it was perceived as the permissible invention of a popular work of entertainment.[18] The story of *Joseph and Aseneth* also begins by presenting the circumstances of Joseph as they would have been known by the readers from biblical history: he becomes Pharaoh's prime minister. But surely the conclusion of the novel would have been read as a deviation from well-known canonical traditions: Joseph supplants Pharaoh's oldest son (after the latter had been killed by Joseph's brothers) and actually comes to rule Egypt between the time that Pharaoh dies and his infant son matures. What is perhaps a more surprising innovation for the historical conception of Jews of the Greco-Roman period is the internecine fighting of Joseph's brothers and their attempt to kill him, *after* he has been reconciled to them in Egypt. This, above all, would appear as a narrative digression wholly outside the scrolls of history.[19] The flights from the biblical ac-

---

[17] See Nickelsburg, *Jewish Literature Between the Bible and the Mishnah,* 108–9.

[18] Fox (*The Redaction of the Books of Esther,* 153) finds in *Esther* 9:20–32 a claim of historicity based on the recording of events in letters. This section, however, is likely a Purim addition, inserted into the older story of Esther to give Purim an appearance of the stamp of authority (Wills, *The Jew in the Court of the Foreign King,* 169–72). But even if this section were not an addition but were instead part of an older stratum, the claim to authenticity would be very tenuous and, one might think, halfhearted, even lighthearted. The reference in *Esther* 10:2 to the "Books of the Chronicles of the kings of Media and Persia" is also more likely an intentional hyperbole than it is actual proof texting.

[19] In regard to *Joseph and Aseneth,* each of the major discrepancies from biblical tradition that were introduced—Joseph as king of Egypt and his brothers' attempt to kill him—are found in later rabbinic literature. Does their attestation in midrashic literature indicate that the rabbis knew them as historical traditions? Not necessarily. Midrashic literature often incorporates

count in *Joseph and Aseneth* were likely seen by the author and audience as fiction, as they were in the other novels.

Beneath the alterations of history, the wish fulfillment of Jewish influence can be seen. In *Esther,* for instance, the queen of Persia is Jewish, but equally important is the final note of the book, where it is stated that Mordecai has become a great prime minister (10:3). The individual legends of *Daniel* 1–6, all beyond the bounds of believability depict Daniel and his three companions as the highest courtiers in the land. In the Book of *Tobit,* Ahikar, the privy counselor to the Assyrian kings, must also be Jewish, since he is Tobit's nephew. The character Achior in *Judith* is evidently the same figure as Ahikar, and although he is not depicted as Jewish, he does become a proselyte. The depiction of Jews in positions of power and respect thus must have been a major attraction of the novels. The historical blunders found in these texts are also associated with the use of irony and humor. Irony is not uncommon in ancient literature, as I noted in Chapter 2, and in these texts it is used for a similar humorous effect, employed quite unstintingly in *Tobit, Judith,* and *Bel and the Dragon.* Graham Anderson has studied the humorous and often self-satirizing effects found in the Greek novels, effects he feels have been underestimated.[20] He notes that educated and sophisticated authors employ humorous effects more than do the less educated authors, but his sampling is too narrow. He considers only the works of those Jewish and Christian authors who are more humorless, such as *Joseph and Aseneth* and the Apocryphal Acts, but not the other novels or *Acts of the Apostles*.

The suggestion that Jewish readers of this period would have perceived these works as fictional is not, however, without its problems. Our first interpreter of *Daniel* 1–6, for example, is the author (or authors) who composed the apocalyptic visions of *Daniel* 7–12 and combined them in the same work. It is difficult to imagine that the eschatologically oriented scribes who penned the visions during the height of the Maccabean Revolt would have knowingly incorporated them into a

---

the antic and the fantastic; the rabbis were attempting to provide edifying and imaginative interpretations of scripture, rather than to establish a line of objective inquiry. One might consider, for example, the cows that sing the praises of God at *Genesis Rabbah* 54:4. Is this historical record or a whimsical narrative world, where cattle can also join in lauding God? For a summary of the motifs concerning Joseph, see Louis Ginsberg, *The Legends of the Jews,* 7 vols. (Philadelphia: Jewish Publication Society, 1968) 5:326 nn. 7–9, 5:350 n. 234, 5:374–75 n. 432. The motif of Joseph as king or vice-regent is alluded to somewhat vaguely at *Testament of Levi* 13:9 and in *Targum Pseudo-Jonathan* regarding *Genesis* 41:44.

[20] Anderson, *Eros Sophistes,* 89.

text that was read as fiction. We further note that at *Daniel* 9:1, Darius the Mede is taken up again, this time with a slight correction. He is now Darius, *by birth* (*mizera*) a Mede, but son of Ahasuerus (Xerxes). Does the author mean to suggest that Darius is only a Mede *by birth* and is now associated with the Persian dynasty (even if the order Xerxes-Darius is inverted)? If so, the author is correcting the tradition as if it were a historical source, as if it did have a referent in past events that needs to be clarified, not as if it were a fiction that could contain an impossible personage. Josephus also incorporates into his *Antiquities* the story of *Esther* (complete with the additions of Greek *Esther*) and the narrative of *Daniel* (interestingly, without the Greek additions). Regarding *Esther,* he follows the tradition in the Greek Bible in confusing Artaxerxes for Xerxes and does not hesitate to recount how Esther, a Jew, became queen of Persia. Regarding *Daniel,* we may detect an attempt to correct or harmonize the text. The narrative of *Daniel* is combined with accounts of Nebuchadnezzar from Berossus, Megasthenes, and other non-Jewish historians, and problematic details are corrected to some extent. Belshazzar, who was never really king of Babylon, is identified by Josephus with Nabonidus, who was, and Darius the Mede is mentioned but is identified as "son of Astyages," who was the last Median king. Josephus further says (*Antiquities* 10.11.4§248) that Darius the Mede "was called by another name among the Greeks," indicating that he chooses to avoid embarrassment by assuming that this figure must be known by two names. These changes indicate that he wanted to render this history more accurately and did not read *Daniel* as fiction.

One could argue that a fact/fiction distinction is a modern fascination, inappropriate for Jewish literature of this period. This would certainly be the case for earlier biblical literature, where authority from God is the truth claim of the text more than a journalistic objectivity, but the Jewish literature in question lies right in the period of fundamental changes in this regard. Herodotus, Thucydides, and Plato all display an interest in utilizing a clear distinction between truth and falsehood, even if their criteria are not precisely our own (see Chapter 1), and this intellectual critique had influenced many historians, who nevertheless continued to struggle with credulity. Already by the third century B.C.E. Demetrius the Chronographer, a Jewish historian, composed a rationalized chronology of biblical history,[21] and although many ancient

---

[21] See the introduction and translation by J. Hanson in James H. Charlesworth, ed., *The Old Testament Pseudepigrapha,* 2 vols. (Garden City, N.Y.: Doubleday, 1985), 2:843–54.

historians—Greek, Roman, and Jewish—continue to exhibit what we would call gullibility in regard to miracles, they also assert that they are involved in a critical reevaluation of received tradition.[22] This much was accepted as an academic ideal. They claimed to know the difference between the truth and a lie, but this is not the same difference as that between fact and fiction. Fiction, the art of creating narratives that do not have a referent in past events, is not really a lie; it is a mutually agreed upon flight of imagination, a playful reflection on what reality is and what it is not. Prose fiction arose in just such a reflection on the academically serious and pretentious genre of history, and it is not clear that everyone appreciated—or even perceived—the humor and irony that is inherent in fiction.[23] Fiction as a plastic art, as a playful counterpart to fact, was a new category that did not immediately gain acceptance. There was, after all, no known word for "novel" even during the period when many were being composed in Greek, Latin, and Hebrew. *Daniel* 9 and Josephus both reflect some attempt to harmonize Darius the Mede with their received historical tradition—they could turn a lie into the truth—but they may have been unable to detect fiction in the tradition. This is especially understandable in the case of *Daniel* 9. The *maskilim,* or sages, who were responsible for combining *Daniel* 1–6 with *Daniel* 7–12 were a pressed sectarian group who were most likely uninterested in the droll possibilities of the Daniel legends. Ironic and satirical effects are sometimes lost on the pious, who in this case were unprepared for the new category of written prose fiction.[24] Josephus,

22 See recently Veyne, *Did the Greeks Believe in Their Myths?*

23 Veyne examines the ancient historians' credulousness about their myths (despite their insistence on a relentless critical evaluation), but his real target, as his last chapter shows, is the analogous credulousness of modern historians who think that they are able to escape the mythology of *their* time and write objective history. Whether or not one accepts his critique, in the process he obscures several points that are crucial for the present study. He attempts to blur the distinction between fact and fiction, on the one hand, and truth and falsehood, on the other. For instance, he asserts that since people *believe* fiction to be true while they are reading it (by the process of the temporary suspension of disbelief), it is no different from history, and history is thus relativized. His epistemological challenge makes for interesting reading, but it is still possible to distinguish *genres* on the basis of the distinctions the reader would likely have made. Whether the Jewish novels do, as I suggest, present a clear *fictitious* world is another question, one I hope to resolve here.

24 An analogous issue is found in the reception of Xenophon's *Cyropaedia.* Plato, who is writing before the flowering of fiction, appears to treat it as history—at least as he conceives it (*Laws* 3.694C–698A)—whereas Cicero, writing much later, felt that it was clearly meant to be taken as fiction (*Ep. ad Quintum fratrem* 1.1.23; see Steven W. Hirsch, *The Friendship of the Barbarians: Xenophon and the Persian Empire* [Hanover: University Press of New England, 1985], 169 n. 11).

likewise, is committed to the most pretentious ideal of the historian and is incapable of telling a good story (unless he is at the center of it). The diverting literature of this period, however, has a logic of its own; it creates a fanciful atmosphere in which historical figures are recast at will—Jews can become the most powerful officials in the land, and the tyrant Nebuchadnezzar is capable of repentance.

Woman's Scene of Self-Debasement and Regeneration

If we look back on the first modern generation of feminist scholarship on the Bible, we note an understandable tendency of some scholars to focus positively on the handful of treatments of women in the Bible. A major step was undertaken, however, when feminists shifted the mode of analysis from women's studies, that is, the study of women and depictions of women, to gender studies, or the study of the construction of gender, male and female. The consideration of *Judith* as a feminist heroine, for example, was replaced by an analysis of the complex gender issues surrounding the depiction and interpretation of Judith. My conclusion is that the novels do not represent a *feminist* treatment of women, if we define a feminist text as one in which the experience of women is viewed from within instead of from without. By that I mean that it (1) begins from the point of view of women's experience, (2) does not prescribe roles for men that are superior to women's (even though they may be described as such), and (3) affirms the value of women's relationships.[25] The sympathetic portrayal of a woman's role is a common motif in popular art, often restricted, however, to a liminal experience of role reversals, after which the woman returns to her place and mundane time is restored. Mordecai resumes his place of authority as leader of the Jews of Persia, a role that actually existed, while "Queen" Esther, a fictional creation, "lives happily ever after." We do not know who

[25] This brief definition of terms is here used merely as a statement of assumptions to facilitate a discussion of the "feminist stance" of the writings in question. Some critics show a tendency to identify any ironic or liminal depiction of a female figure as "subversive" and therefore feminist, a conclusion I would question. (See the discussion in Chapter 5 regarding *Judith.*) The theoretical considerations of Roberta L. Krueger ("Double Jeopardy: The Appropriation of Woman in Four Old French Romances of the 'Cycle de la Gageure,'" in Sheila Fisher and Janet E. Halley, eds., *Seeking the Woman in Late Medieval and Renaissance Writings* [Knoxville: University of Tennessee Press, 1989], 21–50) are helpful here. Ultimately, the question of judging the feminist stance of texts and authors cannot be adjudicated by recourse to objective criteria; to attempt that would even contradict the spirit of much feminist theory.

actually wrote the novels or who read them, but we may suggest that the novels contain male projections of the nature of women or, better, that they are cultural projections that take the male point of view. That they are inherently romanticizing a conservative social and sexual ethic should not surprise us if we consider the similar social function of most of the Greek novels.[26]

A contrast with the book of *Ruth* is quite instructive on this point. Unlike the heroines of the novels, Ruth is not beautiful, or rather, we are never told whether she is beautiful or not. This lack of idealization of the heroine indicates that the work should perhaps be excluded from our genre; there are other indications as well. *Ruth,* like *Jonah,* is much too short (a mere 1200 words in Hebrew), is subdued and economical in its emotionalism, and is realistic in its depiction of social classes. To be sure, despite its brevity, it must be considered one of the great short stories in world literature, but it does not match the particular requirements of the novel. Aside from the problem of dating, there is little exploration of threats or dangers and the emotions associated with them, little exploitation of the effects that are possible within the written medium, especially the description of internal states—they are presumed or suggested but not articulated. In a word, there is little extension of the narrative for the sake of entertainment. But *Ruth* is, by the definition applied here, feminist. It takes women's lives and concerns seriously, is transparent to social categories of male and female, and underscores the importance of the women's relationship by making it the center of the story.

To the reader, the woman in distress may represent the vulnerable and emotional side of the psyche, where an identification with the heroine occurs for both men and women. The sexual and erotic side of these women's scenes may be read differently by men and women—compare, for example, the stripping of Susanna—but the vulnerability of the heroine may resonate similarly for male and female readers: it is the suspension of the woman's soul, usually in penitence, that comes through for the reader (although Judith is penitent for Israel's sins, not her own, and somewhat less anxious). We must posit in this case a very complex involvement of the reader, which would be different for

[26] Brigitte Egger makes similar observations about the absence of a feminist perspective in the Greek novels; they communicate instead "emotional gynocentrism, but factual androcentrism" ("Women and Marriage in the Greek Novels: Fiction and Reality," in Tatum and Vernazza, eds., *Ancient Novel: Classical Paradigms and Modern Perspectives,* 86, and also Egger, "Looking at Chariton's Callirhoe," in Morgan and Stoneman, eds., *Greek Fiction,* 38–39).

men and women and multilayered for both. Given the consensus on the dates of the works under study, there appears to be a steady evolution over time in the length and complexity of this scene. *Tobit* is likely the earliest of the novels, followed by *Judith,* Greek *Esther,* and last of all *Joseph and Aseneth,* with the date of *Susanna* uncertain. Tobit's scene of the female protagonist's distress contains little of the trappings of the others. Mourning was perhaps not unknown to Sarah—she has lost seven fiancés—but it is not *ritual* mourning that is presented (she was not legally and ritually their wife), and there is not a hint, even in the wedding chamber, of the erotic themes we find in the others.

This emphasis on the conjugal couple, the dangers that threaten to separate them, and the joys that are acclaimed by all when they are reunited speak to the new situation of domestic values in the Greco-Roman period. The ideal, separated and isolated relationship between a young man and woman—in essence a "pure" relationship between a man and woman, since any attachments they may have to family, business, government, and so on have been stripped away—is at the core of the Greek novel. It is this ideal relationship that is threatened in a series of adventures. Thus, central themes of the Greek novel, as I stated in the Introduction, are the rootlessness of the individual and the vulnerability to life's changes. Mikhail Bakhtin ties the role of chance and twists of fate in the Greek novel to a sense of alienation: "The world of the Greek romance is an *alien world:* everything in it is indefinite, unknown, foreign. Its heroes are there for the first time (since they have been abducted, stranded, and so on); they have no organic ties or relationships with it; the laws governing the sociopolitical and everyday life of this world are foreign to them, they do not know them; in this world, therefore, they can experience only random contingency."[27] This is the common model for the sense of alienation of the literate class in the Greco-Roman world. It has even been compared to the quest of the inner soul found in Gnosticism, a radical religious orientation that denies the reality of the external world. No matter what bizarre and unreal occurrences threaten the hero and heroine, they retain a chaste inner identity in which each searches out the other.[28] For the Greek reader, the discovery of one's identity in the conjugal mating provides a solace, but the Jewish novels indicate that their readers perceived a different threat and sought a different haven in the storm. The Jewish novels generally

[27] Bakhtin, *The Dialogic Imagination,* 90.
[28] Terry Comito, "Exile and Return in the Greek Romances," *Arion,* n.s., 2 (1975): 58–80.

depict a physical threat to Jews, but the actual problem that may motivate them was the creation and maintenance of ethnic boundaries and
the threats to Jewish identity. Greek *Esther*, Greek *Daniel*, *Judith*, *Third
Maccabees*, and Artapanus's *Moses Romance*, like the Christian martyr-
doms of the next centuries, are perhaps aimed at the social discomfort
of readers who are no longer in mortal danger.

   In the Jewish novels, the woman is more thoroughly integrated into
an extended family than she is in the Greek novels. The extended family
issue is not stated continuously, but it does appear at crucial junctures
in each Jewish novel, like a motive clause. This is not to suggest that
Jews maintained a traditional extended family in the face of the shift to
a nuclear family in the Greco-Roman world at large; there were great
changes in Jewish family structure as well.[29] The extended family does
appear as a literary topos, however, perhaps romantically and anachro-
nistically. The reunion of the conjugal couple, by contrast, receives only
fleeting interest. At the same time that the heroine becomes the focus for
the audience's vulnerability, she also moves through a purification process and, indeed, a change of identity. It is not without its complexities,
and it likely evolved over time, but in *Judith* and Greek *Esther*, a similar
scene is enacted. A heroine who must rise to the occasion and save her
fellow Jews within the context of pagan society declares that her "true"
identity is in her debased state, without, as it were, her makeup on.
Esther and Judith are described as beautiful but with some ambivalence;
after emerging from a scene of purging and cleansing and a figurative
death, they put on a new identity. It is not a "true" identity, however.
They beautify themselves externally to move into the pagan world, and
they intentionally use their beautification—their "false" identities—to
alter history. In *Joseph and Aseneth* the intensity of the woman's scene is
increased, but it is played out in a slightly different way. Aseneth, like
Judith and Esther, also undergoes a ritual death to her old self, losing her
former beauty and her old identity, and like the others she reemerges to

---

[29] The partial breakdown of extended family patterns can be detected quite early in Israel
(Lawrence E. Stager, "The Archeology of the Family in Ancient Israel," *Bulletin of the American Society for Oriental Research* 260 [1985]: 1–36), and family, clan, and tribe designations may
have become more ideal than real even before the Exile. Important shifts toward a nuclear
family have been posited by scholars for the period after the Exile: A. Causse, *Du groupe eth-
nique a la communauté religieuse: Le problème sociologique de la religion d'Israël* (Paris: Librairie Félix
Alcan, 1937), 189–91, and Markham J. Geller, "New Sources for the Origins of the Rabbinic
Ketubah," *Hebrew Union College Annual* 49 (1978): 227–45. See also Isaiah M. Gafni, "The Institution of Marriage in Rabbinic Times," in *The Jewish Family: Metaphor and Memory*, ed. David
Kraemer (New York: Oxford University Press, 1989), 13–30.

put on beautiful clothes and jewels. When she reemerges and beautifies herself, however, it is not a false identity she is projecting but her true identity, her conversion identity. Her beautification, rather than being used as an alluring entrée into the inner sanctums of pagan power, is symbolic of her new status as an authentic love match for Joseph.

Underlying the narrative asceticism of the Jewish novels is evidently a fundamental, almost mythical view of Jewish identity in the Greco-Roman period. Sexual continence of both males and females until marriage was considered a basic foundation of the self-identity of Jews (even if it is the sexuality of women more than that of men that is placed before the reader in novels). As the Alexandrian Jewish philosopher Philo stated it (*On Joseph* 43), writing in the first century C.E.: "Before the lawful union we know no mating with other women but come as virgin men to virgin maidens. The end we seek in wedlock is not pleasure but the begetting of lawful children." Josephus (*Jewish War* 2.8.13 §161) also attributes to one group of Essenes the view that sex is for procreation, not pleasure. Many scholars have noted that Jewish identity in the Greco-Roman period is often distilled into a few piously intoned ideals: monotheism, abhorrence of idolatry, philosophically pure reason, and sexual continence.[30] These ideals are held up in the propagandistic Jewish literature of the period in stark contrast to the supposed ubiquitousness of their opposites in Greek culture (although we will find reason to doubt this contrast below). It is not in the novels alone that women receive a special moral scrutiny; there is a heightened interest in women's ritual purity in the Mishnah as well.[31]

[30] See Collins, *Between Athens and Jerusalem,* esp. 135–74. Howard Clark Kee has noted the lack of a broader Jewish legal "program" in *Testaments of the Twelve Patriarchs* ("Ethical Dimensions of the Testaments of the XII as a Clue to Provenance," *New Testament Studies* 24 [1978]: 259–70), but Dixon Slingerland has argued that he is being too mechanical ("The Nature of *Nomos* [Law] within the *Testaments of the Twelve Patriarchs*," *Journal of Biblical Literature* 105 [1986]: 39–48). A cherished few "public" ideals may be emblematic in the minds of the readers of a whole life of observance, but not necessarily. We do know that many Jews had determined to live their lives in reverence of certain philosophical principles without continuing to observe the particularities of Jewish law (Philo, *Migration of Abraham,* 89–93).

[31] See Wegner, "The Image and Status of Women in Classical Rabbinic Judaism," esp. 77–78, and David Biale, *Eros and the Jews,* esp. 34–42. Biale notes (34–36) that rabbinic strictures on asceticism and the affirmation that procreation is a divine command may reflect a critical stance toward the increasing popularity of celibacy, although the rabbis' stance may be at odds with the Jewish novels, as we shall see below, this chapter. A side issue of great importance for this study is the question of the relationship of the Jewish novels—and the attitudes toward women's roles that they reflect—to Christian novels, where celibacy, especially for women, is a common theme. Lefkowitz ("The Motivations for St. Perpetua's Martyrdom") suggests that celibate relationships and fictive kinship notions among early Christians offered a haven

These themes of the Jewish novels must be placed in the context of intellectual developments of the Greco-Roman period. The "narrative asceticism" of the Jewish novels and the sense of alienation of the Greek are likely related to the same struggle to define the autonomous self and to create a "discourse that was fundamentally concerned with regulating both the physical and mental self." [32] The modern, introspective exploration of what it means to be a "person" is not paralleled in most periods of history, but it does appear to find an analogue in the Greco-Roman world. It arises in the *Confessions* of Augustine, but one can see it earlier as well in the new focus on the physical side of life, the detailed discussion of disease and healing, and the urgent advocacy of a proper lifestyle to carry one through the vicissitudes of existence (or to escape them altogether). An ascetic principle in Roman life is now seen as parallel to the rise of widespread ascetic disciplines among Christians, and parallel concerns are also voiced within the Jewish texts of the period.

The parallels between the ancient and the modern discovery of the individual are reflected in the two periods' novels as well. The novel form itself has been linked in the modern world to the discovery of the individual, the description of a character as problematic and imperfect, that is, three-dimensional. Georg Lukács highlights the individual as the center of the novel's dramatic landscape: "The inner form of the novel has been understood as the process of the problematic individual's journeying towards himself, . . . towards clear self-recognition." [33] The

---

for people—especially women—from actual family relationships that were not as supportive. Whereas the rootless bourgeois of the Greco-Roman period may have found a home in the conjugal marriage, many women may have preferred to sever this tie and create a set of new, family*like* relations. The Jewish novels do not challenge the family bonds, although they do have in common with some of the Christian novels a transformation of the identity of the female protagonist. See also Burrus, *Chastity as Autonomy,* and Kraemer, *Her Share of the Blessings,* "The Conversion of Women to Ascetic Forms of Christianity," and "Monastic Jewish Women in Greco-Roman Egypt."

It is also important to note that the stronger emphasis on ritual purity for women is not confined to Judaism. Compare, for example, a very interesting set of regulations for a pagan house sanctuary that forbids adulterous sexual relations for both men and women but with unequal emphasis: S. C. Barton and G. H. R. Horsley, "A Hellenistic Cult Group and the New Testament Churches," *Jahrbuch für Antike und Christentum* 24 (1981): 7–41. Likewise, Greek medical texts are strongly concerned with menstruation; so Leslie Dean-Jones, *Women's Bodies in Classical Greek Science* (Oxford: Oxford University Press, 1993).

[32] Judith Perkins, "The 'Self' as Sufferer," *Harvard Theological Review* 85 (1992): 246–47; see also Foucault, *The History of Sexuality,* vol. 3, *The Care of the Self,* 39–68; Brown, *The Body and Society;* Aline Rousselle, *Porneia: On Desire and the Body in Antiquity* (Oxford: Basil Blackwell, 1988); and on Jewish asceticism, Fraade, "Ascetical Aspects of Ancient Judaism."

[33] Lukács, *The Theory of the Novel,* 80.

overpowering sense of a central character or characters is certainly present in other art forms, such as epic or drama. What is crucial in the novel is not the reader's discovery of some great "personage" but the discovery of the person within oneself, barely better than average but worthy of scrutiny. The Jewish novels as well, in some cases, problematize the normal individual. *Esther* (especially Hebrew *Esther*), *Joseph and Aseneth* (especially the mystical elaborations), *Testament of Joseph* (especially regarding the *shlemiel*-Joseph whom we encounter in the second half), and Greek *Daniel* (especially *Susanna*) all constitute bold experiments in exploring the self-coming-to-recognition.[34] The ingenuity and originality of the Jewish experiments in discerning the problematic nature of the individual is perhaps greater than anything in the Greek novels and is comparable to that found in the Latin novel *The Golden Ass*. The innovations that are reflected, however, were not carried through to completion, and we are left with the most intriguing building blocks of an essentially unrealized art form. And interestingly, the "person" whom the Jewish novel investigates is almost always a woman. She experiences the vulnerability that must be addressed, and the woman's scene of debasement and redemption becomes programmatic for the discovery of self.

It is true that partial analogues for the woman's scene can be found in the Greek novels, and they provide evidence of the parallel developments of some themes. In Heliodorus's *Ethiopian Story* (6.8–9), the heroine, bereft of her lover, whom she presumes dead, retires to her room during a wedding festival and there pines, in a scene reminiscent of Aseneth's:

> Only Charikleia did not join in [the festivities]; she stole away from the company and withdrew to her room; she locked the doors securely behind her; now she could be sure that no one would disturb her. Possessed by a frenzy of despair, she untied her hair without inhibition; she tore her dress and said: "Come then, let us dance too, in a manner befitting the malign power that controls our destiny. Let us sing him a song of mourning and dance him a dance of sorrow! . . . So this is the nuptial

[34] Many influences could also be mentioned concerning this development, for instance, the topos of the suffering righteous person (*Job, Wisdom of Solomon* 2–5) and the court legends, such as the Esther and Daniel traditions, which had a long transmission before they became novels. As reflected in sources such as the *Testaments of the Twelve Patriarchs* or the works of Philo, the inner moral psyche of the person was analyzed more acutely in Judaism than in the prevailing culture; so Peter Brown, "Late Antiquity," in *A History of Private Life*, vol. 1: *From Pagan Rome to Byzantium*, ed. Paul Veyne (Cambridge: Harvard University Press, 1987), 253–54.

chamber our guiding deity has built for us! This is the bridal room he has appointed for us! There is no one in it but me, no husband beside me. . . . Theagenes, the thought of whom is the one thought that brings me any joy, if you are dead, if I am brought to believe the news that I pray never to hear, I shall not hesitate to join you in death. For the present I make you this offering"—as she spoke, she tore her hair and laid the tresses on the bed [as an offering]—"and I pour you this libation from the eyes that you love"—and straightway the rain of her tears watered her bed. "But if you are alive, as I hope, come and sleep beside me, my love; appear to me in my dreams at least. But even then respect me, my friend, and preserve your bride's virginity for lawful wedlock. . . ." And so saying, she flung herself face downwards on the bed. She held the mattress clasped tight in her arms, sobbing and moaning from the depths of her heart, until her sorrow grew past bearing, and a swirling mist stole over her, plunging her conscious mind into darkness and causing her to slip, despite herself, into a slumber in which she remained till long after daybreak.

Although Aseneth was provoked first by the presence of a bridegroom (Joseph) and then by her sense of guilt and unworthiness, Charikleia is disconsolate over the absence of her lover. Otherwise, however, there are many similarities, including the swooning delirium and the state of symbolic mourning. Virginity is also a key theme in both texts, although the modern reader is often surprised to see it played out so strongly in the Greek novels. What we miss in the Greek novel here, when compared to the Jewish novel, is the *systematic* death and rebirth, or at least the transformation of identity and character, which is accompanied by the reemergence in a new role, and the rerobing and full beautification treatment that follows. Some semblance of this is found elsewhere in the same novel (10.9), when the purity and virginity of the heroine are tested as Charikleia is asked to step onto a golden gridiron that will burn the feet of those who are impure:

Then, before the people supervising the test could tell her what to do, she produced, from a little pouch that she was carrying, her Delphic robe, woven with gold thread and embroidered with rays, and put it on. She let her hair fall free, ran forward like one possessed, and sprang onto the gridiron, where she stood for some time without taking any hurt, her beauty blazing with a new and dazzling radiance as she stood conspicuous on her lofty pedestal; in her magnificent robe she seemed more like an image of a goddess than a mortal woman. . . . Visible proof had been furnished that, for all her youthful charms, the greatest ornament to her beauty was chastity.

This passage reads almost like the conclusion to Aseneth's rerobing scene: Charikleia is robed and apotheosized and becomes a testament to chastity. A psychological kinship does exist between the two works, but it is skewed and uneven. The connection between a purging and penitent experience and a new identity is not clear in the Greek novel. Also, Charikleia, like her lover, Theagenes, will graduate from her chastity to find her identity in her union with him, whereas Aseneth, even though she will find a union with Joseph, will find her *true* identity in her new worship of God and perhaps in an implied union with the Man from Heaven as well. We may at least wonder whether the subliminal message of the work is that the ideal reader's true identity is found in chastity. Judith, we may note, and Esther in Greek *Esther* as well appear to retain their chastity in perpetuity, serving their fellow Jews ever chaste, whereas Susanna and Sarah (Tobit's daughter-in-law) find their fulfillment in a network of extended family loyalties. To return to Philo's quotation above, the difference between Jewish and Greek ideals, as reflected in their respective bodies of novelistic literature, is not so much that Jewish novels affirm the value of sexual continence before marriage, since the Greek novels do also, but that the Jewish works downplay a sexual union after marriage in favor of an affirmation of extended family ties.

From Semantic to Syntactic Roles

In Rick Altman's analysis and integration of semantic and syntactic approaches, the former are the building blocks that are available to the author, and they can be and are utilized in a number of ways. Semantic elements may coalesce in different combinations, but the most important development occurs when they are assembled in a new syntax, that is, when the message of the interrelation of parts has stability and expressive potential within a culture and is repeated throughout many exemplars of the genre.[35] (Recall that repeatability is one of the key characteristics of popular art). Both the historical blunder and the woman's debasement scene are semantic elements in the novel, but the former remains a more incidental aspect of the overall shape of the genre—it can appear at any point in the text—and does not enter into a new syntax, whereas the latter evolves quite significantly in our sampling and

[35] Altman, *The American Film Musical*, 97–102.

becomes a determining part of the syntax of the Jewish novel, relating in a particular way to what happens before it and after it. The novels begin by depicting a threat looming on the horizon, a threat that becomes increasingly menacing to an increasing number of people. Those threatened are typically extensions of the heroine's family, even if there is a leap from her family to all Jews of Persia, as in *Esther,* or to all Jews of Jerusalem and the surrounding area, as in *Judith.* The heroine then withdraws by herself, puts off her clothes, debases and castigates herself in acts of ritual mourning, prays to God, and then reclothes herself and reemerges, ready to move decisively forward to accomplish her ends. Her action as she emerges is often forceful and dramatic, as in Hebrew *Esther* where, after commanding Mordecai to rally the Jews, she summons up her own courage to enter in before the king or as in *Judith* where she marches downhill to emasculate the attacking general. But even in Greek *Esther,* where her first new action upon emerging is to faint, she is no less resolute in fulfilling a new role, that is, the role of the demure romantic heroine who softens the heart of the king. Should we see here the presentation of a change in character or of the development in character, the hallmark of the modern, psychologically oriented novel? The mere focus on a character and her spiritual transformation, mechanical as it is, suggests that we should at points, although it is nowhere carried through to completion. It is noteworthy, however, that the novelistic impulse, even in the hands of "primitive" authors, naturally turns to this element in the exploration of narrative descriptions of more ordinary people; the character change of the female protagonist is beginning to be articulated. Her role, that is, the proper narrative role for a female protagonist, is to be the subject of a psychological transformation, from the most vulnerable to the most worthy.[36] This is the new syntax of the Jewish novel.

Altman's notion of a gradual development of a stable syntax brings us to a most important issue in the description of a genre. Genres are usually discussed as if they are like Plato's forms, which neither wax nor wane and do not change with time. Whether a genre is defined by se-

---

[36] In noting the new interest in personal or psychological development, it is worthwhile to compare the older, much simpler narratives of, say, *Daniel* 3 and 6. Many comparable elements are present, especially the threat to the protagonists and their reemergence. George W. E. Nickelsburg even notes the presence of a crucial decision process in these narratives (*Resurrection, Immortality, and Eternal Life in Intertestamental Judaism* [Cambridge: Harvard University Press, 1972], 49–57) and "The Genre and Function of the Markan Passion Narrative," but the *psychological* dynamic is not explored, except in those narratives, such as *Susanna,* that are part of novelistic development.

mantic elements or by an isolated core syntax of interrelated members, a difficulty is immediately introduced if the question of genre history is raised. Even though we know that discernible changes in members of a genre must occur, they can become a problem for the critic, for criteria that appear in some exemplars and not others, or that disappear entirely, can be challenged as not belonging to the "constitutive" definition. A diachronic definition of a genre requires, first, that a constitutive core be defined but, second, that its transmutations also be mapped. Indeed, shifts in a genre, rather than exposing the weakness of the definitional criteria, can actually confirm the organic interrelatedness of members along a time line. There may not be a single element that is present in every exemplar of a genre, but an inner logic or ethos that *evolves* can be proposed for a diachronic definition of genre.[37]

Alastair Fowler has argued that the evolution of genres occurs in three stages: (1) an innovative combination of old and new elements that expresses an important new sentiment or theme, (2) a classic re-alignment that brings unity to all of the disparate elements and fully exploits the new potentialities of the genre, and (3) a baroque period in which the classic model is reflected upon, inverted, or satirized.[38] But granting that genres evolve, which semantic elements or structural patterns must be present in all cases, from the first pristine creation to the last baroque self-parody? Any genre definition must allow that some elements are added over time while others fall away, but is it possible to describe a genre in which even the "core" elements change? Advocates of syntactic definitions may respond to this challenge by arguing that an unchanging core structure of relationships of elements exists in a genre, even though individual elements may change. But even the structural relationships themselves may sometimes change within the diachronic development of a genre. In Altman's view, after a syntax has become fixed for a genre, a baroque stage can arise in which the classi-

---

[37] As I noted in Chapter 1, genre history or literary history is not simply an accounting of the succession of changing literary works; it is an analysis of the evolution of models and the creation of new ones. See Ducrot and Todorov, *Encyclopedic Dictionary of the Sciences of Language*, 144–45, and Nagy, *Pindar's Homer*, 21 n. 18.

[38] Alastair Fowler, "The Life and Death of Literary Forms," in *Directions in Literary History*, ed. Ralph Cohen (Baltimore: Johns Hopkins University, 1974), 77–94. The division into three stages, as opposed to two or four or fifty, is somewhat arbitrary but serves well for the purposes of reflection on the question of evolution itself, especially *typical* patterns of evolution reflected in different genres. See also, however, the four-stage theory of genre evolution proposed by Henri Focillon, *The Life of Forms in Art*, 2d ed. (New York: George Wittenborn, 1948), 10–15; on a more general level, see Claudio Guillén, *Literature as System* (Princeton: Princeton University Press, 1971), 121, and Todorov, "Introduction" in *The Fantastic*.

cal syntax is intentionally broken, embellished, or satirized. As he puts it, a new syntax is imposed on the old semantic elements.[39] The differences, then, between *Daniel* and *Tobit,* on the one hand, as the earliest novels and *Joseph and Aseneth,* on the other, as the most baroque do not threaten to undermine a definition of the genre; they merely force us to explain the nature of the organic development. The organic relationship among them and the similar contract between author and reader that these works exhibit allow them to be placed together.

Despite the fact that Altman's approach appears at times to subordinate the semantic elements to the new syntactical arrangement, elsewhere he states that the syntax that emerges is only one message of the text, communicated on one level; it is not necessarily *the* message.[40] We might propose, for instance, that the woman's self-debasement scene has a *semantic* importance that is very significant, quite apart from its syntactical meaning. The intense focus on the emotions and psychological states of the moral agent provides for an individuation of the subject that is so typical of the modern novel. The "introspective conscience"[41] is developed not just as a theme but as an empathetic, even purgative experience for the reader. We find here a call to saintliness and an ethic of renunciation for women more often associated with Christian asceticism than with Jewish social ethics. The poetics of the Jewish novel, then, can be described from both a semantic and a syntactic point of view and will ultimately require both. The message—or messages—of the texts of this genre are communicated in several ways simultaneously.

Myth in the Jewish Novel

Finally, we note an aspect of the Jewish novels that has not yet been explicitly explored in this study. At precisely what point do poetic grammars pass over into the category of mythical structures, that is, patterns in literature that correspond to deeply embedded patterns in a culture's self-consciousness? Because myth can have a number of meanings and can be used to refer to fundamental truths communicated on

[39] Altman, *American Film Musical,* 97–99.

[40] Ibid., 96–97.

[41] Krister Stendahl's phrase; see "The Apostle Paul and the Introspective Conscience of the West," *Harvard Theological Review* 56 (1963): 199–215, reprinted in his *Paul among Jews and Gentiles* (Philadelphia: Fortress, 1976), 78–96.

different levels, the precise nature of myth, or a universally applicable definition, is difficult to articulate. Still, some considerations of an adequate working definition are necessary at this point.

Myths are traditions that communicate the most deeply held beliefs of a people. The definition of myth is sometimes limited to narratives—that is, myths must tell a story—and the stories are further limited to traditional narratives that explicitly pertain to events on a cosmic or suprahistorical level.[42] However, both halves of this definition can be challenged. Many scholars of myth seek to penetrate to the level of the truth behind the myth, or what the myth communicates. The narrative is seen both as a deeply held truth in itself and as a means by which some other nonnarrative truth, such as the structure of human society or the metaphysics of human existence, is communicated. Narrative is therefore the means of myth but not necessarily its end. I am interested both in the myth-as-narrative and in the fundamental, often nonnarrative truths reflected in the narratives; both are deeply held truths that are explored in the mythical realm. Likewise, the suprahistorical domain of a narrative is not necessarily a criterion of myth. "Charter myths," those myths that provide the sacred and primeval foundations for important social institutions—kingship, patrilineal or matrilineal organization, and so on—can also be found in everyday social institutions, such as, as Edmund Leach notes, local English football clubs.[43] The presence of a narrative and the suprahistorical domain are not necessary, therefore, for a discussion of myth, even though they are quite often the means by which deeply held truths are communicated. For our purposes, however, what will be considered constitutive of myth is the relationship between two levels of discourse: deeply held, even metaphysical truths of necessity, causality, association, opposition, and so on and the level of everyday discourse in which these truths are lived.[44] It is not sufficient to say that myths "explain" everyday reality,

[42] See Leach, "Introduction," and Nagy, *Pindar's Homer,* esp. 31, 43, 66–67, 331. Nagy also discusses the important relationship between myth and ritual, and the reenactment of myth in ritual, but notes the diminution of references to ritual in literary developments of mythical themes (66–67, 143 n. 40). The "initiatory" aspects of the reading experience (on which see below, this chapter) are at one remove from public ritual but are analogous to the literary developments Nagy analyzes.

[43] Leach, "Introduction." Leach focuses not on the suprahistorical domain of a narrative but on the way that a *corpus* of stories may operate to give varied and even conflicting views of the foundation of an institution.

[44] See Pierre-Yves Jacopin, *La parole generative de la mythologie des indiens yukuna* (Tremblay: Lepettit, 1981), esp. 6–11, 374–77. His work provides many important theoretical insights for the discussion of the relationship between the realm of the mythical and the realm of the

as if they were abstract reflections; they are a lived reality in which the audience comes to take part. Nor can it be said that myth is separated from everyday reality by being concerned with a primeval time frame; myths are often understood as fundamentally present realities.[45] Mythical narratives concerning a suprahistorical realm can be one way that this relationship between two realms is mediated, but these truths can also be experienced as a living reality in the distinctions in clothing, the symbols on dollar bills, or the plot machinations of popular novels. Our task is to ascertain where, if anywhere, the Jewish novels relate these two levels of discourse, to find expressions or intimations of myth within the realistic (or pseudo-realistic) discourse of the novel.

It might still be objected, of course, that the deeply held truths of popular novels are simply themes, important beliefs as far as the author and audience are concerned but hardly the stuff of myth. But the "depth" of a myth is often very difficult to fix. Leslie Fiedler, for example, proposed that in American literature there is a common topos of a white hero and a man of color who is his faithful sidekick: Ishmael and Queequeg, Natty Bumppo and Chingachgook, Huck Finn and Jim, Lone Ranger and Tonto, and so forth.[46] Fiedler senses a fascination of white readers with a homosexual relationship in each case and an American obsession with nature and the coming of culture, in which there is a need to explore the dynamic of a white hero, only half-civilized, who is connected to the natural world through a man of color, also half-civilized. Yet is this commonplace a "myth"? It broadens the perspective only slightly to point out the continuation of this topos in contemporary American police films, which commonly showcase an impetuous white hero and a more reserved African-American partner in the jungle of the city. It may still seem at first limited to an American preoccupation. Our reservations may fall away, however, when the parallel is drawn of Gilgamesh, the Babylonian hero, and Enkidu, his wild companion; if it is 4,500 years old, it must be myth. John G. Cawelti, in his study of modern formula stories in popular art, articulated a simi-

---

real, even though his study is particularly and intentionally focused on a society that lacks a complex division of labor, a far cry from Judaism in the Greco-Roman period.

[45] Emphasized already by Bronislaw Malinowski, *Myth in Primitive Psychology* (New York: Norton, 1926), 18. Literary scholars often assume that myth is an *ancient* narrative that still makes its presence felt only through dreams or the peculiar sensibilities of the artist. Myths must still be operative, even if contemporary myth making is more difficult to ascertain.

[46] Leslie Fiedler, "Come Back to the Raft Ag'in, Huck Honey!" in *The Collected Essays of Leslie Fiedler,* 2 vols. (New York: Stein and Day, 1971), 1:144–54.

lar notion about the mythical stature of some of the protagonists of popular art. He concludes that the supposedly superficial formulae of detective novels, westerns, or melodramas sometimes become cultural myths. The Lone Ranger, Mickey Spillane's *I, the Jury,* or (we may add) Superman "establish themselves so completely that almost everyone in the culture has some knowledge of them and what they stand for. They represent the kind of artistry that can take a popular story formula and present it in such a way that it becomes an expression of a basic pattern and meaning in the consciousness of many members of the audience. This is the kind of creativity through which a formula not only becomes an expression of cultural mythology, but becomes a cultural myth."[47] To be sure, the novel can be seen as a dilution of such older mythical narratives as Gilgamesh and Enkidu. Claude Lévi-Strauss has argued that, whereas myth transcends the historical context, the novel must bring transcendent realities down to the level of the everyday, embed them in a historical context, and remove from them any visible aspiration to a higher order of reality. The novel, especially the popular novel, was born from the "exhaustion of myth."[48] But even if novels do not themselves directly describe a mythical realm in the same way that epic sings it or ritual reenacts it, they still communicate the persistence of deeply held truths, such as the ways that constitutive rules underlie the inexorable progress of events.

One way of avoiding some of these problems in the application of the term *myth* would be to substitute the word *archetype,* which does not imply a narrative of events on the suprahistorical level and which also emphasizes the unconscious nature of the deeply held truths. Fiedler has addressed the deeper levels of reference in popular narratives by recourse to this term: "By 'archetype' I mean a coherent pattern of beliefs and feelings so widely shared at a level beneath consciousness that there exists no abstract vocabulary for representing it, and so 'sacred' that unexamined, irrational restraints inhibit any explicit analysis. Such a complex finds a formula or pattern story, which serves both to embody it, and, at first at least, to conceal its full implications."[49] This term would serve for many of the passages under discussion, but its

---

[47] Cawelti, *Adventure, Mystery, and Romance,* 300.

[48] Claude Lévi-Strauss, *The Origin of Table Manners: Introduction to a Science of Mythology: 3* (London: Jonathan Cape, 1978), 129–31. McKeon compares Lévi-Strauss's view with that of Northrop Frye in a very full assessment of their devaluation of the novel (*The Origins of the English Novel, 1600–1740,* 5–10).

[49] Fiedler, "Come Back to the Raft," 146.

usual connotation is too narrow for others. The conscious utilization of primeval traditions should not be ruled out, nor should the narrative aspect of the deeper level of discourse. The broader term *myth* is preferable, therefore, even if the particular relation of the two levels of discourse must be specified in each case.

It is possible now to turn to the discussion of the mythical beliefs that may be reflected in the novels. Without suggesting that one mythical message is more "true" or "fundamental" than others, we begin by isolating what I would call synchronic myths, repeated narrative and structural patterns that reveal fundamental cultural codes but that may not reflect ancient tradition. Especially intriguing about this line of investigation for popular literature in general is the possibility of elucidating commonly held assumptions of the culture that are nowhere stated explicitly and that remain largely unconscious. (Here the word *archetype* would be as appropriate as *myth*.) Synchronic myths may undergird much of the fabric of daily life, but they are often relatively changeable and culture-specific. Popular art is one window, in some cases perhaps the only available window, to the study of this aspect of cultural history. Among the "everyday myths" that Jewish novels express is the deep distinction between Jew and Other. Although a kind of coexistence is possible and Jews may even succeed in the larger society, a threat of violence hangs over them, and the newly discovered individual person must reclothe her or himself in Jewish identity to protect the interests of the family and the people.[50] The relationship between Jew and Other had undergone enormous transformation since the time of the Exile; the particular angst experienced during the period of the novels was probably new: the first *religious* persecutions that Jews experienced were during the late Hellenistic period, under Antiochus IV Epiphanes

---

[50] The exceptions to this tendency among the novels are equally interesting: *Tobit, Susanna,* and the *Tobiad Romance* reflect less of a tension between Jew and Other but may also predate the high period of the Jewish novel.

Cf. a different approach to mythical patterns in some of the Jewish novels by Carroll, "Myth, Methodology, and Transformation in the Old Testament." The basic pattern Carroll finds in several of the novels can be summarized in this way:
1. Central female who is or was married;
2. Attempted seduction
3. By male of high social standing;
4. Attempt fails.

Although Carroll's article is suggestive, the pattern discerned appears neither deep enough nor broad enough to merit attention as a "mythical" construct. His article is interesting, however, for the way he tries to incorporate Lévi-Strauss's theory of the transformation of one myth into another.

of the Seleucid Empire and Ptolemy VIII Euergetes of the Ptolemaic Empire. The response to a potentially antagonistic world found in the Jewish novels is quite different from the more general sense of malaise in the Greek novels. The latter communicate a sense of rootlessness and alienation and resolve this angst with a full engagement of eroticism and romantic love. The Jewish novels do not presume rootlessness, but rather, rootlessness is as much the enemy as the anti-Jewish agitators. The private life that Greco-Roman culture discovered in this period— the end of the Greek novel is a happy resolution for the private couple— is not a panacea for Jews.

These truths could be expressed as semantic elements—individual motifs of the Greek or Jewish worldviews—or they could be embedded in syntactic narrative structures that emphasize the relationship of A to B or the change from A to B; the narrative brings the truth to realization. In contrast to the Greek novels, the heroine of the Jewish novels is called from private to public life. Esther is called upon to reengage with her fellow Jews, Judith is called out of private mourning to act decisively to save her city and Jerusalem, and Aseneth must intervene to foil a conspiracy and reconcile her husband's brothers. Rootedness is affirmed. The passive and introspective heroine, often associated with the novel ancient and modern, is present in the Jewish novels as well, but she moves to take action, and the alienation from the world is not complete. Concerning another deeply felt if not mythical issue, the conception of the possibility of effective action in the world, Jewish novels are thus significantly removed from the Greek novel and from modern novels as well (as some critics would interpret them).[51] Furthermore, this syntactic message on the political or social level has a counterpart on the level of personal piety. In *Susanna,* Greek *Esther, Judith,* and *Joseph and Aseneth,* we find the following progression: a beautiful woman, both the projected object of the audience's desires (or the male audience's desires) and the subject of their sense of vulnerability, faces an external threat that connives to undo her purity. Purity and danger, in fact, are held in tension as motive forces of the syntactical relationships of the narrative. The woman remains steadfast to her purity and, with God's help, overcomes the danger. The mythical message of these narratives is not so much that God will protect the righteous—that much had been said before—as that the righteousness of the woman is achieved through her ascetic, penitential prayers, which render her innocent and

---

[51] See the discussions in Chapter 1, especially regarding the views of Georg Lukács.

acceptable before God. Reflected here may be a domestication of sexuality for the bourgeois family ethic of an urban, Jewish entrepreneurial class, or perhaps the seed of an ascetic denial of sexuality that was fully developed later.

Other themes may be found expressed in the Jewish novel that carry over mythical concerns of Jewish tradition, and these I will term diachronic myths. This is the usual sense in which scholars speak of "myth and literature." The entire program of Northrop Frye, for instance, to account for the structure and themes of literary works by recourse to ancient mythical patterns would fall into this category.[52] His broad statements about romance (or at least non-Christian romance) might apply equally to the Jewish novels, but my suggestions will necessarily be less ambitious. The focus on the character of the female protagonist, her vulnerability and subjectivity in the moral drama being played out, is likely related to the increased contemporary speculation on the personified female figure of Wisdom (*sophia* in Greek, *ḥokmah* in Hebrew, both words feminine in gender). Briefly, we may note that in the postexilic period Wisdom becomes a cosmological figure who is God's agent of creation, even depicted as his consort, but more to the point, she becomes like the Greek savior goddesses (*soteirai*), such as Isis or Hekate (in her late Hellenistic persona).[53] Wisdom is approachable and protective and is also a vulnerable character in the heavens who in gnostic texts is attacked and barely escapes rape and death. Furthermore, she is not only a consort of God; she becomes a consort of humans as well. Sexual

---

[52] Northrop Frye, *Anatomy of Criticism* (Princeton: Princeton University Press, 1965), and *The Secular Scripture*. Much of the contents of Strelka, ed., *Literary Criticism and Myth*, is concerned in one way or another with this question. The theories of Frye are taken up often and are given a positive assessment by Eva Kushner, "Greek Myths in Modern Drama: Paths of Transformation," 202–3, and a generally negative one by Lillian Feder, "Myth, Poetry, and Critical Theory," 53–57.

[53] John S. Kloppenborg, "Isis and Sophia in the Book of Wisdom," *Harvard Theological Review* 75 (1982): 57–84; Sarah Iles Johnston, *Hekate Soteira* (Atlanta, Ga.: Scholars, 1990); Hans Conzelmann, "The Mother of Wisdom," in James M. Robinson, ed., *The Future of Our Religious Past* (New York: Harper and Row, 1971), 230–43; James M. Reese, *Hellenistic Influence on the Book of Wisdom and Its Consequences* (Rome: Biblical Institute, 1970), 6–12, 36–49. Although the theories of Karl Kerenyi (*Der antike Roman* [Darmstadt: Wissenschaftliche Buchgesellschaft, 1971]) and Merkelbach (*Roman und Mysterium in der Antike*) that the Greek novels contained hidden references to mystery initiations may seem similar here, I would emphasize that it is not an intentionally *hidden* reference to a mystery initiation that is involved in the Jewish novels (nor in the Greek novels) but a parallel operation of two realms. Many scholars have now resurrected Kerenyi's and Merkelbach's theories of the religious associations of the novels by noting that they bespeak a religious or even mythical *worldview;* see Hägg, *The Novel in Antiquity,* 90, and Pervo, *Profit with Delight,* 94. Even "initiation" in the Jewish novel as treated below, this chapter, is not mystery initiation.

and marriage metaphors for the sage's relationship with Wisdom had already existed (*Sirach* 14:20–27, *Wisdom* 7–9), but in keeping with the spirit of the times, contemplation of Wisdom could also be understood as spiritual marriage, the ascetic implications of which were drawn by Philo.[54] Thus Wisdom attains several new emotionally engaging roles in the period of the novel: ideal wife and helpmate, vulnerable subject through whose eyes the cosmic drama of good and evil is perceived, and also the surrogate partner who allows for the transcendence of earthly sexual activity. It should be remembered that these depictions of Wisdom are found in widely divergent schools of Jewish and Christian speculation covering a period of perhaps several centuries. It is still the case, however, that the various options of Wisdom speculation in this period bear some striking resemblances to the issues explored through the female character of the novels. To be sure, this parallel development of goddess–female protagonist need not be limited to Judaism; Isis might equally be compared with the qualities of the female protagonists in the Greek novels. The Jewish novels, however, may prove more interesting than the Greek in this regard, since, first, they are not as balanced with respect to male and female—the female protagonist predominates—and, second, the goddess–female protagonist parallel in Judaism is concerned with what should be a forbidden category, that is, a female divine figure within a monotheistic system (even if she is only a "hypostasized" figure). At any rate, there does appear to be a parallel between the speculation on the cosmic woman, Wisdom, and the investigation of the predicament of the virtuous female protagonist in the Jewish novel.

There are yet other means of representing mythical truths that do not transmit the structures of Jewish myths in particular but, rather, the myths of human cultures in most, if not all, times and places. These are neither synchronic nor diachronic myths but what we may call universal myths, since they are not tied to one culture and they appear to be quite generalized. We recall, for example, the suggestion of Mircea Eliade (Chapter 3, on *Tobit*) that folktales offer, on an imaginary level, the same liminal experience of loss and restoration as do rituals of initiation, with their thick mythical codes.[55] The Greek novel provides a

---

[54] Richard Horsley, "Spiritual Marriage with Sophia," *Vigiliae Christianae* 33 (1979): 30–54. Passages from Philo on spiritual marriage include *Flight* 52, *Cherubim* 42–52, and *Moses* 2.68f. For Horsley's treatment of asceticism in Philo, see especially pp. 38–43, and for asceticism in rabbinic Judaism, see Fraade, "Ascetical Aspects."

[55] Mircea Eliade, *Myth and Reality*, 201–2. Once again, it should be emphasized that initiation here is not a mystery initiation but a process of psychic reintegration.

similar experience of danger and resolution, and its mythical resolution may be seen as the stable union of the conjugal couple, whereas the resolution of the Jewish novel is the reintegration of the reader's sense of identity and belonging within the family and within Judaism. The ends are the same when viewed in this way and when viewed from the point of view of synchronic myths, but the process is highlighted here, and it is this medium of initiation that takes on the compelling tone of a mythical message. The experience of reading can become a personal, even inward quest; the reader is placed in great peril, separated from the networks of family and security, forced to rise to heroic levels of strength to overcome adversaries, and reintegrated into a redeemed social setting. As unheroic, then, as the bourgeois reader may become, the experience of reading the adventure novel is heroic—Lévi-Strauss's devaluations of the popular novel notwithstanding—and connects on a mythical level with the same fundamental human experience in rituals, myths, and tales everywhere.

We most likely possess only a small percentage of the Jewish novels that existed in the ancient world—or of the Greek or Roman novels, for that matter—but from these it appears that the formation of widespread cultural myths are reflected in them. This genre, like all other genres, was not static, and our snapshots of its development do not afford us comprehensive evidence of its full contours. But the apparent growth and evolution of the novelistic experiments of *Daniel* and *Tobit* into the broader and more formulaic domestic melodramas of Greek *Esther, Judith,* and *Joseph and Aseneth* indicate that were we to have at our disposal all of the Jewish novels of antiquity placed in chronological order, we would see more clearly the repeated messages of this popular art form. Either way, the new poetics of popular novels is placed in the service of deeply held but otherwise unarticulated mythical structures.

The Jewish novels invite study on many levels. Our analysis could have been taken up solely with the reconstruction of the social world that is at times reflected in them. The language and ideology of patronage, for example, is striking in Greek *Esther* and *Second Maccabees* and dominates the *Tobiad Romance.* In addition, further research could be undertaken on what I referred to in Chapter 7 as the "morphology of values" found in such popular texts. This study has mainly progressed, however, with a simple interest in a group of texts as literary products and has sought to describe certain aspects of them and to point toward the principles by which they communicate meaning. It is an attempt to investigate the poetics of popular Jewish novels, but not in a narrow sense. The poetics of popular literature is very much bound up with the social fabric of the culture in which it is transmitted, and the novels afford us a glimpse into the social attitudes and dreams of a period in Jewish life.

According to Mishnah *Yoma* 3:10, when the queen of Adiabene—the same of the historical novel of Chapter 7—erected a golden plaque at the temple in Jerusalem, she had inscribed on it *Numbers* 5:12–31, the procedure for the trial-by-ordeal of the suspected adulteress (mentioned in Chapter 2 in regard to *Susanna*). Since the ordeal in the *Numbers* passage is a test of the suspected adulteress, it can establish sexual purity and innocence as well as condemn, and this is perhaps significant for the queen's choice. Just as Aseneth's conversion is associated with the establishment of her purity, so the queen of Adiabene, a convert, affirms the test of innocence. The novels appear to engage an important current of contemporary Judaism to which the queen's plaque, standing over the temple in Jerusalem, also gives voice. They affirm the meaningfulness of denial, a "narrative asceticism" popular with Jews who were likely still fully involved in social and family life.

The *Testament of Abraham* as a Satirical Novel

Throughout this book I have emphasized the parallels, both literary and sociological, between the origins of the Jewish novel and the Greek novel, on the one hand, and the rise of the modern English novel, on the other. Similar goals and methods, related to similar social developments, can be discerned in all three genres. The novelistic impulse transcends a particular set of cultural circumstances and can be found in many different contexts in world history. But one aspect of this set of parallels between ancient and modern novels has not been explored, that is, the question of the existence of Jewish satirical novels, analogous to the satirical novels found among the other two groups.

In the second half of the twentieth century there have been several radically different ways of conceiving the "essence" of the modern European novel, each of which gives rise to different theories of its origins. First, the twin achievements of Ian Watt and Erich Auerbach succeeded in championing a definition of the novel focusing on realism.[1] The novel is quintessentially a genre that treats ordinary people and their trials and experiences seriously, full of tragic potential, and expresses this in the natural language of everyday, unelevated discourse that "mirrors" reality. Watt and Auerbach developed a strong moral sense that this achievement was a triumph in artistic representation, and they had little patience with countervailing tendencies in literature or criticism. They advocated a canon that would include certain works of middle-class representation—*Pamela* and *Madame Bovary*, for example—

---

[1] Watt, *The Rise of the Novel*, and Auerbach, *Mimesis*.

and exclude, or at least downplay in significance, such arch and satirical treatments of bourgeois respectability as Fielding's *Tom Jones*.

Michael McKeon has recently investigated Watt's and Auerbach's approaches to the definition and evaluation of the novel by comparing them to those of other literary and social critics.[2] McKeon points out the challenge brought to this definition by Claude Lévi-Strauss and Northrop Frye. For them, the elevated art forms of premodern history take precedence over the novel; the former express the mythical beliefs of thousands of years of cultural tradition. No matter how the themes are transformed, they still reflect the structural tensions of mythical conflicts and resolutions that transcend history. The novel, however, takes as its setting the domestic interiors of its bourgeois audience; heroic discourse collapses into everyday discourse of natural language. Narrative no longer soars and transcends history in heroic flight; it is embedded in history and the concrete. Lévi-Strauss and Frye, in their lament over the demise of the heroic mode, do not actually disagree with the realists on what the novel *is,* only on whether it is a triumph or a bane.

In McKeon's analysis, it was left to Mikhail Bakhtin to attempt a resolution of these two views. His resolution comes not by way of synthesis of opposite viewpoints (as much as his dialogical method might lead one to expect that) but by valuing differently the process by which the old forms are eradicated. It is not the case that vibrant, heroic forms are supplanted by a discourse that is wedded to the mundane; in Bakhtin's view, the old epic forms are nothing more than cultural reliquaries, repositories for collective memory. The novel is dynamic and living, mainly because it alone of all the literary forms can contain materials of different kinds—dialogue, heterogeneous language systems and styles, voices of different characters, and narrators who are advocates of contradictory positions. The dialogue of levels is not intended to effect a blending, harmony, or synthesis but to retain a dynamic tension in the form as a whole and to undercut stability. The ethos of this form was the interplay of voices that cuts through the seriousness of "monoglot" forms and is essentially parodic, so much so, in fact, that Bakhtin saw it related to all parody, satire, mime, and so on as one intergeneric "immense novel."[3] In his exuberance, Bakhtin includes within this immense novel many parodic forms that are not novels and excludes more earnest works that are.

[2] McKeon, *The Origins of the English Novel, 1600–1740.*
[3] Bakhtin, *The Dialogic Imagination,* esp. 59–60 on this final point.

It is Bakhtin's exclusion of earnest novels, as much as anything, that led McKeon to attempt a truly dialectical redefinition of the origins of the novel. Aside from the dialogue among various voices and levels within the novel (which McKeon would not deny), there is another dialectic between the two types of authorial voices found in different novels. The perfection of realism in the novel is not just reflected in the earnest domestic novels of Richardson, as Watt held, but also in the more cynical and satirical novels of Fielding as well. The earnest and the satiric are two perspectives on the same artistic "problem," which is, What is the affirmation of meaning (or, as McKeon would say, truth and virtue) in a social existence in which older romantic and heroic forms no longer hold sway? The examination of the everyday can be positive and uplifting, promulgating a high standard of moral conduct (Richardson), or it can be satirizing (Fielding), but the methods are quite similar. Thus, we find a dialectical relationship of two perspectives on realism, the earnest and the satirical. It provides a more complicated paradigm for the origin of the English novel than Watt's and a more empirical paradigm than Bakhtin's. If we posit, then, a view of the novel which sees both types as complementary, two answers to the problem of the collapse of transcendent, heroic codes of truth and virtue in everyday life, then it becomes pointless to assert that one or the other is the proper function of the novel or is logically or temporally prior to the other. Even an empirical observation that one form was actually created before the other can generally be challenged on the basis of the definition of what is truly "novelistic." The two perspectives, the earnest and the satirical, are necessarily related to each other and are both characteristic outgrowths (if we may reintroduce the biological metaphor of Chapter 1) of the rise of an entrepreneurial, literate class.

It should be emphasized that the distinction drawn here is not between tragic and comic or between serious and farcical but between a positive affirmation of the moral codes of an everyday reality and a critical, "unconvinced," arch perspective. Humor, parody, and even some forms of satire do not necessarily challenge the authority of given social constraints. And equally, satires on the social order which are merely liminal, which explore a reversal of roles for a temporary experience of exhilaration and release, may merely reinforce deeply held social codes and not strike at the very heart of a mercantile-class worldview. It may be that the key to the satire that McKeon is addressing is alienation—not alienation from the tyranny of the ruling majority but alienation from one's own symbolic universe.

In the ancient world as well as the modern, the novel may arise as a result of the emergence of a new entrepreneurial, literate class no longer bound to the heroic art forms and values of the previous centuries. And likewise, artisans of the novel may look upon the aspirations of this class in either of two ways: with pride and hope or with a satirical questioning. The erosion of traditional expressions of truth and virtue and their replacement with new ones is here also the artistic problem that both kinds of novelists attempt to address: Is the new bourgeois hero truly heroic, or are the ideals of that hero laughable and constricted within a petty universe? Bruce D. MacQueen invokes the distinction between the straightforward novel and the ironic parody and divides the extant Greek novels along these lines: Achilles Tatius and Longus are playing off the pattern of the serious novel but inverting and subverting many of the themes and assumptions.[4] The playful joie de vivre of Longus's *Daphnis and Chloe* and the absence of a travel motif are not problems for MacQueen in including this work with the other Greek novels (as they are for many others); rather, they merely highlight the consciously parodic attitude of the author. Achilles Tatius is simply more cynical in regard to the earnest domestic values of the "typical" Greek novel. Other ancient Greek novels reflect the same cynical or satirical viewpoint, such as the fragments of *Iolaus* or Lollianus's *Phoenician Tale*.[5] *Life of Aesop* should also be considered in this category, as should both of the extant Roman novels, *The Golden Ass* and *Satyricon*.[6]

---

[4] MacQueen, *Myth, Rhetoric, and Fiction*, 117–37. MacQueen does not refer to McKeon (the two books were published at about the same time), but he does draw the parallel between the two-sided origin of the ancient novel and that of the modern novel. Although McKeon and MacQueen apply this principle of dual perspectives quite broadly, the germ of it—but only the germ—was already articulated in classical scholarship some sixty years ago by Haight (*Essays on Ancient Fiction*, 1–45, esp. 19–39; see also the Introduction for a discussion of her theory). She divided the extant fragments of the novella from the classical period—*novella* in the sense of a short, pointed narrative, originally from oral tradition, taken over into a written work—into novella proper and the "tragic tale." The former is a short narrative with "interest of episode, plot or behavior, uncolored by emotion, sometimes enlivened by the ironic comment of a narrator." The latter is "romantic," usually tragic, and "fundamentally colored by emotion." She suggests (p. 43) that there occurred an evolution of such stories into the quasi-realistic novel of antiquity, but she does not proceed to the more far-reaching and detailed theses of McKeon and MacQueen that the two perspectives are complementary ways of viewing reality and are both integral to the development of the novel.

[5] MacQueen, *Myth, Rhetoric, and Fiction*, 224; Albert Henrichs, *Die Phoinikika des Lollianos* (Bonn: Hablet, 1972); Gerald N. Sandy, "A Phoenician Story" and "Iolaus," in Reardon, ed., *Collected Ancient Greek Novels*, 809, 816–17.

[6] On the Roman novels and *Aesop* as satirical, see Winkler, *Auctor & Actor*, 135–79, 276–91.

For wealthier Jews as well within the Greco-Roman world, one kind of novel can affirm the values of a new class—God, family, piety, self-sacrifice, the beginnings of an ascetic principle—while the other kind, if such existed in Judaism, does not. Did such satirical Jewish novels exist? We may begin by considering the differences between the version of *Esther* found in the Hebrew Bible and that found in the Apocrypha, Greek *Esther*. The farcical Hebrew *Esther*, which never mentions the name of God, stands in sharp contrast to Greek *Esther*. The latter reins in the satirical tendencies of the former, consciously or unconsciously, and piously reinterprets all events to the greater glory of God: dramatic visions and pretentious royal decrees are added, and Esther's earnest self-examination becomes the new center of gravity of the work. Although in this case the satirical version, Hebrew *Esther*, likely came first, it is evident that versions prior to the Hebrew Bible could be postulated that were likely more pious. At any rate, the extant versions reflect quite opposite poles. Hebrew *Esther*, however, is not likely satirical in the same way as, say, Fielding or, in MacQueen's view, Longus and Achilles Tatius. We may encounter different sorts of "satire" in the Jewish novels or shades of gray in the attitude toward virtue and truth in everyday life. If Hebrew *Esther* does satirize the social order, it is probably in respect to a non-Jewish social order, one situated in the past, that is, the Persian period. Furthermore, as a Purim reading the experience is festive and liminal only, not permanent. The morning after, Jews must nurse their hangovers and return to work. It is true that in later Jewish history (and originally as well, if we were to entertain the early dating for Hebrew *Esther* in the Persian period), the satire strikes right at the pretensions of the ruling majority, but that would not constitute a questioning of the *Jewish* symbolic universe, only a much-needed opportunity for release. Likewise, *Judith* and *Tobit*, both comical and often satirical to some extent, do not strike at the pretensions of the social order. *Judith*, like many folktales, explores the liminal release occasioned by the reversal of sex roles, and *Tobit* only benignly satirizes the social order. It is questionable whether any of the novels analyzed in the previous chapters, humorous and concerned with the parody or satire of certain foreign figures though they be, is satirical in the way that we are intending here.

The most fascinating candidate for a Jewish satirical novel, however, has never been considered a novel at all and has not been mentioned heretofore in this study because of its surface differences. The *Testament of Abraham* is a remarkable document, dated by most scholars to about 100 C.E.,[7] which relates the last days of the patriarch Abraham. Despite its title, however, and its opening words, it is not typical of the popular testament genre, which generally depicts the predictions and final exhortations of a dying patriarch. The *Testament of Abraham* instead presents a parody of the pious Abraham, the "friend of God." The story begins with a description of Abraham that immediately seems intentionally satirizing. An inflated view of Abraham's piety is recounted, giving way to a tone of mock solemnity:

> Abraham lived all the years of his life in quietness, gentleness, and righteousness. And this righteous man was indeed hospitable: he pitched his tent at the crossroads of the oak of Mamre, and he welcomed everyone, rich and poor, kings and rulers, maimed and handicapped, friends and strangers, neighbors and passing strangers—the saintly, most holy, righteous, hospitable Abraham welcomed them all on equal terms. But he also came at last to that common, inexorable, bitter cup of death and the unforeseen end of his life. (1:1–3)

The archangel (here "commander-in-chief") Michael is sent by God to inform Abraham of his impending death, in order that the latter may have time to make a last will and testament. Abraham plays host to Michael, unaware that the latter is an angel, and brings him into his home, but the angel is so struck with Abraham's abundant hospitality that he cannot bring himself to deliver his message. Stepping outside as if to relieve himself, Michael ascends up to heaven to ask God what he must do. "Return to my friend Abraham," says God, ". . . and I will send my holy spirit upon his son Isaac and place the notion of his death in Isaac's heart as in a vision. He shall see the death of his father in a dream, and when he recounts it, you can interpret the meaning. In that way, Abraham will come to know that he is about to die" (4:7–8). Isaac does awake during the night with a disturbing dream, and Michael interprets it to mean that Abraham is about to die.

---

[7] See, above all, the introductions by Nickelsburg, *Jewish Literature Between the Bible and the Mishnah,* 248–53; E. P. Sanders, "Testament of Abraham," in James H. Charlesworth, ed., *Old Testament Pseudepigrapha,* 2 vols. (Garden City, N.Y.: Doubleday, 1983), 871–902; and John J. Collins, *The Apocalyptic Imagination: An Introduction to the Jewish Matrix of Christianity* (New York: Crossroad, 1984), 201–4. More technical studies can be found in Nickelsburg, ed., *Studies on the Testament of Abraham,* and Francis Schmidt, *Le Testament grec d'Abraham* (Tübingen: Mohr [Paul Siebeck], 1986).

When Michael identifies himself, however, as the one who will escort Abraham's soul to heaven, Abraham refuses to go.[8] Michael transports himself again to heaven and requests further orders from God. God commands Michael to tell Abraham that God has blessed him greatly thus far and thought fit to give him advance word of his death so that he could make a last will and testament. "Do you not know," says God (through Michael) "that if I were to allow Death to come to you, then I would find out whether you would come or not!" Abraham responds by asking Michael to relay an urgent request to God: Abraham only wishes to see the entire world and all the things that God created before he dies. Abraham is granted this request, but as he is taken by Michael over the earth, he sees many sinners: first murderers, then adulterers, then robbers. Abraham immediately beseeches Michael to destroy these sinners, which he does. God now stops their tour of the earth, lest they destroy everyone. God explains to Abraham that he had only delayed the death of these sinners in hopes that they might repent. Abraham, however, who has not sinned, has no mercy on sinners. God then has Michael conduct Abraham to the place of judgment, so that he may witness the horrible postmortem punishments exacted upon sinners. Abraham now repents of his rash requests and asks to have those sinners returned to life whom he had earlier consigned to death.

Abraham is then returned to his home and is once more informed by Michael that his soul is about to depart his body and that he must make his last will and testament. This time, the command is said to come directly from God (15:8–10), but once again he refuses to obey, and once more Michael must ask God what action to take. God decides at this point to summon Death and send him to take away Abraham's soul. Michael has been characterized as unexpectedly ineffectual with Abraham, but Death is presented in an even less prepossessing manner: "When Death heard [God's command to appear], he quaked and trembled, overcome with fear. Coming before the unseen Father, he shuddered in fright, moaning and trembling as he awaited the Master's command" (16:3). He is to be clothed, however, not in his fearsome aspect but in his beautiful raiment, so as not to terrify Abraham. Death comes before Abraham and announces his mission, but Abraham does

---

[8] Much is rightly made of the close parallels to the account of Moses cheating death in *Deuteronomy Rabbah* 11:10, a relatively long continuous narrative in midrashic literature. Both traditions are difficult to date, but Sanders concludes (p. 879) that the Moses tradition has influenced *Testament of Abraham*.

not believe that such a beautiful figure could be Death and refuses to go. Abraham the hospitable now walks about his house apparently sulking, leaving Death to trail after him from room to room: "Abraham arose and went into his house, followed by Death. As Abraham went up to his room, Death followed along behind. There Abraham lay down on his couch, while Death came and remained at his feet. 'Leave me now,' said Abraham, 'I want to rest on my couch.' But Death replied, 'I will not leave until I have taken your spirit from you'" (17:1–3).

When Abraham finally learns, however, that this handsome gentle-man really is Death, he asks to see him not in his beautiful visage but in his horrible state, as he appears to sinners. This horrifying revela-tion results in the death of seven thousand servants and, for the first time, brings upon Abraham the "listlessness of death" (*oligorian thana-tou*, 17:19). From this moment, the tone of the story changes. Abraham, once active and strong, is now increasingly succumbing to the listless-ness of death. Although no clear explanation is given at first for the change that has come over him, he apparently has come to witness more than he can bear. This does not stop him, however, from requesting to see more. After successfully petitioning God to bring the dead servants back to life, Abraham retires to his room again. Death comes and stands beside him once more, but Abraham insists that he will not go with him until he sees all the ways that Death comes to people, by drowning, by the sword, by falling from great heights, and so on. Death recounts the seventy-two ways that people die and asks Abraham once again to come with him. Abraham resists Death but this time with a greater heaviness of spirit: "'Leave me now for just a little while, so that I may rest on my couch. A great listlessness now oppresses me. From the moment I be-held you with my eyes, my strength has left me. All of my limbs are like a lead weight, and my breathing is very weak. Leave then for a while; I cannot bear to look upon your form'" (20:4–5). Abraham has asked to see all aspects of Death but is now overcome by the vision. Death, evidently sensing that he has an advantage, offers his hand for Abraham to kiss. When the patriarch kisses his hand, his soul escapes into Death's possession.[9] From there it is borne to heaven by Michael and the other angels. God receives Abraham into Paradise while his body is buried at the oaks of Mamre.

George W. E. Nickelsburg has noted the careful, suggestive structur-

---

[9] This action reflects a belief of the period that the soul could pass out of a body through kissing. See Sanders, "Testament," 895. See also Josephus, *Against Apion,* 2.24 § 203, on the transference of the soul at birth and death.

ing of *Testament of Abraham* into two parts (here simplified, with many verbal parallels omitted):[10]

Part 1	Part 2
God summons Michael:	God summons Death:
Tell Abraham he will die and to make testament	Tell Abraham he will die
Michael goes to Abraham at Mamre	Death goes to Abraham at Mamre
Abraham and Michael greet	Abraham and Death greet
Abraham hosts Michael	Abraham inhospitable to Death
Michael reveals mission	Death reveals mission
Abraham asks to see whole world	Abraham asks to see Death's ferocity
Abraham asks that sinners die	Death causes servants to die
Abraham prays for dead, who are revived	Abraham and Death pray for dead, who are revived
Michael returns Abraham to Sarah, Isaac, and servants, who rejoice	Isaac, Sarah, and servants mourn
Abraham refuses to make testament	Abraham is suddenly taken
Michael returns to heaven	Michael takes soul to heaven

Nickelsburg also points out one of the oddities of this text: our preconceptions of what a "testament" is are overturned in line after line. The recurring motif of *Testament of Abraham* is that Abraham, unlike most people, is allowed time by God to make a testament. He never does. Other aspects of the work reflect an even broader satirical style. The absurdity of the maneuverings of Michael between heaven and earth would surely not be missed by an ancient audience: the "commander-in-chief" of the angels is so stunned by Abraham's piety that he must absent himself—on the pretext of needing to urinate!—to ask God for further instructions (4:5–6). Sarah, it seems, easily recognizes Michael as one of the three visitors Abraham had entertained at the oaks of Mamre (*Genesis* 18) and sparks a glimmer of recognition in her husband by informing him of this after he has bathed Michael's feet. "Oh, yes!" Abraham seems to say, "I thought I recognized those feet!" (6:6). Furthermore, Abraham's interview with Death, as though

---

[10] Nickelsburg, *Jewish Literature*, 249–50.

the former were a depressed patient on an analyst's couch, and its neat balancing with the interview with Michael indicate some special intention on the author's part, separate from the tour of heaven one would expect to dominate this work.

The comical aspects of the writing are all part of a broader plan of the author to present a meditation on death that overturns many cherished notions of the Judaism of the period. The overwhelmingly pious Abraham, who yet humbly refers to himself as a sinner, seems flighty, self-centered, and plainly disobedient to God. He eventually succumbs to the "listlessness of death" (17:19, 18:8, 19:2, 20:7) but never goes willingly; he is finally deceived by Death into kissing his hand. The import of the biblical hero's testament and the predictions and exhortations that usually accompany it fall conspicuously to the wayside. In vain we would search for easy generic parallels. It is not a testament except by its inverted point of departure. The tour of heaven calls to mind apocalyptic and visionary texts, but the noneschatological nature of the tour and the unusual angelic interpreter—Death!—render this connection problematic, as Martha Himmelfarb and others have noted.[11] The themes of *Testament of Abraham,* indeed, evoke thoughts of writings from many different contexts. Like *Jonah,* it chastises the "man of God" for condemning others too quickly; like some of the Moses literature of this period, it depicts the hesitancy of the heavenly forces to cart away a hero's soul; like *Job,* it resolves the rift between God and a pious rebel irresolutely; like Euripides' *Alcestis,* it places a hero in a position to extricate souls from the hands of Death;[12] like Lucian's *True History,* it lampoons the credulous genres beloved by many others. We may even move out of the ancient period and find parallels in Charles Dickens's *Christmas Carol* and Ingmar Bergman's *The Seventh Seal.* Much of the appeal of the story can indeed be attributed to the enduring folk tradition that underlies it. In the process, *Testament of Abraham* leaps beyond the expected generic associations.

Much about the work, however, is novelistic. It is about the same length as *Tobit,* and it develops a narrative plot line that sustains interest and leaves the reader wondering how the story will be resolved (not

[11] Martha Himmelfarb, *Ascents to Heaven in Jewish and Christian Apocalypses* (New York: Oxford University Press, 1993), 8, 116 n. 15; Enno Janssen, "Testament Abrahams," in *Jüdische Schriften aus hellenistisch-römischer Zeit,* part 3, fascicle 2, ed. Werner Georg Kümmel (Gütersloh: Gütersloher Verlagshaus Gerd Mohn, 1980), 196. Collins disagrees (*Apocalyptic Imagination,* 201–4).
[12] *Alcestis* 28–76, 843–51; see Janssen, "Testament Abrahams," 197.

what the visions will reveal).[13] It also exploits the possibilities of dialogue to a remarkable degree. Finally, there is the issue of Abraham's change of character. The satirical tone of the beginning of *Testament of Abraham* has given way at the end to somber realizations on the part of Abraham that he will not escape Death's command and that the reality of death is horrible. The work as a whole moves away from the category of satire to a philosophical reflection on the inevitability of death. Several scholars attempt an interpretation of *Testament of Abraham* that will make sense of its unusual tone. Nickelsburg manages to wrest a pious conclusion from the work by noting that Abraham (and therefore the readers) can find some consolation in the fact that those who die untimely deaths do not face postmortem judgments.[14] Collins agrees and pushes this line of interpretation further: "If Abraham stands apart from the rest of humanity by his righteousness, he at least shares the instinctive human denial of death. He becomes then a figure with whom we can identify, so that by following through his (fictional) experience we can experience an 'apocalyptic cure' for the fear of death."[15] Under these interpretations, the revelation to Abraham becomes much more important: the consolation for the reader is only present after Abraham's heightened knowledge of heavenly justice. This hopeful doctrine can certainly be abstracted from the text, but it is not at all clear that this is the "message." It is especially significant that this argument does not satisfy Abraham: he resists Death till the end and must be taken by deception. Collins is comfortable grouping the *Testament of Abraham* with apocalypses, despite its tolerant view of judgment, its lack of eschatological and dualistic tendencies, and its individualistic concern with death, but I would aver that it is merely the shell of the testament or the apocalypse that is taken over and that this is done for a satirical purpose.

Even if the more positive interpretation of the ending were accepted, it would not be foreign to the category of satire, just as Job's philosophical questions about the justice of God go hand in hand with a satire on the traditional Jewish wisdom that is heard in the mouths of his interlocutors.[16] But does the *Testament of Abraham*, in its two-part

---

13 Himmelfarb, *Ascents to Heaven*, 8, 116 n. 15.

14 Nickelsburg, *Jewish Literature*, 252.

15 Collins, *Apocalyptic Imagination*, 202.

16 For reasons that were discussed in Chapter 1, it is difficult to consider *Job, Ruth,* or *Jonah* novels, although it is interesting that *Testament of Abraham* is like these works in *theme:* they all explore the philosophical problem of a good person who is somehow alienated from God. Job, according to the interlocutors' view of Jewish wisdom, must have sinned because he is being punished; Jonah disobeys a direct command of God; Ruth is a woman of the Moabites,

progression, satirize the very values that the other Jewish novels would affirm? I would assert that the answer is yes, and it is a satire in the specific sense that I have underscored above; that is, it is a mirror image of the earnest novel, born in the same social conditions but reflecting an experience of alienation.[17] Thus, although *Testament of Abraham* lacks many of the elements of the earnest Jewish novels, it has boldly adapted a wholly different genre—the testament—to a satirical novel. A paradox concerning Jewish novels is clarified by recourse to the history of novels in general: *Testament of Abraham* is a novel not because it is like the other Jewish novels but because it is not. It is a satirical novel, written in the form of a mock testament, that utilizes considerable artistic skill in creating an arch narrative for an alienated readership.

---

who are perennial enemies of Israel; Abraham disobeys God's command to make a testament and accompany Michael.

[17] The fact that the *Testament of Abraham* exists in two recensions only corroborates the theory that the version before us is intentionally satirical. The other version ("short recension," also translated in Charlesworth) contains most of the motifs of the present recension *but not told in a satirical way;* the archangel Michael is not thwarted by Abraham's maneuverings, Death does not dog Abraham's footsteps, and Abraham does not systematically flout God's command to make a testament. See Nickelsburg, "Structure and Message in the Testament of Abraham," in Nickelsburg, ed., *Studies on the Testament of Abraham,* 89–90. The obvious question of whether the short recension should therefore be considered an earnest novel must be answered negatively: it is rather a more typical "tour of heaven."

Bibliography

Adrados, Francisco R. "The 'Life of Aesop' and the Origins of Novel [*sic*] in Antiquity." *Quaderni urbinati di cultura classica* 30 (1979): 93–112.

Albertz, Rainer. *Der Gott des Daniel: Untersuchungen zu Daniel 4–6 in der Septuagintafassung: Sowie Zu Komposition und Theologie des aramäischen Danielbuches.* Stuttgart: Verlag Katholisches Bibelwerk, 1988.

Alonso-Schökel, Luis. *Narrative Structures in the Book of Judith.* Berkeley: Center for Hermeneutical Studies in Hellenistic and Modern Culture, 1975.

Alter, Robert. *The Art of Biblical Narrative.* New York: Basic, 1981.

Altheim, Franz, and Ruth Stiehl. *Die aramäische Sprache unter den Achaimeniden.* 2 vols. Frankfurt am Main: Vittorio Klostermann, 1963.

Altman, Rick. *The American Film Musical.* Bloomington: Indiana University Press, 1987.

Anderson, Graham. *Eros Sophistes: Ancient Novelists at Play.* Chico, Calif.: Scholars, 1982.

Aptowitzer, Victor. "Asenath, the Wife of Joseph—A Haggadic, Literary-Historical Study." *Hebrew Union College Annual* 1 (1924): 239–306.

Ariès, Philippe, and Georges Duby, eds. *A History of Private Life.* Vol. 1, *From Pagan Rome to Byzantium.* Cambridge: Harvard University Press, 1987.

Auerbach, Erich. *Mimesis: The Representation of Reality in Western Literature.* Princeton: Princeton University Press, 1953.

Aune, David. *The New Testament in Its Literary Environment.* Philadelphia: Westminster, 1987.

Bakhtin, Mikhail. *The Dialogic Imagination.* Austin: University of Texas Press, 1981.

Bal, Mieke. "The Elders and Susanna." *Biblical Interpretation* 1 (1993): 1–19.

——. *Femmes imaginaires: L'ancien testament au risque d'une narratologie critique.* Paris: Nizet, 1986.

——. *Lethal Love: Feminist Literary Readings of Biblical Love Stories.* Bloomington: Indiana University Press, 1987.

——. *Narratology: Introduction to the Theory of Narrative.* Toronto: University of Toronto Press, 1985.

Baskin, Judith R., ed. *Jewish Women in Historical Perspective.* Detroit: Wayne State University Press, 1991.

Beard, Mary, et al., eds. *Literacy in the Roman World.* Ann Arbor: Journal of Roman Archaeology, 1991.

Beaton, Roderick, ed. *The Greek Novel,* A.D. *1–1985.* London: Croom Helm, 1988.

Becker, Jürgen. *Untersuchungen zur Entstehungsgeschichte der Testamente der zwölf Patriarchen.* Leiden: Brill, 1970.

Berg, Sandra Beth. *The Book of Esther: Motifs, Themes, and Structure.* Missoula: Scholars, 1979.

Berlin, Adele. *Poetics and the Interpretation of Biblical Narrative.* Sheffield: Almond, 1983.

Biale, David. *Eros and the Jews: From Biblical Israel to Contemporary America.* San Francisco: HarperCollins, 1992.

Biale, Rachel. *Women and Jewish Law.* New York: Schocken, 1984.

Bickerman, Elias. "The Colophon of the Greek Book of Esther." *Journal of Biblical Literature* 63 (1944): 339–62. Reprinted in Bickerman, *Studies in Jewish and Christian History,* vol. 2, 225–45. Leiden: Brill, 1976.

——. *Four Strange Books of the Bible.* New York: Schocken, 1967.

——. "Héliodore au Temple de Jérusalem." In *Studies in Jewish and Christian History.* Pp. 2:159–191.

——. *The Jews in the Greek Age.* Cambridge: Harvard University Press, 1988.

——. "Notes on the Greek Book of Esther." In *Studies in Jewish and Christian History.* Pp. 2:246–74.

Blenkinsopp, Joseph. "Biographical Patterns in Biblical Narrative." *Journal for the Study of the Old Testament* 20 (1981): 27–46.

Bow, Beverly, and George W. E. Nickelsburg. "Patriarchy with a Twist: Men and Women in Tobit." In Levine, ed., *Women Like This.* Pp. 127–43.

Bowman, Alan, and Greg Woolf. *Literacy and Power in the Ancient World.* Cambridge: Cambridge University Press, 1994.

Braun, Martin. *History and Romance in Graeco-Oriental Literature.* New York: Garland, 1987.

Brenner, Athalya. "Esther Through the Looking Glass" (in Hebrew). *Bet Mikra* 86 (1981): 267–78.

——. *The Israelite Woman: Social Role and Literary Type in Biblical Narrative.* Sheffield: Journal for the Study of the Old Testament Press, 1985.

Brenner, Athalya, and Fokkelien van Dijk-Hemmes. *On Gendering Texts: Female and Male Voices in the Hebrew Bible.* Leiden: Brill, 1993.

Brichto, Herbert Chanan. *Toward a Grammar of Biblical Poetics.* New York: Oxford University Press, 1992.

Brown, Peter. *The Body and Society: Men, Women, and Sexual Renunciation in Early Christianity.* New York: Columbia University Press, 1988.

Burchard, Christoph. *Der dreizehnte Zeuge: Traditions- und kompositionsgeschichtliche Untersuchungen zu Lukas' Darstellung der Frühzeit des Paulus.* Göttingen: Vandenhoeck & Ruprecht, 1970.

——. "The Present State of Research on Joseph and Aseneth." In *Religion, Literature, and Society in Ancient Israel, Formative Christianity and Judaism*. Ed. Jacob Neusner et al. Lanham, Md.: University Press of America, 1987. Pp. 31–52.

——. *Untersuchungen zu Joseph und Aseneth*. Tübingen: Mohr (Paul Siebeck), 1965.

Burrus, Virginia. *Chastity as Autonomy: Women in the Stories of the Apocryphal Acts*. Lewiston, Me.: Edwin Mellen, 1987.

Carroll, Michael P. "Myth, Methodology, and Transformation in the Old Testament: The Stories of Esther, Judith, and Susanna." *Studies in Religion/Sciences Religieuses* 12 (1983): 301–12.

Carson, Anne. "Putting Her in Her Place: Woman, Dirt, and Desire." In *Before Sexuality: The Construction of Erotic Experience in the Ancient Greek World*. Ed. David M. Halperin, John J. Winkler, and Froma I. Zeitlin. Princeton: Princeton University Press, 1990. Pp. 135–69.

Cawelti, John G. *Adventure, Mystery, and Romance: Formula Stories as Art and Popular Culture*. Chicago: University of Chicago Press, 1976.

Cazelles, Henri. "Notes sur la composition du rouleau d'Esther." In *Lex tua veritas: Festschrift für Hubert Junker*. Ed. H. Gross and F. Mussner. Trier: Paulinus, 1961. Pp. 17–29.

Chase, Mary Ellen. *Life and Literature in the Old Testament*. New York: Norton, 1955.

Chesnutt, Randall D. "Conversion in Joseph and Aseneth: Its Nature, Function, and Relation to Contemporaneous Paradigms of Conversion and Initiation." Ph.D. diss., Duke University, 1986.

Clark, Elizabeth A. *Ascetic Piety and Women's Faith*. Lewiston, Me.: Edwin Mellen, 1986.

Clines, David J. A. *The Esther Scroll: The Story of the Story*. Sheffield: Journal for the Study of the Old Testament Press, 1984.

Cohen, Ralph. "Genre Theory, Literary History, and Historical Change." In *Theoretical Issues in Literary History*. Ed. David Perkins. Cambridge: Harvard University Press, 1991. Pp. 85–113.

Cohen, Shaye J. D. "Menstruants and the Sacred in Judaism and Christianity." In *Women's History and Ancient History*, ed. Sarah B. Pomeroy. Chapel Hill: University of North Carolina Press, 1991.

Collins, John J. *The Apocalyptic Vision of the Book of Daniel*. Missoula: Scholars, 1977.

——. *Between Athens and Jerusalem: Jewish Identity in the Hellenistic Diaspora*. New York: Crossroad, 1983.

——. "The Court-Tales in Daniel and the Development of Apocalyptic." *Journal of Biblical Literature* 94 (1975): 218–34.

——. "Daniel and His Social World." *Interpretation* 39 (1985): 131–43.

Craven, Toni. *Artistry and Faith in the Book of Judith*. Chico, Calif.: Scholars, 1983.

Danahy, Michael. "Le Roman est-il chose femelle?" *Poetique* 25 (1976): 85–106.

Dancy, J. C. *The Shorter Books of the Apocrypha*. Cambridge: Cambridge University Press, 1972.

Darr, Katheryn Pfisterer. *Far More Precious Than Jewels: Perspectives on Biblical Women*. Louisville: Westminster John Knox, 1991.

Day, Peggy L., ed. *Gender and Difference in Ancient Israel*. Minneapolis: Augsburg Fortress, 1989.

Delling, Gerhard. "Die Kunst des Gestaltens in 'Joseph und Aseneth.'" *Novum Testamentum* 26 (1984): 1–40.

Deselaers, Paul. *Das Buch Tobit: Studien zu seiner Entstehung, Komposition, und Theologie.* Göttingen: Vandenhoeck & Ruprecht, 1982.

Donner, Herbert. *Die literärische Gestalt der alttestamentlichen Josephsgeschichte.* Heidelberg: Carl Winter, 1976.

Doran, Robert. *Temple Propaganda: The Purpose and Character of 2 Maccabees.* Washington: Catholic Biblical Association, 1981.

Dubarle, A. M. *Judith: Formes et sens des diverses traditions.* 2 vols. Rome: Pontifical Biblical Institute, 1966.

Ducrot, Oswald, and Tzvetan Todorov. *Encyclopedic Dictionary of the Sciences of Language.* Baltimore: Johns Hopkins University Press, 1979.

Engel, Helmut. *Die Susanna-Erzählung.* Göttingen: Vandenhoeck & Ruprecht, 1985.

Feldman, Louis H. "Hellenizations in Josephus' Version of Esther." *Transactions of the American Philological Association* 101 (1970): 143–70.

——. *Jew and Gentile in the Ancient World.* Princeton: Princeton University Press, 1992.

Fenz, Augustinus Kurt. "Ein Drache in Babel. Exegetische Skizze über Daniel 14, 23–42." *Svensk exegetisk arsbok* 35 (1970): 5–16.

Fewell, Danna Nolan. *Circle of Sovereignty: A Story of Stories in Daniel 1–6.* Sheffield: Almond, 1988.

Foley, John Miles, ed. *Oral Tradition in Literature: Interpretation in Context.* Columbia: University of Missouri Press, 1986.

——. *The Theory of Oral Composition: History and Methodology.* Bloomington: Indiana University Press, 1988.

Foucault, Michel. *The History of Sexuality.* Vol. 3, *The Care of the Self.* New York: Pantheon, 1986.

Fowler, Barbara Hughes. *The Hellenistic Aesthetic.* Madison: University of Wisconsin Press, 1989.

Fox, Michael V. *Character and Ideology in the Book of Esther.* Columbia: University of South Carolina Press, 1991.

——. *The Redaction of the Books of Esther.* Atlanta: Scholars, 1991.

Fraade, Steven D. "Ascetical Aspects of Ancient Judaism." In *Jewish Spirituality.* Ed. Arthur Green. 2 vols. New York: Crossroad, 1986. Pp. 1:253–88.

Frye, Northrop. *The Secular Scripture.* Cambridge: Harvard University Press, 1976.

Frymer-Kensky, Tikva. *In the Wake of the Goddesses: Women, Culture, and the Biblical Transformation of Pagan Myth.* New York: Free Press, 1992.

Fuchs, Esther. "Who Is Hiding the Truth? Deceptive Women and Biblical Androcentrism." In *Feminist Perspectives on Biblical Scholarship.* Ed. Adela Yarbro Collins. Chico, Calif.: Scholars, 1985. Pp. 137–44.

Funk, Robert W. *The Poetics of Biblical Narrative.* Sonoma, Calif.: Polebridge, 1988.

Gan, Moshe. "The Book of Esther in Light of the Story of Joseph in Egypt" (in Hebrew). *Tarbiz* 31 (1961–62): 144–49.

Gendler, Mary. "The Vindication of Vashti." *Response* 18 (1973): 154–60. (*Response* vol. 18 was also published separately as *The Jewish Woman,* ed. Liz Koltun. Waltham, Mass.: Jewish Educational Ventures, 1973.)

Gill, Christopher, and T. P. Wiseman. *Lie and Fiction in the Ancient World*. Exeter: University of Exeter Press, 1993.

Ginsberg, H. L. "The Composition of the Book of Daniel." *Vetus Testamentum* 4 (1954): 246–75.

——. *Studies in the Book of Daniel*. New York: Jewish Theological Seminary of America, 1948.

Goldman, Stan. "Narrative and Ethical Ironies in Esther." *Journal for the Study of the Old Testament* 47 (1990): 15–31.

Goldstein, Jonathan A. *1 Maccabees*. Garden City, N.Y.: Doubleday, 1976.

——. *2 Maccabees*. Garden City, N.Y.: Doubleday, 1983.

——. "Tales of the Tobiads." In *Christianity, Judaism, and Other Greco-Roman Cults*. Ed. Jacob Neusner. 3 vols. Leiden: Brill, 1975. 3:85–123.

Good, Edwin M. "Apocalyptic as Comedy: The Book of Daniel." *Semeia* 32 (1984): 41–70.

Goody, Jack, ed. *Literacy in Traditional Societies*. Cambridge: Cambridge University Press, 1968.

Goody, Jack, and Ian Watt. "Consequences of Literacy." *Comparative Studies in Society and History* 5 (1963): 304–45.

Graham, William A. *Beyond the Written Word: Oral Aspects of Scripture in the History of Religion*. Cambridge: Cambridge University Press, 1987.

Greenstein, Edward L. "A Jewish Reading of Esther." In *Judaic Perspectives on Ancient Israel*. Ed. Jacob Neusner, Buruch A. Levine, Ernst Frerichs. Philadelphia: Fortress, 1987. Pp. 225–44.

Gunkel, Hermann. *Esther*. Tübingen: Mohr (Paul Siebeck), 1916.

——. *The Folktale in the Old Testament*. Sheffield: Almond Press, 1987.

——. *Was bleibt vom Alten Testament?* Göttingen: Vandenhoeck & Ruprecht, 1916.

Haag, Ernst. *Die Errettung Daniels aus der Löwengrube*. Stuttgart: Katholisches Bibelwerk, 1983.

——. *Studien zum Buch Judith*. Trier: Paulinus, 1963.

Hackett, Jo Ann. "In the Days of Jael: Reclaiming the History of Women in Ancient Israel." In *Immaculate and Powerful: The Female in Sacred Image and Social Reality*. Ed. Clarissa Atkinson, Constance H. Buchanan, and Margaret R. Miles. Boston: Beacon, 1985. Pp. 15–38.

Hadas, Moses. "Cultural Survival and the Origin of Fiction." *South Atlantic Quarterly* 51 (1952): 253–60.

——. *Hellenistic Culture*. New York: Norton, 1972.

——. *The Third and Fourth Book of Maccabees*. New York: Ktav, 1953.

Hägg, Tomas. "The Beginnings of the Historical Novel." In Beaton, ed., *The Greek Novel, A.D. 1–1985*. Pp. 169–78.

——. "*Callirhoe* and *Parthenope*: The Beginnings of the Historical Novel." *Classical Antiquity* 6 (1987): 184–204.

——. *Narrative Technique in Ancient Greek Romances*. Stockholm: Swedish Institute in Athens, 1971.

——. *The Novel in Antiquity*. Berkeley and Los Angeles: University of California Press, 1983.

Haight, Elizabeth Hazelton. *Essays on Ancient Fiction*. New York: Longmans, Green, 1936.

Harpham, Geoffrey Galt. *The Ascetic Imperative in Culture and Criticism*. Chicago: University of Chicago Press, 1987.

Harris, William V. *Ancient Literacy*. Cambridge: Harvard University Press, 1989.

Hartman, Geoffrey H., and Sanford Budick, eds. *Midrash and Literature*. New Haven: Yale University Press, 1986.

Havelock, Eric A. *The Origins of Western Literacy*. Toronto: Ontario Institute for Studies in Education, 1974.

Hawkes, Terence. *Structuralism and Semiotics*. London: Methuen, 1977.

Hengel, Martin. *Acts and the History of Earliest Christianity*. Philadelphia: Fortress, 1980.

——. *Judaism and Hellenism: Studies in Their Encounter in Palestine During the Early Hellenistic Period*. 2 vols. Philadelphia: Fortress, 1974.

Hock, Ronald F. "The Greek Novel." In *Greco-Roman Literature and the New Testament*. Ed. David Aune. Atlanta: Scholars, 1988. Pp. 132–41.

Hollander, Harm W. "The Ethical Character of the Patriarch Joseph." In Nickelsburg, ed., *Studies on the Testament of Joseph*. Pp. 47–104.

Humphreys, W. Lee. "A Life-Style for Diaspora: A Study of Esther and Daniel." *Journal of Biblical Literature* 92 (1973): 211–23.

——. "Novella." In *Saga, Legend, Tale, Novella, Fable*. Ed. George W. Coats. Sheffield: Journal for the Study of the Old Testament Press, 1985. Pp. 82–96.

Jacobus, Mary. "Judith, Holofernes, and the Phallic Woman." In *Reading Women: Essays in Feminist Criticism*. New York: Columbia University Press, 1986. Pp. 110–36.

Jakobson, Roman. "The Metaphoric and Metanymic Poles." In *Critical Theory Since Plato*. Ed. Hazard Adams. New York: Harcourt Brace Jovanovich, 1971. Pp. 113–16.

Jameson, Fredric. "Magical Narratives: Romance as Genre." *New Literary History* 7 (1975): 135–63.

Jason, Heda. "Aspects of the Fabulous in Oral Literature." *Fabula* 19 (1978): 14–31.

——. *Ethnopoetry: Form, Content, Function*. Bonn: Linguistica Biblica, 1977.

——. "Genre in Folk Literature: Reflections on Some Questions and Problems." *Fabula* 27 (1986): 167–94.

Jason, Heda, and Aharon Kempinski. "How Old Are Folktales?" *Fabula* 22 (1981): 1–27.

Jones, Bruce William. "Two Misconceptions about the Book of Esther." *Catholic Biblical Quarterly* 39 (1977): 171–81.

Junod, Eric. "Créations romanesques et traditions ecclésiastiques dans les Actes apocryphes des Apôtres: l'alternative fiction romanesque–vérité historique: une impasse." *Augustinianum* 23 (1983): 271–85.

Kee, Howard Clark. "The Socio-Cultural Setting of Joseph and Asenath." *New Testament Studies* 29 (1983): 394–413.

——. "The Socio-Religious Setting and Aims of Joseph and Asenath." In *Society of Biblical Literature 1976 Seminar Papers*. Ed. George MacRae. Missoula: Scholars, 1976. Pp. 183–92.

Kelber, Werner. *The Oral and the Written Gospel*. Philadelphia: Fortress, 1983.

Kirkpatrick, Patricia G. *Old Testament and Folklore Study*. Sheffield: Journal for the Study of the Old Testament Press, 1988.

Kolenkow, Anitra Bingham. "The Narratives of the TJ (*sic*) and the Organization of the Testaments of the XII Patriarchs." In Nickelsburg, ed., *Studies in the Testament of Joseph*. Pp. 37–45.

Konstan, David. *Sexual Symmetry: Love in the Ancient Novel and Related Genres*. Princeton: Princeton University Press, 1994.

Kraemer, Ross S. "The Conversion of Women to Ascetic Forms of Christianity." *Signs* 6 (1980): 298–307.

———. *Her Share of the Blessings: Women's Religions Among Pagans, Jews, and Christians*. New York: Oxford University Press, 1992.

———. "Jewish Women in the Diaspora World of Late Antiquity." In Baskin, ed., *Jewish Women in Historical Perspective*. Pp. 43–67.

———. "Monastic Jewish Women in Greco-Roman Egypt: Philo Judaeus on the Therapeutides." *Signs* 14 (1989): 342–70.

———, ed. *Maenads, Martyrs, Matrons, Monastics: A Sourcebook on Women's Religions in the Greco-Roman World*. Philadelphia: Fortress, 1988.

Kratz, Reinhold Gregor. *Translatio imperii: Untersuchungen zu den aramäischen Danielerzählungen und ihrem theologiegeschichtlichen Umfeld*. Neukirchen-Vluyn: Neukirchener Verlag, 1991.

Kuch, Heinrich, ed. *Der antike Roman: Untersuchungen zur literarischen Kommunikation und Gattungsgeschichte*. Berlin: Akademie-Verlag, 1989.

Küchler, Max. *Schweigen, Schmuck und Schleier: Drei neutestamentliche Vorschriften zur Verdrängung der Frauen auf dem Hintergrund einer frauenfeindlichen Exegese des Alten Testaments im antiken Judentum*. Göttingen: Vandenhoek & Ruprecht, 1986.

Kugel, James L. *In Potiphar's House: The Interpretive Life of Biblical Texts*. San Francisco: HarperCollins, 1990.

Lacocque, André. *The Feminine Unconventional: Four Subversive Figures in Israel's Tradition*. Minneapolis: Augsburg Fortress, 1990.

Leach, Edmund. "Introduction." In M. I. Steblin-Kamenskij, *Myth*. Ann Arbor: Karoma, 1982. Pp. 1–20.

Lefkowitz, Mary R. "Influential Women." In *Images of Women in Antiquity*. Ed. Averil Cameron and Amélie Kuhrt. Detroit: Wayne State University Press, 1983. Pp. 49–64.

———. "The Motivations for St. Perpetua's Martyrdom." In *Heroines and Hysterics*. New York: St. Martin's Press, 1981. Pp. 53–58.

Levenson, Jon D. "The Scroll of Esther in Ecumenical Perspective." *Journal of Ecumenical Studies* 13 (1976): 440–52.

Levine, Amy-Jill. "Diaspora as Metaphor: Bodies and Boundaries in the Book of Tobit." In *Diaspora Jews and Judaism*. Ed. J. Andrew Overman and Robert S. MacLennan. Atlanta: Scholars, 1992. Pp. 105–17.

———. "Sacrifice and Salvation: Otherness and Domestication in the Book of Judith." In VanderKam, ed., *No One Spoke Ill of Her*. Pp. 17–27.

———, ed. *"Women Like This": New Perspectives on Jewish Women in the Greco-Roman World*. Atlanta: Scholars, 1991.

Licht, Jacob. "The Book of Judith as a Literary Creation" (in Hebrew). In *Baruch Kurzweil Memorial Volume.* Ed. M. Z. Kaddari, A. Saltman, and M. Schwarcz. Tel Aviv: Schocken, 1975. Pp. 169–83.

Loader, J. A. "Esther as a Novel with Different Levels of Meaning." *Zeitschrift für die alttestamentliche Wissenschaft* 90 (1978): 417–21.

Lord, Albert B. "The Merging of Two Worlds: Oral and Written Poetry as Carriers of Ancient Values." In *Oral Tradition in Literature: Interpretation in Context.* Ed. John Miles Foley. Columbia: University of Missouri Press, 1986. Pp. 19–64.

Loretz, Oswald. "Roman und Kurzgeschichte in Israel." In *Wort und Botschaft.* Ed. Josef Schreiner. Würzburg: Echter, 1967. Pp. 290–307.

Lukács, Georg. *The Historical Novel.* Lincoln: University of Nebraska Press, 1983.

———. *The Theory of the Novel.* Cambridge: MIT Press, 1971.

MacQueen, Bruce D. *Myth, Rhetoric, and Fiction: A Reading of Longus's "Daphnis and Chloe."* Lincoln: University of Nebraska Press, 1990.

Martin, Wallace. *Recent Theories of Narrative.* Ithaca, N.Y.: Cornell University Press, 1986.

McGuire, Errol. "The Joseph Story: A Tale of Son and Father." In *Images of Man and God: Old Testament Short Stories in Literary Focus.* Ed. Burke O. Long. Sheffield: Almond Press, 1981. Pp. 9–25.

McKeon, Michael. *The Origins of the English Novel, 1600–1740.* Baltimore: Johns Hopkins University Press, 1987.

Meinhold, Arndt. "Die Gattung der Josephsgeschichte und des Estherbuches: Diasporanovelle." *Zeitschrift für die alttestamentliche Wissenschaft* 87 (1975): 306–24; 88 (1976): 79–93.

Merkelbach, Reinhold. *Roman und Mysterium in der Antike.* Munich: Beck'sche, 1962.

Milik, J. T. "Daniel et Susanne à Qumrân?" In *De la Tôrah au Messie.* Ed. Maurice Carrez, Joseph Doré, and Pierre Grelot. Paris: Desclée, 1981. Pp. 337–59.

———. "Les modèles araméens du livre d'Esther dans la grotte 4 de Qumrân." *Revue de Qumrân* 59 (1992): 321–406.

———. " 'Prière de Nabonide' et autres écrits d'un cycle de Daniel." *Revue Biblique* 63 (1956): 411–15.

Milne, Pamela J. "Folktales and Fairy Tales: An Evaluation of Two Proppian Analyses of Biblical Narratives." *Journal for the Study of the Old Testament* 34 (1986): 35–60.

———. *Vladimir Propp and the Study of Structure in Hebrew Biblical Narrative.* Sheffield: Sheffield Academic Press, 1988.

Montley, Patricia. "Judith in the Fine Arts." *Anima* 4 (1978): 37–42.

Moore, Carey A. *Daniel, Esther, and Jeremiah: The Additions.* Garden City, N.Y.: Doubleday, 1977.

———. *Judith.* Garden City, N.Y.: Doubleday, 1985.

———, ed. *Studies in the Book of Esther.* New York: Ktav, 1982.

Morgan, J. R., and Richard Stoneman. *Greek Fiction: The Greek Novel in Context.* London: Routledge, 1994.

Müller, Hans-Peter. "Märchen, Legende und Enderwartung. Zum Verständnis des Buches Daniel." *Vetus Testamentum* 26 (1976): 330–41.

——. "Die weisheitliche Lehrerzählung im Alten Testament und in seiner Umwelt." *Die Welt des Oreints* 9 (1977): 77–98.

Nagy, Gregory. *The Best of the Achaeans*. Baltimore: Johns Hopkins University Press, 1979.

——. "Homeric Questions." *Transactions of the American Philological Association* 122 (1992): 17–60.

——. "Mythological Exemplum in Homer." In *Innovations of Antiquity*. Ed. Ralph Hexter and Daniel Selden. London: Routledge, 1992.

——. *Pindar's Homer*. Baltimore: Johns Hopkins University Press, 1990.

Neusner, Jacob. "The Conversion of Adiabene to Judaism." *Journal of Biblical Literature* 83 (1964): 60–66.

Nickelsburg, George W. E. *Jewish Literature Between the Bible and the Mishnah*. Philadelphia: Fortress, 1981.

——, ed. *Studies on the Testament of Abraham*. Missoula: Scholars, 1976.

——, ed. *Studies on the Testament of Joseph*. Missoula: Scholars, 1975.

Niditch, Susan. "Eroticism and Death in the Tale of Jael." In Day, ed., *Gender and Difference in Ancient Israel*. Pp. 43–57.

——. "Father-Son Folktale Patterns and Tyrant Typologies in Josephus' *Ant* 12:160–222." *Journal of Jewish Studies* 32 (1981): 47–55.

——. "Legends of Wise Heroes and Heroines." In *The Hebrew Bible and its Modern Interpreters*. Ed. Douglas A. Knight and Gene M. Tucker. Philadelphia: Fortress, 1985. Pp. 445–63.

——. "Portrayals of Women in the Hebrew Bible." In Baskin, ed., *Jewish Women in Historical Perspective*. Pp. 25–42.

——. *Underdogs and Tricksters: A Prelude to Biblical Folklore*. San Francisco: Harper and Row, 1987.

——, ed. *Text and Tradition: The Hebrew Bible and Folklore*. Atlanta: Scholars, 1990.

Niditch, Susan, and Robert Doran. "The Success Story of the Wise Courtier." *Journal of Biblical Literature* 96 (1977): 179–93.

Niehoff, Maren. *The Figure of Joseph in Post-Biblical Jewish Literature*. Leiden: Brill, 1992.

Ong, Walter J. *Orality and Literacy*. London: Routledge, 1982.

Pardes, Ilana. *Countertraditions in the Bible: A Feminist Approach*. Cambridge: Harvard University Press, 1992.

Perry, B. E. *The Ancient Romances*. Berkeley and Los Angeles: University of California Press, 1967.

——. *Studies in the Text History of the Life and Fables of Aesop*. Haverford, Pa.: American Philological Association, 1936.

Pervo, Richard I. "Aseneth and Her Sisters: Women in Jewish Narrative and in Greek Novels." In Levine, ed., *Women Like This*. Pp. 145–60.

——. "Joseph and Aseneth and the Greek Novel," *Society of Biblical Literature 1976 Seminar Papers*. Ed. George MacRae. Missoula: Scholars, 1976. Pp. 171–81.

——. *Profit with Delight: The Literary Genre of the Acts of the Apostles*. Philadelphia: Fortress, 1987.

——. "The Testament of Joseph and Greek Romance." In *Studies on the Testament of Joseph*. Ed. Nickelsburg. Pp. 15–28.

Pfeiffer, Robert H. *History of New Testament Times*. New York: Harper and Brothers, 1949.

Philonenko, Marc. "Joseph and Aseneth." In *Encyclopedia Judaica*. 16 vols. New York: Macmillan, 1971–1972. P. 10:223.

———. *Joseph et Aséneth: Introduction, texte critique, traduction et notes*. Leiden: Brill, 1968.

Praeder, Susan Marie. "Luke-Acts and the Ancient Novel." *Society of Biblical Literature 1981 Seminar Papers*. Ed. Kent Harold Richards. Chico, Calif.: Scholars, 1981. Pp. 269–92.

Propp, Vladimir. *The Morphology of the Folktale*. Austin: University of Texas Press, 1968.

Rad, Gerhard von. "Biblische Joseph-Erzählung und Joseph-Roman." *Neue Rundschau* 76 (1965): 546–59.

———. "The Joseph Narrative and Ancient Wisdom." In *The Problem of the Hexateuch and Other Essays*. New York: McGraw-Hill, 1966. Pp. 292–300.

Radday, Yehuda T. "Esther with Humour." In Radday and Athalya Brenner, eds., *On Humour and the Comic in the Hebrew Bible*. Sheffield: Almond, 1990.

Radford, Jean, ed. *The Progress of Romance: The Politics of Popular Fiction*. New York: Routledge and Kegan Paul, 1986.

Radway, Janice A. *Reading the Romance: Women, Patriarchy, and Popular Literature*. Chapel Hill: University of North Carolina Press, 1984.

Reardon, B. P., *The Form of the Greek Romance*. Princeton: Princeton University Press, 1991.

———. ed. *Collected Ancient Greek Novels*. Berkeley and Los Angeles: University of California Press, 1989.

Richlin, Amy, ed. *Pornography and Representation in Greece and Rome*. New York: Oxford University Press, 1992.

Rimmon-Kenan, Shlomith. *Narrative Fiction: Contemporary Poetics*. New York: Routledge and Kegan Paul, 1983.

Rohde, Erwin. *Der griechische Roman und seine Vorläufer*. 5th ed. Hildesheim: Georg Olms, 1974.

Ruiz-Montero, Consuelo. "The Structural Pattern of the Ancient Greek Romances and the *Morphology of the Folktale* of V. Propp." *Fabula* 22 (1981): 228–38.

Ruppert, Lothar. "Das Buch Tobias—Ein Modellfall nachgestaltender Erzählung." In *Wort, Lied, und Gottesspruch: Festschrift für Joseph Ziegler*. Ed. Josef Schreiner. Würzburg: Echter Verlag, 1972. Pp. 109–19.

Sänger, Dieter. *Antikes Judentum und die Mysterien. Religionsgeschichtliche Untersuchungen zu Joseph und Aseneth*. Tübingen: Mohr (Paul Siebeck), 1980.

Sasson, Jack M. "Esther." In *The Literary Guide to the Bible*. Ed. Robert Alter and Frank Kermode. Cambridge: Harvard University Press, 1987. Pp. 335–42.

Schiffman, Lawrence H. "The Conversion of the Royal House of Adiabene in Josephus and Rabbinic Sources." In *Josephus, Judaism, and Christianity*. Ed. Louis H. Feldman and Gohei Hata. Detroit: Wayne State University Press, 1987. Pp. 293–312.

Scholes, Robert. *Approaches to the Novel: Materials for a Poetics*. San Francisco: Chandler, 1966.

Scholes, Robert, and Robert Kellogg. *The Nature of Narrative.* New York: Oxford University Press, 1966.

Scobie, Alexander. *Aspects of the Ancient Romance and Its Heritage.* Meisenheim: Anton Hain, 1969.

Slingerland, H. Dixon. "The Testament of Joseph: A Redactional-Critical Study." *Journal of Biblical Literature* 96 (1977): 507–16.

Smith, Morton. *Palestinian Parties and Politics That Shaped the Old Testament.* New York: Columbia University Press, 1971.

Snyder, Jane McIntosh. *The Woman and the Lyre: Women Writers in Classical Greece and Rome.* Bristol: Bristol Classical Press; Carbondale, Ill.: Southern Illinois University Press, 1989.

Soll, William. "Tobit and Folklore Studies, with Emphasis on Propp's Methodology." *Society of Biblical Literature 1988 Seminar Papers.* Ed. David J. Lull. Atlanta: Scholars, 1988. Pp. 39–53.

Sprödowsky, Hans. *Die Hellenisierung der Geschichte von Joseph in Ägypten bei Flavius Josephus.* Greifswald: Verlag Hans Dallmeyer, 1937.

Starr, Raymond J. "The Circulation of Literary Texts in the Roman World." *Classical Quarterly* 37 (1987): 213–23.

Stephens, Susan A., and John J. Winkler. *Ancient Greek Novels: The Fragments.* Princeton: Princeton University Press, 1993.

Stern, David. *Parables in Midrash: Narrative and Exegesis in Rabbinic Literature.* Cambridge: Harvard University Press, 1991.

Stern, David, and Mark Jay Mirsky. *Rabbinic Fantasies: Imaginative Narratives from Classical Hebrew Literature.* Philadelphia: Jewish Publication Society, 1993.

Sternberg, Meir. *The Poetics of Biblical Narrative.* Bloomington: Indiana University Press, 1985.

Stiehl, Ruth. "Das Buch Esther." *Wiener Zeitschrift für die Kunde des Morgenlandes* 53 (1956): 4–22.

Stone, Michael. *Scriptures, Sects, and Visions: Profile of Judaism from Ezra to the Jewish Revolts.* Philadelphia: Fortress, 1980.

Stone, Nira. "Judith and Holofernes: Some Observations on the Development of the Scene in Art." In VanderKam, ed., *No One Spoke Ill of Her.* Pp. 73–93.

Stoneman, Richard. "Introduction." In *The Greek Alexander Romance.* London: Penguin, 1991. Pp. 1–27.

Strelka, Joseph P., ed. *Literary Criticism and Myth.* Yearbook of Comparative Criticism 9. University Park: Pennsylvania State University Press, 1980.

Szepessy, Tibor. "L'Histoire de Joseph et d'Aseneth et le roman antique." *Acta Classica Universitatis Scientiarum Debreceniensis* 10–11 (1974–75): 121–31.

Tatum, James, ed. *The Search for the Ancient Novel.* Baltimore: Johns Hopkins University Press, 1994.

Tatum, James, and Gail M. Vernazza. *The Ancient Novel: Classical Paradigms and Modern Perspectives.* Hanover, N.H.: International Conference on the Ancient Novel, 1990.

Tcherikover, Victor. *Hellenistic Civilization and the Jews.* New York: Atheneum, 1977.

——. "The Third Book of Maccabees as a Historical Source of Augustus' Time." *Scripta Hierosolymitana* 7 (1961): 1–26.

Thomas, Rosalind. *Literacy and Orality in Ancient Greece*. Cambridge: Cambridge University Press, 1992.

Todorov, Tzvetan. *The Fantastic: A Structural Approach*. Ithaca, N.Y.: Cornell University Press, 1975.

——. *Mikhail Bakhtin: The Dialogic Principle*. Minneapolis: University of Minnesota Press, 1984.

——. *The Poetics of Prose*. Oxford: Blackwell, 1977.

Tolbert, Mary Ann. *Sowing the Gospel: Mark's World in Literary-Historical Perspective*. Minneapolis: Augsburg Fortress, 1989.

Tomashevsky, Boris. "Thematics." In Lemon, Lee T., and Marion J. Reis, eds., *Russian Formalist Criticism: Four Essays*. Lincoln: University of Nebraska Press, 1965. Pp. 61–98.

Trebilco, Paul. *Jewish Communities in Asia Minor*. Cambridge: Cambridge University Press, 1991.

Trenkner, Sophie. *The Greek Novella in the Classical Period*. Cambridge: Cambridge University, 1958.

Trible, Phyllis. *God and the Rhetoric of Sexuality*. Philadelphia: Fortress, 1978.

——. *Texts of Terror: Literary-Feminist Readings of Biblical Narratives*. Philadelphia: Fortress, 1984.

VanderKam, James C., ed. *"No One Spoke Ill of Her": Essays on Judith*. Atlanta: Scholars, 1992.

Veyne, Paul. *Did the Greeks Believe in Their Myths?* Chicago: University of Chicago Press, 1988.

——. "La famille et l'amour sous le haut-empire romain." *Annales (Économie, Sociétés, Civilizations)* 33 (1978): 35–63.

Walfish, Barry Dov. *Esther in Medieval Garb*. Albany: State University of New York Press, 1992.

Watt, Ian. *The Rise of the Novel*. Berkeley and Los Angeles: University of California Press, 1957.

Wegner, Judith Romney. *Chattel or Person? The Status of Women in the Mishnah*. New York: Oxford University Press, 1988.

——. "The Image and Status of Women in Classical Rabbinic Judaism." In Baskin, ed., *Jewish Women in Historical Perspective*. Pp. 68–93.

Weimar, Peter. "Formen frühjudischer Literatur: Eine Skizze." In *Literatur und Religion des Frühjudentums*. Ed. Johann Maier and Josef Schreiner. Würzburg: Echter, 1973. Pp. 123–62.

West, S. "Joseph and Asenath: A Neglected Greek Novel." *Classical Quarterly* 68 (1974): 70–81.

White, Sidnie Ann. "Esther: A Feminist Model for Jewish Diaspora." In Day, ed., *Gender and Difference in Ancient Israel*. Pp. 161–77.

——. "In the Steps of Jael and Deborah: Judith as Heroine." In VanderKam, ed., *"No One Spoke Ill of Her": Essays on Judith*. Pp. 5–16.

Williamson, Margaret. "The Greek Romance." In Radford, ed., *The Progress of Romance*. Pp. 23–45.

Wills, Lawrence M. "The Depiction of the Jews in Acts." *Journal of Biblical Literature* 110 (1991): 631–54.

——. *The Jew in the Court of the Foreign King: Ancient Jewish Court Legends*. Minneapolis: Fortress, 1990.

——. "The Jewish Novellas." In Morgan and Stoneman, eds., *Greek Fiction: The Greek Novel in Context*.

Winkler, John J. *Auctor & Actor: A Narratological Reading of Apuleius' Golden Ass*. Berkeley and Los Angeles: University of California Press, 1985.

——. *The Constraints of Desire*. New York: Routledge, 1990.

Zenger, Erich. "Der Juditroman als Traditionsmodell des Jahweglaubens." *Trierer Theologische Zeitschrift* 83 (1974): 74–80.

Zimmermann, Frank. *The Book of Tobit*. New York: Harper and Brothers, 1958.

General Index

Index of Modern Authors

MYTH AND POETICS

A series edited by

GREGORY NAGY

Homer and the Sacred City
by Stephen Scully
Singers, Heroes, and Gods in the Odyssey
by Charles Segal
The Mute Immortals Speak: Pre-Islamic Poetry and the Poetics of Ritual
by Suzanne Pinckney Stetkevych
Phrasikleia: An Anthropology of Reading in Ancient Greece
by Jesper Svenbro
translated by Janet Lloyd
The Jewish Novel in the Ancient World
by Lawrence M. Wills